Satyam Shivam Sundaram

Truth Godliness Beauty

Extemporaneous talks given by Osho at OSHO International Meditation Resort, Pune, India

OSHO

Satyam Shivam Sundaram

Truth Godliness Beauty

MACMILLAN

First published in the Indian subcontinent 2015 by Macmillan
This updated edition published 2024 by Macmillan
an imprint of Pan Macmillan Publishing India Private Limited
707 Kailash Building
26 K. G. Marg, New Delhi 110001
www.panmacmillan.co.in

Pan Macmillan, The Smithson, 6 Briset Street, Farringdon, London EC1M 5NR
Associated companies throughout the world
www.panmacmillan.com

ISBN 978-93-82616-25-2

The material in this book is a transcript of a series of original OSHO Talks, Satyam Shivam Sundaram, given to a live audience. All of Osho's talks have been published in full as books, and are also available as original audio recordings. Audio recordings and the complete text archive can be found via the online OSHO Library at www.osho.com/library

1 3 5 7 9 8 6 4 2

Typeset in Adobe Garamond Pro by R. Ajith Kumar, New Delhi
Printed and bound in India by Gopsons Papers Pvt. Ltd., Noida

Contents

Preface

> Osho,
> The nature of ultimate truth has been described as truth, satyam, beauty, sundaram and goodness, shivam. Are these the characteristics of godliness?

These are not the qualities of godliness. Rather, they are our experiences of it. They do not belong to the divine as such; they are our perceptions. The divine, by itself, is unknowable. Either it is every quality, or no quality at all. But as the human mind is constituted, it can experience the divine through three windows: you can have the glimpse either through beauty, or through truth, or through goodness. These three dimensions belong to the human mind. They are our limitations. The frame is given by us; the divine itself is frameless.

It is like this...We can see the sky through a window. The window looks like a frame around the sky, but the sky itself has no frame around it. It is infinite. Only the window gives it a frame. In the same way, beauty, truth and goodness are the windows through which we can glance into the divine.

Human personality is divided into three layers. If intellect is predominant, then the divine takes the shape of truth. The intellectual approach creates the window of truth, the frame of truth. If the mind is emotional, if one comes to reality not through the head but through the heart, then the divine becomes beauty. The poetic quality is given by you. It is only the frame. Intellect gives it the frame of truth; emotion gives it the frame of beauty. And if the personality is neither emotional nor intellectual – if action is predominant – then the frame becomes goodness.

Osho
The Psychology of the Esoteric

A Note about Language

Spoken Words: Osho's books are not "written" but rather are transcribed from recordings of his talks. These talks are extemporaneous, without reference to notes other than copies of questions, stories or scriptures he has been asked to comment upon, or jokes he might use to drive home a particular point. He has asked his editors to preserve that quality of the spoken word in his printed books.

Pronouns: When hearing him speak, it is quite clear to the listener that generally when Osho talks about "man" he is referring to "human beings." His use of "he" as a default pronoun simply serves an ease and flow of speaking – in no way does it imply that "she" (or "they") is being dismissed or disregarded.

Osho's unique vantage point is good to keep in mind:

A meditator is neither a man nor a woman,
because meditation has nothing to do with your body;
neither does it have anything to do with your mind.
In meditation you are simply and purely consciousness.
And consciousness is neither male nor female.

– Osho

Introduction

Every few thousand years an individual appears who irrevocably changes the world around him in ways that are never immediately apparent, except to the most perceptive.

Osho is one such individual: his spoken words will resonate for centuries to come.

All those words have been recorded and transcribed into books like this one; written words that can carry a transforming message to the reader.

For Osho, all change is individual. There is no 'society' to change – it can only happen to each one of us, one at a time. So, no matter what the subject matter of the book, the thread that runs through all Osho's words is like a love song that we can suddenly, mysteriously, hear at just the right moment. And strangely, no matter what the words seem to be referring to, they are really only referring to us.

And this is no ordinary love song; it is more an invitation to open our hearts to hear something beyond the words, beyond the heart... a silence beyond all understanding. Where we all belong.

1

Truth, Virtue, Beauty: The Ultimate Reality

Osho,
What is the mystic conception of ultimate reality?

The mystic's conception of the ultimate reality is the only authentic and real experience. It is not a thought or a concept, but an existential experience.

The mystic does not deal with the mind. His whole effort is to get rid of the prison of the mind. The mystic is not a philosopher; his world is beyond all philosophies. Philosophies are simply by-products of mental processes. They do not reflect the reality, they only reflect you. That's why there are so many philosophies in the world contradicting each other.

The reality is one. How can there be so many philosophies? There are not so many mystical experiences. There is only one experience: neither time nor space changes it. For millennia, the mystic in every country, in every race, in every age has experienced the same reality. The philosopher thinks about reality, the mystic simply drops all thinking. In his silence – his utter silence and serenity – he becomes a mirror, and the reality reflects itself.

The mystic is the greatest flowering of human consciousness. His ultimate vision can be described in three beautiful words that have been used for thousands of years, and there has not been any improvement on them. They are three words from the ancient-most sources: *satyam shivam sundaram.*

Satyam means the truth – not what you think about it, but what it is; not your idea about it, but its reality. To know this truth you have to be utterly absent. Your very presence will distort the vision – because your presence means the presence of your mind, your prejudices, your conditionings. You are nothing else but a bundle of all that has been forced upon you by the religions, by the society, by the so-called leaders of humanity.

Your absence means the absence of all prejudices, of all borrowed knowledge: absence of the Christian, absence of the Hindu, absence of the Mohammedan; just a pure sky, a pure being. I am using the word *absence* to deny all that is not you.

But don't misunderstand me: this absence of you is your real presence. Only the prejudices are absent. The ego is absent, your knowledgeability is absent but your being shows in its utter purity. You disappear as a personality and there remains only a pure presence. So on one side it is absence of all that is false in you, and on the other side it is presence of all that is real in you. In this state you don't think, you simply see.

This seeing of existence is the first experience of the mystic contained in the word *satyam*. *Satyam* means the truth: not any conception about it, but truth itself.

The second word, *shivam*, means virtue: all that is good, all that is valuable, all that is the most precious in you; the ultimate good. The man who comes to experience the truth starts living the truth immediately. There is no other alternative. His living the truth is *shivam*. *Shivam* means truth in action, truth in your life, truth in your love, truth in your friendship, truth in your eyes and truth in your heart. *Shivam* is the action of truth. Truth itself is the center of the cyclone, but if you experience the truth, the cyclone around you becomes *shivam*. It becomes pure godliness.

A man of truth is the only proof that the world is divine. No argument can prove that the world is divine.

I am reminded of one of the greatest mystics, Ramakrishna. When asked by a logician, "What is truth? Do you have any argument, any evidence for it?" Ramakrishna laughed hilariously.

He said, "I am the argument, and if you cannot see in my eyes the proof and the evidence, you will not find it anywhere else. I am the only proof that existence is not dead, that existence is not only matter; that existence is not only available to science, that existence is much more than matter, that you are much more than the body, that you are much more than the mind."

But this "much more" cannot be proved by any logician, any scientist. Only the mystic is the proof. He also cannot prove it by words, but only by his way of life. The way of life of the mystic is the only possibility of coming in contact with the divine, which is all around you. You are living in the very ocean of the divine, but the mystic becomes your first window through which you can see the nonmaterial, the spiritual, the beyond.

Shivam is the mystic in action: his gestures, the music in his words, the poetry of his life, the light and the depths of his eyes. And whatever he does – whether he is chopping wood or carrying water from the well – you can see that there is a subtle difference. He is total in his every act, and that totality brings the third word, *sundaram*.

Sundaram means beauty. So this is the mystic trinity: *satyam*, the truth; *shivam*, the good, the divine; and *sundaram*, the beauty.

You have seen the beauty of the flowers, you have seen the beauty of the stars, you have seen the beauty of a bird on the wing, you have seen beauties upon beauties of sunsets and sunrises. But the greatest beauty is to see the totality, the intensity of the mystic. That is the greatest flowering in existence – of consciousness itself. It is available only to those who are humble enough to receive it, who are not living a closed life of fear, of paranoia, but who are living a life of love with all the windows open. And they are ready to go with life wherever it leads.

These receptive souls are the only real seekers in the world. These receptive souls are blessed with their experience of *sundaram*: the beautiful rose that is opening in the heart of the mystic. These three words are so unique, so incomparable, there is nothing parallel to them.

Truth is the experience, *shivam* is the action that comes out of the experience, and beauty is the flowering of consciousness of the man who has experienced truth. These three are the ultimate reality for those who are on the mystical path.

This is a mystery school. All my effort is not to give you knowledge, but to take all knowledge away from you; to make you so innocent, just like a newly born child who is fully conscious, sensitive, alert, but knows nothing. His not knowing makes every child's experience something that is available only to the greatest sages of the world.

To understand the psychology and the development of religious consciousness, I would like you to start with the child. It is the child's experience that haunts intelligent people their whole life. They want it again: the same innocence, the same wonder, the same beauty. Now it is a faraway echo; it seems as if you have seen it in a dream. But the whole of religion is born out of the haunting of the childhood experience of wonder, of truth, of beauty, of life in its beautiful dance all around. In the songs of the birds, in the colors of the rainbows, in the fragrance of the flowers the child goes on remembering deep in his being that he has lost a paradise.

It is not a coincidence that all the religions of the world have this idea in their parables: that man once lived in paradise and somehow, for some reason, he has been expelled from that paradise. There are different stories, different parables, but signifying one simple truth. These stories are just a poetic way of saying that every man is born in paradise and then loses it.

The retarded, the unintelligent completely forget about it but the intelligent, the sensitive, the creative go on being haunted by the paradise that they had once known. And now only a faint unbelievable memory has remained with them. They start searching for it again.

The search for paradise is the search for your childhood again. Of course your body will no longer be a child's, but your consciousness can be as pure as the consciousness of the child. This is the whole secret of the mystical path: to make you a child again – innocent, unpolluted by any knowledge, not knowing anything, still aware of everything that surrounds you, and with a deep wonder and a sense of a mystery that cannot be demystified.

This is something of fundamental importance to understand. The scientist is trying to demystify existence. His whole effort is to make everything known. The very word science means knowledge. The work of the mystic is exactly the opposite of the work of a scientist. The mystic does not want to demystify existence; on the contrary he wants to become part of this enormous mystery itself. He does not want to become a knower; he wants to disappear in the mystery of existence.

I am reminded of a beautiful story. Of course it cannot be true, but it is so significant that I don't care whether it is true or not.

A Chinese emperor called all the painters in his empire. It was one of the greatest empires in the world. He himself was deeply in love with painting and he asked the painters, "I want to declare one of you the master painter of my empire. You are going to be my guests and you have to paint. I will come to see your paintings and whichever painting proves to be the best, that painter will become part of my royal court and the master painter of the whole empire – with many rewards."

Thousands of painters participated in this competition. One old painter said to the king, "It will take at least three years for me to complete the painting, and I have a few conditions. While I am making the painting, nobody should enter into my house. I don't want anybody to see the incomplete painting. When the painting is complete, I will invite you."

The king said, "Three years? That is too much."

The painter said, "Then I must get out of the competition. Three years is nothing because you don't know what I am going to paint."

Reluctantly the emperor agreed. All the other painters finished their work: somebody in one week, somebody in two weeks – at the most four weeks. But the king was not satisfied. He was waiting for the old man. Without seeing his painting he could not declare his judgment.

After three years the old man came and asked the emperor, "Now the painting is complete. You are welcome." He had been painting in the king's palace itself. He had been given a beautiful place that was guarded twenty-four hours a day so that nobody could enter for three years. Let the painter do his work unhindered, not interfered with.

The emperor was waiting for three years. It is a long time and he was old and afraid that perhaps death may come before then. But fortunately he was still alive. With great wonder in his heart he entered the palace where the painter had done his work. He had painted on a whole wall of the palace, a beautiful forest with a small river flowing, and a small footpath going into the deep forest and disappearing into the mountains that he had painted.

The king could not believe his eyes. It was almost miraculous, magical. He was in awe. After a long silence he asked the painter only one question: "I am very much interested in this little footpath that goes around the forest, is sometimes seen around the mountains and then disappears. Where does it go?"

The painter said, "There is no other way to know unless you walk on it." And the king completely forgot that it was only a painting. He was so overwhelmed by the beauty that he took the painter's hand in his hand and they both walked on the path and disappeared into the mountains.

They have not yet returned.

This is the way of the mystic. He disappears into existence not to return.

The scientist always remains an outsider: speculating, dissecting, analyzing, but he is not part of what he is doing. He is just a neutral objective observer. The mystic is not an observer. The mystic joins the dance. He dances with the trees, he dances in the rain, he dances with the peacocks. He sings songs with the birds. He slowly, slowly merges and melts into existence. He does not demystify it; he makes it more mysterious. He glorifies it, he gives it its splendor, its majesty. He makes it the most profound orgasmic experience.

The mystic is a lover not a knower. His path is of love not of knowledge. Love is his God, not logic. Through his love he has come to realize three things: *satyam shivam sundaram* – the truth, the godliness of existence and the tremendous beauty, the unbelievable poetry, the song of the silence, the music without sounds. Only the mystic knows without any knowledge.

The scientist has knowledge but knows nothing. A man of the caliber of Albert Einstein said to his friends before dying, "If there is another life, I would not like to be a scientist or a physicist again. This has been a sheer wastage. I have known so much, but I know nothing about myself. What is the use of all this knowledge? My inner world remains dark and I have been watching faraway stars and the galaxies and the nebulas and I have not looked at myself."

Only a man of tremendous intelligence can see the point: Albert Einstein was not dying with contentment, with joy, but with a deep frustration and disappointment. The world may think that he was one of the greatest, most successful men – perhaps the greatest scientist that has ever walked on the earth. But ask him, he has missed all that is beautiful, he has missed all that is divine, he has missed all that makes life a rejoicing.

The mystic's concern is to create a song in your heart and a dance to your feet and a joy that never fades in your very being.

Remember these three words. They are the most beautiful words ever uttered by anyone, and they reveal the very essence of the ultimate reality: *satyam shivam sundaram*.

Osho,

I was reading an article about women being fed up and the responsibility is man's. Is it true?

It is true, but only half true. Man is also fed up, and the responsibility is of the women. In fact we are all in the same boat. Man or woman, all are fed up because our way of life is utterly wrong. Neither are men responsible for women's boredom nor are women responsible for men's frustration.

You will have to go deep into the psychology of frustration. The first thing to remember is that you are frustrated, you are fed up, you are bored only if you were expecting otherwise. If you were not expecting anything...

I am not fed up, and I don't see any possibility... To the very last breath I will remain with the same wondering eyes that I was born with. I am also living in the same world in which you are living. I am not bored because I never expected anything. Hence frustration is impossible.

Women are fed up because they have been expecting too much from man, and the poor man cannot fulfill all that. Women are more imaginative. They make a hero out of any Tom, Dick or Harry. With their romantic eyes, idiots appear to be Gautam Buddhas. And slowly, slowly as they come closer to their great heroes, they don't find the giants, they find ordinary, poor human beings. Then great frustration sets in. They magnify and exaggerate but you cannot live in exaggerations and you cannot go on living looking through a magnifying glass. Sooner or later you have to come to terms with reality, and the reality is just the henpecked husband, and utterly uninteresting.

And the man – he is not so imaginative but his biological instinct makes him almost intoxicated, and when he is intoxicated by his biological instinct then any ugly woman appears like a Cleopatra. His eyes are covered with biological madness. The people who called love blind were not wrong. He starts seeing with closed eyes. He is afraid to open his eyes because the reality may not be so great. But how long can you go on living with closed eyes? Sooner or later you have to see the woman you have been infatuated with.

The biological infatuation disappears very soon. It is chemical, hormonal. Once you are sexually satisfied with the woman, all blindness, all madness disappears. You are again rational, sane, and you see just an ordinary woman. Naturally, to avoid her you start reading the newspaper. Men are sitting before their TV's. In America they have done a survey: the average American man looks at the TV seven and a half hours per day. And naturally the woman feels fed up.

I have come to know that people are even making love to each other and watching the television at the same time! Even the greatest sexologists – Vatsyayana, Pundit Koka, Sigmund Freud, Havelock Ellis – have not dreamed about a day when people will make love while they are watching the television. They are so bored with everything. Television is a refuge.

But the psychology is simple: you start expecting things from others and you start believing in your expectations. Soon your expectations are shattered against the reality. That is the reason why men are fed up, women are fed up – everybody is fed up. The world is full of bored people.

Boredom is perhaps the most significant phenomenon that has happened to the twentieth century. Man was never so bored before. In ancient days, when man was a hunter and there was no marriage and no possibility of monotony, he was not bored. There was no time to be bored. The woman was not bored: there were possibilities of choosing new men. Marriage settled everything in the name of safety and security, but it took away the joy of exploration.

One of the Urdu poets has a beautiful song in which he says, "If you..." he is addressing God, "...if you were in favor of marriage, then why did you give me eyes, then why did you give me intelligence?" Idiots are not bored! And you will be surprised: blind people are not bored.

The more intelligent you are the sooner you will be bored. That is the criterion. The most intelligent, sensitive, creative people are the most bored people because one experience is enough. To repeat it is only for the idiots.

As the world has become more and more settled financially and socially: marriage, children, education, retirement, pension, insurance – in advanced countries people are even paid for their unemployment – it has taken away all the joy of exploration. Everything has become so settled and controlled that in the West particularly, there seems to be only one possibility left to explore, and that is suicide. Only that has remained unknown.

They have experienced sex and found it is just foolishness. They have experienced drugs and found that it is just deceiving yourself. Now there seems to be no adventure, no challenge. More and more people are committing suicide. It is something to be noted that the suicide rate is not increasing in the poor countries. The poor people seem to be less bored, less fed up because they have to think about food and clothes and shelter. They don't have time for boredom. They cannot afford it.

The richer the society, where everything is available... How long can you go on living in a settled, monotonous, secure, insured, guaranteed lifestyle? People of great intelligence start committing suicide.

The East has also known times of richness, but fortunately the East has found a better substitute for suicide, and that is sannyas. When people became fed up, like Gautam Buddha... Because he had all the luxuries possible, and how long can you go on repeating the same luxuries every day? By the age of twenty-nine he was finished with the world. He had experienced everything; there were no more possibilities in the world.

One dark night he escaped from his kingdom, his security, his safety. He dropped all of that and became a beggar in search of something which will be eternally fresh, which will never become old, which will never become boredom. The search for the eternally fresh is the search of sannyas.

There is a source within you that is eternally fresh. It never becomes old, you can never get fed up with it. And when I am saying this, I am saying it from the same source. My words are coming from the same source. If you can taste them, if you can feel them, you may have some glimpse of a faraway land where everything goes on becoming new every moment, where dust does not gather on any mirror.

And that world is within you – but you are interested in a woman, and the woman is interested in you. The woman cannot find your eternal source of joy, neither can you find your eternal source of joy because you are focused on the woman. We are all focused on others, and that which can give you a continuous joy is within you. But you never look within.

People are ready to go to Everest, people are ready to go to the moon, to Mars in search – but you don't know that even if you reach Everest you will simply look stupid. What will you do there? How long did Edmund Hillary remain on the top of Everest? Not more than two minutes! And he risked his life. Hundreds of others had died before him, trying to reach the same peak. And as far as I can see, Edmund Hillary standing on the highest Himalayan peak in the world must have looked very embarrassed. It was good that there was no one to see him. After two minutes he was bored: Go back home!

What are you going to do on the moon? It is a strange situation with man.

When Yuri Gagarin, the first Russian astronaut in the history of man to reach close to the moon came back, he was asked by the journalists, "What was your first thought when you were close to the moon?"

He said, "The first thought: I looked at the earth. It was looking so beautiful from there. It is eight times bigger than the moon, and from space it shines exactly as the moon shines, but eight times more. And the moon becomes just as ordinary as the earth."

It is only from far away that you catch the reflected rays of the sun. The moon has no light of its own: when you reach the moon, it is the most deserted, the ugliest spot possible because there is no water, no greenery, no roses. Nothing happens there at all. It is just a desert, utterly dead.

"But from space," Yuri Gagarin said, "my first thought was, 'My beautiful earth!'" Strange! When you live on the earth, you don't bother about the earth. Yuri Gagarin had lived his whole life on the earth and he had never thought, "My beautiful earth!"

And the second thing he said was, "When I uttered to myself 'My beautiful earth!' I remembered that I am a communist and I belong to the Soviet Union, but from space the earth is no longer divided into the Soviet Union and Germany and Japan and America and India." All these stupid lines that we have created on the map don't exist on the earth. From close to the moon, for the first time he felt one humanity, one earth – and so beautiful.

Yuri Gagarin was in India. I met him in New Delhi and I asked him, "Since you have been back on the earth, have you ever thought 'How beautiful is my earth' again?"

He looked at me, shocked. He said, "Nobody has asked that question. And I have never thought that about the earth again."

Man always looks to faraway things. He seems to be completely unaware of that which is obvious, that which is close. You are the closest to you, that's why you go on missing it. And there is no way to take you away from yourself. Wherever we will take you, you will be – you cannot be separated from yourself. Hence you cannot say, "My beautiful being!" You will have to learn the art of entering into yourself. You will have to be more subjective than objective.

Subjectivity is the essence of mysticism. You will have to start looking inwards: that's what we call meditation. It is nothing but looking inwards, reaching to the point of your very life source. And once you have touched your very life source, there is no boredom. Your life is a constant celebration. Otherwise, whether you are man or woman, to be bored is going to be your destiny.

Becky Goldberg was becoming extremely upset and lonely because all her husband, Hymie, did all day and all night was watch television. So she went to the pet shop to find a companion.

"If you are looking for an unusual pet," said the shop owner, "this cage contains a giant goony bird, whose beak and claws are capable of destroying anything."

"How horrible," said Becky.

"Not at all," the man replied. "The goony bird is remarkably well- behaved, completely obedient. He will only destroy something if he is given the command, such as 'Goony bird, the chair,' or 'Goony bird, the table.' Then he will fly into action.'"

"Could he destroy a TV set?" asked Becky.

"Of course," said the man. "He will turn it into a pile of scrap in a matter of seconds."

So Becky bought the goony bird and took him home. Sure enough, Hymie was in front of the TV, so she opened the bird's cage.

Hymie looked up and said, "What sort of pet did you buy, dear?"

"I bought a goony bird," said Becky, preparing to give the command. Hymie went back to watching TV and said, "Goony bird, my ass!"

2

Tears Are Your Songs

Osho,
The other morning when I heard you talking about sexual energy, AIDS and birth control, I felt such a pure rightness about each thing that you said. You are the intellectual giant of the century: there is no competition. I also feel a sense of urgency. What can I do to spread your words, or is that something only you can do?

The question you have asked has raised many questions.

First, I am not an "intellectual giant of the century." That kind of misunderstanding is very possible, particularly because whatever I have to say has to be said through the intellect. But intellect is only a means, a vehicle, a medium; it is not the source of what I am saying. It is not the meaning of my life and my being. I am not an intellectual. In fact, I am the most anti-intellectual person who has ever existed on this earth. I will have to explain to you.

Intellect is thinking about things you do not know. How can you think about things you do not know? It is simply groping in the dark. I am reminded of the old definition of a philosopher. A philosopher is purely intellectual. The old definition of a philosopher is of a man who is blind, and in the darkest night, in a house that has no light, he is searching for a black cat that does not exist.

The intellectuals go on doing great gymnastics of the mind. They go on thinking about things that they do not know. Naturally, they never come to any conclusions. And it is impossible to come to any conclusion, to any realization through intellectual processes; hence the whole philosophical effort of the world has been an exercise in utter futility.

All philosophy is bunk. No philosopher has contributed any new insight, any new consciousness, any new festivity to the world, any new celebration to man's consciousness. No philosopher has contributed to the beauty of this planet and this humanity. But they have been doing tremendous work all their lives creating great systems of thought which are nothing but castles in the air, soap bubbles.

The greatest intellectuals and philosophers of the world are just children, playing on the sea beach, making castles out of sand. You cannot live in those castles; in fact, just a little breeze and your castle disappears.

Mind can be used in many ways. One is the way of the intellectual: he goes round and round and round, about and about and about. He moves in a circle, which is of course unending. Every circle is unending. He travels much but he never reaches anywhere. This is the most futile use of your mind.

The other way is to use the mind not in circles but as a straight, horizontal line – one-dimensional. That's how the scientific, the mathematical, the logical genius uses the mind. He moves in a straight line, but horizontally. He comes to certain conclusions, he comes to certain discoveries, he comes to certain inventions. He enriches the world as far as matter is concerned, as far as technology, machines and knowledge about objects is concerned.

At least his effort is not absolutely useless. It may be harmful, but it is not useless. Because the one-dimensional man is blind, he goes on searching, seeking, but does not know what the ultimate purpose of all his seeking and searching is. Hence even a man like Albert Einstein ends up finding atomic energy.

He was not a man who was violent or destructive. He was a man of peace. But if you are blind and you go on searching in directions without knowing where you are going, you are bound to end up in areas which are not healthy, which are not life-affirmative, which may even be dangerous to human beings. And that's what Albert Einstein's whole life's effort has proved: Hiroshima and Nagasaki are the ultimate conclusion of his discoveries.

Science is a blind search. It has no sense of direction; it does not know the meaning, the significance of human life. It does not understand that man is not only matter. The horizontal, straight, line of science can never discover anything more than matter; hence science has become confined to a materialist conception of the world.

It is one of the most dangerous conceptions because a man like Karl Marx – a great genius, a giant as far as intellectuality is concerned – ended up with materialism. He concluded that man is nothing more than a by-product of matter, an epiphenomenon. The moment the body dies, nothing remains, everything dies. There is no difference between a man and a machine. A machine has no soul, neither does man have a soul.

The ultimate result was that his follower, Joseph Stalin, killed thirty million Russians after the revolution without any difficulty. If man is only a machine, there is no question of compassion and love, and there is no question of violence either. If you destroy a bicycle you will not feel any prick in your conscience. You have not killed anybody, you have not murdered anybody. A bicycle has no consciousness, no life; it is already dead. How can you murder a dead thing?

Because of Karl Marx's materialist communism, Joseph Stalin was able to kill thirty million people from his own land without any trouble, without feeling any disturbance in his mind about what he was doing for a single night. He tortured more men than any other man in the whole of history. It was possible for Adolf Hitler to destroy six million Jews in Germany and altogether nearabout forty million people in the Second World War. A materialist conception about man is going to be destructive because it is coming out of a blind search.

Mind can also be used as a ladder going downward. That's how the psychologist uses it: from consciousness to sub-consciousness, from sub- consciousness to unconsciousness, from unconsciousness to collective unconsciousness – as yet they have only reached so far. One rung of the ladder has still to be reached. They will certainly reach it: they are groping toward it and that will be the final conclusion of all our psychological in-depth research.

The last rung of the ladder will be the cosmic unconsciousness, utter darkness – a darkness that knows no dawn. Psychology is moving into the darker chambers of human beings; it is making man more and more at ease with his animality because those dark chambers belong to his animal past. This is not the right use of the mind either.

There is one more use. This is the way the mystic uses the mind, in just the diametrically opposite dimension than the psychologist. The ladder

is going upward from our so-called consciousness – which is very thin, almost negligible. Just scratch it a little bit and it will disappear and your unconsciousness arises. In the East this consciousness is only called the so-called consciousness. It is so thin, skin-thin, that it has no bearing on our spiritual growth.

If you move upward, for the first time you reach the authentic consciousness that comes through meditation, awareness, alertness, witnessing. Your consciousness becomes a tremendous force. Your whole life starts revolving around your consciousness. It is no longer possible for anyone to drag you into unconscious worlds, no longer possible for anybody to drag you backward into the animal past – those dark nights of the soul that we have passed but which are still dormant in our beings.

This small consciousness that we have is not enough to fight with the nine times more powerful unconsciousness. That's why you decide one thing but you do something else. Perhaps you have never looked into the fact of your decision-making: small decisions, not of any great importance. You decide to wake up early in the morning at five o'clock, and even when you are deciding it, deep down you know it is not going to happen – and it does not happen.

At five o'clock the alarm clock goes off, you pull your blanket over you, you start convincing yourself that it is too cold, too early, "I am still not fully satisfied with sleep. In fact, just now I was going more deeply into sleep and this crazy alarm clock disturbed me. And there is no hurry. Tomorrow I can wake up at five o'clock."

And this has been going on your whole life. There are millions of people who have never seen the beauty before the sun rises: the utter silence of the sky, the tremendous magnificence of the stars, the music of celestial silence. In fact, between four and six when the sun rises, those two hours are perhaps the most peaceful, the most magnificent in your twenty-four-hour day. But there are millions of people in the world who will never know about it – although they have decided many times.

But what goes wrong? Your consciousness decides and your unconsciousness cancels. You have heard the proverb: Man proposes and God disposes. There is no God, but I know that there is somebody who disposes: it is your unconsciousness, it is your dark layers of being. Your thin consciousness decides, but your thick layers of darkness cancel, dispose. They have never known about your decision. There is no communication between your consciousness and unconsciousness.

Going beyond this consciousness is the whole alchemy of meditation: attaining to an authentic consciousness which cannot be canceled or overruled by any unconsciousness that may be dormant in your being. Then the emperor has arisen in you, the master has arisen in you.

The second layer, beyond authentic consciousness, is superconsciousness. You become open to the beyond, to the mysterious and to the miraculous. Beyond the super-conscious is the collective super- conscious: you start losing your "I," your ego, your separateness from existence. Your dewdrop starts melting into the ocean. Collective super- consciousness – and you are almost on the threshold of the divine.

Beyond the collective super-consciousness there is only one step more and that is cosmic super-consciousness. This cosmic super-consciousness has been called *samadhi* by Patanjali, nirvana by Gautam Buddha, *kaivalya* by Mahavira. In the East there are a thousand and one words for that ultimate experience. No language is so rich as to be able to translate all those words with their different nuances, different fragrances. In English we are utterly poor, with faraway echoes not authentic translations. The words being used are *enlightenment, self-realization, illumination, the ultimate awakening*, but these are very poor words.

And why don't they exist in thousands of languages in the world? – because the experience has not existed in those languages. For example, Eskimos have eleven words for snow. No other language has eleven words for snow, but because Eskimos live with it day and night – all the year round, their whole lives – they experience snow in different ways. They know the subtle differences.

In the same way, the cosmic super-consciousness has been expressed by different awakened beings according to their own taste, according to their own choice. Mahavira calls it ultimate aloneness, *kaivalya*, because he enjoys the freedom of being absolutely alone. Everything else has disappeared: only aloneness, and the purity of it and the utter virgin silence of it. There is no "other" to create any hell, just absolute silence. And when there is no other, aloneness is only a word – because how can you be alone without the other? The very word *alone* loses all meaning if there is no comparison and context with the other. Mahavira is aware of it. He says this word *kaivalya* comes closest to the experience, but the experience is beyond it.

The mystic uses intellect to transcend intellect. Therefore, I say unto you, I am not an intellectual. My whole effort is to help you to go beyond intellect, to reach to the cosmic consciousness, to go beyond thinking. Those who are thinking are still children, playing on the sea beach. Only the mystic is mature, only the mystic goes beyond the horizon. Only he has the courage of an eagle to fly across the sun.

I am not an intellectual. I am simply a mystic. I don't think about reality, existence, truth. I am experiencing them. They are my very being.

But it is not only you. There are many very sincere people, very honest, who commit the same mistake. Just the other day I saw a review of my two books, *The Rebellious Spirit* and *The New Man*, by one of the best and the most honest, sincere and courageous journalists in India, M.V. Kamath. And he says the same thing you are saying: that I am the greatest intellectual of the second part of the twentieth century. He thinks he is praising me – and he has an honest intention. But he does not understand me.

As I looked at his review, things became more and more clear. He is an intellectual and naturally that is his only measure. He knows nothing of mysticism and he commits the fallacy of all the intellectuals. With all good intentions he says in his review that if I were not a controversial man, always surrounded by controversies, I would have had many more admirers in the world.

Now, he does not understand a simple thing: that no great intellectual has ever existed in the world without controversy. Intellect is intrinsically controversial. Only idiots are not controversial.

And secondly, he says I would have had many admirers. He says that with great love, but the misunderstanding is there – with all the good intentions and love and respect. The intellectual likes admirers; the mystic does not care at all. The intellectual, the artist, the showman, the politician all exist on the admiration of people. Their whole life is how to get more and more admiration. That is their nourishment. That's how they go on inflating their egos.

The mystic has no concern at all about admiration. He is so fulfilled, so contented, that there is no need for any other nourishment. His nourishment showers over him from the beyond. He has found the very life source: he does not live upon the opinions of others. He can stand alone against the whole world.

And that's what I have been doing all my life: standing all alone – the majority of one against the whole world. And the reason why I can manage to be against the whole world is because I have found my own life source. I don't depend on anyone. I don't need any admiration, any compliments, any rewards, any Nobel Prizes. I am enough unto myself.

I am not an intellectual, I am not a giant. I am a simple person who is utterly lost into the beauty of this glorious existence. I have disappeared into the whole. I don't exist separately.

If the outsiders think like this – and M.V. Kamath is an outsider and perhaps deep down afraid of coming closer to me because he ends his review by saying, "Osho needs to be read. You don't have to listen to him and you don't have to see him. You have just to read him. He is the master of words. He brings magic to ordinary words."

Now, he does not know that I am not a master of words, I am not a poet, I am not a creative artist. I use words just out of sheer necessity, always feeling guilty because no word is big enough to convey what I want to say. Every moment I utter a word I am committing a certain crime against truth because no word is capable of bringing truth to you. But it is perfectly okay for an outsider.

It is not okay for you. You know that if my words have a certain beauty, it is not of the words. It comes from my silence, it comes from my wordless innermost fragrances. Because these words are coming from my heart, they carry some beats of my heart with them. But you know me: you have heard me, and you have seen me, and you have felt me. And you are perfectly aware that if the written word impresses a man like M.V. Kamath and he thinks that is enough, more than enough, he is unnecessarily clinging to a limitation.

I speak words only to provoke you to come to me. If you become satisfied with my words, that is a calamity. Those words were only provocations, invitations, calling you forth: "Don't be afraid, come a little bit closer" – because the spoken word is alive, the written word is dead. The written word may be beautiful but it is a corpse. The spoken word is still warm, is still carrying the silences of the heart. And to say that there is no need to see me is just showing your blindness.

My words say something. My silences say more. My presence says all.

If you can be in tune with my presence, if my heartbeats can become your heartbeats, only then will you understand my words and the transcendental meaning that surrounds them but becomes visible only to those who drink from my well. Otherwise, to the outsider, it remains invisible.

You have to become an insider. You have to taste the presence of a master, of a mystic. Only then will you know that man is not just what you see in the world; man contains worlds beyond worlds, skies beyond skies.

A mystic is a window into the ultimate, a finger pointing to the moon.

I am not an intellectual, but the fallacy is created because I am compelled to use intellect and words to convey that which is not intellectual, which is not logic: that which is pure love. Out of sheer necessity I have to speak, but my speaking is not that of an orator. I am not a master of words: my speaking is just a simple conversation. At the most, I am only a storyteller, a man who loves to touch your hearts by different devices. Words are only one of my devices.

You are also saying, "there is no competition." In the world, everywhere, there is competition. Only in the inner, in the subjective, there is no competition – ever. Between two Gautam Buddhas there is no competition.

It happened... I have told you many times; I love it so much. I rejoice in telling it.

It happened that two great mystics, Kabir and Farid, had a meeting. The meeting continued for two days. The disciples of both were immensely excited in the beginning, thinking that something great is going to be communicated by Kabir to Farid or by Farid to Kabir.

But as time passed, their excitement turned into great frustration because neither Kabir nor Farid spoke. Both remained absolutely silent. Sitting side by side, holding each other's hand in deep love, once in a while smiling, giggling. And those smiles and those giggles irritated the disciples even more, but they never uttered a single word. And the day of departure came soon...

Farid had had to go; he was on a pilgrimage and just because Kabir's village was nearby, his disciples had told him, "It will be a great occasion if we stay at least for one or two days with Kabir." And Kabir's disciples had also asked him: "It will not look right if we don't invite Farid, who is passing by the side of the village."

Farid had agreed, and Kabir himself came to receive Farid outside the village. They hugged each other, and two days passed in utter silence. Those two days appeared to the disciples like two centuries. After two days they hugged each other again, had a good belly laugh, and departed.

As they parted, the disciples of both masters, who had been keeping themselves controlled with great difficulty because of the presence of the other master and *his* disciples... When they were left alone, the disciples of Kabir were very angry – and it was the same situation with the disciples of the other master. They said, "You have been talking to us every day and... what happened to you? You simply became as if you didn't know how to speak!"

Kabir said, "You don't understand. We are both in the same space: two bodies, one soul. Who is going to speak to whom? And what is there to speak? He knows it, I know it."

And the reply of Farid to his disciples was the same: "Don't be stupid! That fellow is exactly where I am. You are not perceptive enough, otherwise you could have seen. Our bodies were separate, but our beings were merging and melting into each other. There was no need to say anything. Everything was understood without being said."

In the world of the mystics there is no competition ever. Even if all the mystics of all the ages gathered together, there would not be any competition. There would be great rejoicing, dancing, singing, but there would not be any addresses, any lectures, any discourses. And there would be no question of competition.

Competition is a word belonging to the ego, and the mystic comes into existence when the ego disappears. There is no question of any hierarchy – who is higher, who is lower, who is greater. All these childish categories are left far behind.

And finally you say, "I also feel a sense of urgency." That's beautiful. Every one of you should feel the sense of urgency because you are blessed with the presence of a master. You are blessed to be in tune with a mystic. In me you have seen Gautam Buddha, Jesus Christ, Zarathustra, Kabir, Farid. They are all one with me.

You should feel the urgency because the whole world needs what I am saying to you, and needs it urgently.

And don't think that only I can spread the message. I can ignite you, I can make you aflame. Then go and shout from the rooftops and spread the fire around the world. If you are touched by me, if you are thrilled and your heart has started dancing, then go with deep compassion for anyone who is ready to share your joy.

Share it, spread it. Humanity needs it more than ever.

Osho,
Why do I always have to cry when I am touched by love?

You are fortunate. If love cannot bring tears to your eyes, then that love is dead.

It is a great misfortune that tears have become associated with sadness, with sorrow. That is only one dimension of their being. But their more significant manifestation is in love, in gratitude, in prayerfulness, in silence, in peace. When you are feeling so full, tears are just the overflow of your contentment, of your joy.

Tears have to be given a new meaning, a new poetry and a totally new dimension – which they have lost because humanity has lived in misery, and tears have become part of that misery.

Secondly, because humanity has been dominated by man, he has made it a point of his ego and pride that he will not cry: "It is feminine to cry, it is womanish to have tears." This is not true. It is an ugly, male chauvinist idea. Not only ugly, but unnatural and untrue because a man's eyes have as many tear glands as a woman's eyes have. Nature has not made any difference in tear glands.

It is obvious that the intention of nature is not to discriminate between man and woman, but for centuries man has been very egoistic and he feels that tears are a kind of weakness. He has stopped his tears, but he is not aware what the consequence of this has been: he has also stopped his love. And he has also created situations for himself that are dangerous.

More men go mad than women for the simple reason that man goes on controlling. A moment comes that the repression becomes too much and there is a breakdown. The woman does not control. When she feels like crying, she cries. She is more natural than man. That has given her a few more experiences which man has missed. The woman is healthier, she lives longer – five years more than man. She is more calm and quiet. Fewer women go crazy, fewer women commit suicide – although they talk about it! Sometimes they even try it, but very half-heartedly.

But man goes on collecting, and a point comes where he is no longer in control. Either he commits suicide or he commits murder or he goes mad.

Just sitting here is one of my attorneys from America, Swami Prem Niren. He came into deeper and deeper contact with me when I was in American jails for those twelve days. He followed me from jail to jail and he was the only person who was seeing me during all those days, almost every day. His eyes were always full of tears and I could see how much he loves me and how helpless he felt. He was doing everything that it was possible to do.

All the other attorneys were paid. Naturally they were simply doing their job. He was the only attorney who was not a servant, who was a lover; who was not being paid. He was one of my sannyasins; my life was at risk, and it was natural for him to fight with totality and intensity. The last day, when I was released from the jail, we were sitting in the hotel. We had our own hotel, our own disco, and our own restaurant in Portland, Oregon, America.

In our own hotel, he was sitting by my side with another of my sannyasins, Isabel, and he was crying like a child. And just the other day he was sitting on this side of me and then I again saw tears. Two years ago I had left him in America with tears, and yesterday I found him again with tears.

But perhaps he is not even aware of his tears. When he came here just a few days ago, he talked to one of my secretaries, Anando: "Why does Osho go on saying this, that 'my attorneys had tears in their eyes'?"

When I heard this, I could not believe it – just yesterday he was sitting here with tears. Perhaps thousands of years of conditioning have blocked his awareness of his own tears, of his own love, of his own feminineness.

A better world, a better humanity, and more people will enjoy tears. They are such a blessing.

You are asking, "Why do I always have to cry when I am touched by love?" What do you want? What more do you want? Certainly you are thinking that those tears are something wrong. Is crying when touched by love something wrong? You are carrying a wrong conditioning. It is absolutely right. When touched by love, what can you do? Words won't help; only tears can convey what is happening deep down in your heart. Tears are the most valuable treasure that you have.

But man has been distorted in every way. Man's nature has been pruned according to the ideas of the vested interests. Nations need armies and they do not want man to be at all touched by love. Their tears have to be dried up and their love has to be blocked, otherwise they will not be able to kill and murder and massacre people – people who are just like you, and people who have not done anything wrong to you, and people whose wives, whose children, whose old parents may be waiting for them just as your parents, your wife, your children are waiting for you.

But to create the soldier, man has to be destroyed completely. He has to be made into a robot – and robots don't cry, robots are not touched by love. Because armies were needed, man was distorted. Because women were not needed in the armies, they were left to the side. It was good for women because they have remained more natural.

Never be ashamed of your tears. Be proud that you are still natural. Be proud that you can express the inexpressible through your tears. Those tears are your songs, unuttered. Those tears are your heart, which cannot use words.

Never feel ashamed of your tears. Eyes that have lost their tears have lost their most beautiful, their most glorious treasure.

I would like my people in particular to be absolutely natural, to be utterly innocent, uninhibited. And when tears are flowing, rejoice! You are still alive! Because don't you know dead people cannot cry, dead people cannot have tears? And the people, who think they are alive and cannot cry and cannot have tears, are living in a fallacy. They have died long ago. The day their tears died, they also died, because their love died.

Except love you don't have any soul.

3

Living with the Eternal

Osho,

Why am I not curious about anything anymore?

Devageet, seven hundred and fifty years ago there was a mystery school exactly like this. The mystery school belonged to one of the greatest Sufis, Mevlana Jalaluddin Rumi. The Turkish word *mevlana* means "beloved master." It has never been used for anyone else.

In front of his mystery school was written in bold letters: "This place is not for those who are only curious."

Curiosity has no spiritual meaning. Curiosity is something like itching in your mind: if you itch it goes, if you don't itch it also goes. Curiosity has no passion in it; it is very superficial – just by the way. An inquiry, a question arises in you, but it is not your quest, you are not going to dedicate your life to searching for the answer for it. You are not even going to commit yourself to the exploration.

Curiosity is cheap. If somebody answers, good. If nobody answers, that too is okay. You are not deeply interested. It is not arising out of your heart. Curiosity has to disappear before you can attain to a passionate inquiry into existence.

So, Devageet, it is not a bad sign, but a tremendously important indication that you are on the right path. The path does not belong to the curious ones. It belongs to those who are committed, dedicated; who are ready even to sacrifice their lives for the experience of truth. As the curiosity disappears you are no longer a student; you become a disciple.

That's the only difference between the student and a disciple. The student is only curious, gathering knowledge from all the sources without much concern. It is not his essential search – just gathering knowledge to cover up his ignorance. But the ignorance remains there, and the more it is covered, the more dangerous because you start forgetting it. And a man who has forgotten his ignorance is a man utterly lost.

To go on remembering that you are ignorant is to go on remembering that the night is not over and your morning has not yet come: that you still have a long way to go before the darkness disappears and you see the first signs on the horizon of the sun rising with all its colors and all its beauty and all its blessings.

The curious person is not at all accountable for anything deep. The moment you become passionately interested to know, it becomes a question of life and death. Without knowing, your life seems to be just a desert without any oasis anywhere. You *have* to know; only then will your life have some significance, some meaning, some relevance, some reason why you should go on existing.

But the disciple is only a beginning, not the end: the right beginning. A moment comes when your passionate longing to know turns into still deeper waters. It becomes a longing not just to know, but to *be*. Knowledge is always something *there*. There is a distance between you and the known. You are not one with it; the knower is separate from the known. That is the state of knowledge. It cannot quench your thirst. The water is there, you are there, but there is no connecting link.

Your thirst will become even more fiery. That great moment also comes in the life of the disciple when he drops the quest for knowing and starts the quest for being. The curious person is only interested in information. The disciple is interested in knowledge.

The devotee is interested in transformation. He is not content to know the truth. He will be contented only when he becomes the truth. And in fact it is just poverty of language that I have to use the word *becoming*. No one ever becomes the truth because everyone is already the truth.

Truth is your very being, not your becoming. It is not a process, it is not a path that has to be traveled, it is not some faraway goal that you have to reach. It is something in your innermost being that has always been there from eternity to eternity. Whether you know it or not, whether you realize it or not, whether you recognize it or not – it does not matter. It is there.

The devotee does not become the truth; he discovers that he is the truth. And this discovery is the greatest discovery possible for human consciousness. So it is perfectly good that you are not curious about anything anymore. It is a sign of maturity, of moving from the state of the student to the disciple. And as I know you, Devageet, you have already moved even from the state of the disciple to the ultimate glory of being a devotee. Your quest, your inquiry is no longer a dry exploration. It has become your love, it has become your very heartbeat. Naturally, all curiosity will disappear.

One day you will realize that even to know about truth, to know about godliness, to know about beauty... You are no longer interested in knowing. Because knowing about water is not going to help, even knowing scientifically that it consists of oxygen and hydrogen is not going to quench your thirst.

The most glorious moment on the path comes when your whole interest and passion become concentrated on a single point: of discovering yourself; of discovering that you have always been, that you are – even in this moment – and irrespective of whether you understand or not, you will always remain your authentic, your essential, your existential being. It contains all: *satyam shivam sundaram* – the truth, the godliness and the tremendous beauty that arises from the recognition of your being truth, of your being part of a divine existence.

Your every gesture becomes a dance, your every silence becomes a song, your words become aflame with a new fire, with a new light. Your whole life becomes a source of a magnetic force.

Just a few days ago, a child was born in France. The mother had been working in an atomic plant. While she was pregnant, for nine months she was exposed to atomic radiation and the doctors and the surgeons were very interested to know how it would affect the child. And they were surprised. The child was very healthy, very radiantly healthy. They were thinking he might be blind, they were thinking he might be crippled. Those people had never seen such a beautiful child – so alive and so vibrant.

But then there was another shock and surprise: as they put the child on the table all the surgeons and the doctors' instruments started moving toward the child. The child had become a magnetic force.

Exposure to continuous radiation in very minute doses has been found by Japanese scientists to be very health-giving. Bigger doses can kill. As the quantity becomes bigger it becomes dangerous. A qualitative change comes in through greater quantity. At the very minimum, soft doses of radiation can create immense health and well-being.

One scientist in Japan has been working for twenty years in Hiroshima and Nagasaki on this particular project: Is there any possibility of a certain quantity of radiation being life-affirmative? And when he came back after twenty years to the university he belongs to, his colleagues could not believe it. They had all aged twenty years and that man seemed to have become younger than when he had gone. He is sixty-five but he looks forty-five. He had discovered a tremendous thing.

He loves me immensely, and he has sent me a few small things. You cannot think that they cost twenty thousand dollars, just a small bottle of radioactive material. He has been using it for one year. He just puts it in his bathtub and the water becomes radioactive, but in a very soft and minimum dose. He has sent me a belt that he has been using for one year. It is filled with radioactive material from Hiroshima, and that belt, he feels, has taken away his old age, has taken away his diseases.

He was immensely concerned about my health. He is going to come. I have not used those things that he has sent because what is a soft dose to one person may be too much to another, and I have a very delicate physical structure. So I am waiting for him first to see the difference between me and himself, and then to decide.

As you move from the disciple to the state of the devotee, suddenly you start radiating something that has been dormant in you for centuries. You become a magnet – not an ordinary magnet, but a spiritual magnet. People will start moving toward you, not knowing why, but a tremendous desire to be with you and a great feeling of well-being and a great turning inwards.

I started my journey alone, and without informing anybody I have found that my caravan is becoming bigger and bigger and bigger. People have come from faraway lands around the world – wondering why they are going, not knowing the inner pull.

Devageet has a heart of a small child, utterly innocent. His transformation from disciplehood to the glorious space of being a devotee has come to him very naturally, very spontaneously, without any effort on his part. Just being in my presence, just being with me, he has moved millions of light-years.

It is natural, Devageet, that your curiosities will disappear. Soon you will find another thing disappearing: your longing for knowledge. These are good indications of coming back home. Perhaps just one step more and you will have forgotten curiosities, questions, quest for knowledge – and you will simply relax in the new light that you have found within yourself: perfectly at ease, cool and calm, not a single worry in the world, at ease with the trees and the birds and the ocean and the stars.

You love to laugh, you have a great sense of humor – and according to me all the religions in the past have missed the great religious quality of the sense of humor. The reason was that they were all against life. They could not be for laughter: they were all against love – how could they be in favor of laughter? They were life-denying not life-affirming ideologies.

Hence you don't see a single instance in the life of Jesus when he would have laughed. Even before he was crucified he lived as though he was continuously being crucified. The crucifixion of Jesus seems to be the ultimate outcome: "This guy will never be satisfied unless he is crucified."

"Why were you kissing my young daughter in that dark corner last night?" said the angry father.

"Now that I've seen her in the daylight," said Ernie, "I sort of wonder myself."

In the darkness you have been curious and you have been many more things, but in the light you start sort of wondering, "What have I been doing?"

It was the couple's twenty-fifth wedding anniversary and the wife said, "Darling, you have been a very good husband over the years and I would like to show you my appreciation. Is there anything that you would like on this special day?"

The husband thought for a while and then said, "Yes, actually there is. You have always forbidden me to look into the top drawer of your cupboard. I would really like to see what is in there."

His wife agreed and he opened it. Inside there were two eggs and about ten thousand dollars in cash. "What are the eggs for?" he inquired.

"Well," said his wife, "I guess it's time you should know. Every time I was unfaithful to you, I put an egg in the drawer."

"Twice in twenty-five years," smiled the husband, "that's understandable. But what is all that money?"

"Well, darling," she replied, "Each time I had a dozen eggs, I sold them."

Devageet, it is very good not to be curious about unnecessary things, because one never knows...

> Osho,
> I really enjoy meditation and am absolutely contented with my life. But now it has been so long since I had any great passion or great joy or great pain that I am wondering if I have become dull and stuck, or if this is the way things are supposed to be.

It is part of this great pilgrimage. The moment you become contented, in the beginning it feels like the journey is over and you are tremendously blissful. But as time passes, contentment settles down. You are peaceful, you are happy, you are at ease, but an old habit of millions of lives starts raising its head: there seems to be no excitement. Have you become dull or have you died? This is just an old habit and it has to be understood.

Excitement is for those who are miserable. Without excitement they cannot live; their misery will be too heavy. A little excitement in their lives, a new love affair, getting a lottery opened in their name – these small things keep them going. These excitements function like lubrications and they go on in their miserable lives hoping another excitement may be coming. And what are your excitements? Moving into a new house and you are excited? Purchasing a new car and you are excited?

I have heard about a man who was tired of his beautiful house. Finally, everything becomes tiring, boring. The house was beautiful and just behind the house was a beautiful lake and beyond the lake the mountains and the forest – but the same scene every day, morning, afternoon, evening. There was no excitement.

He called a real estate agent and told him that he wanted to sell this boring house. The real estate man was completely puzzled. He had never in his life seen such a beautiful house with such peaceful surroundings. It was almost paradise. So he said, "I will advertise it and it will be sold, there is no problem." And he advertised it in the newspapers.

The next day the man read the advertisement and he was so excited: a beautiful marble house surrounded by a lake – and just beyond the lake a primeval forest, thick, with trees so high as if they are trying to touch the stars. The description was so poetic, and of course there was no mention of his name or his address, only the phone number of the real estate man.

He immediately phoned and said, "Whatever the price, I want to purchase this house."

The real estate man said, "This is too difficult a problem. This is your house!"

He said, "My God, you have written such a poetic piece about it. I had completely forgotten the lake; I had started taking it for granted. The forest, the mountains... Yes, I remember now; when I entered this house for the first time there was so much excitement."

But excitement is a momentary thing. You cannot remain excited forever; otherwise your blood pressure will rise so high you will simply pop off! Excitement always means going up to a certain point and then going down. It is always up and down. Falling back into misery, searching again for some excitement; this is the ordinary run of life.

But when you attain contentment through meditation – when you come to a peaceful inner space where nothing moves, where time stops – in the beginning it is a tremendous ecstasy, not only excitement. But soon you will become accustomed to it, and that's what is happening to you. You have neither become dull, nor are you stuck. It is just natural. It is the way things are supposed to be.

You have to learn a new art of seeing your contentment, your peace, your silence, your happiness – not as something that you had yesterday too. You have to learn to forget the past completely. To be more exact, you have to die to the past so that every day your peace and your contentment are fresh, ecstatic, as if you have discovered them just now.

Die every moment to the past and be reborn again and again. Each moment has to be a death and a resurrection. Unless you learn the art of dying and resurrecting you will feel a little bored because it is the same, always the same, nothing changes.

You have lived your millions of lives in the past only through changes, hoping for some excitement. Arriving, you have to learn some new art. Some new dimension has to open into your being: how to live with the eternal. You have known only living with the changing, with the impermanent, with the ephemeral. Now learn the new art of living with the eternal, the unchanging, the absolutely still, unmoving – something beyond time and space.

Once you have learned this new art, you will find every day new flowers in your contentment, new stars in your silence, new showers of blissfulness and ecstasy. But you have to forget your yesterdays otherwise it will look like the same repetition.

I am not bored, and I have lived in utter contentment, in absolute peace. Nothing moves within my being. All is totally silent and still. But because I never think of yesterdays I am immensely ecstatic every moment. What is past is past; I have never looked back. It is the same contentment, the same peace, the same silence – but because I go on dropping the past it is always new for me.

Learn the art of keeping the eternal always fresh. Don't allow any dust to gather on the mirror of the eternal.

A Zen story... In the world of Zen it is a beautiful tradition that masters send their disciples to other masters just to see the reality from some other angle. Even masters who have been contradicting each other their whole lives exchange disciples, so the disciple can see the truth from a totally different standpoint.

It happened...

One disciple was always getting into the same space as you. He was utterly content, there was no complaint, nothing was missing. But this eternal silence without any change was against the old, very deep-rooted habit of the search for excitement. Now there was no excitement possible.

The master called him – he had not been calling him for many days – and then slapped him. The disciple could not believe it. He had not said anything. He had not done anything. He asked, "Why have you hit me?"

The master said, "You needed a little change. And moreover you have to go to the opposing monastery of my eternal enemy. Now you have to live with that master!"

The disciple said, "But you have always been contradicting him. You have never agreed on any point with that man, neither has he ever agreed with you. Why are you sending me to him?"

The master said, "Never ask the master why. He knows, and there is no need for you to know it. Simply go and ask the other master to accept you as a disciple."

His whole contentment, meditation, silence – everything was disturbed. Tidal waves of thought that he had completely forgotten – this was too much! For what was he being punished? He forgot all about boredom and all about life having no excitement any more. Now there was great excitement. But if the master says, "You have to go..."

He went to the other master very reluctantly, very unwillingly, almost in a state of split. He knew that this man was wrong: he had been listening to his master and he was so logical in his refutation of the other man.

But finally he knocked on the door of the monastery. The master himself came out and he said, "What is the matter? What do you want? You belong to my enemy."

The disciple said, "I know. I never wanted to come here but your enemy, my master, has sent me to request that I should be accepted as your disciple."

The master said, "This is very strange. And you followed whatever he said?"

The disciple said, "I had to. He has also hit me very hard – and he is a dangerous fellow! If I don't follow, he will beat me every day: morning, afternoon, evening, in the middle of the night. He is not reliable. I thought it prudent to come to you."

The master closed his door in his face and said, "Your master is very compassionate. Go back to him."

This was even more puzzling. He said, "You have been contradicting my master, writing books against him, teaching your disciples not to listen to him – not even to talk to his disciples – and suddenly today you have changed your mind. You say, 'Your master is very compassionate.'"

The old man laughed and he said, "Yes, he is very compassionate. He disturbed you out of compassion, to give you a sense of: 'Don't be stupid! You are settling. All the waves in your mind are disappearing, all the thoughts becoming silent.' It is out of his compassion that he has disturbed you and he has sent you to me so that I can disturb you more. I am against him, I am against everything that he says, but I am sorry: I cannot accept you. You will have to go back. You have already arrived; just one step more!"

He went back to his master and said, "He has rejected me and the reason he gives is: 'Your master is too compassionate. Go back to him.'"

The master said, "Start meditating again."

And it was again excitement, and again a beginning into the unknown, but soon – because he was already a great adept – things settled; contentment, peace. But now there was no desire for excitement any more. It was stupid.

But it comes to everybody out of a deep-rooted inheritance of your past lives. It is so deep-rooted that it has gone into your blood, into your bones, into your marrow.

You are not becoming dull and you are not stuck. You yourself are saying, "I really enjoy meditation and am absolutely contented with my life, but now it has been so long since I had any great passion or great joy or great pain that I am wondering if I have become dull and stuck, or if this is the way things are supposed to be." This is the way things are supposed to be.

Bernie had been out of town and was surprised when he got back to find his wife, Stella, in bed with a strange man. The stranger, naked and obviously well satisfied, was sprawled on the bed.

"Why you son-of-a-bitch!" Bernie exploded.

"Wait, darling," cried Stella. "You know that fur coat I got last winter? This man gave it to me. Remember the diamond necklace you like so much? This man gave it to me. And remember when you could not afford a second car and I got a Toyota? This man gave it to me."

"For God's sake, it's drafty in here!" shouted Bernie. "Cover him so he doesn't catch cold!"

Just be a little understanding. Everything is going perfectly beautifully.

Just a few jokes for you – not to disturb you, but just as a little holiday from your contentment. Just for a few moments to forget your meditation and contentment.

It was a late night again in the bar when the door opened and a voice called out, "MacTavish your house is on fire!"

One man rushed out and after running a hundred yards down the street, suddenly skidded to a halt. "Wait a minute!" he said to no one in particular. "My name is not MacTavish."

The veteran preacher was instructing a class of new ministers on the importance of facial expressions harmonizing with their sermons.

"When you speak of heaven," he said, "let your face light up, let it be bright with a heavenly gleam, let your eyes shine with reflected glory. But when you speak of hell – well, your ordinary face will do."

A Frenchman, a Swiss and an Italian are on a flight to Italy in their little private plane. As the weather gets bad they get lost in the clouds. The Frenchman puts his hand out of the window and suddenly says, "I touched the Eiffel Tower. This must be France."

After a while the Swiss man puts his hand out of the window and says, "We are home. This is Switzerland; I touched the mountains."

Finally the Italian sticks his hand out of the window and says, "This must-a be Italy."

"How do you know?" asked the others.

The Italian pulls his hand in and says, "They stole-a my watch-a."

4

Except Pure Love, There Is No God

Osho,

How can I love better?

Love is enough unto itself; it needs no betterment. It is perfect as it is; it is not in any way to be more perfect. The very desire shows a misunderstanding about love and its nature. Can you have a perfect circle? All circles are perfect; if they are not perfect, they are not circles.

Perfection is intrinsic to a circle and the same is the law about love. You cannot love less, and you cannot love more because it is not a quantity; it is a quality that is immeasurable.

Your very question shows that you have never tasted what love is, and you are trying to hide your lovelessness in a desire of: "how to love better." No one who knows love can ask this question. Love has to be understood not as a biological infatuation. That is lust. That exists in all the animals: there is nothing special about it. It exists even in trees. It is nature's way of reproduction. There is nothing spiritual in it, and nothing especially human.

So the first thing is to make a clear-cut distinction between lust and love. Lust is a blind passion; love is the fragrance of a silent, peaceful, meditative heart. Love has nothing to do with biology or chemistry or hormones. Love is the flight of your consciousness to higher realms – beyond matter and beyond body. The moment you understand love as something transcendental then love is no longer a fundamental question. The fundamental question is: how to transcend the body, how to know something within you which is beyond – beyond all that is measurable. That is the meaning of the word *matter*. It comes from a Sanskrit root, *matra*, which means measurement. It means that which can be measured. The French word *metre* comes from the same root.

The fundamental question is: how to get away from the measurable and how to enter into the immeasurable – in other words, how to go beyond matter and open your eyes toward more consciousness. And there is no limit to consciousness. The more you become conscious, the more you realize how much more is possible ahead. As you reach one peak, another peak arises in front of you. It is an eternal pilgrimage.

Love is a by-product of a rising consciousness. It is just like the fragrance of a flower. Don't search for it in the roots; it is not there. Your biology is your roots, your consciousness is your flowering.

As you become more and more an open lotus of consciousness, you will be surprised, taken aback, with a tremendous experience that can only be called love. You are so full of joy, so full of bliss; each fiber of your being is dancing with ecstasy. You are just like a rain cloud that wants to rain and shower. The moment you are overflowing with bliss, a tremendous longing arises in you to share it. That sharing is love.

Love is not something that you can have from someone who has not attained to blissfulness. And this is the misery of the whole world: everybody is asking to be loved and pretending to love. You cannot love because you don't know what consciousness is. You don't know the *satyam*, the *shivam*, the *sundaram*.

You don't know truth, you don't know the experience of the divine, and you don't know the fragrance of beauty. What have you got to give? You are so empty, you are so hollow; nothing grows in your being, nothing is green. There are no flowers within you, your spring has not yet come.

Love is a by-product. When the spring comes and you suddenly start flowering, blossoming, and you release your potential fragrance – sharing that fragrance, sharing that grace, sharing that beautitude is love. And there is no question of making it better. It is already perfect; it is *always* perfect. If it is, it is perfect. If it is not perfect, it is not there. Perfection and love cannot be separated.

If you had asked me, "What is love?" it would have been more truthful, honest, sincere, authentic. But you are asking me, "How can I love better?" You have already accepted as a fact that you know what love is – not only that, your question implies that you already love. Now the question is how to better it.

I don't want to hurt you, but I am helpless. I have to say the truth to you: you don't know what love is. You can't know because you have not yet gone deeper in your consciousness. You have not experienced yourself. You know nothing of who you are. In this blindness, in this ignorance, in this unconsciousness, love does not grow. This is a desert in which you are living. In this darkness, in this desert, there is no possibility of love blossoming.

First you have to be full of light and full of delight – so full that you start overflowing. That overflowing energy is love. Then love is known as the greatest perfection in the world. It is never less and never more. But our very upbringing is so neurotic, so psychologically sick that it destroys all possibilities of inner growth. You are being taught from the very beginning to be a perfectionist, and then naturally you go on applying your perfectionist ideas to everything – even to love.

Just the other day I came across a statement: A perfectionist is a person who takes great pains, and gives even greater pains to others. And the outcome is just a miserable world.

Everybody is trying to be perfect. And the moment somebody starts trying to be perfect, he starts expecting everybody else to be perfect. He becomes a condemner. He starts humiliating people. That's what all your so-called saints have been doing down the ages. That's what your religions have done to you – poisoned your being with an idea of perfection.

Because you cannot be perfect, you start feeling guilty, you lose respect for yourself. And the man who has lost respect for himself has lost all the dignity of being human. Your pride has been crushed, your humanity has been destroyed by beautiful words like perfection.

Man cannot be perfect. Yes, there is something that man can experience but which is beyond the ordinary conception of man. Unless man also experiences something of the divine, he cannot know perfection.

Perfection is not something like a discipline, it is not something that you can practice, it is not something for which you have to go through rehearsals – but that is what is being taught to everybody. And the result is a world full of hypocrites, who know perfectly well that they are hollow and empty, but go on pretending all kinds of qualities which are nothing but empty words.

When you say to someone, "I love you," have you ever thought what you mean? Is it just biological infatuation between the two sexes? Then once you have satisfied your animal appetite, all so-called love will disappear. It was just a hunger and you have fulfilled your hunger and you are finished. The same woman who was looking the most beautiful in the world, the same man who was looking like Alexander the Great – you start thinking how to get rid of this fellow!

It will be very enlightening for you, to understand this letter written by Paddy to his beloved Maureen.

My darling Maureen,

I met you last night but you did not show up. Next time I will meet you again whether you show up or not. If I am there first, I will write my name on the gatepost to let you know. And if it is you that is first, rub out my name and nobody will be any the wiser.

Darling Maureen, I would climb the highest mountain for your sake, and swim the wildest sea. I would endure any hardships to spend a moment by your side.

Your ever-loving,

Paddy.

PS I'll be over to see you on Friday night if it is not raining.

The moment you say to someone "I love you," you don't know what you are saying. You don't know that it is just lust hiding behind a beautiful word, love. It will disappear. It is very momentary.

Love is something eternal. It is the experience of the buddhas, not the unconscious people of whom the whole world is full. Only very few people have known what love is – and these same people are the most awakened, the most enlightened, the highest peaks of human consciousness.

If you really want to know love, forget about love, remember about meditation. If you want to bring roses into your garden, forget about roses and take care of the rosebush. Give nourishment to it, water it, take care that it gets the right amount of sun, water. If everything is taken care of, the roses are destined to come in the right time. You cannot bring them earlier, you cannot force them to open up sooner, and you cannot ask a roseflower to be more perfect.

Have you ever seen a roseflower that is not perfect? What more do you want? Every roseflower is perfect in its uniqueness. Dancing in the wind, in the rain, in the sun – can't you see the tremendous beauty, the absolute joy? A small ordinary roseflower radiates the hidden splendor of existence.

Love is a roseflower in your being, but prepare your being. Dispel the darkness and the unconsciousness. Become more and more alert and aware, and love will come of its own accord, in its own time. You need not worry about it. And whenever it comes it is always perfect.

Love is a spiritual experience – nothing to do with sexes and nothing to do with bodies, but something to do with the innermost being.

But you have not even entered into your own temple. You don't know at all who you are and you are asking about love. First be thyself; first know thyself – and love will come as a reward. It is a reward from the beyond. It showers on you like flowers, fills your being. And it goes on showering on you, and it brings with it a tremendous longing to share. That sharing can only be indicated in human language as "love." It does not say much, but it indicates the right direction. Love is a shadow of alertness, of consciousness.

I teach you to be more conscious. And love will come as you become more conscious: it is a guest that comes, that comes inevitably to those who are ready and prepared to receive it. You are not even ready to recognize it.

If love comes to your door, you will not recognize it. If love knocks on your doors, you may find a thousand and one excuses. You may perhaps think it is some strong wind, or some other excuse. You will not open the doors. And even if you open the doors you will not recognize love because you have never seen love before. How can you recognize it?

You can only recognize something that you know. When love comes for the first time and fills your being, you are absolutely overwhelmed and mystified. You don't know what is happening. You know your heart is dancing, you know you are surrounded by celestial music, you know fragrances that you have never known before, but it takes a little time to put all these experiences together and to remember that perhaps this is what love is. Slowly, slowly it sinks into your being.

Love is not to be found in poetry. My own experience is that the people who write poetry about love are the people who do not know love. I am personally acquainted with great poets who have written beautiful poetry about love, and I know they have never experienced love. In fact their poems are just substitutes, consolations. By writing about love they are deceiving themselves and others that they know love.

Only mystics know love. Other than mystics there is no category of human beings who have ever experienced love. Love is absolutely the monopoly of the mystic. If you want to know love you will have to enter into the world of the mystic.

Jesus says, "God is love." He has been part of a mystery school of the Essenes, an ancient school of mystics. But perhaps he did not graduate from the mystery school because what he is saying is just not right. God is not love; love is God. And the difference is tremendous; it is not just a change of words.

The moment you say God is love you are simply saying that love is only an attribute of God. He is also wisdom, he is also compassion, he is also forgiveness. He can be millions of things besides love. Love is only one of the attributes of God. And, in fact, even to make it a small attribute of God is very irrational and illogical. Because if God is love then he cannot be just; if God is love then he cannot be cruel enough to throw sinners into eternal hell, if God is love then God cannot be the law.

One great Sufi mystic, Omar Khayyam, shows more understanding than Jesus when he says, "I will go on just being myself. I am not going to take any notice of the priests and the preachers because I trust that God's love is great enough. I cannot commit a sin that can be greater than his love. So why be worried? Our hands are small and our sins are small. Our reach is small – how can we commit sins that God's love cannot forgive? If God is love then he cannot be present on the last judgment day to sort out the saints and throw the remaining millions and millions of people into hell for eternity."

The teachings of the Essenes were just the opposite. Jesus quotes them wrongly. Perhaps he was not very deeply rooted in their teachings. Their teaching was "Love is God." That is such a tremendous difference. Now God becomes only an attribute of love; now God becomes only a quality of the tremendous experience of love. Now God is no longer a person but only an experience of those who have known love. Now God becomes secondary to love. And I say unto you, the Essenes were right.

Love is the ultimate value, the final flowering. There is nothing beyond it; hence, you cannot perfect it. In fact, before you attain it you will have to disappear. When love will be there you will not be there.

A great Eastern mystic, Kabir, has a very significant statement – a statement that can be made only by one who has experienced, who has realized, who has entered into the inner sanctum of ultimate reality. The statement is: "I had been searching for truth, but it is strange to say that as

long as the searcher was there, truth was not found. And when the truth was found, I looked all around – I was absent. When the truth was found, the seeker was no more; and when the seeker was, truth was nowhere."

Truth and the seeker cannot exist together. You and love cannot exist together. There is no coexistence possible: either you *or* love. You can choose. If you are ready to disappear, melt and merge, leaving only a pure consciousness behind, love will blossom. You cannot perfect it because you will not be present. And it does not need perfection in the first place. It always comes as perfect.

But *love* is one of those words that everybody uses and nobody understands. Parents are telling their children, "We love you," and they are the people who destroy their children, they are the people who give their children all kinds of prejudices, all kinds of dead superstitions. They are the people who burden their children with the whole load of rubbish that generations have been carrying. And each generation goes on transferring it to another generation. The madness goes on, becoming mountainous.

Yet all parents think they love their children. If they really loved their children, they would not like their children to be their images because they are just miserable and nothing else. What is their experience of life? – pure misery, suffering. Life has not been a blessing to them but a curse. And still they want their children to be just like themselves.

I was a guest in a family. I was sitting in their garden in the evening. The sun was setting and it was a beautiful, silent evening. The birds were returning back to the trees, and the small child of the family was sitting by my side. I just asked him, "Do you know who you are?"

And children are more clear, more perceptive than the grown-ups because the grown-ups are already spoiled, corrupted, polluted, with all kinds of ideologies, religions. That small child looked at me and he said, "You are asking me a very difficult question."

I said, "What is the difficulty in it?"

He said, "The difficulty is that I am the only child of my parents, and as long as I can remember, whenever some guests come, somebody says my eyes look like my father's, somebody says my nose looks like my mother's, somebody says my face looks like my uncle's. So I don't know who I am because nobody says anything looks like me!"

I said, "This is really difficult."

But this is what is being done to every child. You don't leave the child alone to experience himself, and you don't leave the child to become himself. You go on loading your own unfulfilled ambitions on the child.

My personal physician is Dr. Amrito. His father was also a well-known physician. His father has left a strange condition in his will: Amrito will be able to get his inheritance if he fulfills the condition – and the condition is that the day he is accepted by the Royal College of Physicians as a fellow of the society, he will be able to get the money from the bank. If he never becomes a fellow, if he is not accepted by the Royal College of Physicians – which is the most significant fellowship in the whole world as far as physicians are concerned.

When I came to know about it I could see the incomplete ambition of the poor father. He would have longed his whole life to become a fellow of this royal society. Now he is burdening his son with his ambition. He will be gone, but still he wants his ambition to be fulfilled. And if the son cannot fulfill the condition he will be left as a beggar on the streets, he will not be able to inherit his father's lifelong savings. And he is the only son, the money will rot in the bank, but he cannot get it.

Fortunately he managed, and managed far better than the father would ever have dreamed of. He was accepted as a Fellow of the Royal College of Physicians – the youngest in their whole history. People are accepted when they become old, experienced, when they have written many books and papers and done many researches and contributed much. Amrito did everything very quickly. He was the youngest fellow of the Royal College.

Every parent wants his child to be in his image. But a child has a destiny of his own. If he becomes your image he will never become himself. And without becoming yourself you will never feel contentment, you will never feel at ease with existence. You will always be in a condition of missing something.

Your parents love you, and they also tell you that you have to love them because they are your fathers, they are your mothers. It is a strange phenomenon and nobody seems to be aware of it. Just because you are a mother does not mean that the child has to love you. You have to be lovable; your being a mother is not enough. You may be a father; that does not mean that you automatically become lovable. Just because you are a father does not create a tremendous feeling of love in the child.

But it is expected, and the poor child does not know what to do. He starts pretending, that's the only possible way. He starts smiling when there is no smile in his heart; he starts showing love, respect, gratitude – and all are just false. He becomes an actor, a hypocrite from the very beginning, a politician. We are all living in this world where parents, teachers, priests – everybody has corrupted you, displaced you, has taken you away from yourself.

My effort here is to give your center back to you. I call this centering, meditation. I want you simply to be yourself, with a great self-respect, with a dignity that existence needed you. And then you can start searching for yourself. First come to the center, and then start searching for who you are.

Knowing one's original face is the beginning of a life of love, of a life of celebration. You will be able to give so much love because it is not something that is exhaustible, because it is immeasurable it cannot be exhausted. The more you give it, the more you become capable of giving it. And the greatest experience in life is when you simply give without any conditions, without any expectations of even a simple "thank-you."

On the contrary, a real, authentic love feels obliged to the person who has accepted his love. He could have rejected it.

When you start giving love with a deep sense of gratitude to all those who accept it, you will be surprised that you have become an emperor – no longer a beggar asking for love with a begging bowl, knocking on every door. And those people on whose doors you are knocking cannot give love to you. They are themselves beggars.

I have heard about two great astrologers. Every morning they used to meet on a certain crossroad. From there their paths separated; they practiced in different parts of the city. But it was almost a daily ritual: meeting on the crossroad before departing toward their sections of the city. They used to show their hands to each other, asking, "What is my destiny today?" And they were great astrologers! They were telling people their destinies and they did not know their own destinies for which they had to consult another astrologer who was consulting them! They each read the lines of the other and predicted.

Beggars are asking each other for love and feel frustrated, angry because the love is not coming. But this is bound to happen. Love belongs to the world of emperors, not of beggars. And a man is an emperor when he is so full of love that he can give it without any conditions.

Then comes an even greater surprise: that when you start giving your love to anybody, even to strangers – because the question is not to whom you are giving it; just the very joy of giving is so much that who cares who is on the receiving end? When this space comes into your being, that you go on giving to each and everybody; not only to human beings but to animals, to the trees, to the faraway stars because love is something that can be transferred even to the farthest star just by your loving look. Just by your touch, love can be transferred to a tree – without saying a single word. It can be conveyed in absolute silence.

And when I am saying it, I am not only saying it. I am a living example of whatever I am saying to you. Can't you feel my love? – although I have never said it to you. It need not be said; it declares itself. It has its own ways of reaching into the very depths, into your being.

First be full of love, then the sharing happens. And then the great surprise, that as you give you start receiving from unknown sources, from unknown corners, from unknown people; from trees, from rivers, from mountains. Love starts showering on you from all the nooks and corners of existence. The more you give, the more you get. Life becomes a sheer dance of love.

To me, this is the state of enlightenment: pure love. And except pure love, there is no God.

Osho,
Could you tell me if you are crucifying me or burning me?

Jayesh, just now I have been talking about love. Your question opens another dimension of love.

There is a cross on which a man like Jesus was crucified. It is of destruction and death; hate, violence and anger. It does not create anything; it only destroys. It is ugly.

But there is also another cross, the cross of love. It destroys in you all that is false, and it resurrects in you all that is authentic, all that is true. It kills you on one hand, and it revives you on the other hand. It kills only that which you are not, but what you have been identifying yourself with. It destroys your false identity, your personality, your hypocrisy.

And as your falseness is destroyed, your truth shines forth, radiates with tremendous beauty. The ancient seers of the East have called the master a death and a resurrection. The disciple goes through the being of the master. All that is false will be burned, and all that is true will come out in its immense glory and splendor, freed from all chains and bondages, in absolute beauty, freedom, grace and eternal joy.

Jayesh, I am certainly crucifying you – but this is the "you" that you are not. Every creator has to destroy to create. Just see a master sculptor...

I am reminded of a very beautiful story about Michelangelo. He was passing through the market where marble rocks were sold, and in front of the greatest shop he saw a huge marble rock lying on the other side of the road. He asked the shopkeeper, "How much will it cost for me to take that rock?"

The shopkeeper said, "It has been lying there for almost a decade. Nobody seems to have any interest in it. You are the first man in these ten years who has even inquired about it. I will give it to you for free. Just take it away; it is unnecessarily taking up my space. It is so ugly and so strange that I don't think you can make anything out of it."

The sculptor took it, and after three years he came back to the shop and invited the owner to see something that he had made. He had made a beautiful statue of Jesus with his mother, when Jesus was brought down from the cross. He is lying almost dead, bleeding, unconscious, in the lap of his mother.

Just a few years ago the statue was destroyed by a madman. It was thought to be one of the greatest pieces of art – and the madman destroyed it and said in the court, "I have destroyed it deliberately to become world famous." He became world famous. His picture was all over in all the magazines and papers; his name suddenly became known throughout the world.

But this beautiful statue – I have seen a picture of it. Jesus looks so beautiful, and his mother with tears in her eyes – the statue looks so alive that it seems Jesus is going to stand up. It is one of the most mysterious creations of man.

The owner of the shop could not believe it when the sculptor said, "It is from the same rock that you gave me for free."

The shopkeeper asked him, "But how could you even dream that that ugly rock could be transformed into such a beautiful piece?"

The sculptor said, "I did not dream about it. In fact, as I was passing by the side of the rock, Jesus called, 'I am encaged in this rock. Help me to be freed.' And all that I have done is not to create Jesus and Mary; I have simply taken away the unnecessary parts of the rock. My work has been only that of eliminating the false, the unnecessary, and what has remained is God's grace."

The function of the master is the same – to take away all that is false in you. And the real, the true and the authentic will be revealed the moment the false is taken away. The master never gives you anything. He only takes away the false, and the truth is already there. Just the unnecessary has to be eliminated.

Yes, Jayesh, I am crucifying you so that you can have a resurrection. But my cross is that of love; it is not to kill you. In fact you are dead as you are. It is to give you a taste of eternal life. It is to revive you, it is to call you from your grave to come out. Yes, in the beginning it looks like crucifixion, but it is really part of the process of resurrection.

Your question is significant. And you are also asking me, "Could you tell me if you are crucifying me or burning me?" As far as burning is concerned...

Just the other day, a woman came from England. Her sister was a sannyasin. Almost ten years ago, in an accident – and it was her own fault – she burned herself. We tried everything that was possible here and when we saw that perhaps she would not be able to recover in India – all her skin had been burned – I sent one of our doctors to take the girl back to England where better and more up-to-date facilities are available.

He took her to England. We arranged all the expenses for her traveling, for her medical care in England, but she could not be cured. She died. And after ten years this woman comes very angrily, saying, "We cannot ever forget it. My mother is still angry and I am angry that you killed my sister."

Amrito said, "This is strange. It was her own fault she got burned. We managed every expense here, and seeing that perhaps she needs better facilities, more up-to-date technology, we took her to England. We made every arrangement. Accidents can happen anywhere."

When I heard this I said, "These people seem to be absolutely stupid. They don't know anything about India." Here, everybody finally gets burned! There is of course one alternative. You can get burned and then you can die, or you can die first and then you can be burned. The choice is yours. Most people choose the second, it is just a question of liking, but everybody here in this country has to be burned finally.

So if you are asking about burning, it will happen – but not right now, Jayesh. There is much more for you to do. And as far as you are concerned, burning is not your problem. It is the problem of other sannyasins. You will be dead – unless you choose the other alternative.

You are too young yet to think about such things. I will give you a few maxims to think over instead:

"The saints are the sinners who keep on trying" – meditate over it.

"Take a risk. Even a turtle gets nowhere until he sticks his neck out."

"A man does not need twenty-twenty eyesight to appreciate a thirty- six, twenty-four, thirty-six vision."

"Nothing wrong ever happens at the right time."

"Save your money." It is particularly significant for Jayesh because he is my treasurer. "Save your money. You never know when your friends will need it."

Jayesh is a busy man, extremely busy, hence a special maxim for him: "A busy man is usually a happy man, unless he is busy scratching."

"Never judge a woman's feet by the shape of her shoes."

"Success is when you have your name in everything except the phone book."

"Salesmanship is the difference between rape and rapture."

"Whiskey may not cure a cold, but no remedy fails with such satisfaction."

"Not all philosophers are married men, but all married men become philosophers."

Jayesh, this is not the time for you to be burned, this is the time to have a good time.

The priest, traveling on a first class sleeper train, had a double compartment all to himself. Having just finished his dinner in the dining car, he returned to his compartment, but was shocked to find two scantily-dressed, sexy- looking girls inside.

He immediately cried out, "You girls are in the wrong compartment. I'm a respectable man, the pillar of my community, and there has never, ever been the smallest whiff of scandal about me in my whole life. So," the priest continued, pulling himself up to his full height, "*one* of you girls will have to go!"

Jayesh, when the burning will come, it will come. We will celebrate it – it is a promise. Meanwhile, enjoy life as much as you can. It is none of your business to worry about things that are going to happen after your death.

Life is so precious. Not a single moment has to be wasted in thinking what will happen after death. Here in India, it is certain that burning will happen. So you can be absolutely unworried and unconcerned. You will not be the one who will have to take care of the burning, and you will not be the one who will be burned on the funeral pyre. You will be a witness standing in the crowd of the celebrant sannyasins. The only difference will be that you will not be visible anymore.

But that is not a misfortune. Just think of the great adventures when you become invisible!

5

The Art of Let-go

Osho,

Why is it so difficult to be in a state of let-go?

The world needs workaholics. It needs people to be slaves, to be proletarians, to be laborers and function just like machines; hence all the so-called moralists and puritans have been teaching people that work has some intrinsic value. It has none.

It has some value, but of the lowest kind: it is a need. Because people have stomachs, they need bread and butter, and they need clothes and a roof over their heads. This natural need has been exploited to the extreme. People are forced to work, but whatever they produce does not come to them. It goes to the people who don't work.

The society has been forever an exploitative society. It has been divided into the "haves" and the "have-nots." The "have-nots" have to work just to survive, and the "haves" go on accumulating mountains of money. It is a very ugly situation – inhuman, primitive, insane. The people who work are poor, hungry, starving. They don't have time for literature, for music, for paintings. They can't even conceive that there are worlds of tremendous beauty, of art; they cannot even imagine that there is something like meditation. It is enough for them to get one meal a day. Just the other day I was informed that Ethiopia is ready for another famine. Just a year ago millions of people died in Ethiopia and the whole world watched. It not only watched: America destroyed billions of dollars worth of foodstuff in the ocean – but it could not be given to the poor who are starving. The countries of Europe destroyed even more because they had so much surplus – mountains of butter. And the new crops were coming so they needed the old crops to be taken out of their warehouses. They were short of warehouses and just by their side one thousand people in Ethiopia were dying every day, just out of hunger.

And the European countries spent two billion dollars just to destroy the surplus foodstuff. It is not known how much the cost of the food was that they destroyed in the ocean; two billion dollars is only the cost of destroying it.

And now, again, Ethiopia is facing another calamity. And the European countries have agreed with Ethiopia that they will give their surplus, but only on one condition. Man seems to be one of the most useless things in the world. It seems man exists for all kinds of conditions and ideologies, not vice versa. The European countries had a condition because in Ethiopia there is a Marxist government, and they made it a condition that: "We will give you food – we have a surplus, there is no problem – but you will have to stop your Marxist plans absolutely."

The food was supposed to have reached by now, but it has not even moved from the warehouses in Europe. And the reason the European countries are giving is that: "You are still continuing your Marxist plans." Can you see the insanity of it? They are more concerned with Marxist plans, which have nothing to do with them. They are not concerned with millions of people dying again. And it is not only a question of other countries – naturally nobody has the responsibility for other countries. In the same country, for example, in America, thirty million people are on the streets without food, without clothes, without shelter. And it is a strange, ironical coincidence that exactly the same number of Americans, thirty million, are dying in hospitals, in nursing and care homes because they have stuffed their bodies with too much food, and they cannot stop.

They will die because of eating too much, and a similar number of people will die because they don't have anything to eat.

These thirty million people are eating the share of the other thirty million who are on the streets. They are ready to work, but there is no work. And when there is no work, nobody is interested in feeding the poor. The poor are fed only if they are needed for work.

Down the ages the majority has been poor, and their survival was dependent on their utility as productive mechanisms. The moment they were not needed they were left to die in hunger and starvation. And they are the real owners of the whole wealth of the world because they are the producers. But cunning people have managed conspiracies with politicians, with priests, to keep the society divided into two different categories: those who are really human beings – the people who are rich, super-rich – and those who are just human beings in name, but are being used as commodities, as productive mechanisms.

Because of this situation the vested interests have been teaching only one thing down the ages: that is work, and work hard so that you can produce more, and the rich can become even richer.

The value of work is only to produce enough for everybody. Perhaps four or five hours work a day would be enough for the whole of humanity to live peacefully and comfortably. But this insane desire to be rich, this insane greed which knows no limits; without any understanding that the more money you have the less value your money has.

It is a simple law of economics: the law of diminishing returns. You have one house: it is valuable, you have to live in it, you need it. You have two houses, you have three houses, you have hundreds of houses... The value goes on diminishing as the number of houses goes on growing.

But there is a small class in the world, which has absolutely valueless money. For example, the richest man in the world is now a

Japanese who has twenty-one billion dollars cash in his banks. What is he going to do with it? Can you eat it? And money attracts more money: just from sheer interest that man will go on becoming more and more rich. Beyond a certain limit money loses all value. But greed is absolutely mad. The whole human society has lived under a kind of insanity.

That's why it is so difficult to be in a state of let-go because it has always been condemned as laziness. It is against the workaholic society. Let-go means you start living in a saner way. You are no longer madly after money; you don't go on working continuously. You work just for your material needs, but there are spiritual needs too. Work is a necessity for material needs, let-go is necessary for spiritual needs. But the majority of humanity has been completely boycotted from any spiritual growth.

Let-go is one of the most beautiful spaces. You simply exist, doing nothing, sitting silently, and the grass grows by itself. You simply enjoy the songs of the birds, the greenness of the trees, the multidimensional, psychedelic colors of the flowers. You don't have to do anything to experience existence; you have to stop doing. You have to be in an absolutely unoccupied state, with no tensions, with no worries.

In this state of tranquility you come into a certain attuning with the music that surrounds us. You suddenly become aware of the beauty of the sun. There are millions of people who have never enjoyed a sunset, who have never enjoyed a sunrise. They cannot afford it. They are continuously working and producing – not for themselves, but for the cunning vested interests: those who are in power, those who are capable of manipulating human beings.

Naturally they teach you that work is something great – it is in their interest. And the conditioning has become so deep that even you don't know why you cannot relax.

Even on holidays people go on doing something or other. They cannot enjoy a holiday, just relaxing on the sea beach and enjoying the ocean and the very fresh and salty air. No, they will do any stupid thing. If they have nothing to do they may take their refrigerator apart – which has been functioning perfectly well – or they may destroy an old grandfather clock, which has been functioning for centuries. They are trying to improve upon it, but basically they cannot sit silently, that is the problem. They have to do something, they have to go somewhere.

On every holiday people are rushing to health resorts, sea beaches – not to rest there; they don't have time to rest because millions of people are going there. Holidays are the best time to remain at home because the whole city has gone to the sea beach. Cars are going bumper to bumper, and by the time they reach the beach it is full of people; they cannot even find a small place to lie down. I have seen pictures of sea beaches. Even the ocean must be laughing at the stupidity of these people.

For a few minutes they will lie down, and then they need ice cream and they need Coca-Cola. And they have brought their portable television sets and everybody is listening to his transistor... And then again the marathon race back home because the time is over. More accidents happen in the world on holidays than on any other days: more people are killed, more cars are crashed. It is strange! And for five days in the week – the working days – people are hoping, waiting with great longing for the holiday. And in those two days, which are the weekend, they are simply waiting for their offices and their factories to open. People have completely forgotten the language of relaxation. They have been made to forget it.

Every child is born with an inner capacity; you don't have to teach the child how to relax.

You just watch a child – he *is* relaxed, he *is* in a let-go. But you won't allow him to enjoy this state of paradise. You will soon civilize him – because every child is primitive, uncivilized. And the parents and the teachers, everybody, is after the children to civilize them, to make them part of the society – and nobody bothers that the society is absolutely insane. It will be good if the child remains as he is, is no longer initiated into the society and your so-called civilization.

But with all good wishes the parents cannot leave the child alone. They have to teach him to work, they have to teach him to be productive, they have to teach him to be competitive. They have to teach him, "Unless you are at the top you have failed us."

So everybody is running to be at the top. How can you relax?

When, for the first time in India, railway lines were being laid down... I have heard a beautiful story...

The British engineer who was overseeing the work that was going on was amazed to see that every day a young Indian, a villager, would come and lie down under the shade of a big tree and watch the workers working and the engineers instructing them. The engineer became interested: This is a strange fellow! He comes every day, he brings his food with him, he takes his lunch and rests, he sleeps in the afternoon under the shade of the tree.

Finally the engineer could not resist the temptation and he asked the villager, "Why don't you start working? You come every day anyway, and you waste your time just lying down, watching."

The villager asked, "Working? But for what?"

The engineer said, "You will earn money!"

The villager asked, "But what will I do with the money?"

The engineer said, "Stupid, you don't know what can be done with the money? When you have money you can relax and enjoy!"

The poor villager said, "This is strange because I am already relaxed and enjoying! Going in such a roundabout way: working hard, earning money and then enjoying and relaxing – but I am doing it already!"

Children come with the intrinsic, intuitive quality of let-go. They are utterly relaxed. That's why all children are beautiful. Have you ever thought about it? All children, without exception, have a tremendous grace, aliveness and beauty. And these children are going to grow, and all their beauty and their grace will disappear. It is very difficult to find a grown-up man with the same grace, with the same beauty, with the same aliveness.

If you can find a man with childlike innocence and relaxation, you have found a sage.

That's how we have defined the sage in the East: he attains his childhood again. After experiencing all the ups and downs in life, finally he decides – the decision comes by itself out of experience – that before death comes, he has to be again the same as he was in his childhood.

I teach you let-go because that's the only thing that can make you a sage. No church will help, no theology, no religion because none of them teach you let-go. They all insist on work, on the dignity of labor. They use beautiful words to enslave you, to exploit you. They are in conspiracy with the parasites of the society.

I am not against work; work has its own utility – but only utility. It cannot become your life's be all and end all. It is an absolute necessity that you need food, that you need clothes, that you need a shelter. Work, but don't become addicted to work. The moment you are out of work, you should know how to relax. It does not need much wisdom to relax. It is a simple art, and it is very simple because you already knew it when you were born. So it is already there; it just has to be made active from a dormant position, it has to be provoked.

All methods of meditation are nothing but methods to help you to remember the art of let-go. I say remember because you know it already. And you know it still, but that knowledge is being repressed by the society.

Simple principles have to be remembered. The body should be the beginning. Lying down on your bed – and you lie down on your bed every day, so there is no special necessity to do so. When you lie down on the bed, before sleep comes, start watching with closed eyes the energy from your feet. Move from there, just watch inside: Is there some tension somewhere – in the legs, in the thighs, in the stomach? Is there some strain, some tension? If you find some tension somewhere, simply try to relax it, and don't move from that point unless you feel the relaxation has come.

Go through the hands because your hands are your mind; they are connected with your mind. If your right hand is tense, the left side of your brain will be tense. If your left hand is tense, the right side of your brain will be tense. So first go through the hands – they are almost the branches of your mind – and then reach finally to the mind.

When the whole body is relaxed the mind is already ninety percent relaxed because the body is nothing but extensions of the mind. Then simply watch the ten percent tension that is in your mind, and just by watching the clouds will disappear. It will take a few days for you. It is a knack. And it will revive your childhood experience – when you were so relaxed.

Have you ever watched? Children go on falling every day, but they don't get hurt, they don't get fractures. You try it; whenever the child falls you also fall.

A psychoanalyst tried an experiment. He announced in the newspapers, "I will pay enough money if somebody is ready to come to my house and just follow my child for the whole day. Whatever my child does, you have to do that."

A young wrestler turned up and he said, "I am ready. Where is the child?"

But by the middle of the day the wrestler was flat on his back! He already had two fractures because everything that the child was doing he had to do. And the child got excited because this was strange, so he would jump unnecessarily, and the wrestler had to jump; he would climb the tree, and the wrestler had to climb; and he would jump from the tree, and the wrestler had to jump.

And this continued. The child completely forgot about food, about everything; he was enjoying the misery of the wrestler so much.

By the afternoon the wrestler simply refused. He said to the psychoanalyst, "Keep your money! This child of yours will kill me by the end of the day. I am already ready to go to the hospital. This child is dangerous! Don't do this experiment with anybody else."

Every child has so much energy, and still he is not tense. Have you watched a child sleeping? Have you watched a child just sucking his own thumb – enjoying it, dreaming beautiful dreams? His whole body is in a deep let-go.

It happens, it is a known fact: every day, all over the world, drunkards fall, but they don't get fractures. Every morning they are found in some gutter and brought home. But it is a strange fact that they go on falling.

I have heard about a drunkard who was coming home and got hit on the head by an electric pole. He looked at the pole and he saw at least eight poles. He said, "My God, how am I going to reach home?"

He tried this way and that way, but nothing helped. Every time the same electric pole would hit him hard. Finally he shouted for help.

A policeman came and asked, "What is the matter?"

He said, "I am surrounded by electric poles and I cannot get out. And you know my wife! I have to reach home. I have been struggling for almost two hours. Who has done this? – because in the day I saw that there was only one electric pole!"

The policeman took him away from those imaginary poles. He had been struggling for two hours, but he was not hurt because a drunkard is relaxed.

I have known accidents in which only drunkards remained unhurt; everybody else was hurt.

Once a train fell from a bridge. That happens almost every year in India, two or three times. Bridges simply collapse, particularly the newly built bridges because there are so many people to be bribed before you can get the government's permission to build the bridge. Finally the constructor, the builder, has to make money out of the bridge – he has spent so much. You have to bribe almost every person who is concerned.

Naturally he does not use cement, but only sand. So the first time the train comes onto the bridge, the whole train goes into the river with the bridge.

Once it happened just near my village. I rushed to look. Only one man had remained unhurt, and that was the village drunkard. When I saw him he asked me, "What has happened? In fact, I don't know why I was traveling in this train. Some idiots put me in the train. I resisted, but before I could get out, the train moved and then suddenly I found myself swimming in the river. I don't know what happened in the middle. The middle portion of the story is completely missing."

I said, "Just come home with me because everybody else has to go to the hospital." A few people were unconscious, a few had died, a few had many fractures – multiple fractures. Everybody was in a mess except that drunkard, who was asking me, "What has happened?"

I took him back home. He was asking me again and again on the way, "You can tell me, I will not tell anybody."

I said, "I don't know. You were on the train!"

He said, "That I know. I remember a few people pushed me into the train, and I was absolutely reluctant because I didn't want to go anywhere. I was going to my home. I thought, 'Perhaps the train is going toward my home.' And then finally I found myself in the river! But in a way it is good because for at least two, three months I have not taken a bath. And the cold water in the river has also made my senses come back. I am a little conscious."

The drunkard will not get hurt because he does not know he is falling, so he does not become tense. He simply falls without becoming tense. It is the tenseness that gives you fractures. If you can fall in a relaxed way you will not be hurt. Drunkards know it, children know it – how did you manage to forget?

Start from your bed, every night, and within a few days you will be able to catch the knack. Once you know the secret – nobody can teach it to you, you will have to search within your own body – then even in the day, at any time, you can relax. And to be a master of relaxation is one of the most beautiful experiences in the world. It is the beginning of a great journey toward spirituality because when you are completely in a let-go, you are no longer a body.

Have you ever observed a simple fact: that you become aware of your body only when there is some tension, some strain, some pain? Have you ever become aware of your head without a headache? If your whole body is relaxed, you simply forget that you are a body. And in that forgetting of the body is the remembering of a new phenomenon that is hidden inside the body: your spiritual being.

Let-go is the way to know that you are not the body, but something eternal, immortal. There is no need for any other religion in the world. Just the simple art of let-go will turn every human being into a religious person – because religion is not believing in God, religion is not believing in the Pope, religion is not believing in any ideological system. Religion is knowing that which is eternal within you – *satyam shivam sundaram* – that which is the truth of your existence, that which is your divinity, and that which is your beauty, your grace, your splendor.

The art of let-go is synonymous with experiencing the immaterial, the immeasurable: your authentic being.

There are a few moments when, without being aware, you are in a let-go. For example, when you are really laughing – not just from the head but also from your belly, belly laughter – you are relaxed without your knowing, you are in a let-go. That's why laughter is so health-giving. There is no other medicine which can help you more in attaining well-being. But the same conspirators who have stopped your awareness of let-go have stopped laughter. The whole of humanity has been turned into a serious, psychologically sick mass.

Have you heard the giggle of a small child? His whole body participates in it. And when you laugh, it is very rare that your whole body laughs – it is just an intellectual, heady thing.

My own understanding is that laughter is far more important than any prayer because prayer will not relax you. On the contrary, it may make you more tense. In laughter you suddenly forget all the conditioning, all the training, all seriousness. Suddenly you are out of it – just for a moment. Next time you laugh, be alert about how relaxed you are. And find out other times when you are relaxed.

After making love you are relaxed, although the same company of conspirators does not allow you to be relaxed even after making love. The man simply turns to the other side and pretends to go to sleep, but deep down he is feeling guilty that he has committed the sin again. The woman is crying because she feels she has been used. And it is absolutely natural to feel so because she gets no nourishment from love. She never gets any orgasmic experience. Just fifty years ago there was not a single woman in the whole world who had experienced orgasm. In India it is extremely difficult to find a woman who knows what orgasm is.

There cannot be a greater conspiracy against humanity. The man wants to finish the whole thing as quickly as possible. Inside him he is carrying The Bible, the Koran, Shrimad Bhagavadgita, and they are all against what he is doing. He is also convinced that he is doing something wrong. So naturally, the quicker it is over the better. And afterward he feels tremendously bad. How can he relax? He becomes more tense. And because he is so quick the woman never comes to the peak. By the time she starts, he is finished! Naturally, the woman starts believing that man is something more like an animal.

In the churches, in the temples, you will find only women, old women particularly. And when the priest talks about sin, they know! It was absolutely sin because they had gained no pleasure out of it; they were used like any commodity – sexual objects. Otherwise, if you are free of guilt, free of all inhibitions, love will give you a tremendous experience of let-go.

So you have to look into your life, for where you can find some natural experience of let-go. Listening to me you can experience a let-go. It happens every day, but you are not aware of it. I can see your faces changing, I can see your silences deepening. I can see when you laugh that your laughter is no longer chained and handcuffed, that your laughter is now your freedom. I can observe every day that you go on becoming more and more relaxed: as if you are not listening to a talk but listening to soft music, not to words but to my silences. If you cannot experience a let-go in my presence here, it will be very difficult for you to find it anywhere else.

But there are moments when you are swimming... If you are really a swimmer, you can manage just to float, not to swim. And you will find tremendous let-go, just going with the river, not even making any movement against the current; becoming part of the current.

You have to gather experiences of let-go from different sources, and soon you will have the whole secret in your hands. And it is one of the most fundamental things, particularly for my people. It will free you from workaholic conditioning.

It does not mean that you will become lazy. On the contrary, the more relaxed you are, the more powerful you are, the more energy gathers when you are relaxed. Your work will start having a quality of creativity – not production. Whatever you will do, you will do with such totality, with such love, and you will have tremendous energy to do it.

So let-go is not against work. In fact, let-go transforms work into a creative experience.

A few jokes for you and for you all. Have a total laugh, which takes away all tensions from your face, from your body, from your stomach, and you will suddenly feel a totally different kind of energy within you. Otherwise most people are continuously feeling knots in their stomachs.

Nathan Nussbaum went to consult a world-famous specialist about his medical problem.

"How much do I owe you?" asked Nat.

"My fee is five hundred dollars," replied the quack.

"Five hundred dollars? That's impossible!" exclaimed Nathan.

"In your case," the specialist replied, "I suppose I could adjust my fee to three hundred dollars."

"Three hundred dollars for one visit? Ridiculous!" cried Nathan.

"Well then," asked the doctor, "can you afford one hundred and fifty dollars?"

"Who has so much money?" Nathan moaned.

"Listen," said the quack, "just give me fifty dollars and be gone."

"I can give you twenty dollars," said Nathan. "Take it or leave it."

"I don't understand you," said the specialist. "Why did you come to the most expensive doctor in New York?"

"Listen, doctor," explained Nathan, "when it comes to my health, nothing is too expensive."

Paddy's friend, Joe, was taking a night course in adult education. "Who is Ronald Reagan?" he asked Paddy.

"I don't know," Paddy replied.

"He is the president of the United States," said Joe. "Now, do you know who Margaret Thatcher is?"

"No," said Paddy.

"She is the prime minister of Britain," said Joe. "You see? You should go to night school like I do."

"Now I have a question for you," said Paddy. "Do you know who Mick O'Sullivan is?"

"I don't," admitted Joe.

"Well," said Paddy, "he is the guy who is screwing your wife while you are at night school."

Jesus and Moses are out one Sunday afternoon for a round of golf. Moses drives first and the ball goes straight down the fairway. Jesus gets ready and on his first drive slices the ball into some tall grass.

"Holy Moses!" cries Jesus. But Moses, being a good fellow, offers Jesus the chance to place his ball on the fairway with no penalty. But Jesus is stubborn and turns down the offer. Moses then says, "Come on Jesus, you can't take a shot in such tall grass."

"If Arnold Palmer can do it," replies Jesus, "so can I." Jesus then takes a smash and knocks the ball, "splash!" into a pond. Then Moses hits his second shot straight onto the green and returns to watch Jesus. Jesus is rolling up his jeans.

"Jesus, please!" cries Moses, "I implore you to just place your ball on the fairway. It will take a miracle to make such a shot!"

"If Arnold Palmer can do it," replies Jesus, "so can I," and he strides off across the top of the water.

A gardener, who has been watching the scene, approaches Moses and says, "Just who does that guy think he is, Jesus Christ?"

"No such luck," replies Moses. "He thinks he is Arnold Palmer!"

Osho,

What is it to give and what is it to receive? I understand now that I am only just beginning to glimpse these. Receptiveness feels like dying to me, and automatically everything inside goes on red alert! Help! Existence seems so huge.

Prem Dhiresha, I can understand what is troubling you. It is troubling almost everybody. It is good that you have recognized it because now, changing the situation is possible. Unfortunate are those who are suffering from the same problem but are not aware of it. Because of their unawareness there is no possibility of any transformation.

You have taken courage to expose yourself. I am immensely glad about it. I want all my people to be courageous enough to expose themselves, howsoever ugly it seems.

The conditioning is to go on hiding the ugly and go on pretending about the beautiful. That creates a schizophrenic situation. You go on showing yourself – what you are not; and you go on repressing yourself – what you are. Your life becomes a continuous civil war. You are fighting with yourself, and any fight with yourself is going to destroy you. Nobody can win.

If my right hand and left hand start fighting, do you think any hand can win? I can manage sometimes to let the right hand feel good as a winner, and sometimes to change the situation and let the left hand feel it is the winner. But nobody can really be the winner because they are both *my* hands.

Almost every human being is carrying a split personality. And the most significant fact is that he identifies himself with the false part and he denies his reality. In this situation you cannot hope to grow up as a spiritual being.

What Dhiresha is saying is tremendously important to understand. She is asking, "What is it to give?" Have you ever asked yourself what it is to give? You think you are already giving too much to your children, to your wife, to your girlfriend, to the society, to the Rotary Club, to the Lions Club – you are giving so much. But the fact is, you don't know what it is to give.

Unless you give yourself you don't give at all.

You can give money, but you are not the money. Unless you give yourself, that means unless you give love, you don't know what giving is.

"...And what is it to receive?" Almost everybody thinks he knows what it is to receive. But Dhiresha is right in questioning and exposing herself that she does not know what it is to receive. Just as unless you give love you don't know what it is to give, the same is true about receiving: unless you are capable of receiving love, you don't know what it is to receive. You want to be loved, but you have not thought about it: are you capable of receiving love?

There are so many hindrances which won't allow you to receive it. The first is that you don't have any self-respect; hence when love comes toward you, you don't feel yourself adequate, enough to receive it. But you are in such a mess that you cannot even see a simple fact, that because you have never accepted yourself as you are, you have never loved yourself, how can you manage to receive somebody else's love? You know you are not worthy of it, but you don't want to accept and recognize this stupid idea that has been fed to you – that you are not worthy of it.

So what do you do? You simply refuse love. And to refuse love you have to find excuses.

The first and the most prominent excuse is, "It is not love. That's why I cannot accept it." You cannot believe that somebody can love you. When you yourself cannot love you, when you have not seen your beauty and your grace and your grandeur, how can you believe it when somebody says, "You are beautiful. I can see a depth in your eyes, unfathomable, of tremendous grace. I can see in your heart a rhythm, in tune with the universe."

You cannot believe all this; it is too much. You are accustomed to being condemned, you are accustomed to being punished, you are accustomed to being rejected, you are accustomed to not being accepted as you are. These things you can take very easily.

Love will have a tremendous impact on you because you will have to go through a great transformation before you can receive it. First you have to accept yourself without any guilt. You are not a sinner as the Christians and other religions go on teaching you.

You don't see the stupidity of the whole thing. Some guy far away in the past, one Adam, disobeyed God – which is not much of a sin. In fact, he was absolutely right to disobey him. If anybody committed a sin it was God, by prohibiting his own son, his own daughter, from eating the fruit of knowledge and eating the fruit of eternal life. What kind of father? What kind of God? What kind of love?

Love demands that God should have told Adam and Eve: "Before you eat anything else, these two trees have to be remembered. Eat as much from the Tree of Wisdom and eat as much from the Tree of Eternal Life as you like, so that you can also be in the same space of immortality in which I am."

That should be a simple thing for anyone who loves. But God prohibiting Adam from wisdom means he wants him to remain ignorant. Perhaps he is jealous, afraid, apprehensive that if Adam becomes wise, he will become equal to him. He wants to keep Adam in his ignorance so that he remains inferior. If he eats the fruit of eternal life, then he will be a god himself.

This God who prevented Adam and Eve must have been very jealous, utterly ugly, inhuman, unloving. And if all these things are not sin, then what can sin be? But religions have been teaching you, Jews and Christians and Mohammedans, that you are still carrying the sin that Adam committed. There is a limit to stretching lies out for so long. Even if Adam had committed a sin, you cannot carry it. According to these religions, you were created by God but you are not carrying godliness. You are carrying Adam and Eve's disobedience.

This is the Western way to condemn you: you are a sinner. The Eastern way comes to the same conclusion but from different premises. They say everybody is loaded with immense sin and evil deeds, committed in millions of past lives. In fact, the burden of a Christian or a Jew or a Mohammedan is far less. You are only carrying the sin that Adam and Eve committed. And it must have become very diluted, centuries upon centuries. You are not a direct inheritor of Adam and Eve's sin. It has passed through many millions of hands: by now the quantity must be almost homeopathic!

But the Eastern concept is even more dangerous. You are not carrying somebody else's sin. In the first place, you cannot carry somebody else's sin. Your father commits a crime – you cannot be sent to jail. Even ordinary human common sense will say that if the father has committed the sin or the crime, he has to suffer. The son or the grandson cannot be sent to the gallows because the grandfather committed a murder.

But the Eastern concept is much more dangerous and poisonous: it is your own sin that you are carrying, not that of Adam and Eve. And it is not a small quantity; it has been growing with each life! And you have lived millions of lives before this life, and each life you have committed so many sins. They have all accumulated on your chest. The burden is Himalayan; you are crushed under it.

This is a strange strategy to destroy your dignity, to reduce you into a subhuman being. How can you love yourself? You can hate, but you cannot love. How can you think that somebody may be able to love you? It is better to reject it because sooner or later the person who is offering you his love is going to discover your reality, which is very ugly – just a long, long burden of sin. And then that person is going to reject you. To avoid rejection it is better to reject love. That's why people don't accept love.

They desire it, they long for it. But when the moment comes and somebody is ready to shower you with love, you shrink back. Your shrinking has a deep psychology. You are afraid. "This is beautiful, but how long will it last? Sooner or later my reality will be revealed. It is better from the very beginning to be alert."

Love means intimacy, love means two persons coming closer, love means two bodies but one soul. You are afraid. Your soul, a sinner's soul, burdened with the evil deeds of millions of lives... No, it is better to hide it; it is better not to come into a position where the person who wanted to love you rejects you. It is the fear of rejection that does not allow you to receive love.

You cannot give love because nobody has ever told you that you are born a loving being. They have told you, "You are born in sin!" You cannot love and you cannot receive love either. This has diminished all possibilities of your growth.

Dhiresha is saying, "I understand now that I am only just beginning to glimpse this."

You are fortunate because there are millions of people in the world who have become completely blind to their own conditionings, to the ugly burdens that the older generation has given them. It is hurting so much that it is better to forget all about it.

But by forgetting it you cannot remove it. By forgetting a cancer you cannot operate upon it. By not recognizing it, keeping it in the dark, you are taking the greatest unnecessary risk against yourself. It will go on growing. It needs darkness; it needs you not to know about it. Sooner or later it will cover up your whole being, and nobody else will be responsible for it except you.

So if, Dhiresha, you feel that you are glimpsing, a few windows are opening in you.

"Receptiveness feels like dying to me." Have you ever thought about it, that receptiveness feels like dying to you? But it is true. Receptiveness feels like dying because receptiveness looks like humiliation. To receive something, particularly love, means you are a beggar. Nobody wants to be on the receiving end because that makes you inferior to the giver.

"Receptiveness feels like dying to me and automatically everything inside goes on red alert." This red alert is implanted in you by the society that you have always respected, by the same people you thought were your well-wishers. And I don't say that they are intentionally trying to harm you. They have been harmed by others and they are simply transferring whatsoever they have received from their parents, from their teachers, from the older generation.

Each generation goes on giving its diseases to the new generation, and naturally the new generation becomes more and more burdened. You are the inheritor of all the superstitious, repressive concepts from the whole of history. What goes on red alert is not something that belongs to you, Dhiresha. It is your conditioning that goes on red alert. And your last sentence is just an effort to find a rationalization for it.

That is also one of the great dangers everybody has to be aware of. Don't rationalize. Go to the very roots of every problem, but don't find excuses because if you find excuses you cannot remove those roots.

The last statement of Dhiresha's is a rationalization. Perhaps she has not been able to see its intrinsic quality. She says, "Help! Existence seems so huge."

Now she is thinking that she is afraid of receiving because existence is so huge, she is afraid of giving because existence is so huge. What is the point of giving your small love, just like a dewdrop, to the ocean? The ocean will never know about it; hence there is no point in giving and there is no point in receiving either. Because the ocean is so huge, you will be drowned in it. Hence it looks like death. But this is your rationalization.

You don't know anything about existence; you don't know anything about yourself – which is the closest point of existence to you. Unless you start from your own being, you will never know existence. That is the starting point, and everything has to begin from the very beginning.

Knowing yourself, you will know your existence. But the taste and the fragrance of your existence will give you courage to go a little deeper into the existence of others. If your own existence has made you so blissful, it is a natural longing to enter into other mysteries that surround you: human mysteries, mysteries of the animals, mysteries of the trees, mysteries of the stars...

And once you have known your existence you are no longer afraid of death. Death is a fiction; it does not happen, it only appears. It appears from the outside.

Have you ever seen your own death? You have always seen somebody else dying, but have you seen yourself dying? Nobody has; otherwise even this minimum of life would become impossible. You see every day that somebody is dying, but it is always somebody else; it is never you.

The poet who wrote, "Never ask for whom the bell tolls; it tolls for thee," has a deeper understanding than you. He must have been a Christian because when somebody dies in a Christian village the church bell rings to inform everybody – people who have gone to their farms, to their orchards, people who have gone to work somewhere. The church bell reminds them: somebody has died. So they all have to come back to give the last farewell.

But the poet has a tremendous insight when he says, "Never ask for whom the bell tolls; it tolls for thee."

But in your actual life it never rings for thee. One day it will ring, but then you will no longer be here to hear it. You never think of yourself at the threshold of death – and everybody is standing on the threshold. You always see somebody else dying; hence the experience is objective, not subjective.

The other is not really dying, but only changing houses. His life force is moving into a new form, into a new plane. Only the body is left without life energy – but the body never had it.

It is just like in a dark house when a candle is burning and the whole house is lighted. Even from the outside you can see the light: from the windows, from the doors – but the house does not have the light as an intrinsic part of it. The moment the candle finishes, the house will be in darkness. In fact it has always been in darkness; it was the candle that was the light.

Your body is already dead. What gives you the impression that it is alive is your life force, your being, which radiates through the body, which fills the body with aliveness. All that you see when people die is that something has disappeared. You don't know where it has gone – whether it has gone anywhere or simply ceased to be. So from the outside the fiction of death has been created.

Those who have known themselves know, without any doubt, that they are eternal beings. They have died many times, yet they are alive.

Death and birth are only small episodes in the great pilgrimage of the soul. The moment you come in contact with yourself, your fear of death will immediately disappear. And that opens a totally new sky to be explored. Once you know that there is no death, all fear disappears: the fear of the unknown, the fear of the dark; whatever the form, all fears disappear. For the first time you start being a real adventurer. You start moving into different mysteries that surround you. For the first time existence becomes your home.

There is nothing to be feared: it is your mother; you are a part of it. It cannot drown you, it cannot destroy you. The more you know it, the more you will feel nourished; the more you know it, the more you will feel blessed; the more you know it, the more you will be. And then you can give love because you have it. And then you can receive love because there is no question of rejection.

Prem Dhiresha, your question will be helpful to all my people. I thank you for your question and for your courage to expose yourself.

This courage is needed by everyone because without this courage you cannot hope for any possibility of transformation – into a new world, into a new consciousness, into your authentic being, which is the door to ultimate reality and to ultimate benediction.

6

Wings for Your Freedom

Osho,

I don't understand why enlightened masters are critical of each other. Are they not all working toward the higher good? Are they not different flavors of the same truth?

The question you have asked is almost impossible to answer for the simple reason that you are not enlightened yet. You don't know the ways of the enlightened ones. You don't know their devices, you don't know their methods; hence the misunderstanding.

An ancient story may help you. In a great city there were two big sweet shops, and one day the owners of both the shops started fighting with each other for some reason. Naturally, they had no other way to fight, so they started throwing sweets at each other. And the whole city gathered and people were enjoying the sweets that were falling on the street.

When two enlightened masters criticize each other it brings tremendous joy to those who can understand. Its taste is just unbelievable. They are not enemies: their fight is not of the ego. Their fight has a totally different context.

They fight because they know one thing: that the goal is one, but the paths are many. And each master has to defend his path, knowing perfectly well that the other paths are as valid as his. But if he starts saying that all the paths are valid, he will not have the impact, the influence on his people. The journey is long and he needs absolute trust.

He is not a philosopher propounding a system of philosophy. His basic concern is that your commitment to the path should be total. To make it total he condemns all other paths, he criticizes all other ways. It is just out of compassion for you. He knows the people on the other path will also reach, and he knows that out of compassion the master on the other path has to criticize him, has to criticize his ways.

This is just a simple methodology to protect the disciple from influences that can take him astray. And the mind is very, very clever in going astray. If all the paths are valid, then what is the necessity of commitment? If all the paths are valid, then what is the necessity of being total?

If all the paths are valid, then why not travel all the paths? Why not go on changing, enjoying different ways, different methods, different sceneries? Each path will pass through different lands: there are paths that will go through the desert, and there are paths that will go through the mountains, and there are paths that will pass through beautiful, flowering trees.

But if you travel for some time on one path and then you change the path, you will have to start again from *ABC*. Whatever you have learned on one path is invalid on another path, and if you go on keeping it within you it is going to create tremendous confusion. You are already in a great mess. No master wants you to be more confused.

Your mind always wants change. It does not know devotion; it loves fashions, its interest is always in some novelty. So it will go on moving from one path to another path, becoming more and more confused because each path has its own language, each path has its own unique methods, and each master is going to defend his path against all the other paths.

If you move on many paths you will collect contradictory arguments; you will become so much divided you will not know what to do. And if it becomes your habit to change paths – because the new has a certain attraction for the mind – you will move a few feet on one path, a few feet on another path, but you will never complete the journey.

One day Jalaluddin Rumi took all his students, disciples and devotees to a field. That was his way to teach them things of the beyond, through the examples of this world. He was not a theoretician; he was a very practical man. The disciples were thinking, "What could be the message, going to that faraway field and why can't he say it here?"

But when they reached the field, they understood that they were wrong and he was right. The farmer seemed to be an almost insane man. He was digging a well in the field – and he had already dug eight incomplete wells. He would go a few feet and then he would find that there was no water. Then he would start digging another well – and the same story continued. He had destroyed the whole field and he had not yet found water.

The master, Jalaluddin Rumi, told his disciples, "Can you understand something? If this man had been total and had put his whole energy into only one well he would have reached the deepest sources of water long ago. But the way he is going he will destroy the whole field and he will never be able to make a single well. With so much effort he is simply destroying his own land, and getting more and more frustrated, disappointed. What kind of a desert has he purchased? It is not a desert, but one has to go deep to find the sources of water."

He turned to his disciples and asked them, "Are you going to follow this insane farmer? Sometimes on one path, sometimes on another path, sometimes listening to one, sometimes listening to another... You will collect much knowledge, but all that knowledge is simply junk because it is not going to give you the enlightenment that you were looking for. It is not going to lead you to the waters of eternal life."

Masters tremendously enjoy criticizing others. If the others are really enlightened, they also enjoy being criticized. They know that the purpose of both is the same: to protect the vagrant mind of the disciple, to keep him on one track. They have to deny that there is any other path anywhere that can lead you except this one.

This is not said out of an egoistical attitude; this is said out of love. This is simply a device to make you committed, devoted. The journey is long, the night is long, and if you go astray you can go on round and round for eternity without finding anything.

But in your unconscious state of mind, in your unenlightened space of being, the question seems to be relevant. You are asking: "I don't understand why enlightened masters are critical of each other."

Don't bother why they are critical about each other; you will understand it when you become enlightened. Before that it is none of your business! If enlightened people enjoy criticizing, they must have some reason of their own, and you are not in a state to understand.

Gautam Buddha, one of the most famous enlightened persons in human history, had eight contemporaries who were enlightened in the same small state of Bihar in India. Even the name "Bihar" came about because eight enlightened masters were continuously wandering, finding their people, searching for those who could fall in tune with them. *Bihar* means wandering; the name has come from those eight enlightened people. And they were condemning each other like anything.

Two out of the eight have left traditions that are still alive. One was Gautam Buddha; the other was Vardhaman Mahavira. Gautam Buddha has left the great tradition of Buddhism. Mahavira has left another tradition, Jainism. Both were in the same space, but immensely critical of each other – no agreement on any single point.

It happened many times that they were in the same city. Once it happened that they were staying in the same *caravanserai*. Half of the *serai* was occupied by Gautam Buddha and his disciples and half of the serai was occupied by Mahavira and his disciples. Traditionally it has been asked why they did not meet. Neither the Buddhists have the answer, nor the Jain have the answer. Both were enlightened; it would have been tremendously beautiful for them to have met.

But I know why they did not meet. They did not want their disciples to be confused because Mahavira had a totally different approach: of utter austerity, of great discipline, of arduous effort. His way was the way of the warrior. Gautam Buddha's approach was not that of a warrior, but that of an utterly relaxed human being. In comparison to Gautam Buddha's path, Mahavira was an extremist – while Gautam Buddha insisted on the middle way: avoid all extremes. Just be exactly in the middle and you are right. Every extreme is dangerous because it excludes the other extreme, and the truth should not exclude anything. The truth should be inclusive of all. So just be in the middle and both the extremes become just like the two wings of a bird and the bird is just in the middle. And you can use both the extremes to fly across the sun to the farthest star.

Mahavira's standpoint was: unless you choose a single dimension of effort and unless you are totally devoted to it, without being worried that you are becoming an extremist – because only from the extreme point can you jump into the beyond.

Now, both are right. But if a person who has never followed any path hears that both are right, he will be simply confused. Before your enlightenment you have to choose. After your enlightenment you are absolutely free to declare that all paths lead to the same place. But while you are leading people on the path you have to be consistently insistent that except this path everything else has to be completely forgotten.

You have to be one-pointed, just like an arrow moving toward the target, not bothering about other arrows moving from different angles, different aspects. If the arrow starts thinking of different angles and different aspects it is not going to reach the target. It will be lost in utter confusion.

People who have followed Mahavira have arrived and people who have followed Gautam Buddha have also arrived. If you ask me what brings them home, it is totality, absolute dedication and unconditional commitment. It does not matter which path you are on, these conditions will have to be fulfilled. In fact, the path does not matter at all: what matters are these three conditions. If you can fulfill these three conditions, even the wrong path will lead you to the right goal. And if you cannot fulfill these three conditions, the path may be absolutely right, but you are not going anywhere.

And one thing more has to be understood. I was saying this about the enlightened ones, but there are many who are simply fakes. You cannot make the distinction.

Just a few days ago I received a big letter from one of my very learned sannyasins, Swami Doctor Amrito. He has many Ph.D.'s and D.Litt.'s, and has written many books. He has written eight books about me. Now there is some man who talks as if he were enlightened, and many sannyasins in Holland are going to him. Seeing the situation my international secretary, Prem Hasya, has announced in all the newspapers that the man is a fake and sannyasins should not go there.

Amrito himself was going there, so he was very much shocked because he was also thinking that the man seems to be enlightened. And without knowing him I know that man cannot be enlightened because I know his master. I don't know that man; I know his master. He used to live in Mumbai and once I went just to have a look at him.

He was known as Beedie Baba because he was continuously smoking beedies. Great enlightenment! Except that I could not see any indication of enlightenment. A great chain-smoker...

This Dutchman became his follower. He was surrounded by a few uneducated, uncultured Indians because he used to smoke beedies and talk about the ultimate. In India every village has one or two idiots doing the same business. This is the country of idiots and enlightened ones!

But for centuries the enlightened people have talked and the idiots have gathered all the beautiful words. It is very easy to talk about the ultimate, *brahma*, and quote a few statements from the scriptures. Every Indian is spiritual, but just on the surface. Deep down I have not seen a more materialistic people anywhere in the world: so much greed, so much ambition, so much repressed lust – and on the surface, a parrot- like spiritual talk.

The Indian consists not of one person, but two. The real population of India is not nine hundred million, it is double that because each Indian is two Indians! One is the real, which is hidden in darkness, and one is the unreal, which goes on repeating beautiful phrases.

The Western seekers don't have any understanding about these parrots, so when they hear great words about which their tradition knows nothing... Their minds are conditioned by a very poor Christianity, mundane, ordinary, which does not have great philosophical flights.

But in India you can talk to anybody and you will be surprised that everybody knows about reincarnation, and everybody is afraid of death. Strange! If you know about reincarnation, why should you be afraid of death? Indians are the most cowardly people in the whole world. And when I say this I have absolute evidence for it. There is no other country in the world that has been enslaved for two thousand years continuously.

Why did India remain enslaved for two thousand years? A country that knows about reincarnation, which knows that the soul is eternal, which knows that you cannot be killed... But this knowledge is only parrot-knowledge; when the time comes, this knowledge is not of any help.

Small tribes have ruled over this big, vast continent because nobody wants to get into trouble unnecessarily. And because for centuries this country has been hearing beautiful words, tremendous revelations, by and by everybody has become saturated with them. So they are capable of rationalizing everything, even slavery.

For twenty centuries Indian scholars, Indian saints were even rationalizing the state of slavery: that it is a fire test of your patience, of your trust in God, of your nonviolence. And behind these beautiful words there was nothing but cowardliness – because Indians are afraid of being killed. That's why they don't kill others: it is dangerous. If you start killing others, you have to risk your life too. Indians have chosen not to fight and they have made a great philosophy out of it, of "nonviolence." It is protective of their cowardly souls.

They are the poorest people in the world. Half of the population is starving and any day in the coming thirteen years, five hundred million people are going to die in this country. But still they will go on rationalizing that it is fate, it is destiny; that everything is in the hands of God. Not even a leaf on a tree moves without God's orders; everything happens according to God. If he wants us to be slaves, what can we do? If he wants us to be poor, what can we do? If he wants us to have more and more children, what can we do?

The rich go on becoming richer and the poor go on producing more and more children.

Even the poorest beggar knows more about metaphysics, about great ideologies. And when the Western man comes – he may be well educated but his education is in science, his education is in logic, his education makes him a great intellectual. But in the heart he remains very naive. Then any Beedie Baba, any idiot can make a great impact on him.

This Dutch man lived for months together with Beedie Baba. He does not mention his well-known name, Beedie Baba; he mentions only his legal name, Nisarg Datta Maharaj. He has written many books on Nisarg Datta Maharaj; he has made Nisarg Datta famous all over the world. I have looked through those books – sheer nonsense!

Now Amrito has written to me, "Osho, you have to tell Hasya to withdraw her statement because I have seen this Dutch man and to me he looks enlightened."

Enlightened people don't look enlightened, they are enlightened! And poor Amrito, this is not for the first time... He gets caught anywhere; it has happened many times. And he is going round and round. He met another idiot's follower, that idiot was Muktananda, and he had an American follower, Baba Free John. Now he has changed his name because now he declares himself enlightened and he has dropped any connection with Muktananda. Now he has become Da Free John.

And Amrito went there and inquired of me, "Can I write a book on Da Free John?"

I said, "Amrito, if your whole life is just to write about any idiot you come across, then don't waste your time in Holland – come to India, and you will find so many people. Go on writing."

He has written about Sri Aurobindo, he has written about J. Krishnamurti, he has written about Da Free John, he has written about me, and now he is caught up with this other Dutch fellow.

I said, "If this is going to be just your profession, to write, if you are some kind of spiritual journalist, then it is okay. But this is not going to lead you toward enlightenment."

He became very confused. It was bound to happen because when he read my statement about Sri Aurobindo – that he was not enlightened – Amrito was shocked. Now, what can I do about it? I know he was not enlightened and he was befooling people. He was declaring to people – and that was the only attraction because thousands of people around the world became interested in Sri Aurobindo for a single reason.

He was telling people, "Up to now there have been enlightened people, self-realized people; they have attained immortality. But now I have come to bring a new experience to the world and that experience is physical immortality. Spiritual immortality many have attained; I have brought the whole alchemy of making you physically immortal."

Naturally all kinds of people who are afraid of death immediately became interested – and these kinds of statements have a beauty. Naturally, you cannot contradict Sri Aurobindo while he is alive; he is the proof that he is immortal. And you cannot contradict him when he dies – who to contradict!

One day he died. And, one of my friends was also there in his ashram. "For three days," he told me, "it was not declared to the world that Sri Aurobindo had died." They kept it a secret because this would shatter all the following and the whole business.

But how long can you keep a dead body? And in Sri Aurobindo's ashram they were thinking and believing that he had gone deep into *samadhi*, that he would come back. But instead of coming back, his whole body started stinking. When the body started stinking, they became worried: "It seems the fellow is gone!"

Then they declared to the world: "Sri Aurobindo has gone so deep in his samadhi that the doctors are saying he is dead."

So they have made a beautiful marble grave for him and they still believe... Many have left, but a few idiots are absolutely impossible – they are still waiting for that one day when he will knock from inside. He has gone in search of the alchemy for his disciples to become physically immortal.

Then there was a woman who was really running the ashram. She was a film actress from France, and she had become attracted to the idea of immortality. Women will be very much attracted to it, particularly film actresses whose professional life is very short, just five to seven years. Before that they are extras, after that again they are extras. Naturally they want physical immortality, and if in the middle of youth they can become physically immortal, they can remain always on the top of the list of celebrities.

This French actress became the mother of the ashram. After Sri Aurobindo died, and while she was alive, she managed the false and absolute lie of Aurobindo. She said, "He has gone in search of a few missing links. But I am here; I am immortal." And by coincidence she lived for almost a hundred years, so naturally she created the idea in many that perhaps she was the chief disciple and Aurobindo had made her immortal. But one day she also popped off!

And when I told Amrito, "Don't get into all this nonsense," he said, "I had never thought about all this." But he goes on from one person to another person. Just curiosity; it seems to be an unquenchable curiosity.

Not only do enlightened people criticize other enlightened people; they also have to criticize those who are not enlightened and are pretending to be so. It is an absolute necessity that the false should be exposed. That too is part of compassion, so you don't get caught up with the false.

And you are asking, "Are they not all working toward the higher good?" You cannot understand anything about the people who are enlightened. They are not working at all – neither for higher good nor for anything else. They are simply delighting and sharing their love, their light, their life – everything they have, their blissfulness and their peace and their silence. And this is simply a delight; it is not a work. They are not working for some higher good. They themselves are the highest good. There is no need for them to work for any higher good – that is Christian language.

I have told you that the man who is enlightened is *satyam shivam sundaram*. He is the very truth itself, he is not working for any other truth. He is godliness himself; he is not working for any other good. And he is beauty himself; he is not trying to lead you toward some beauty.

He is present. You can drink out of his well and be absolutely contented, right now, this very moment. A man of enlightenment is no longer interested in the future. There is no future as far as he is concerned; everything is always in the present. Existence is always in the present. His whole joy is not to lead you toward some good, but just to bring you back to yourself – because all that is beautiful, all that is good and all that is great is within you, not anywhere else.

And finally you are asking, "Are they not different flavors of the same truth?"

By the very nature of the situation you cannot ask the right question. And I am compelled to give you the right answer although you are asking the wrong question: every enlightened man has all the flavors of truth. It is not that one enlightened man has one flavor, another enlightened man has another flavor; that this one has a different perfume, that one has a different perfume.

The moment you are enlightened truth blossoms in you with all the flavors together simultaneously. Every enlightened man is complete and perfect in himself. There is nothing missing in him.

It will be good for you, rather than asking about enlightened people and worrying about what they are doing and why they are doing it... The simple way is to become enlightened and you will know!

Between enlightenment and the state of unenlightenment, it is a very long distance call! And languages are different: something is said, something else is heard – and this has been going on for centuries, misunderstanding upon misunderstanding.

The phone rang at the maternity hospital and an excited voice at the other end of the line said, "Send an ambulance quickly. My wife Maureen is about to have a baby!"

"Calm down," replied the nurse. "Tell me, is this her first baby?"

"No," said Paddy, "this is her husband speaking."

Paddy was very, very ill indeed, so Maureen sent for the doctor. After a brief examination the doctor announced that Paddy was dead.

"I am not," said Paddy from his bed.

"Be quiet!" said Maureen. "Do you think you know better than the doctor?"

"My wife, Bridget," Sean confided to Paddy, "is an angel."

"You are lucky," said Paddy, "my wife Maureen is still alive."

Hymie Goldberg was having his first session with the psychoanalyst.

"Do you cheat on your wife?" asked the shrink.

"My God," said Hymie, "who else could I cheat on?"

A Californian psychiatrist was driving along in his car, when he saw a man lying on the sidewalk. He stopped his car and got out. It turned out the man had been mugged and left for dead.

"Quick," said the shrink, "tell me who did this to you; he needs help immediately!"

An Indian businessman who had made millions after a childhood of poverty was on his deathbed giving advice to his son.

"Listen, son," he said, "I owe my success to two principles: honesty and wisdom. Honesty is if you promise to deliver some goods, no matter what happens, even if it means bankruptcy, deliver!"

"I will try to remember, father," replied the boy. "And what about wisdom?"

"Wisdom is simple, my boy," continued the father. "Never make any promises."

From the place where you are, don't be worried about the actions of people who are existing on a totally different plane. If you really want to understand them, reach to the same consciousness and you will understand without fail.

I have been acquainted with almost all the enlightened people who have lived on the earth. My whole life I have been searching in every nook and corner of the earth, and a few things have emerged out of my research into the enlightened being.

They are absolutely perfect in all dimensions possible, with all flavors. And it is a sheer necessity for them to criticize others, knowing perfectly well that the people they are criticizing will understand their compassion. They may have moved through different paths; they *have* moved. It is almost like a mountain: you can move from different directions, you can choose different pathways, you will have different experiences on the way, but when you reach to the top it is the same experience, absolutely the same sweetness, the same fragrance.

But if you belong to the category of the arhats you may remain silent, without criticizing anybody because you don't have any followers.

There are two categories of people who have achieved enlightenment; one is called the arhat. The literal meaning of the word is one who has conquered. The second is the bodhisattva; the literal meaning is one who has awakened. The ultimate experience is the same, whether you are an arhat or a bodhisattva. But there are differences in their actions and in their words.

Therefore arhats have remained silent. Naturally there is no question of criticizing anybody. They have never asserted any truth, they have never tried to manifest any of their experience. They have never bothered that somebody may be there who can be helped. They never become saviors of anybody. They have a very small boat; only one can sit in their small boat, and they go to the further shore alone. And because they don't have disciples, there is no question of any criticism. They are the silent ones.

But the bodhisattvas are people of immense compassion. The arhats in comparison look a little hard, unconcerned about others who are struggling in darkness and death. Bodhisattvas are tremendously interested in giving you a hand and pulling you up from your ditch and putting you on the right path. And of course the right path is the path that they have followed; that is the only path they know exactly. They don't know about any other path because they have never followed it. And it is absolutely correct to make it completely clear to the disciple that this is the only path, so he does not go astray.

By the time the arhats and the bodhisattvas reach to the peak, they experience the same light and the same bliss and the same ecstasy. But the arhats still remain silent. Bodhisattvas still remain concerned about people who have been left behind on the path.

There is a beautiful story about Gautam Buddha, who is a bodhisattva. When he reached the gate of paradise there was a great celebration because never before had such a great enlightened being reached paradise. He has a beauty of his own, a grace that is incomparable, and a compassion that is infinite.

The doors were wide open; there was celebration in paradise. But the story is that Gautam Buddha refused to enter paradise, on the grounds that he had left many on the way. He would stand at the gate until the last human being had entered the gate. He would be ultimately the last.

The story says that he is still standing outside the gate, waiting for his disciples and devotees whom he has promised. He cannot go against his promise.

Gautam Buddha criticized the seers of the Vedas, he criticized the seers of the Upanishads, he criticized Mahavira, he criticized everybody that he could find – Krishna, Rama, all the Hindu gods. For forty-two years continuously he was criticizing every old scripture, every old prophet, every old savior – but he is not an enemy of anyone. He was criticizing all those people so that you can be unconditioned, so that you can be freed from the clinging with the past – which cannot help you.

When a living enlightened being is present, he cannot allow you to remain clinging with the dead, which can only be a weight on your heart but cannot become wings for your freedom.

It needs tremendous insight and meditative understanding to have a little glimpse of the world of the enlightened person. I have criticized many. Only a few of them were enlightened; most of them were simply frauds. The frauds have to be absolutely exposed to humanity.

Even those who were enlightened have become only a tradition, a convention, a dead belief. You have to be freed from their grip too because they cannot help you, they can only hinder your path. They can become your chains, but they cannot become your freedom.

I can become your freedom. I *am* your freedom.

When I am gone I hope there may still be courageous people in the world to criticize me, so that I don't become a hindrance on anybody's path. And those who will criticize me will not be my enemies; neither am I the enemy of those whom I have criticized. The working of the enlightened masters just has to be understood.

You should remember only one word, and that is compassion – compassion for you, compassion for all those who are still not centered in their being, who are still far away from themselves, who have to be called back home.

7

How Watching Leads to No-mind

Osho,
How does watching lead to no-mind? I am more and more able to watch my body, my thoughts and feelings and this feels beautiful. But moments of no thoughts are few and far between. When I hear you saying, "Meditation is witnessing," I feel I understand. But when you talk about no-mind, it doesn't sound easy at all. Would you please comment?

Meditation covers a very long pilgrimage. When I say, "meditation is witnessing," it is the beginning of meditation. And when I say, "Meditation is no-mind," it is the completion of the pilgrimage. Witnessing is the beginning, and no-mind is the fulfillment. Witnessing is the method to reach to no-mind. Naturally you will feel witnessing is easier. It is close to you.

But witnessing is only like a seed, and then comes the long waiting period. Not only waiting, but trusting that this seed is going to sprout, that it is going to become a bush; that one day the spring will come and the bush will have flowers. No-mind is the last stage of flowering.

Sowing the seeds is of course very easy; it is in your hands. But bringing forth the flowers is beyond you. You can prepare the whole ground, but the flowers will come on their own accord; you cannot manage to force them to come. The spring is beyond your reach – but if your preparation is perfect, spring comes; that is absolutely guaranteed.

The way you are moving is perfectly good. Witnessing is the path and you are starting to feel, once in a while, a thought-less moment. These are glimpses of no-mind, but just for a moment.

Remember one fundamental law: that which can exist just for a moment can also become eternal because you are given not two moments together, but always one moment. And if you can transform one moment into a thought-less state, you are learning the secret. Then there is no hindrance to changing the second moment, which will also come alone with the same potential and the same capacity.

If you know the secret you have the master key, which can open every moment into a glimpse of no-mind. No-mind is the final stage: when mind disappears forever and the thoughtless gap becomes your intrinsic reality. If these few glimpses are coming, they show you are on the right path and you are using the right method.

But don't be impatient. Existence needs immense patience. The ultimate mysteries are opened only to those who have immense patience.

I am reminded... In old Tibet it was customary, respectful, that every family should contribute to the great experiment of expanding consciousness. So the first child of each family was given to the monasteries to be trained in meditation. Perhaps no country has done such a vast experiment in consciousness.

The destruction of Tibet at the hands of communist China is one of the greatest calamities that could have happened to humanity. It is not only a question of a small country; it is a question of a great experiment that was going on for centuries in Tibet. The first child was given to the monasteries when he was very small – five, or at the most six, years old. I am reminded of one incident: there would have been millions like it...

A six-year-old child... Tibet knew that children can learn witnessing better than grown-ups. The grown-ups are already utterly spoiled.

The child is innocent and as yet the slate of his mind is empty. To teach him emptiness is absolutely easy. But the entrance of a child into a monastery was very difficult, particularly for a small child. I am telling you about only one incident but there would have been hundreds of incidents happening like this. It is bound to be so.

A small child, six years old, is leaving. His mother is crying because life in a monastery for a small child is going to be so arduous. The father tells the child, "Don't look back! It is a question of our family's respectability. In the whole history of our family a child has never looked back – not even once. Whatever the entrance test for the monastery is, even if your life is at risk, don't look back. Don't think of me or your mother and her tears.

"We are sending you for the ultimate experiment in human consciousness with great joy, even though the separation is painful. But we know you will pass through all the tests. You are our blood, and of course you will keep the dignity of your family."

The small child rides on the horse with a servant riding on another horse. A tremendous desire arises in him when the road turns, just to have a look again back to the family house, to its garden. His father must be standing there, his mother must be crying, but he remembers that his father has said, "Don't look back."

And he does not look back. With tears in his eyes, he turns with the road. Now he cannot see his house anymore and one never knows how long it will take – perhaps years and years – until he will be able to see his father and mother and his family again.

He reaches the monastery. At the gate of the monastery the abbot meets him, receives him gracefully, as if he is a grown-up, bows down to him as he bows down to the abbot. And the abbot says, "Your first test will be to sit outside the gate with closed eyes, unmoving, unless you are called in." The small child sits at the gate, outside the gate with closed eyes. Hours pass, and he cannot even move. There are flies sitting on his face, but he cannot remove them. It is a question of the dignity that the abbot has shown to him. He does not think any more like a child; so respected, he has to fulfill his family's longing, the abbot's expectations.

The whole day passes, and even other monks in the monastery start feeling sorry for the child. Hungry, thirsty – he is simply waiting. They start feeling that the child may be small, but he has great courage and guts.

Finally, by the time the sun is setting and the whole day has passed, the abbot comes and takes the child in. He says, "You have passed the first test, but there are many more peaks ahead. I respect your patience, being such a small child. You remained unmoving, you did not open your eyes. You did not lose courage, you trusted that whenever the time is right you will be called in."

And then years of training in witnessing: the child was only allowed to see his parents again after perhaps ten years, twenty years had elapsed. But the criterion was that until he experienced no-mind, he could not be allowed to see his parents, his family. Once he achieves no-mind, then he can move back into the world. Then there is no problem.

Once a man is in a state of no-mind, nothing can distract him from his being. There is no power bigger than the power of no-mind. No harm can be done to such a person. No attachment, no greed, no jealousy, no anger – nothing can arise in him. No-mind is an absolutely pure sky without any clouds.

You say, "How does watching lead to no-mind?"

There is an intrinsic law: thoughts don't have their own life. They are parasites; they live on your identifying with them. When you say, "I am angry," you are pouring life energy into anger because you are getting identified with anger.

But when you say, "I am watching anger flashing on the screen of the mind within me," you are not giving any life, any juice, any energy to anger anymore. You will be able to see that because you are not identified the anger is absolutely impotent, has no impact on you, does not change you, does not affect you. It is absolutely hollow and dead. It will pass on and it will leave the sky clean, the screen of the mind empty.

Slowly, slowly you start getting out of your thoughts. That's the whole process of witnessing and watching. George Gurdjieff used to call it "non-identification." In other words you are no longer identifying with your thoughts. You are simply standing aloof and away – indifferent, as if they might be anybody's thoughts. You have broken your connections with them. Only then can you watch them.

Watching needs a certain distance. If you are identified there is no distance, they are too close. It is as if you are putting the mirror too close to your eyes: you cannot see your face. A certain distance is needed. Only then can you see your face in the mirror.

If thoughts are too close to you, you cannot watch. You become impressed and colored by your thoughts. Anger makes you angry, greed makes you greedy, lust makes you lustful because there is no distance at all. They are so close that you are bound to think that you and your thoughts are one.

Watching destroys this oneness and creates a separation. The more you watch, the bigger is the distance. The bigger the distance, the less energy your thoughts are getting from you. And they don't have any other source of energy. Soon they start dying, disappearing. In these disappearing moments you will have the first glimpses of no-mind.

That is what you are experiencing. You say: "I am more and more able to watch my body, my thoughts and feelings, and this feels beautiful." This is just the beginning. Even the beginning is immensely beautiful – just to be on the right path, even without taking a single step, will give you immense joy for no reason at all.

And once you start moving on the right path, your blissfulness, your beautiful experiences are going to become more and more deep, more and more wide, with new nuances, with new flavors, with new fragrances.

You say, "But moments of no thoughts are few and far between." It is a great achievement because people don't know even a single gap. Their thoughts are always in a rush hour: thoughts upon thoughts, bumper-to-bumper – the line continues, whether they are awake or asleep. What you call your dreams are nothing but thoughts in the form of pictures because the unconscious mind does not know alphabetical languages. There is no school, no training institute that teaches the unconscious language.

The unconscious is very primitive; it is just like a small child. Have you looked at the books of your small children? If you want to teach the child, you have to make a big picture first. So in children's books you will see pictures, colorful pictures, with very little writing. The child is more interested in the pictures. He is primitive, he understands the language of pictures.

Slowly, slowly you make the pictures and the language associate. Whenever he sees the mango he knows, "it is a mango," and he starts learning that underneath the picture of the mango there is a certain word describing it. His interest is in the mango, but the word *mango* slowly becomes associated. As the child grows, the pictures will become smaller and there will be more language. By the time he enters university, the pictures will have disappeared from the book; only language will remain.

By the way, this reminds me to tell you that television has brought humanity back to a primitive stage because people are again looking at pictures. There is a danger in the future: it is already apparent that people have stopped reading great literature. Who bothers to read, when you can see the film on the TV? This is a dangerous phenomenon because there are things that cannot be reproduced in pictures. Great literature can be only partially reproduced in pictures. The danger is that people will slowly start forgetting language and its beauty and magic, and they will again become primitives, watching the television.

Now the average American is watching television for seven and a half hours every day. This is going to destroy something that we have achieved with great difficulty. Now, this man who is watching television for seven and a half hours per day – you cannot expect him to read Shakespeare, Kalidas, Rabindranath Tagore, Herman Hesse or Martin Buber or Jean Paul Sartre. The greater the literature, the less the possibility of putting it into pictures.

Pictures are colorful, exciting, easy, but they are no comparison to language. The future has to be protected from many things. Computers can destroy people's memory systems because there will be no need. You can keep a small computer the size of a cigarette packet in your pocket: it contains everything that you will ever need to know. Now there is no need to have your own memory. Just push a button and the computer is ready to give you any information you need.

The computer can destroy the whole memory system of humanity that has been developed for centuries with great difficulty. Television can take away all great literature, and the possibility of people like Shelley or Byron being born again in the world. These are great inventions, but nobody has looked at the implications. They will reduce the whole of humanity into a retarded state.

What you are feeling is a great indication that you are on the right path. It is always a question for the seeker whether he is moving in the right direction or not. There is no security, no insurance, no guarantee. All the dimensions are open: how are you going to choose the right one?

These are the ways and the criteria of how one has to choose. If you move on any path – any methodology – and it brings you joy, more sensitivity, more watchfulness, and gives a feeling of immense well-being, this is the only criterion that you are going on the right path. If you become more miserable, more angry, more of an egoist, more greedy, more lustful, those are the indications you are moving on a wrong path.

On the right path your blissfulness is going to grow more and more every day, and your experiences of beautiful feelings will become tremendously psychedelic, more colorful – colors that you have never seen in the world, fragrances that you have never experienced in the world. Then you can walk on the path without any fear that you can go wrong.

These inner experiences will always keep you on the right path. Just remember that if they are growing, that means you are moving. Now you have only a few moments of thoughtlessness. It is not a simple attainment; it is a great achievement because in their whole lives people do not know even a single moment when there is no thought. These gaps will grow.

As you become more and more centered, more and more watchful, these gaps will start growing bigger. And if you go on moving without looking back, without going astray, if you keep going straight the day is not far away when you will feel for the first time that the gaps have become so big that hours pass and not even a single thought arises. Now you are having bigger experiences of no-mind.

The ultimate achievement is when twenty-four hours a day you are surrounded with no-mind.

This does not mean that you cannot use your mind. That is a fallacy propounded by those who know nothing about no-mind. No-mind does not mean that you cannot use the mind; it simply means that the mind cannot use you.

No-mind does not mean that the mind is destroyed. No-mind simply means that the mind is put aside. You can bring it into action any moment you need to communicate with the world. It will be your servant. Right now it is your master. Even when you are sitting alone it goes on, yakkety- yak, yakkety-yak – and you cannot do anything, you are so utterly helpless.

No-mind simply means that the mind has been put in its right place. As a servant it is a great instrument. As a master it is very unfortunate, it is dangerous, it will destroy your whole life.

Mind is only a medium for when you want to communicate with others. But when you are alone, there is no need of the mind. So whenever you want to use it, you can use it.

And remember one thing more: when the mind remains silent for hours, it becomes fresh, young, more creative, more sensitive, rejuvenated through rest.

Ordinary people's minds start somewhere around three or four years of age, and then they go on continuing for seventy years, eighty years without any holiday. Naturally they cannot be very creative. They are utterly tired – and tired with rubbish. Millions of people in the world live without any creativity. Creativity is one of the greatest blissful experiences. But their minds are so tired, they are not in a state of overflowing energy.

The man of no-mind keeps the mind in rest, full of energy, immensely sensitive, ready to jump into action the moment it is ordered. It is not a coincidence that the words of the people who have experienced no- mind, start having a magic of their own. When they use their mind, it has a charisma, it has a magnetic force, it has tremendous spontaneity, and the freshness of the dewdrops in the early morning before the sun rises. And the mind is nature's greatest, evolved medium of expression and creativity.

So the man of meditation – or in other words, the man of no-mind – changes even his prose into poetry. Without any effort, his words become so full of authority that they don't need any arguments. They become their own arguments. The force that they carry becomes a self-evident truth. There is no need for any other support from logic or from scriptures. The words of a man of no-mind have an intrinsic certainty about them. If you are ready to receive and listen, you will feel it in your heart – the self-evident truth.

Look down the ages: Gautam Buddha has never been contradicted by any of his disciples; neither has Mahavira, nor Moses, nor Jesus. There is something in their very words, in their very presence that convinces you. Without any effort to convert you, you are converted. None of the great masters have been missionaries; they have never tried to convert anyone, but they have converted millions.

It is a miracle – but the miracle consists of a rested mind, of a mind that is always full of energy and is used only once in a while.

When I speak to you, I have to use the mind. When I am sitting in my room almost the whole day, I forget all about the mind. I am just a pure silence, and meanwhile the mind is resting. When I speak to you, those are the only moments when I use the mind. When I am alone, I am utterly alone, and there is no need to use the mind.

You say: "When I hear you say, 'Meditation is witnessing,' I feel I understand. But when you talk about no-mind, it doesn't sound easy at all."

How can it sound easy? It is your future possibility. You have started meditation: it may be in the beginning stages but you have a certain experience of it that makes you understand me. But if you can understand meditation, don't be worried at all.

Meditation surely leads to no-mind, just as every river moves toward the ocean without any maps, without any guides. Every river, without exception, finally reaches the ocean. Every meditation, without exception, finally reaches the state of no-mind.

But naturally, when the Ganges is in the Himalayas wandering in the mountains and in the valleys, it has no idea what the ocean is, it cannot conceive of the existence of the ocean. But it is moving toward the ocean because water has the intrinsic capacity of always finding the lowest place, and the oceans are the lowest place. So rivers are born on the peaks of the Himalayas and start moving immediately toward lower spaces, and finally they are bound to find the ocean.

Just the reverse is the process of meditation. It moves upwards to higher peaks, and the ultimate peak is no-mind. No-mind is a simple word, but it exactly means enlightenment, liberation, freedom from all bondage, the experience of deathlessness and immortality.

Those are big words and I don't want you to be frightened, so I use a simple word, *no-mind*. You know the mind, you can conceive of a state when this mind will be non-functioning.

Once this mind is non-functioning, you become part of the mind of the cosmos, the universal mind. When you are part of the universal mind your individual mind functions as a beautiful servant. It has recognized the master, and it brings news from the universal mind to those who are still chained by the individual mind.

In fact when I am speaking to you, it is the universe using me. My words are not my words; they belong to the universal truth. That is their power, that is their charisma, that is their magic.

Osho,

Are there real differences in different races, or is it just superstition?

There are differences not only between the races, but even in the individuals. Each individual has a uniqueness about himself. There is no other individual exactly like you. You are alone.

And this is the dignity of the individual – that he is not a replica, not a repetition, not a carbon copy. What is true about individuals is in a different way true about races. Because each race of humanity has passed through a different terrain, a different history, it has grown different psychologies, different minds. It is absolutely natural that the Eskimos will certainly be different from the people who have not even known how it feels when snow is falling.

Eskimos have eleven names for snow. No other language has eleven names for snow because only Eskimos know the slight differences which make the eleven names, which are not synonymous. But to know those slight and subtle differences you have to be in the same geography, in the same climate, and you have to pass through the same experiences.

Different races have passed through different lands, through different experiences, and naturally they have grown certain characteristics. According to me, that makes the earth more beautiful because it gives variety.

But your question is: "Are there real differences... or is it just superstition?"

There are real differences – and there are many more which are only superstitions, which are not real differences. Naturally, a man born in Tibet will have different superstitions from a man born in India. For example: heaven, according to the Indian tradition, is a very cool place, almost air-conditioned; cool breezes all day long, never hot. But Eskimos and Tibetans will not agree with this heaven! They are tired of the cold.

In fact, in Tibet for centuries there has been a strange tradition that whenever a child is born, he is immediately dipped into ice-cold water nine times – a newborn child! Nine children out of ten die, but the reasoning behind such an act is out of a deep understanding of Tibet. If a child is not strong enough to survive those nine dips in the ice-cold water it is better for him to die because he will remain sick, unhealthy, miserable his whole life.

It looks cruel because it is killing almost nine children out of ten. But it is out of compassion, not out of cruelty. They know perfectly well what is ahead. If the child is not capable, has not the stamina to face Tibetan ice – eternal ice that has never melted all year round – if he is weak from the very beginning, his whole life will be miserable. It is better to die before suffering a life of unnecessary pain and misery. And the child who survives certainly proves he is capable of living in the eternal snows, perfectly healthy.

Tibetans are very healthy people, but the reason is that the unhealthy ones have been canceled from the very beginning. Their heaven is warm and remains warm all the year round. Snow never falls in their heaven; it falls in their hell. Their hell is utterly cold, far worse than Tibet.

These are all superstitions: they also make differences.

One of my friends, a professor of Sanskrit, wanted to go to Tibet. He was doing some research on a few Sanskrit scriptures that had disappeared from India. But their translations were in existence in Tibet: he wanted to translate them back into Sanskrit.

Those were very important scriptures, particularly concerned with Gautam Buddha. Perhaps Hindus burned those scriptures in India, but because Tibet became Buddhist, before they were destroyed they were translated into Tibetan. They exist in Chinese, they exist in Japanese; only in Indian languages do they not exist

– and Buddha was born in this land, he was speaking the language of the people of this land.

So this man's research was really very significant in bringing Buddha back to his own land. But he was a high-caste brahmin, and he had learned Tibetan with great effort. Of course Sanskrit was his family language. He belonged to a very learned family; they used Sanskrit in their family instead of any other language of the people, so he was perfectly capable of translating from Tibetan into Sanskrit.

But I told him, "I expect to see you back within three days."

He said, "What are you saying? It will take at least three years."

I said, "Forget all about it! I know you – and I know something about Tibet."

He said, "I don't understand, you always make strange statements."

He went to Tibet. He was a high-caste brahmin with all the superstitions of the brahmins. The brahmin has to take a cold bath in the river before sunrise; then he has to do his religious worship – and only after that can he take his breakfast. As he reached Tibet, he remembered me. My statement was not wrong. He took only one bath and that was enough. He forgot all about translations.

By the third day I had to receive him at the airport. I said, "What do you think about my statement?"

He said, "I would have been killed in three years. Just one day was enough. Even now I am still shivering; the coldness has entered into my bones. Without taking a bath before sunrise I cannot even take my breakfast. So the choice was either to live without food or to have a cold bath before sunrise."

I said, "That's why I had said what I said. You are a fanatic brahmin; you will not drop your stupid idea. It is perfectly good in India, in fact the best time to take a bath is before the sun rises; only then is it cool. As the sun rises things become hotter. The moments before sunrise are the most beautiful in India. But that is not the case with Tibet."

Now, the Dalai Lama, the head of the state of Tibet and also the head of the Buddhist church of Tibet, has escaped from Tibet. He lives in India and thousands of Tibetans have come with him.

I was giving a meditation camp in Bodhgaya, where Gautam Buddha became enlightened, and thousands of Tibetans had come just to pay their respects to Gautam Buddha and the place and the tree under which he became enlightened. Hearing that I was also staying just near the place where Gautam Buddha became enlightened, and that hundreds of my people were meditating there, they became curious. They came to see me.

I have never felt so miserable in my life because they stink and I am allergic to smells. They are the smelliest fellows in the whole world! Their holy scripture says: "At least one bath every year is absolutely necessary." They are covered with the dust of Indian roads, perspiring – but they will not take a bath. Only one bath per year is allowed. They use the same clothes they were using in Tibet, many layers of clothes. It is very difficult to make a Tibetan naked: you take off one layer of clothes, another layer; you take that off and you find another layer. And each layer becomes dirtier!

I had to tell my people, "Prevent these people from coming to me. They have been living for years now in India, but they have not changed their superstition."

A more intelligent humanity will not follow superstitions, will not follow what is right in one place but may not be right in another place. Intelligence demands that you respond to the situation in which you are. So there are superstitious differences, and those differences make humanity not beautiful, they make humanity stupid.

I believe in the old saying: When in Rome, act like the Romans – order spaghetti. That is why I have refused my sannyasins... They have been continuously trying to persuade me to come to Italy and I am saying, "No. Either spaghetti or me!" And this is not a superstition!

One of my secretaries was a beautiful Italian woman, well educated. She was a professor in the university of Rome. She had all the degrees in philosophy, post graduation, Ph.D., D.Litt., and she was the first Italian to come into contact with me. She destroyed my interest in spaghetti because one day she prepared spaghetti for me.

That woman never used to take a bath, I don't think she had ever taken one in her whole life. Her face had layers of powder, centuries old! She went on putting on more powder but she would not take a bath. I used to tell her to sit a little far away.

Very lovingly she brought the spaghetti. I could not refuse – it looked too unmannerly – so I said to her, "Leave it on my dining table, but you leave the room."

She said, "I would just like to see you eating spaghetti."

I said, "Please leave the room, and then I will take care of the spaghetti." And as I went close to my dining table, the spaghetti smelled exactly like the woman smelled. I had to throw it down the toilet. Even after twenty years, whenever I remember I start smelling the spaghetti. I don't know the real smell of spaghetti, but I don't want to know.

But there are beautiful differences that should be protected. Humanity should remain a beautiful garden with all kinds of flowers. Even the wild flowers should be protected. They all make life richer, more beautiful, more adventurous.

The people that run international car shows have discovered that the nationality of the visitors can be determined by the way in which the visitors approach a car. If a visitor opens the hood to look at the engine, he is a German. If he is interested in the style and the lines of a car, he is French. If he tries the horn, he is Italian. And if he checks the size and the price tag, he is a Jew.

"Man, am I scared!" confided Paddy to Seamus, looking furtively around the pub. "I just got a card from a guy saying that he would shoot me if I did not stay away from his wife."

"Well, stay away from his wife," advised Seamus, "and you have got no problem."

"How can I?" moaned Paddy, "he did not sign his name."

Hymie Goldberg was telling his friends about his sailing holiday and how his boat had capsized in rough weather, throwing him into the water.

"I had abandoned all hope," said Hymie, "and as I sank for the third time, my past lives seemed to rise up before me in a series of grim, realistic pictures."

A murmur of sympathy came from the group listening. But before Hymie could continue, his friend Moishe Finkelstein spoke up sharply saying, "And did you happen to notice a picture of me lending you five dollars late in 1960?"

The sun never sets on the British Empire because God would not trust an Englishman in the dark.

Nathan Nussbaum from Israel is visiting Paris. He goes to a brothel and insists on the services of a girl called Gloria. Gloria is unavailable, but when Nathan shows a thousand-dollar bill, she is brought to him and they spend the night together.

On the following two nights again a thousand-dollar bill changes hands and Nathan and Gloria spend the nights in passion.

Finally Gloria asks why she is receiving such generous attention.

"Well," says Nathan, "you see, I am from Israel."

"Why, so am I," exclaims Gloria.

"Yes, I know," replies Nathan. "It happens that your grandmother lives in the same building as my parents and when she heard I was going to Paris, she asked me to give you the three thousand dollars you asked for."

8

Accept Yourself

Osho,
Why am I scared to accept myself the way I am?

Everybody is in the same situation. Everybody is scared to accept himself the way he is. This is how all the past centuries of mankind have cultivated, conditioned every child, every human being.

The strategy is simple but very dangerous. The strategy is to condemn you and to give you ideals so that you are always trying to become someone else. The Christian is trying to become a Jesus, the Buddhist is trying to become a Buddha. To distract you from yourself seems so clever a device that perhaps the people who have been doing it are themselves unaware of it.

What Jesus said on the cross – his last words to humanity – is immensely significant in many ways, particularly in this context. He prayed to God, "Father, forgive these people because they know not what they are doing."

This is applicable to every father and to every mother, to every teacher and every priest and every moralist; to the people who manage culture, society, civilization, and who try to mold every individual in a certain way. Perhaps they also don't know what they are doing. Perhaps they think they are doing everything for your good. I don't suspect their intentions, but I certainly want you to be aware that they are ignorant, they are unconscious people.

A small child is born into the hands of an unconscious society. And the unconscious society starts molding the child according to its own ideals, forgetting the one thing which is the most fundamental: that the child has a potential of his own. He has to grow, not into a Jesus or into a Krishna or into a Buddha. He has to grow to be himself.

If he misses growing into being himself he will remain utterly miserable his whole life. His life will become just a hell and a curse, and he will not know what has gone wrong. He has been put in the wrong direction from the very beginning.

And he thinks the people who have put him in the wrong direction love him, are his benefactors. Actually they are his greatest enemies. The parents, the teachers, the priests and the leaders of the society are the greatest enemies of every individual who has been born on the earth up to now. Without being aware, they are distracting you from yourself.

And to distract you, you have to be absolutely conditioned about one thing: that you are unworthy, undeserving, of no use at all as you are. Of course you can become worthy of respect, dignity, if you follow the rules and regulations given to you by others. If you are able to manage to be a hypocrite you will be a prestigious citizen of the society.

But if you insist on being sincere, honest, authentic, yourself, you will be condemned by everybody. And it needs tremendous courage to be condemned by everybody. It needs a man with a steel spine to stand on his own and declare: "I am not going to be anybody else but myself. Good or bad, acceptable or not acceptable, prestigious or not prestigious, one thing is certain – that I can be only myself and nobody else."

This needs a tremendously revolutionary approach toward life. This is the basic revolt that each individual needs if he wants ever to be out of the vicious circle of misery.

You are asking me: "Why am I scared to accept myself the way I am?" Because you have not been accepted by anyone the way you are. They have created the fear and the apprehension that if you accept yourself you will be rejected by everybody.

This is an absolute condition of every society and every culture that has existed up to now: that either you accept yourself and be rejected by all, or you reject yourself and gain the respect and honor of your whole society and culture. The choice is really very difficult.

Obviously the majority is going to choose respectability. But with respectability come all kinds of anxieties, anguishes; a meaninglessness, a desert-like life where nothing grows, where nothing is green, where no flower ever blossoms, where you will walk and walk and walk and you will never even find an oasis.

I am reminded of Leo Tolstoy. Just a few days ago in Moscow there was an international exhibition of books, and one of my sannyasins, Lani, was there. She was surprised – and my Russian sannyasins were there, and they were also surprised: world-famous publishing houses were exhibiting their books, but our stall was the most crowded. At any one time there were not less than one hundred people there the whole day that the exhibition was open.

One old man, looking at my picture, asked Lani, "Is this man something like Leo Tolstoy?" – just because of my beard. Tolstoy had a beautiful beard.

Tolstoy used to have a dream that psychoanalysts of different schools have been interpreting for almost the whole century. The dream was very strange, but not to me. To me it needs no psychoanalysis, but simple common sense. The dream was repeated every night continuously for years. It was strangely nightmarish, and Tolstoy awoke in the middle of every night, perspiring, although there was no danger in the dream.

But if you can understand the meaninglessness of the dream... That was the problem that became the nightmare. This dream represents almost everybody's life. No psychoanalytic school has been able to figure out what kind of dream it is because there is no parallel, it is unprecedented.

The dream used to be the same every night. A vast desert, as far as you can see just desert and desert and two boots, which Tolstoy recognized as his, go on walking. But he is missing, just the boots go on making noise in the sand. And it continues because the desert is endless. They never reach anywhere. Behind he can see the prints of the boots for miles, and ahead he can see the boots going on walking.

Ordinarily you will not think it is a nightmare. But if you think a little more closely: every day, every night the same dream of utter futility, reaching nowhere. There seems to be no destiny, and nobody is in the boots, they are empty.

He told all the well-known psychoanalysts of his day in Russia. Nobody could figure out what it meant because there is no book that describes any dream which can even be called a little bit similar to this. It is absolutely unique.

But to me there is no question of any psychoanalysis. It is a simple dream, representing every human being's life. You are walking in a desert because you are not walking toward the goal that is intrinsic in your being. You are not going to reach anywhere. The more you go away, the more you will be going away from yourself. And the more you look for any meaning the more you will find utter emptiness and nothing else. That is the meaning. The man is missing; only the boots are walking.

You are not in what you are doing. You are not in what you are being. You are not in what you are pretending. It is utter hollowness, pure hypocrisy.

But the way it has been created is a simple method: Tell everybody, "As you are, you are absolutely undeserving – even to exist. As you are, you are just ugly, an accident. As you are, you should be ashamed of yourself because you don't have anything worthy of honor and respect." Naturally, every child starts doing things that are supposed to be honorable. He goes on becoming more and more false, more and more phony, more and more distant from his authentic reality, his very being – and then the fear arises.

Whenever a longing is felt to know yourself, it is immediately followed by great fear. The fear is that if you find yourself you are going to lose respect for yourself – even in your own eyes.

The society is too heavy on every individual. It makes every effort to condition you so heavily that you start thinking that you are the conditioning – and you become part of the society, against your own being. You become a Christian, you become a Hindu, you become a Mohammedan, and you forget completely that you were born just as a human being, with no religion, with no politics, with no nation, with no race. You were born just a pure possibility of growth.

According to me, sannyas is to bring you back to yourself, whatsoever the consequences, whatsoever the risk. You have to come back to yourself. You may not find a Jesus there. There is no need: one Jesus is enough. You may not find a Gautam Buddha. It is perfectly okay because too many Gautam Buddhas in existence will be simply boring.

Existence does not want to repeat people. It is so creative that it always brings something new in each individual, a new potential, a new possibility, a new height, a new dimension, a new peak.

Sannyas is a revolt against all societies and all cultures and all civilizations, for the simple reason that they are against the individual. I am absolutely for the individual. I can sacrifice every society and every religion and every civilization – the whole history of mankind – just for a single individual. The individual is the most valuable phenomenon because the individual is part of existence.

You will have to drop your fear. It has been imposed on you; it is not natural. Watch every small child: he accepts himself perfectly; there is no condemnation, there is no desire to be anybody else. But everybody, as he grows, is distracted. You will have to gather courage to come back to yourself. The whole society will prevent you; you will be condemned. But it is far better to be condemned by the whole world than to remain miserable and phony and false and live a life of somebody else.

You can have a blissful life and there are not two ways, only one single way. This is: you have just to be yourself, whatever you are. From there, from that deep acceptance and respect for yourself, you will start growing. You will bring flowers of your own – not Christian, not Buddhist, not Hindu – just absolutely your own, a new contribution to existence.

But it needs immense courage to go alone on a path leaving the whole crowd on the highway. To be in the crowd one feels cozy, warm; to go alone, naturally one feels afraid. The mind goes on arguing within that, "the whole of humanity cannot be wrong, and I am going alone." It is better just to be part of the crowd because then you are not responsible if things go wrong.

Everybody is responsible. But the moment you depart from the crowd you are taking your responsibility in your own hands. If something goes wrong, you are responsible.

But remember one very fundamental thing: responsibility is one side of the coin and the other side is freedom. You can have both together or you can drop both together. If you don't want to have responsibility, you cannot have freedom, and without freedom there is no growth.

So you have to accept responsibility for yourself and you have to live in absolute freedom so that you can grow, whatever you are. You may turn out to be a rosebush, you may turn out to be just a marigold flower, you may turn out just to be a wild flower that has no name. But one thing is certain: whatever you turn out to be, you will be immensely happy. You will be utterly blissful.

You may not have respectability – on the contrary, you may be condemned by everybody – but deep inside, you will feel such an ecstatic joy that only a free individual can feel. And only a free individual can grow in higher layers of consciousness, can reach to the heights of the Himalayan peaks.

Society has kept everybody retarded, it has made everybody stupid. It needs idiots; it does not want intelligent people around. It is afraid of intelligence because intelligence is always in revolt against slavery, against superstition, against all kinds of exploitation, against all kinds of stupidities, against all discriminations between races, nations, classes, colors. Intelligence is continuously in revolt.

Only the idiot is always obedient. Even God wanted Adam to be an idiot because it was his vested interest that Adam and Eve remain idiots so they could go on worshipping him.

In my vision the Devil is the world's first revolutionary, and the Devil is the most significant person in the whole of history. The whole civilization and progress owe much to the Devil – not to God at all. God wanted only a stupid Adam, a stupid Eve; and if Adam had followed God you would still be chewing grass in the Garden of Eden!

Man has moved because he revolted against God. God was the establishment. God represents the establishment, authority, the power and the domination. Anybody who is intelligent cannot be converted into a slave; he would rather die than become a slave. He cannot be exploited and he cannot be dragged away from his own center.

My people have to learn the fact that I believe only in the religion of revolt. Except that, there is no religiousness. Except that, there is no possibility of your consciousness rising to the highest potential that you are carrying as dormant energy.

Paddy had recently joined his local skydiving club and had gone up for his first jump. Everything was going perfectly until it was Paddy's turn to jump.

"Hold it," shouted his instructor, "you are not wearing your parachute!"

"Oh, that's okay," replied Paddy, "we are just practicing, aren't we?"

Society needs these idiots. They are perfectly obedient, docile, ready to be exploited, ready to be reduced almost into animals.

Don't be afraid of accepting yourself. That's where your real treasure is, that's where your home is. Don't listen to the so-called wise – they are the poisoners who have killed millions of people, destroyed their lives, taken away all meaning and significance.

It does not matter who you are. What matters is that you should remain exactly what you are because from there starts growth.

A few sutras for you to meditate upon, perhaps they may give you some courage, some intelligence.

"Everybody is ignorant, only on different subjects." So don't be worried about being ignorant; everybody is.

"All men are born free, but some get married." So just be alert, and freedom is yours!

"Illusion is the first of all pleasures." Remember, the life of growth goes beyond the mundane life of pleasures. Pleasure is not something very significant; it is just like scratching your skin: it feels pleasant, but just for a little while. If you go on scratching you will bring blood to your skin, and then pleasure turns into pain. And you all know that you have turned all your pleasures into pain.

A man of intelligence searches for something that can never be turned into pain and anguish and anxiety and suffering. What I call bliss is not pleasure because bliss cannot be turned into its opposite. There is no opposite of it.

The search should be for the eternal, and everybody has the capacity to experience the eternal. But the pleasures of the physical body or biological infatuation or the pleasures of eating food keep people engaged and take away the small time they have here on this earth to grow.

I have heard...

A man went to a psychiatrist and said, "I am very much concerned. My wife goes on eating and eating and she spends the whole day sitting on the sofa looking at the television. And even while she is looking at the television she is eating something – ice cream – or if she is not eating something, at least she is chewing gum. But her mouth continues.

"Now she has lost all beauty; she has become just a bag of skin with no curves anywhere. What am I supposed to do?"

The psychiatrist said, "Try one thing. It is a sure success; I have tried it on many patients." He gave the man a photograph of a beautiful nude girl.

The man said, "My God! How is this picture going to help?"

The psychiatrist replied, "You have to understand the whole strategy. Put it inside your refrigerator. Stick it with real German glue, so your wife cannot take it away. Whenever she opens the refrigerator she will see herself, and this beautiful girl. Perhaps she will start reducing her weight. Just give her a comparison."

For three or four months the psychiatrist waited and waited, and finally he went to the man's home to find out what had happened. He could not believe it: the man was sitting on the sofa; he had become so fat and he was watching television, chewing gum. The psychiatrist said, "What is the matter? What happened to you?"

The man said, "It is that damned picture! Because of the picture I started going to the refrigerator, just to have a look. But when you open the refrigerator then naturally you want something, the very flavor of so many nice things. So each time I open the refrigerator I start eating. Your device worked, but it backfired."

People are behaving so stupidly in their lives. People who go on eating. The doctors are prohibiting it; everybody is telling them that it is dangerous. What pleasure do they have? Just a small patch on the tongue experiences taste; once the food has passed that small patch you don't know any taste, any pleasure. It must be utter stupidity.

But people are after all kinds of pleasures. They are not even aware that they are wasting immensely valuable time: this is the time when somebody becomes a Gautam Buddha, this is the time when somebody becomes a Socrates – the same time, the same energy, the same potential. But you are wasting it in running after things that are meaningless.

"Chivalry is a man's attempt to defend a woman against every man except himself."

"Even when you are on the right track you will get run over if you just sit there."

"To do nothing is the most difficult thing in the world."

Everybody is doing something. Only very few people know the art of sometimes not doing anything. When you are not doing anything you are simply and purely your being.

Doing and being are two ways of living your life, two styles of living your life. The life of doing is mundane; the life of being is sublime, is divine. I am not saying drop all doing, I am saying doing should be secondary in your life and being should be primary. Doing should be only for the necessities of life, and being should be your real luxury, your real joy, your real ecstasy.

"To be perfectly happy one must be perfectly stupid."

Whenever you see a happy person, remember it. Stupid people are very happy because they don't know what they are here for. They don't know that there is some task to be fulfilled. They are almost like retarded children who go on playing with teddy bears. Your teddy bears can change their shape: somebody's teddy bear is money and somebody's teddy bear is women, and somebody's teddy bear is men – but whatever you are doing you are feeling very happy that money is accumulating, that you have found a new girlfriend, that you are promoted to a higher position. You are utterly happy. Unless you are stupid this is not possible.

A man of intelligence will be able to see without fail that all these small things of life are preventing you from the beyond. They keep you engaged here, and this is not your home. They keep you engaged in a life that is going to end up in a graveyard.

The intelligent man starts asking – and this becomes his fundamental search and quest – "Is there something beyond the graveyard or not? If there is nothing beyond the graveyard, then this whole life is just a dream and meaningless. Unless there is something beyond, life cannot be significant and life cannot be meaningful." But the stupid person is immensely happy with any toys that the society provides him. Don't be stupid!

"To err is human, to admit it is divine."

It is absolutely human to commit mistakes. To admit it, without any guilt, brings a transformation in your being. You are simply admitting your humanity by admitting your mistake. Something of the divine, something of the beyond starts opening up.

"Every cloud has a silver lining and even old clothes have their shiny side."

"If it were not for the optimist, a pessimist would never know how happy he isn't."

People are continuously comparing themselves with others. They become happy, they become unhappy because of the comparisons.

I had a meeting with a very famous Hindu saint. He told a few other people who had gathered to listen to what transpired between us, "The secret of happiness is always to look to those who are unhappy. Look at the crippled and you will feel happy that you are not crippled. Look at the blind and you will feel happy that you are not blind. Look at the poor and you will feel happy that you are not poor."

I had to stop this idiot! I said, "You don't understand a simple fact. Once a person starts comparing he cannot stop at only comparing with those who are unfortunate. He will also look at those who are richer than him, who are more beautiful than him, who are stronger than him, who are more respectable than him. Then he will be miserable. You are not giving him the secret of happiness; you are giving him the secret of being in absolute misery."

It has been taught down the ages in almost all the religious scriptures, in different words, but the essential secret is the same: Feel contented because there are people who are so miserable. Thank God that you are not so miserable.

But this cannot remain one-sided. Once you learn the way of comparison, you cannot compare yourself only with those who are inferior to you. Inevitably you will also have to compare yourself with those who are superior to you – and then there will be immense misery.

In fact, comparison is not the right thing to do. You are yourself, and there is nobody else with whom you can be compared.

You are incomparable. So is the other person. Never compare.

Comparison is one of the causes that is keeping you tethered to the mundane – because comparison creates competition, comparison creates ambition. It does not come alone; it brings all its companions with it. And once you become competitive there is no end to it; you will end before it does. Once you become ambitious you have chosen the most stupid path for your life.

Henry Ford was once asked... And he seems to be one of the wisest men of this century because his small statements make so much sense. He was the first man to say that "history is bunk," and that is absolutely true.

He was asked, "What have you learned through your successful life?" He was one of the most successful men you can conceive of; from poverty he rose to be the richest man in the world. What he said has to be remembered.

Henry Ford said, "Through all my successful life I have learned only one thing: I have learned to climb staircases, to climb ladders. And then when I reach the last rung of the ladder I feel so stupid and so embarrassed because there is no longer anywhere to go.

"And I cannot say to the people who are behind me, struggling hard to reach the same ladder where I am feeling stupid, what I have been struggling for. And nobody will listen to me if I say to them, 'Stop wherever you are. Don't waste time because there is nothing. Once you reach the top you are stuck. You cannot get down because that looks like falling back. You cannot go ahead because there is nowhere to go ahead.'"

The presidents and prime ministers of countries just feel stuck. Now they know there is only one thing that can happen, and that is the fall. There is nothing to rise to; there is nowhere to go except to fall from the place that they have reached. So they cling to their seats.

But this is not the right kind of life. First you go on climbing ladders, struggling with people; then ultimately you are stuck and you cling to the last rung so that nobody can take you away from it. Is this a madhouse?

Man has turned this planet into a madhouse. If you want to be sane, first be yourself – without any guilt, without any condemnation. Accept yourself with humbleness and simplicity.

This is a gift of existence to you. Feel grateful, and start searching for what can help you to grow as you are not to become a carbon copy of somebody else, but just to remain your original self.

There is no ecstasy greater than to be your original face.

Osho,
Is there any possibility that I will ever grow up?

I love the way you have asked the question. It is out of a sincere humbleness. And just because it is arising out of a simple humbleness it opens the doors for your growth.

You are asking, "Is there any possibility that I will ever grow up?" There are all the possibilities. For the humble heart everything is possible, for the egoist nothing is possible. For a person who can accept that "I am nobody," all doors suddenly open, all the mysteries of existence become available. For the man who can say, "I do not know," a miracle becomes possible. In his acceptance of not knowing he starts becoming wise because he starts becoming like a child, utterly innocent.

There is every possibility of your growing up. And particularly in this buddhafield, if you are not functioning out of your ego, if you have left your ego outside the Gateless Gate, then everything is possible for you, then the whole existence is available for you. The only thing that blocks is the small ego.

One sometimes wonders why this small ego, phony, false, prevents people from growing. Logically it seems very ridiculous, but existentially it is something like a small speck of dust falling into your eyes and the whole existence disappearing. Your eyes are closed, you cannot open your eyes. Those small pieces of dust have taken the whole of existence away from you. The rainbow in the clouds and the sun and the rain – all have disappeared.

Logically it should not be so: that such small dust particles prevent the view of the whole sky. But in reality they do. So it is not a question of logic; it is question of actual, existential reality.

The small ego functions just like a small dust particle in your vision, and it prevents you from looking at all the possibilities that are available, which have always been available. Just remove that small particle from your eyes. Nothing is changing, all was always available – your eyes were just not capable of seeing it.

With your humbleness great miracles are possible. Just remain humble, innocent, receptive, available, waiting for the guest to knock on your doors.

Two nuns were walking through the woods one evening when they were jumped on by two men who dragged them into the bushes and began to rape them. Sister Mary, bruised and battered, looked up at the sky and began to pray softly, "Forgive him Lord, for he knows not what he is doing."

Sister Teresa looked over and said, "That's a pity, mine does."

A gorgeous blonde walked into the dentist's office and was obviously very nervous. "Oh doctor," she cried, "I'm so scared. You know, I think I would rather have a baby than have a tooth filled."

"Okay," said the dentist warily, "but make up your mind before I adjust the chair."

Just remain innocent and laughing and rejoicing and you need not be worried about your growth. It will be happening on its own accord. You don't have to do anything for it; you have just to create the right atmosphere.

And we have already created that atmosphere here. You can benefit from this atmosphere if you don't remain an outsider – just a spectator or a curious person.

If you are here, then melt and merge in this beautiful communion which is incomparable in the sense that nowhere on the earth is anything similar happening. Where people are laughing, rejoicing, dancing, singing, melting into each other, the growth will come on its own accord.

Just learn to laugh, learn to dance, learn to sing, learn to be yourself, utterly fulfilled and grateful to existence.

Paddy and Maureen had just had their eighteenth child, so Maureen went to the doctor and asked if he could give her a hearing aid. "A hearing aid?" asked the doctor. "How will that help you plan your family more effectively?"

"Well," said Maureen, "I'm a little bit deaf, so every night when Paddy says, 'Would you like to go to sleep or what?' I always say, 'What?'"

9

The Middle Path

Osho,
I feel and know in my heart, I am your disciple. I don't feel I am yet a devotee although I aspire to be one. Is it the nature of being a devotee that one knows one has become one? Or does the innocence of the devotee make the awareness of it not possible?

Antar Farid, the question you are asking is certainly significant. Its significance is very subtle. I will have to go step by step to make it clear to you.

These are the stages a seeker moves through: the student, the disciple, the devotee. The fourth is also there but it does not belong to the seeker, it belongs to the one who has arrived; that's why I am not counting it. The seeker is on the path. The student is not aware that he is a student. He may think he is a disciple, he may think he is a devotee; he functions absolutely unconsciously.

I am reminded of a case – it happened in the life of a Sufi mystic, Junnaid:

A man came; he wanted to be a disciple. Junnaid looked at him for a long time. The man started feeling a little nervous: Why is he looking at him for so long and so silently?

Finally Junnaid said, "To be a disciple is very difficult."

The man said, "Then I am ready to be a devotee."

Junnaid said, "That is even more difficult. The only thing that is not difficult here is to be a master."

The man said, "If that is the case, I am ready to be the master."

Junnaid told his disciples and devotees, "This is a case of unconsciousness. He is not even a student, but the longing is to be a master if it is easier."

The student comes almost accidentally. Perhaps he reads a book, perhaps a friend talks to him and he becomes curious. But curiosity is so superficial; it cannot make you committed and devoted for a long journey. It is very momentary; hence the student is not accepted in the mystery schools. He is too unripe; he has to wander a few days more or perhaps a few lives more before he can be accepted by a master as a disciple. Another Sufi story will explain it to you clearly...

A man left his home and his village in search of a master. Just outside the village he met an old man sitting under a tree, so silently and so peacefully that he thought, "Perhaps he may know somebody who is a master; otherwise, how am I going to find...?"

Each master is so unique that there are no symptoms that can be recognizable. The young man went to the old man sitting under the tree and asked him, "Do you know a master?"

The old man said, "Certainly. Do you also want to know him?"

He said, "That's why I have asked you. Show me how I can reach the master and how I will recognize him."

The old man said, "It is easy. He will be very old – at least thirty years older than me – and he will be sitting under a tree." And he described the tree, what kind of tree it would be, and he described the moment of meeting. He described it in such detail that the young man was puzzled, how he could manage to describe even the moment of meeting?

But the old man said, "It will take at least thirty years for you to find him."

The young man thanked the old man and went on in search. Now he has some signs, some indications: a certain tree that he can recognize in the evening when the sun is setting, an old man who will be thirty years older than the man he has just left. Of course it is going to be a long journey, wandering here and there, but the old man said things with such authority, with such certainty, that it was almost indubitable.

He wandered in the desert, and he never came across the tree that was described, he never met a man who was thirty years older than the old man. Every evening when the sun was setting he looked all around. No master appeared.

Utterly frustrated and disappointed, now himself becoming old, tired and tattered with the journey in the desert, he came back home. Strangely enough, the old man was still sitting under the tree.

The last time when he was there and the old man was describing the tree – its leaves, its flowers, its fruit, its height, its foliage, its deep shade even in the middle of a sunny day – he had never looked at the tree under which the old man was sitting. He was describing the same tree, but now the man recognized it. After wandering for thirty years looking at every tree, he had become almost accustomed to looking at the tree first.

"My God," he said, "this is the tree! I never came across the same tree anywhere." And the old man was certainly thirty years older, and all the descriptions that he had given about the master were absolutely apparent in the old man – and the sun was setting.

The old man said, "So you have come! I had to wait so long. I was already old enough and ready to die, but just for you I had to wait thirty years."

The young man said, "This is so stupid! Why didn't you tell me at the first moment of meeting that this is the tree and you are the master?"

The old man laughed. He said, "I had told it in every possible way, but you were not ripe. Your understanding was almost absent. These thirty years have ripened you and now you can recognize that which you failed to recognize when you met me. I am your master."

The student is very accidental. There is every possibility that he will never become a disciple. He may go from one place to another, he may gather much knowledge, but he will never become aware of his own being – which is the only true knowledge in existence; the only knowledge that takes you away from darkness to light, away from death to immortality and away from ignorance to innocence. It is the only knowledge that is not information but transformation.

The student is not aware that he is accidental, that he is only curious, that the search has not begun yet because deep in his heart he is not ready to go on a long pilgrimage.

The disciple knows perfectly well that he is a disciple. The first rays of understanding, awareness, have penetrated his being. He knows for sure that he is no longer a student. He feels it deep in his heart, without any doubt, that the miracle has happened: he has become a disciple. He feels the dedication, he feels the love, he feels the commitment. Even if it takes lives to reach, he knows he is on the right path and he will certainly reach. He knows perfectly well that he has found the master.

It is not an intellectual understanding; it is something intuitive, just like love. In fact, the Zen masters have called it "the great affair." Love is a small affair, but to find a master is a great affair because there is no other love that will be deeper and more fragrant and more profound than that which exists between the disciple and the master. And the disciple is perfectly aware of it.

But the devotee is again a totally different phenomenon. The devotee never knows – not because he is unconscious like the student. Devotion comes so slowly, not making any noise. You don't hear the footsteps.

The disciple simply grows just as the child grows and becomes a young man and the young man grows and one day becomes old, but you cannot find when it happened. The disciple grows slowly, slowly into a devotee. And to be a devotee is such a total transformation that only the master becomes aware that you have changed from the disciple to the devotee. You yourself cannot be aware of it.

But the difference between the unawareness of the student and the absence of awareness of the devotee is tremendous. The devotee is so full that there is no place left from where he can stand aloof and be aware of what is happening. He is completely enveloped with the experience, and it is so absorbing that he cannot be watchful of it.

To be watchful, to be alert, you need a certain distance. The devotee has lost all distance. It is the master who recognizes for the first time the change, that the climate has changed: the disciple is no longer a disciple.

Another Sufi story may help you. Sufis have such beautiful stories, such unparalleled stories, that each story opens a new vision.

This Junnaid I mentioned was himself once a seeker. He used to tell his disciples, "When I met my master, the master never looked at me for three years. I was sitting from morning till evening. So many people were coming and going and he was talking to people and he did not look at me – as if I did not exist for him yet. But I was persistent because I had felt the presence of the master and I had tasted the sweetness of his surroundings. I remained. In fact the more he ignored me, the more I became certain that there is some secret in his ignoring me."

After three years the master looked at him for the first time. That was the recognition that he was not a student but a disciple. A student would have got lost in three years. No student can stay that long, waiting just for a look. And then another three years passed and he never looked again.

After three years the master looked again and smiled too. And his smile almost went just like a sharp sword into the heart of Junnaid. Why had he smiled? But the master did not give him a chance to ask. He started talking to other disciples.

Three years passed again, and one day he called him close and kissed his forehead and said, "My son, now you are ready. Now you can go and spread the message."

But no message had been given to him. For nine years he had been there and the only message was that once he was looked at, once he was smiled at, and once he had been kissed on his forehead.

But if the master is saying "You are ready," it must be so. Touching the feet of the master in gratitude, he left.

He used to tell his disciples: "I met a very strange man. In nine years he prepared me without even looking at me – but at each change he made the indication. When he became certain that I was a disciple and whatever happened I was going to stay there, he looked at me. But his look was such a shower of love – I could have waited for it for three lives. Three years were nothing. I was immensely glad: the way he looked at me, with such deep love and compassion, I was almost bathed in a new experience.

"Without telling me anything... In those three years my mind had stopped functioning. I just went on looking at the master, his every gesture, and slowly, slowly there was nothing to think about. I even forgot for what purpose I was sitting there – and that was the day he looked at me and I knew the purpose, and I was immensely fulfilled.

"But then three years again passed, and when he smiled the whole of existence smiled. Every fiber of my being felt his smile, such a soft touch, but it went deep into my heart. I knew something had happened, but I was not aware at that time what had happened. I had passed from disciplehood into devoteehood.

"And the day he kissed my forehead, he sealed my certificate as a master. His kiss on my forehead was his only final message. It took me years to figure out slowly what he had meant."

The kiss of the master to the disciple, to the devotee, is a declaration that the merger has happened, the melting has happened, and now you are ready to spread the fragrance that you are filled with all around.

The student is unconscious. The disciple starts becoming conscious. The devotee is so conscious that he cannot be conscious of his consciousness. It has to be a recognition from the master because from the devotee the distance between himself and the master is absolutely nil. From the devotee one grows into a master, but it is a spontaneous and natural growth.

Farid, I remember these Sufi stories because of your name. Farid is the name of a great Sufi master. You are right: "I feel and know in my heart, I am your disciple." I agree with you.

You say "I don't feel I am yet a devotee although I aspire to be one." Just drop the aspiration and you are one. Only the aspiration is blocking the way. Aspiration is simply a beautiful name for desire, for greed.

Just drop the aspiration and there is no hindrance to your being transformed, transmuted from disciplehood into the wider world of a devotee. And you have certainly stumbled upon a beautiful fact, which cannot be possible just through intellect. You say, "Is it in the nature of being a devotee that one knows one has become one, or does the innocence of the devotee make the awareness of it not possible?"

The second part of your statement is correct; the very nature of the devotee makes it impossible for you to recognize it. There is no space left to stand aside and see. Every knowledge, every awareness needs a distance. You have to stand aside: then you can see and watch, and you can know and you can be aware.

But the devotee has lost all distance between himself and his knowing. He himself has become awareness. Now who is there to be aware of awareness?

This has to be understood: you cannot be aware of your awareness because if you can be aware of your awareness you will be falling into a very logical regress. Then you will have to be aware of your awareness of your awareness, and there is no end to it.

Finally you will always have to decide "Now, this is enough!" In fact you cannot be aware of your awareness because you *are* awareness. It comes from the recognition of the master. He can see the transformation, the change of the climate in your being. And every master has many things to do. One of the most important things, the final thing, is to give you the indication, the kiss on your forehead recognizing that you have entered into the most mysterious experience of life.

Farid, you will never become aware of your being a devotee, but your longing to be a devotee is a hindrance. Drop it immediately! Don't take time dropping it, don't postpone.

There are things that should never be postponed because the tomorrow is never certain. There are things that have to be done just here, immediately, and you will see many doors opening which your aspiration was blocking.

But once you enter into those mysteries you will not be aware because you will become the mystery itself.

Osho,
What does it mean to be in the middle?

To be in the middle means many things. I will have to start my answer from Gautam Buddha because he was the first man to use the words "to be in the middle," and of course nobody has been able to improve upon the meanings that he gave to the word *middle*.

He called his path "the middle path." The first meaning is that if you can avoid both the extremes – the rightist and the leftist – if you can be exactly in the middle of both the extremes, you will not be in the middle. You will have transcended the whole trinity of the extremes and the middle. If you drop both the extremes, the middle disappears on its own accord. Middle of what?

Gautam Buddha's insistence on the middle is not on the middle; it is in fact a subtle way to persuade you for transformation. To tell you directly to be transformed may make you apprehensive, afraid, but to be in the middle seems to be very simple.

Gautam Buddha played with the word out of sheer compassion. His own word for the middle is *majjhim nikai*, the middle path. Every extreme has to exclude the other extreme; every extreme has to be in opposition to the other polarity. The negative is against the positive, the minus is against the plus, death is against life. If you take them as extremes, they naturally appear as opposites.

But the man who can stop exactly in the middle immediately transcends all the extremes and the middle as well. And from the higher standpoint of the transformed being, you can see there is no opposition at all. The extremes are not opposites, not contradictory, but only complementary.

Life and death are not enemies, they are part of one single process. Death does not end life, it simply renews it. It gives it a new form, a new body, a new plane of consciousness. It is not against life; looked at rightly, it is a process of refreshing life, of rejuvenating life. The day is not against the night.

In existence there is no opposition in anything; all opposites contribute to the whole. Existence is an organic unity. It does not exclude anything from it. It is all-inclusive.

The man who can stop in the middle comes to know this tremendous experience: that there are no opposites, no contradictories. The whole existence is one, and in that oneness all contradictions, all oppositions, all contraries disappear into a single unity. Then life includes death, then day includes night.

A man who can experience this organic unity becomes fearless, without any anguish and angst. For the first time he realizes his vastness because he is as vast as the whole existence.

One of the great disciples of George Gurdjieff, P. D. Ouspensky, has written a book. I must have seen thousands of books, and perhaps no other man in the whole world can claim to know more about books than I know. But in this whole experience of thousands of books I have never come across another book that can be compared in any way with P. D. Ouspensky's *Tertium Organum.*

Tertium Organum means the third canon of thought. He gave this name to this great and incomparably unique book because there have been two other books in the past. The first was written by Aristotle, and he called it *The First Organum*, the first principle of thought; and the second was written by Bacon, and he called it *Novum Organum*, a new canon of thought.

Then Ouspensky wrote *Tertium Organum*, the third canon of thought, and he declared just in the beginning of the book that "although I am calling it the third canon of thought, it existed before the first canon of thought ever existed." This book contains so many mysteries that each page, almost each paragraph, each sentence seems to be so pregnant with meaning.

I used to love underlining my books. That's why I have never been interested in reading books from any library. I cannot underline a book that has been borrowed from a library; I cannot put my stamp on it. And I hate to read a book which has been underlined by somebody else because those lines which have been underlined stand out and they unnecessarily interfere in my own conception, my own flow.

This is the only book that I started underlining and I recognized after a few pages that every line has to be underlined. But I could not be unjust to the book. All my books in the library are underlined. Knowing perfectly well after a few pages that this book could be left not underlined but that that would be unjustified, I had to underline the whole book. In that book there are so many things. One that is significant is the reference I am talking about.

P. D. Ouspensky was one of the greatest mathematicians of his time. He knows perfectly well what he is writing, and he says that in mathematics the part can never be bigger than the whole. It is obvious: how can the part be bigger than the whole? But he goes on to say that mathematics is not all: "I have come to know the mystical experience with my master, George Gurdjieff, and now I can say there is a higher mathematics, the mystical mathematics, where the part can not only be equal to the whole, but sometimes it happens that it is bigger than the whole."

Now you are entering into a strange world, where the part cannot only be equal to the whole, sometimes it can be bigger than the whole. It is simply absurd as far as logic is concerned, and from the mouth of a man who is one of the greatest mathematicians, and he knows it. He makes it clear that "I am embarrassed making this statement. As a mathematician I should condemn it. But what can I do against the existential experience? When it comes to experience, then mathematics or no mathematics, I have to state it exactly as it is."

The moment somebody transcends the opposites and comes to know them as complementaries, he is not only part of the whole, he becomes the whole.

And let me tell you the final absurdity. Once in a while – in a man like Gautam Buddha, or in a man like Mahavira, or Chuang Tzu, or Lao Tzu – it happens that the part becomes bigger than the whole: absolutely illogical, absolutely unmathematical, but still absolutely right.

A Gautam Buddha not only contains the whole but because of his transformation he is a little bit more than the whole. The whole is not aware of its complementariness. Gautam Buddha is aware of its complementariness, and that's where he transcends and becomes bigger than the whole although he is just a part of it.

To be in the middle is one of the great methods of transforming yourself into the ultimate. To prepare yourself for being in the middle you will have to drop all extremist ideas. And all your ideas are extremist – either leftist or rightist, either Christian or Mohammedan, either Hindu or Buddhist. You have chosen. You have not allowed a choiceless consciousness, accepting everything that is.

All your prejudices are your choices. I am against all your prejudices for a simple reason: to bring you into the middle.

The pope heard that a certain lady in Ireland had produced ten children, so he sent one of his cardinals to grant her his blessings.

When he met the lady the cardinal was disgusted to learn that she was not a Catholic. "Do you mean to say," he thundered, "that I have come all this way to meet a sex-mad Protestant?"

If she had been a Catholic, she would have received the blessings of the pope. But unfortunately she is a Protestant. Immediately the prejudiced mind changes its position: from blessings; he starts cursing. He calls that poor woman "a sex-mad Protestant!" This is the way of all prejudices.

A sannyasin is one who has no prejudices, who has not chosen any ideology to be his own, who is choicelessly aware of all that is. In this choicelessness you will be in the middle. The moment you choose, you choose some extreme. The moment you choose, you choose against something; otherwise there is no question of choice. Being in a choiceless awareness is another meaning of being in the middle.

It happened that a very beautiful young prince, whose name was Shron, listened to Gautam Buddha for the first time. Buddha was visiting the capital of the young man's kingdom, but listening to Gautam Buddha, the prince immediately asked to be initiated. He was well known as a sitar player and he was also well known for luxurious living, utterly luxurious.

It was said that even when he was going upstairs, rather than having a railing on the staircase, naked, beautiful women used to stand all along the staircase so that he could move from one woman's shoulder to another woman's shoulder. That was his way to go upstairs. He used to sleep the whole day because the hangover of the night before was too much; the whole night was a night of celebrations, drinking, eating, music, dance. There was no time for him to sleep in the night.

All these things were known, well known to the people. Gautam Buddha had never hesitated to give initiation to any man before.

Now he hesitated. He said, "Shron, I know everything about you; I would like you to reconsider. Think it over. I am still going to stay in this capital for the four months of the rainy season."

In the rainy season, Gautam Buddha never used to move around, nor did his sannyasins. Eight months of the year they were continuously wandering and sharing their experiences of meditation and higher states of consciousness. But because twenty-five centuries ago there were only mud roads, and Buddha had not allowed his disciples to have any possessions – not even an umbrella, no shoes, and just three pieces of cloth. One was for any emergency, and two so that you could change every day after the bath; more than three was not allowed. In the rainy season when it was pouring it would have been difficult to keep those three cloths dry, and to walk in the mud, in the pouring rain might make many poor sannyasins sick.

For that reason he had made it a point that for four months you remain in one place, and those who want to see you can come. For eight months you should go to every thirsty person; for four months let others come to you.

So he said, "There is no hurry, Shron."

But Shron said, "Once I have taken a decision I never reconsider. You have to give me initiation right now."

Buddha still tried to persuade him that "there is no harm in reconsidering it because you have lived a life of utter luxury. You have never walked on the road, you have been always in a golden chariot. You have never come out of your luxurious palace and gardens. You have lived continuously with beautiful women, with great musicians, with dancers. All that will not be possible when you become a sannyasin – not even two meals a day." A Buddhist sannyasin is expected only to have one meal.

Gautam Buddha's insight has been proved correct by science after twenty-five centuries of criticism. Now science has come to the same conclusion: if you can reduce your food to half, your diseases, sicknesses, illnesses will also be reduced to half, and your life will be doubled. Now it can be said scientifically that Buddha was right. It was not a deprivation; it was really a very healthy measure.

He told Shron, "You will not be able. And I don't like anybody to return to the world because that makes him lose his self-respect. That's why I say, 'Consider.'"

Shron said, "I have considered again and again and I still want to be initiated right now. The more you tell me to consider the more I become adamant and stubborn."

Gautam Buddha had to relent and give him initiation, and from the very second day there was trouble – but a trouble that no sannyasin of Gautam Buddha had expected. A trouble that perhaps Gautam Buddha had expected started happening.

When all the sannyasins had three pieces of cloth, Shron started living naked – from one extreme to the other extreme. When all the Buddhist sannyasins were walking on the road, Shron would always walk by the side of the road in the thorns. When the other sannyasins were resting under the shade of the trees, Shron would always stand in the hot sun in the middle of the day.

Within just six months a beautiful young prince became almost old, a skeleton, black; one could not recognize that this was the man who used to be a great prince and was famous for his utterly luxurious life. His feet were bleeding, his whole body had shrunk, and one night after six months Gautam Buddha went to the tree under which he was sleeping. It is one of the rare occasions when Buddha went in the night to any sannyasin for any reason. There is no other incident, at least in the Buddhist scriptures, this is the only incident.

He woke Shron up and asked him a very strange question: "I have heard that when you were a prince you were also the greatest sitarist in the country. Is that right?"

Shron said, "You could have asked at any time. I don't see the point in the middle of the night."

Gautam Buddha said, "Just wait a little, you will see the point."

Shron said, "Yes, it is true."

Buddha said, "Now the second question is, if the strings of the sitar are too tight, will there be any music born out of those strings?"

Shron said, "Of course not. If they are too tight they will be broken."

Buddha said, "If they are too loose, will there be any music?"

Shron said, "You are asking strange questions in the middle of the night. When the strings are too loose they cannot create any music. A certain tension is needed. In fact, to play on a sitar is simple. The real mastery is to keep the strings exactly in the middle, neither too tight nor too loose."

Buddha said, "This is the point I came to make to you. Life is also a musical instrument: too tight and there is no music, too loose and there is no music. The strings of life have to be exactly in the middle; neither too tight, nor too loose. Only then is there music. And only a master knows how to keep them in the middle. Because you have been a master sitarist I would like you also to become a master of life. Just don't move from one extreme to another, from luxury to austerity, from pleasures to self-torture. Try to be exactly in the middle."

In a sense Gautam Buddha is one of the most profound psychologists that the world has produced: to be in the middle in every action of your life. Always find the middle and you have found the path of meditation and the path of liberation.

Osho,
When I enter the "Gateless Gate" my body is filled with some type of uncontrollable vibration. Sitting in your presence in Buddha Hall with closed eyes my whole body vibrates and tears flow from my eyes. I feel the vibration deepening as if someone has touched me. However, I get lost in the darkness with closed eyes and I am very much frightened of what's happening. Then I try to stop all this by keeping my eyes wide open. Osho, would you please comment?

It is natural that when something from the unknown starts happening one feels afraid. Although you are seekers and you want the whole sky to open for you – you want the unknown to touch your heart, you want the stars to enter in your being – you are not aware that when things start happening you will be afraid and trembling.

Now whatever is happening to you is absolutely good. But the fear is natural, and you will have to overcome your fear. It is perfectly good to sit with closed eyes when so much is happening around you and you are feeling strange vibrations and a soft touch to your heart.

Don't close your eyes out of fear; close your eyes for deeper exploration. There is nothing to be afraid of. This is our existence, this is our world, and there are many, many things of which we are unaware.

As you become more receptive, you will become aware of subtle vibrations and naturally you will start thinking, "Am I going mad or what?" You will start feeling things which, if you are not aware and clear, can drive you nuts.

Close your eyes with love for a deeper contact with those vibrations. Those are the vibrations of a buddhafield. You are fortunate that they are touching you, but your fear can stop the whole process. If you want to be afraid, be afraid only of your fear. Except that, there is nothing to be afraid of. Close your eyes.

But when you close your eyes, another fear comes – of darkness. There is nothing in darkness to be afraid of. It is so silent, so beautiful, so vast. In the light you are always surrounded by a crowd of people or trees – but you are always crowded. Only in darkness are you absolutely alone. That aloneness creates fear.

But our whole effort is to teach you aloneness, to teach you to love without any choice. Light or darkness, both should be explored. Light has its own beauties, its own colors, its own rainbows, its own flowers. Darkness also has its own silences. Light comes and goes, darkness remains.

Darkness is far more eternal than light. It is always there; it does not need any fuel, it is not dependent on anything, on any cause. You cannot destroy darkness; you can destroy light without much difficulty. You cannot do anything directly with darkness; it is there and it will remain forever. Search for its beauties, search for its depth. Out of fear, first you close your eyes. Then another fear grips you – of darkness – so you open your eyes, but then the whole experience starts disappearing. Get out of this misunderstanding.

If you can, just trust me a little bit. I give you the guarantee that what is happening to you is for your good, for your well-being. You are not only entering the Gateless Gate, you are really entering into the gateless gate within you.

Allow it to happen. Rejoice in it so that it can happen more. Dance. In welcoming it, allow your whole heart to be receptive to all these vibrations. You have entered a mystery school. You have to prepare yourself for many more mysteries ahead, but if you misunderstand you will lose something great that was beginning to grow within you.

Be absolutely assured that what is happening to you is going to happen to all. These experiences happen like a chain. If one person becomes absolutely immersed in these unknown vibrations, he will become infectious, contagious to others. Spread your vibrations to others.

Sitting by the side of someone, focus with your eyes closed on the person; particularly, if you can, focus with closed eyes on the neck of the person. Sit behind him. The neck is the most receptive center – and those vibrations will start moving into the other person too. You will see that he is becoming fidgety, looking all around – what is happening?

Every day sit behind somebody else. You have a great and a very enjoyable task. Just sit behind Avirbhava, and you will see the explosion. But don't misunderstand what is happening to you. Welcome it.

A young lady living in Canada received a present from a friend in Mexico. It was a tiny Chihuahua dog, the so-called Mexican hairless breed.

During the Canadian winter the tiny dog, which was used to tropical heat, began to shiver uncontrollably. No matter how many blankets she put on it, the poor dog could not get warm.

In desperation the girl jumped on her bicycle and pedaled down to the village drugstore. She asked the druggist if he could give her something to keep her Chihuahua warm and maybe grow some hair on it.

The druggist blushed and said, "Miss, I think that is something you should see your doctor about."

The girl was about to leave when the man added, "But I will tell you one thing, miss. Riding that bicycle is only going to make things worse!"

10

Friendship Is Small, Compared to Friendliness

Osho,

Rig Veda says, "Let noble thoughts come to us from every side." Do you agree with this statement?

I do not agree with Rig Veda and its statement. It appears only to the intellectuals as true.

But those who know, know perfectly well that thoughts are simply thoughts. They are neither noble nor ignoble. They are all chains, prisons; how can they be noble? Mind itself is your slavery, how can it be noble? And the ugliest thing in the statement of Rig Veda is that it is asking, "Let noble thoughts come to us from every side." You are already too full of all kinds of crap – and you are inviting more crap to come to you from every side?

How can I agree with this statement? It may have been made by a great Hindu seer and saint, but because of this statement, this very statement, whoever has made it has shown his ignorance about human consciousness. He does not know the state beyond the mind.

Unless you know the state beyond the mind you are as blind as anyone else, as ignorant as anyone else, with only one difference:

you are a hypocrite, you are a pretender, you are showing the world a false face and hiding your reality. Any man who has made this statement is utterly ignorant about spiritual reality. It does not matter that the statement is contained in the ancientmost holy book of the Hindus. To me, each statement has to stand on its own authority. It doesn't matter from where it comes, who utters it. The statement itself intrinsically is wrong. It shows only one thing: that whoever uttered it was also wrong.

The whole process of religious consciousness is getting rid of thoughts. Yes, noble thoughts are included in this. It doesn't matter whether your chains are made of gold or just steel. In fact, the chains that are made of gold are more dangerous than the chains made of steel because the chains made of gold can be misunderstood as ornaments; you can start being attached to them and then there is no possibility of freedom at all.

To call any thoughts "noble" is one of the most dangerous statements to make. It goes against all mystical experience. No thought is noble, and therefore no thought is ignoble either. Thoughts are just thoughts. Their function is to keep you clouded so that you cannot see the sun. Their function is to keep you in darkness so you cannot see the light of the day. They surround you in thick layers and keep you disconnected from existence. This separation is our misery. This is our anguish, this is our hell.

All thoughts have to be removed, irrespective of whether they are made of gold or of steel. Whether they appear to be good or bad, whether they come in moral packages or immoral packages does not matter. In fact, again I would like to repeat: thoughts that appear to be noble are more dangerous than those that are apparently ignoble because there is a tendency within you to get attached to anything that is noble, moral, puritan.

Once you get attached to your chains, how are you going to be free? Once you become attached to your cage, how are you going to open your wings in the sky?

Rig Veda is certainly the ancientmost scripture in the world. That does not make it in any way significant; it simply makes it more primitive than any other scripture. It was written by more barbarous and more primitive people, less civilized, less cultured – and you can see it in the lifestyles of the Vedic seers.

You can see the difference between a Gautam Buddha and any seer, any sage of the Vedas. They had many wives – and not only that, they had many other women, purchased in the slave markets. Can you conceive of Gautam Buddha purchasing a woman auctioned in the marketplace? It is simply inconceivable to reduce a woman to a commodity; just a sexual object to be used. And all the Vedic seers, without any exception, had many wives and many women purchased from the auctions in the marketplace.

You will be surprised to know... Sometimes words go through such a transformation that one becomes absolutely unaware of their meaning. The word *vadhu* has lost all its original meaning. Now it means the newly-wed wife, but in the times of the Vedas, *vadhu* meant a woman who had been purchased from the marketplace. You can treat her as a wife, you can use her as a sexual object, but her children will not be legitimate. They will be orphans, illegitimate and condemned by the society.

Strange, the people who are producing them are praised as seers and sages. Their very act of purchasing women is so ugly that to call them sages is simply stupid; they are not even worthy to be called human. And then to produce from those women children who will be condemned for their whole lives as illegitimate...

I say unto you, there is not a single child in the whole world who is illegitimate. Parents may be illegitimate, but not children. How can a child be illegitimate? Every child comes from the same source of life and existence, with the same purity and dignity. No child brings a certificate that "I am legitimate;" and no child comes with a seal on his forehead that he is illegitimate.

But these so-called seers were accumulating immense money. They were in favor of the ugly caste system of India – in fact they created it. One fourth of the country is condemned to live like cattle, and the responsibility goes to the Vedas. They were very ordinary people. If you look at the prayers that they have written in the Vedas, you can see their utter ordinariness.

And that has continued to be the inner unconscious of the Indian mind. They were greedy people: they possessed lands, slaves, and they were very jealous, jealous of each other. They were not humble people, and they were jealous even of their own wives. They had many wives, and they had many purchased women who were almost like prostitutes, but they wanted their wives to be absolutely dedicated only to them. They were very angry people, ready to curse anybody – not only for this life but even for future lives – on any slight provocation. And they still have a certain existence in the Indian mind.

Just a few days ago Jayesh was telling me – because he is looking after all the problems that the Indian government and the Indian bureaucracy have created for this place – one ex-attorney general of Maharashtra appeared to be very much interested in me.

Jayesh asked him, "Have you ever heard Osho, have you ever read anything?" He said, "I have not read anything, I have never heard him." Jayesh said, "Then in what ways are you interested in him? And why do you want to help me in solving the legal problems against the ashram, which are absolutely invalid?"

He said, "I simply want to help because it is a blessing to work for Osho." Jayesh was very much influenced, but in the next sentence the man said, "I will work just for the sheer joy and the blessings that will come to me from working for Osho. But money is also needed..."

Jayesh asked me what to do with such people. "He does not know you, he has never read you, he has never heard you. He talks about blessings, looks very spiritual – and ends up with the sentence that money is also needed."

I said to him, "Ask him to choose between the two: either the blessings or the money." He said, "Osho, you will destroy my whole work! He is the man I am depending on." I said, "But make it clear because he cannot have both." He said, "It was better not to have told you. Now I am in a fix. I know he needs money, I know he is working for money. And if I ask this question, he will certainly be very much annoyed."

This greed, this money infatuation, this materialism comes exactly down from the seers of the Rig Veda. It still constitutes the unconscious of the Hindu mind. On the surface, everything is spiritual. Underneath, everything is so ugly, so obscene, and the beauty of it is that the Indians go on condemning the whole world as materialist; they are the only spiritual people.

But my own experience is that I have not come across a more materialist people in the whole world than the Indians. Yes, they have a spiritual mask that the others don't have, so the others appear to be materialistic. And Indians are very much conditioned to talk about spirituality, the ultimate reality. It is just common heritage to talk about great things. But when you scratch a little bit, you will find the most ugly human beings in the world – and the responsibility goes to such people.

The man who said: "Let noble thoughts come to us from every side," has been praised by Hindu scholars down the ages. I am the first in the whole history of mankind who is condemning this man and his statement. His statement shows absolutely clearly that he knows nothing of meditation.

Noble thoughts are simply noble chains, noble prisons, noble poisons. Every thought has to be dropped. Whether it is good or bad – that is immaterial. You have to rise into a state of thoughtlessness. That state is the only nobility in the world. That is the only authentic spirituality.

But the moment you go beyond thought, you are no longer a Christian, no longer a Hindu, no longer a Jew, no longer a Buddhist – because all these are thoughts. To be a Hindu means you have certain kinds of thoughts; to be a Mohammedan means you have chosen a different collection of thoughts. What is the difference between a Hindu and a Christian? – just the thoughts. Once they both go beyond thoughts, what will be the difference? In the silences of the heart, everybody is exactly the same open sky, without any clouds.

A few sutras for your meditation. You need them urgently because you are reading the wrong kind of literature.

The first sutra: "Not all saints are playing a practical joke on the public. Some are genuinely mad."

Second: "If everyone does what they believe to be right, there will be assuredly utter chaos in the world."

Third: "If you see the good in everybody, you are an optimist or you may be simply nuts."

Fourth: "Just when I nearly had the answer, I forgot the question."

Osho,
What is real authentic friendliness?

The question you have asked is very complex. You will have to understand a few other things before you can understand what real authentic friendliness is.

The first is friendship. Friendship is love without any biological tones to it. It is not the friendship that you understand ordinarily – the boyfriend, the girlfriend. To use the word *friend* in any way associated with biology is sheer stupidity. It is infatuation and madness. You are being used by biology for reproduction purposes. If you think you are in love, you are wrong; it is just hormonal attraction. Your chemistry can be changed and your love will disappear. Just an injection of hormones and a man can become a woman and a woman can become a man.

Friendship is love without any biological tones. It has become a rare phenomenon. It used to be a great thing in the past, but a few great things in the past have completely disappeared. It is a very strange thing that ugly things are stubborn, they don't die easily; and beautiful things are very fragile, they die and disappear very easily.

Today friendship is understood either in biological terms or in economic terms, or in sociological terms – an acquaintance, a kind of acquaintance. But friendship means that if the need arises you will be ready even to sacrifice yourself. Friendship means that you have made somebody else more important than you; somebody else has become more precious than you yourself. It is not a business, it is love in its purity.

This friendship is possible even the way you are now. Even unconscious people can have such a friendship. But if you start becoming more conscious of your being, then friendship starts turning into friendliness.

Friendliness has a wider connotation, a far bigger sky. Friendship is a small thing compared to friendliness. Friendship can be broken, the friend can turn into an enemy. That possibility remains intrinsic in the very fact of friendship.

I am reminded of Machiavelli giving guidance to the princes of the world in his great work, *The Prince*. One of his guidelines is: Never tell anything to your friend which you would not be able to say to your enemy because the person who is a friend today may turn into an enemy tomorrow.

And the suggestion following that is: Never say anything against the enemy because the enemy can turn into a friend tomorrow. Then you will be very embarrassed. Machiavelli is giving a very clear insight: that our ordinary love can change into hate, our friendship can become enmity any moment. This is the unconscious state of man: where love is hiding hate just behind it, where you hate the same person you love but you are not aware of it.

Friendliness becomes possible only when you are real, you are authentic and you are absolutely alert of your being. And if love arises out of this awareness, it will be friendliness. Friendliness can never change into its opposite. Remember this as a criterion: that the greatest values of life are only those which cannot change into their opposite – in fact there is no opposite.

You are asking, "What is real authentic friendliness?"

It will need a great transformation in you to have a taste of friendliness. As you are, friendliness is a faraway star. You can have a look at the faraway star, you can have a certain intellectual understanding, but it will remain only an intellectual understanding, not an existential taste.

Unless you have an existential taste of friendliness, it will be very difficult, almost impossible to make a distinction between friendship and friendliness.

Friendliness is the purest thing you can conceive about love. It is so pure that you cannot even call it a flower, you can only call it a fragrance which you can feel and experience, but you cannot catch hold of. It is there, your nostrils are full of it, your whole being is surrounded by it. You feel the vibe, but there is no way to catch hold of it. The experience is so big and so vast and our hands are too small.

I said to you that your question is very complex – not because of the question, but because of you. You are not yet at the point from where friendliness can become an experience. Be real, be authentic and you will know the purest quality of love – just a fragrance of love surrounding you always. And that quality of the purest love is friendliness. Friendship is addressed to someone, somebody is your friend.

Once Gautam Buddha was asked, "Does the enlightened man have friends?" and he said, "No." The questioner was shocked because he was thinking the man who is enlightened must have the whole world as his friend.

But Gautam Buddha is right, whether you are shocked or not. When he says, "The enlightened man has no friends," he is saying he cannot have friends because he cannot have enemies. They both come together. Friendliness he can have, but not friendship.

Friendliness is unfocused, unaddressed love. It is not any contract, spoken or unspoken. It is not from one individual to another individual; it is from one individual to the whole existence, of which man is only a small part because trees are included, animals are included, rivers are included, mountains are included, stars are included. Everything is included in friendliness.

Friendliness is just the way of your being real and authentic; you start radiating it. It comes on its own accord, you don't have to bring it. Whoever comes close to you will feel the friendliness.

That does not mean that nobody will be your enemy. As far as you are concerned, you will not be an enemy of anyone because you are no longer a friend to anyone. But your height, your consciousness, your blissfulness, your silence, your peace will annoy many, will irritate many, will make many – without understanding you – your enemies.

In fact the enlightened men have more enemies than the unenlightened. The unenlightened may have a few enemies, a few friends. The enlightened men have almost the whole world antagonistic toward them, because blind people cannot forgive the man who has eyes, and the ignorant cannot forgive one who knows. They cannot feel love toward a man who has attained to his fulfillment because their egos are hurt.

Just the other day, I received four letters from four different American prisons. All the four prisoners are asking for sannyas. One American prisoner has been reading my books. Since I was in that prison for one day, the authorities became interested, the prisoners became interested, so they must have ordered my books. The prisoner has been reading those books.

Although he is an American, he writes, "Osho, reading your books, listening to you on the television... And when you were in this prison for one day, I was also here." He has been there for almost five years. "It was a blissful experience for me and I will never forget the day we were together in the same cell. It was been the most important day of my life.

"And I have been carrying something in me which I want to express to you. You have not committed any sin. Of that I was absolutely certain the moment I saw you. But to be innocent seems to be a greater crime than any other, and because you were talked about on the radio, on the television, your books were read all over the country, there came a moment when you were a more important figure than the president of America. That's what triggered the whole process of destroying your commune, imprisoning you – just to humiliate you."

I was surprised that a prisoner would have such a deep insight. He is saying "People like you are bound to be condemned because even the greatest, most powerful people look like pygmies before your consciousness and your height. It is your fault," he is saying to me. "If you had not been so successful, you would have been ignored. If your commune had not been so successful, nobody would have bothered about you."

The enlightened man has no friends, no enemies, but only a pure love, unaddressed. He is ready to pour into anybody's heart who is available. That is real, authentic friendliness.

But such a man will provoke many egos, will hurt those who think they are very important and powerful people. The presidents and the queens and the prime ministers and the kings will become immediately worried, concerned. A man who has no power has suddenly become the focus of attention of the people, attracts more people than the people who have power and money and prestige. Such a man cannot be forgiven. He has to be punished whether he has committed any crime or not. And a man of enlightenment cannot commit a crime; that is just a sheer impossibility.

But to be innocent, to be friendly, to be loving for no reason at all, just to be yourself is enough to trigger many egos against you. So when I say, "The enlightened man has no enemies," I mean that from his side he has no enemies. But from others' side, the greater his height, the more will be their antagonism against him, the more will be the enmity, hatred, condemnation. This is how it has been happening for centuries.

Nirvano was just telling me the other day that the day I was fined four hundred thousand dollars – more than half a crore rupees – knowing perfectly well that I don't possess a single paisa, a single cent, the attorney who was working for Nirvano told her, "They have done it again."

She asked him, "What are you saying?" and he said, "Yes, they have done it again. They have again crucified Jesus, they have again punished a man who is utterly innocent – but his innocence hurts their egos."

Just an intellectual understanding will not be enough – although it is good to have some intellectual understanding because that may help you move toward existential experience. But only the experience will give you the full taste of the tremendous sweetness, the beauty, the godliness and the truth of love.

> Osho,
> Can it be true that sex is already over? I have been your sannyasin for four and a half years and my body is thirty-one years of age. I never planned to drop sex, but now it feels like it has dropped me. Am I a "quicky" or what?

Dhyan Satyama, the place you are in and the space you are in – four and a half years is really too long. You can understand by the laughter of the people. They are in the same boat.

If you meditate, sex is going to drop by itself. Sex is part of your unconsciousness, and it is a blissful experience if it drops by itself. If you force it to drop, it never drops. On the contrary, it becomes perverted; it starts finding ways from the back door. Unless it drops by itself, it never drops.

Meditation is the secretmost method of going beyond the body and all that the body contains. Sex is part of your body, your biology. It is not part of your consciousness. The moment you start rising up in your consciousness, sex is left far behind. Naturally, at the age of thirty-one one starts wondering, "Something seems to have gone wrong." Nothing has gone wrong, everything has gone right. You should feel blessed that you are free from the greatest imprisonment of your being.

Adam and Eve were standing underneath the Tree of Knowledge, looking at the apple in Eve's hand. Eve turned to Adam and said, "After we have eaten the apple, we are going to do *what*?"

Naturally the poor woman was not yet aware about "what" – and they had eaten only one apple! It seems you have been eating too many apples; then one becomes a quicky.

Little Ernie's mother was worried about his progress at school, so she took him to see the psychiatrist. The shrink decided to give him an aptitude test and asked the nurse to put a hammer, a wrench and a screwdriver on the table. "If he grabs the hammer," said the shrink, "he will be a carpenter. If he grabs the wrench, he will be a mechanic. If he grabs the screwdriver, he will be an electrician."

Ernie fooled them all. He grabbed the nurse.

It does not matter what your age is; sex has nothing to do with age. It can disappear at any moment or it may not disappear even when one leg is in the grave. It all depends whether your life is just a horizontal phenomenon or something vertical also.

That verticalness can happen any moment – particularly for those who are in meditation. You can start moving differently than any other animal is capable of – except a few men. It is unfortunate that I have to say "except a few men." Intrinsically, every man is capable of going beyond sex.

But people think sex is life. They think the moment sex disappears now there is no point in going on living. Sex was their meaning, their very salt. These are the poorest people in the world, who have not known anything beyond the lowest. They have never raised their eyes toward the stars.

"A man has reached old age when he can't take yes for an answer."

So it doesn't matter, at the age of thirty-one you have become a wise old man. And the beauty of a wise old man is tremendously valuable in comparison to the foolishness of all those who are just young. The young people are bound to fool around; it is rare at this age, to be capable of getting out of this stupidity that we call youth.

Dhyan Satyama, you are exactly what I would like every sannyasin to be. This place is a place for transformation, and the only energy you have got to be transformed is sex.

Sex is your basic life force. If you transform it into higher forms, it is going to disappear from its lower manifestations. But you are not going to miss anything. At each higher state the energy will give you more and more blissfulness. The higher it rises, it becomes a tidal wave of blissfulness. You start feeling orgasmic in every fiber of your being. Sexual orgasm seems to be a faraway echo, almost as if you have seen it in a dream, just a faint memory.

Because what you are now experiencing is so authentic and so real, so solid, you will not need a companion. That too is one of the basic dependencies, and that's why all couples are in a constant fight. The reason is that nobody wants to be dependent on anyone. It takes away your dignity, your individuality, your freedom. In a subtle sense it makes you a slave.

The man who loves a woman will hate the woman because that woman has become a necessity and one hates to be dependent on anyone. And the same is the case for the woman. Every woman hates the husband, has to hate him because she has become dependent on him for momentary pleasures that don't last long.

A meditator finally comes into a space where he does not need anyone to give him pleasure. He is full of blissfulness, overflowing.

He can share, he can fill the whole world with his blissfulness, his very being has become orgasmic.

Now that is something tremendously significant to be remembered. You are both: man and woman together. Because you are born of a father and a mother – half of your being has been contributed by your father and the other half by your mother – naturally you cannot be just man or just woman. It is a fallacy perpetuated for centuries that man is man and woman is woman. It is absolutely wrong.

Every man has his woman within him and every woman has her man within her. Only the meditator comes to know his whole being. Suddenly his inner woman and the inner man melt and merge into each other. That creates an orgasmic state in him. Now it is no longer a momentary experience that comes and goes; it is something that continues, day in, day out, like heartbeat or breathing. Every moment he is in an orgasmic state.

Naturally, sex disappears. A greater experience has come in. The sun has risen; what is the use of having a candle unnecessarily burning? You are bound to blow it out. If somebody keeps his candle burning in the sun, it only shows one thing: that man is blind.

A meditator comes to know such a vast experience of joy that all other pleasures simply fade away.

You are asking, "Can it be true that sex is already over?"

Yes, it is true, and you need not repent for it. Don't look back. Look ahead. Something greater is going to open in your being, something like a lotus, which will give you absolute fulfillment and contentment, and freedom, independence, individuality. For the first time, you will feel you are able to fly alone into the vast sky of existence. Your need for the other has disappeared – that is what sex is, the need for the other – and in this state of orgasmic experience within yourself, without the help of anyone else you become capable of sharing your love, not bargaining, not even hoping for something in return.

In other words, this is what I was just talking about – friendliness, friendliness toward the whole existence. Nothing is greater, more glorious. Nothing is more of a splendor and a miracle.

You are saying, Satyama, "I have been your sannyasin for four and a half years and my body is thirty-one years of age." The body can be of any age...

There are two things which are not necessarily of the same age as the body. The lowest of these two is well understood by the psychoanalyst; the higher is still beyond them. Psychology is still struggling to stand up. It is crawling on the ground at the lowest level of human energies; hence, about the lower it has found a few fundamental truths.

One is the mental age: a man may be seventy years old, yet his mental age may be only fourteen – or vice versa. In cases like Mozart, when he was only four years of age he was able to play on musical instruments like a great master; at the age of five he was already becoming famous. Even great masters of music could not believe the phenomenal energy of Mozart. At the age of five, he was almost as mature mentally as very few people become at the age of seventy.

Psychology has accepted that body and mind don't grow together. Sometimes, most of the time, the mind is lagging behind and the body goes on growing. A few times, in rare cases, the mind grows ahead and the body lags behind.

When Emerson, a great creative and sensitive man, was asked about his age, he said, "Three hundred and sixty years." The people who were present could not believe it. They could not believe that Emerson, a man of truth, a very innocent man, a man loved and respected by all those who could understand the heights of consciousness; why should he lie about such a thing? Three hundred and sixty years old? He does not look more than sixty. What to make of it?

Finally, one man asked, "Perhaps I could not rightly hear what you said. Will you please repeat it?"

Emerson laughed and said, "Why are you going in a roundabout way? Why don't you say directly that you cannot believe that my age is three hundred and sixty years?"

Then another man said, "Now we have to ask you. You look only sixty at the most; you will have to give us evidence that you are three hundred and sixty years of age. And a man of your integrity is expected not to lie."

Emerson said, "I am not lying. I have lived as much in sixty years as you will be able to live only in three hundred and sixty years. According to my intensity and totality of life, I have lived in sixty years as much as an ordinary man will live in three hundred and sixty years. I am not lying. It all depends how you live."

Meditation changes your life pattern completely.

This has still to be recognized by psychology. But the psychology of the enlightened ones knows perfectly well that consciousness can go on growing. It need not grow simultaneously with the body.

Adi Shankara, the founder of a systematic, philosophical system for the Hindus, died at the age of thirty-three. He became enlightened somewhere about the age of seven. His father had died when he was seven. He was the son of a poor father, a poor Brahmin. His mother was only living for him, the only son. At the age of seven, Adi Shankara asked his mother – he wanted to renounce the world. Can you conceive of a child of seven years old thinking of renouncing the world? He must be another Mozart, a Mozart of spirituality.

The mother said, "Your father has died and you want to renounce the world. Don't you think of me?"

Adi Shankara said, "I can only promise you one thing: before you die I will be present so in your last moments you can die peacefully. But right now, allow me to renounce the world. I want to become a sannyasin and to go in search." The mother refused. Not to hurt her, Shankara remained for a few days more.

One day he went to the river. He used to go for his bath every day, but that day he insisted that his mother should also come with him. The mother was a little concerned. Why was he so insistent? But then he became absolutely adamant: "If you don't come, I will not go for the bath. Then I cannot worship and then I cannot eat either," the mother had to go.

The mother was standing on the riverbank and the little child, seven years old, was caught by a crocodile. A crowd gathered, but there was nothing that could be done. Both the feet of the boy were inside the mouth of the crocodile, and Shankara shouted to the mother, "Now there are only two possibilities: either you give me permission to renounce the world and become a sannyasin or the crocodile is going to eat me. It is up to you to decide. Be quick!"

It is a strange story. How did the crocodile conspire in this? And the mother of course immediately shouted, "I allow you! You can become a sannyasin. Even this much will be a solace to me, that you are still alive."

And the story goes that the crocodile immediately left him and disappeared. It must have been a very saintly crocodile! Whatever the case – perhaps it is only a parable – one thing is certain: at the age of seven Adi Shankara must have convinced his mother that either she had to allow him to be a sannyasin or she had to be ready for his death. How he managed this is a different matter. But one thing is certain: he gave her the clear-cut choice, either death or sannyas. Obviously the poor mother had no choice; she allowed him.

At the age of seven, Adi Shankara became a sannyasin. In the whole history of the world there is no other case parallel to Shankara. Somewhere between the age of seven and eleven – there is no historical record of it, but it seems just between seven and eleven – he must have become enlightened. At the age of eleven he started writing his great commentaries on the Upanishads, and on one of the greatest and most complicated scriptures that exists in India, Badrayana's *Brahma Sutras*.

At the age of eleven it is almost impossible even to understand it – and Shankara wrote the greatest commentary. It has defeated all the great commentators of the past and all the great commentators that came after him. Nobody has been able to go beyond these flights of consciousness and bring such tremendous meaning to the almost dead scripture of Badrayana's *Brahma Sutras*. The way he interprets is possible only after enlightenment. Each small word, the way he gives a turn to its meaning... Something that was looking very ordinary immediately becomes extraordinary. He has the touch that transforms everything into gold.

By the time he was thirty-three, he had written all the great commentaries on all the great scriptures, and he had traveled all over the country and defeated all the so-called great philosophers, theologians, and priests. At the age of thirty-three he died.

Consciousness is not limited to your physical age. Consciousness can go far ahead of you, your body.

So don't be worried, Satyama. You are saying, "I never planned to drop sex, but now it feels like it has dropped me." That's the right way. You should never drop sex with conscious effort because that is only repression. You should not pay any attention to sex. Your whole focus should be toward meditation, and one day sex is going to drop just like an old leaf dropping from the tree; not making even any noise, silently falling into the earth and disappearing.

I have given you the name Satyama. I would like to explain to you that that name belonged to an ancient seeker. He was also in the same category as Adi Shankara.

When he was just nine years old, he asked his mother, "I would like to go to a forest monastery and learn all about myself, before it is too late."

The mother said, "My son, you are creating a difficulty for me. But if you have decided, then I will not stand in your way. Just one thing you have to remember: in that forest monastery the first question that will be asked will be, 'What is the name of your father?' – and I don't know the name of your father. When I was young, being poor I used to serve in many houses, and I have been sexually abused by so many rich people. I was so poor I could not fight back, neither was anybody ready to believe me. Those people were powerful, and my whole concern was you. I don't know who your father was out of so many people who have made forced love to me against my will.

"So when you are asked in the university, you have to say the simple truth. Your name is Satyakama, and your mother's name is Jawali. As far as your father is concerned, your mother has said that while young she has been abused, exploited by so many rich people, that she does not know who exactly your father is: 'So please call me not by my father's name, call me by my mother's name. My name is Satyakama, my mother's name is Jabali. You can call me Satyakama Jabali.'"

He went to the forest university. And the first thing the *kalpati* of the university, the head of the university asked him was, "What is your caste?"

He said, "I don't know."

"Who is your father?"

He said, "I don't know. I asked my mother, and this is the story she has told me. You can call me Satyakama Jabali."

The old man could not believe that a mother could be so truthful as to say this to her own son, and that the son also could be so truthful as to repeat it to a stranger without feeling any guilt or any humiliation – with utter dignity, with absolute acceptance: whatever is the case is the case. The old man must have been a man of immense understanding. He said, "You are accepted, Satyakama Jabali, because at the age of nine you are so truthful. And your mother is also great. Her respect for truth is immense. You don't know your caste. I know your caste. You are a born brahmin" – the highest caste in India. "Because of your truth, I can deduce logically that you must belong to the highest caste. You are accepted." One day this Satyakama became enlightened.

I have given you the name Dhyan Satyama – just another form of Satyakama. Remain truthful to yourself and to the world and the day of your illumination is not far away.

11

True Humbleness Is Simply Egolessness

Osho,
What is the difference between being humble, being shy, and just hiding out of fear?

Anand Shantideva, the difference between being humble, being shy, and just hiding out of fear is immensely great. But man's unawareness is such that he is not even capable of making distinctions between his own actions and responses to reality; otherwise, the difference is so clear that even to ask the question is useless.

First you have to go deeper into the word *humble*. All the religions have given it a wrong connotation. By *humble* they mean just the opposite of the egoist. It is not so, because even the exact opposite of the ego will still be ego, hiding behind facades. It is shown once in a while in the so-called humble man. He thinks he is more humble than anybody else. That is the ego. Humility knows no such language.

I have told you the story of three Christian monks. Their monasteries were close by in the mountains and they had to pass each other at the crossroads every day. One day it was too hot and they decided to rest a little and to talk to each other a little. After all they are all Christians; they may belong to different sects, but their fundamentals are Christian.

As they sat down under the shade of a tree, the first one said, "It is absolutely clear that your monasteries may have something, but you cannot find such wisdom, such scholarship as you will find in our monastery."

The second one said, "You have raised the question, hence I have to say this: your monastery may have scholarship, but that is not the question. Nobody is more austere, disciplined than the people of our monastery. Their austerity is incomparable, and in the ultimate moment of judgment, remember, scholarship will not be counted. What will be counted will be austerity."

The third man laughed and he said, "You both are right about your monasteries, but you don't know the real essence of Christianity, and that is humbleness. We are the tops in humbleness."

Humbleness and "the tops"? Then it is simply a repressed ego. Out of greed, out of tremendous greed to enter into paradise and to enjoy all its pleasures, a man is capable of repressing his ego and becoming humble. Before I can tell you what true humbleness is you have to understand false humbleness. Unless you understand the false it is impossible to define the true. In fact, in understanding the false, the true arises on its own in your vision.

False humbleness is just repressed ego, pretending to be humble but desiring to be at the top. Authentic humbleness has nothing to do with ego. It is absence of the ego. It has no claim of being superior to anybody. It is a simple and pure understanding that there is no one who is superior and there is no one who is inferior. People are just themselves; incomparably unique. You cannot compare them as superior or inferior.

Hence, the authentic humble man is very difficult to understand because he will not be humble in the way you understand it. You have known hundreds of humble people, but they were all egoists and you are not insightful enough to see their repressed ego.

Once a Christian missionary woman, a young, beautiful woman came to my house. She presented me with the Holy Bible and a few other pamphlets, and she was looking very humble. I told her, "Take all this rubbish away from here. This Holy Bible of yours is one of the most unholy scriptures in the world," – and immediately she exploded; she forgot all humbleness. I told her, "You can leave the Bible. It was just a device to show you who you are. You are not humble; otherwise you would not have been hurt."

Only the ego is ever hurt. You cannot hurt a humble man.

True humbleness is simply egolessness. It is dropping all personality and the decorations that you have accumulated around you, and just being like a small child who does not know who he is, who does not know anything about the world. His eyes are clear; he can see the greens of the trees more sensitively than you can see.

Your eyes are full of the dust that you call knowledge. And why have you collected this dust that is making you blind? – because knowledge in the world gives a tremendous energy to your ego. You know and others don't. The humble man knows nothing. He has come back full circle to his childhood innocence. He is full of wonder. He sees mysteries everywhere. He collects stones and seashells on the sea beach, and rejoices as if he has found diamonds and emeralds and rubies.

In my childhood, my mother was very much troubled by me – and so was my tailor because I used to tell him, "Make as many pockets as possible."

He said, "On only one condition: that you don't tell anybody who has made this dress. Because of you I am losing customers. They say, 'This tailor has gone a little cuckoo,'" because I had pockets in front, at the back, on the side, on the pants, as many...

I told him, "Wherever you can find a little space, make a pocket." He said, "Are you mad or something?" I said, "You can think anything, but I need that many pockets," because by the river of my village there were so many beautiful colored stones, and I had to collect them, and I needed different pockets for different colors.

My mother was very angry because I would go to sleep with all my stones in my pockets. And then when I was asleep, she would start pulling my stones out of my pockets: "How can you sleep with so many stones?" I told her that this is cheating; nothing should be done to me while I am asleep.

Childhood has an immense clarity. In that clarity, in that transparency, in that perspective, the whole world looks a miracle.

The humble man comes back to this miraculous existence. We take it for granted, but you don't see how from the same soil a lotus flower blossoms, and a rosebush, and millions of other flowers. The earth has no colors; from where do those beautiful colors come? The earth is very rough; from where do the velvety roses come? The earth has no greenery; from where do the green trees come?

The humble man is a child again. He has no claim, but only gratitude: gratitude for everything, even gratitude for things for which you cannot conceive how one can be grateful.

A Sufi mystic, Junnaid, was on a religious pilgrimage with his disciples. In his mystery school it was almost a routine for the disciples to pray with the master. And his prayer was always the same, ending with thankfulness to God: "How am I going to pay? You are giving me so much, you are pouring so much bliss over me, and you never think how I am going to pay for it. I don't have anything other than gratefulness. Forgive me for my poverty, but I thank you for all the great things that you have given to me."

Nobody had objected to it. The mystery school of Junnaid was flourishing, people were coming from faraway places; it had become one of the richest schools of the Sufis. But on the pilgrimage the disciples started wavering about the last part of the prayer.

One day they passed through a fanatic village. Mohammedans don't believe that Sufis are real Mohammedans, and Sufis are the only real Mohammedans in the whole world. Mohammedans – the orthodox Mohammedans, the priests – condemn Sufis: they have gone astray because they have left the crowd and they have started moving on their own lonely paths. They don't bother about tradition, and they declare clearly: "If something is wrong in the tradition we are going to correct it."

For example, Mohammedans pray to God, praise him, and end the prayer saying that the God of the Mohammedans is the only God; there is only one God, and there is only one holy book, the Koran, and there is only one prophet, Hazrat Mohammed.

Sufis never complete the whole thing; they simply say there is only God – and nothing else. They drop the two points that there is only one holy book, the Koran, and there is only one prophet, Hazrat Mohammed. This hurts the orthodox Mohammedans.

Sufis are very humble people and open to receive from all the sources. They don't bother whether it comes from Christian sources, or Jewish sources, or Hindu sources. Truth is truth; from what door it enters into your being is immaterial.

That fanatic village did not give them shelter, did not give them food, did not even allow them to drink from their well. It was a desert country and it continued to happen for three days. They were sleeping in the cold night in the desert – shivering the whole night – hungry, thirsty, rejected, condemned. And in one last village they were even stoned. Somehow they survived by escaping.

But the master continued his prayer, just the same as he had been doing it in his mystery school: "How much you have given to us! Your compassion is infinite – and you know our poverty. We cannot give you anything except our heartfelt gratitude."

Now this was too much. Three days: no food, no shelter, cold nights in the desert. The disciples could not tolerate it – Junnaid is going a little too far. One of the disciples said to him, "At least for such days, drop this last part."

Junnaid said, "You don't understand. God has given us these three days as a fire test. His compassion is infinite: he was just trying to see whether our trust is also infinite or not, whether our trust has some conditions. If you had been received by these three villages, welcomed, given good food, shelter to rest..." because Mohammedans very much respect people who are going for a holy pilgrimage "...then you would have agreed with my prayer – because until now you have never disagreed. For the first time God is giving me the opportunity to show that it is not only on good days that I am grateful; whatever happens, my gratefulness will remain unwavering. Even in my death I will be dying with the same words on my lips."

A humble man lives an unconditional life of gratitude – not only gratitude to God, but gratitude to human beings, to trees, to stars, to everything.

Being shy is another way of the ego. It has been converted into something almost ornamental. A person who feels shy, particularly women in the East, are thought to be very graceful because they are so shy – but they are shy because it is thought to be great.

In the West, this shyness is slowly, slowly disappearing from the women because it is no longer thought to be of any value. It simply shows a long tradition of slavery. The modern woman in the West has thrown it away because it was also a binding chain, and for liberation it needs to be broken.

What are the moments when you start feeling shy? Those are the moments when somebody praises you. Those are the moments when somebody says, "You are so beautiful!" And you know that it is not true; there are not so many beautiful people around. But almost everybody will come across an idiot who will say, "You are so beautiful!" And then a shyness comes because you know it is not true, but it is very ego-fulfilling.

You can try. You can tell the ugliest man or the ugliest woman, "My God, the world has not yet discovered the mystery of you! You are so beautiful that even Cleopatra would have been nothing in comparison to you." And even the ugliest woman will not deny it. In fact, she will say, "You are the only person who has the sensitivity."

It happened that I was expelled from a college. I was expelled from many colleges and many universities. That way it gave me great richness. Nobody has belonged to so many colleges and so many universities. In the city where I was there were twenty colleges; a time came when not a single college was ready to accept me.

I asked those principals, "What is the problem?"

They said, "You are not the problem. Certainly we cannot say you are the problem, because from every other college you have been expelled – not because you are a problem, but because you create such situations that professors start resigning. Nothing can be said against you because you are only asking relevant questions. But because the professors cannot answer them they feel very humiliated. We don't want our staff to be disturbed."

Only one college remained, and I thought now it was better not to approach directly but to find some indirect way. So rather than going to the college office, I inquired about the principal – his qualities, what he likes and what he does not like. And from every source I collected knowledge about him. They said, "He is a very religious man. Early in the morning, at four o'clock, he disturbs the whole neighborhood because he is a very big fellow, very fat, and he is a devotee of Mother Kali of Kolkata. He has a big statue in his house, he has made a temple, and when he starts shouting what he calls prayer, he is the only man in the city who can address a meeting of ten thousand people without a microphone. And he becomes so utterly intoxicated by his own words."

I said, "That will do." I went to the principal's house early in the morning at exactly four o'clock. He was in his temple. Just a small cloth was wrapped around him – otherwise he was almost naked – and he was shouting continuously, "Jai Kali! Jai Kali! Jai Kali..." The words mean, "Victory to the Mother-Goddess."

I was sitting in the corner of his temple and I also started shouting, "Jai Kali!" He looked around because this was the first time that anybody had joined him. I shouted with all my strength because I cannot speak without a microphone. But it was an absolute necessity.

He asked me, "Who are you?" I said, "Just a devotee of the Mother Goddess of Kolkata. But I am a small devotee; you are a big devotee. I have just come to sit at your feet because in this whole city you are the only religious man."

He said, "You are the only man who has ever understood me. Otherwise all the neighbors are reporting me to the police, and my staff in the college think me a little cuckoo."

I said, "All those idiots are of no importance. A man of heart and love declares you to be the greatest devotee of Mother Kali. You are the most spiritual man I have ever come across."

He said, "Can I do something for you?" I said, "Nothing much. I just want to be admitted to your college. Although there are twenty colleges, when I have the opportunity and chance to be under your grace, I would not get entrance into any other college."

He said, "You are admitted. And the day you come, sign the forms. I am giving you a scholarship. And if you want to move into the hostel you will not be charged because you are the only person who has understood me. In my whole life nobody thinks that I am sane, not even my wife, not even my children. 'Something is wrong.'"

I went to his college. He welcomed me at the gate. Even his own staff of professors and students could not believe it. He took me by his side into his office and he told me, "You are not going to pay anything in this college. But as people came to know that you were being admitted... They are as afraid of you as they are afraid of me, so there is only one condition – because I don't want to disturb the whole staff. They are all against you, and I know they are all against me too. They are all irreligious, materialist people, so you will have to forgive me. Just one condition: you should not attend any classes."

I said, "I don't care about classes. Can I attend the temple?"

He hugged me, with tears in his eyes. He said, "Even at this early age you have such a pure heart. The doors of my temple will always be open for you. I keep it locked because there is fear of the neighbors destroying the statue. But I will give you a copy of the key. Whenever you want you can go there. Lock the door from the inside. Even if a crowd gathers, don't be worried; these kinds of distractions always come on the path of religious seekers."

I said, "Don't be worried."

When I graduated from his college I had not attended a single lecture. I was moving to another city for my post-graduation, so I thought it was better to tell him the truth. I went to him, met him in the temple, and I said, "It is very heavy on my heart; I want to tell you the truth. You said that I understand you, and I am the only person who understands you. I beg your pardon, but I don't understand you either – and I am absolutely certain that some nuts and bolts are either loose or tight."

He said, "What are you saying?"

I said, "I have graduated and now there is no problem. It was a simple bribe, a spiritual bribe."

When I had said to him, "You are the greatest religious person I have come across," even that fat and very big man looked shy. It is the ego again, playing a different game.

The egoless person never feels shy because if you say anything untrue about him, he will refute it himself. He wants to expose himself in his absolute authenticity.

And the last thing: "...just hiding out of fear." All are different expressions of the ego: a false humbleness, being shy – knowing perfectly well that what is being said is not true – and the third, hiding out of fear. Except ego, there is no element in you which ever feels fear because ego is the only false thing that has to die. Neither will your body disappear – it will just go back to its basic elements – nor is your consciousness going to die. It will move in its journey to higher levels and forms of expression, or finally it may disappear into the universal consciousness. But that is not death. That is becoming greater, vaster, infinite and eternal. It is not a loss.

The only thing that is going to die, and has been dying continuously each time you have died... The body goes to the material elements, the consciousness goes to the universal consciousness or into a new form of consciousness, but one thing dies again and again, and that is the ego.

So ego is the root cause of all fear in you. A man who is egoless is also fearless.

Shantideva, it is just intellectual discrimination as far as you are concerned. It is not intellectual distinction as far as I am concerned; it is my experience. The day my ego disappeared, I found a totally new kind of humbleness. I have found that there is nothing to be shy about, and I have not been hiding in any way out of fear. This can become your experience too, and unless it becomes your experience, just intellectual understanding will not be enough.

Meditation can help you to get rid of the ego and all these three things will disappear. But in an unconscious state it is very difficult to make a distinction between the authentic humbleness and the bogus.

A man was saying to me, "Not only do I not know what tomorrow will bring, I'm still not exactly sure what yesterday brought." We are all living like a somnambulist who walks in his sleep. Our consciousness is so thin, and our unconsciousness is so deep. All our actions come from our unconscious; all our decisions come from our conscious. That's why our decisions and our actions are never synonymous. You say something but you do something else because within you there is a great split.

The doer is the unconscious, and the conscious mind is so small it can only do the talking. So everybody talks beautifully. What even the greatest poets, painters, artists of different dimensions are doing with painting or sculpture or poetry is only from their conscious minds. It is their way of talking; it is their way of expressing, communicating with others. But it is a very unfortunate experience if you come in contact with these people personally. They are more ordinary than the ordinary people – and they have written such golden poetry.

I happen to know almost all the great poets of this country because I was traveling all over the country, and every kind of person was meeting me. I was surprised. I had read their poetry, and I had loved their poetry, but I could not believe that these ordinary men could rise to such heights. Slowly, slowly I became aware of a split. The conscious mind talks and it talks beautifully, but the unconscious mind does not know anything about your conscious.

As far as action is concerned and your lifestyle is concerned, it is going to come from your unconscious. It is vast: it is your heritage of millions of years of human evolution. It is tremendously powerful. Remember, if you are in the grip of the unconscious, there is no way to see things exactly as they are.

Except meditation, there is no other way to bring light into the unconscious darkness of your being. As your meditation grows your consciousness grows, your unconsciousness diminishes. At the ultimate point your consciousness is total, and your unconsciousness has disappeared completely. That is the moment when your words and your life and you are all synonymous. Then there is no split, no division, no antagonism.

As far as ordinary humanity is concerned, it may appreciate beautiful paintings, but its appreciation is again an expression of the ego.

I have heard about a very rich woman who had purchased a Picasso. She was keeping the Picasso painting in her drawing room. She could not understand what it was; she could not even figure out whether it was hanging upside-down or the right side up. Many times even Picasso was puzzled: what has he painted?

He was certainly a great artist, but not a conscious artist. He has poured the colors in the most beautiful combinations, but his paintings don't have any headings to them. He himself could not figure out what it was all about, and when he was asked he was very angry. He said, "Nobody asks the rose, nobody asks the trees, nobody asks the sun and the moon, what is their meaning. Then why do you harass me, continuously asking, 'What is the meaning of the painting?' It is just beautiful, it has no meaning."

The woman was just an exhibitionist. She wanted to show that she has a Picasso painting – one million dollars worth. But it happened many times. A critic would come to look and would say, "It is fake." Immediately the painting would be removed. Then another critic would come and say, "I want to see the painting" and it had been thrown in the basement. He would say, "Who says it is fake? It is absolutely authentic" and again it would come into the drawing room. This happened many times.

Your ego is a very subtle phenomenon. If anything fulfills it, it is good. If it does not fulfill it, it is bad. And everybody pretends to appreciate great music – just to show that he understands great music, great poetry, great literature; just to show that he understands. But the reality is totally different. Ego never wants to accept one thing: ignorance.

Little Ernie was getting very tired of the long sermon at the church. In a loud whisper he asked his mother, "If we give him the money now, will he let us go out?"

This is pure innocence: If he is after money, give him the money and let us get out. Why get tortured? But only a child can say that, and I would like all my sannyasins to be children again.

"Boys," said Father O'Flanagan to his Bible class, "you should never lose your temper. You should never swear, or get excited or angry. I never do. Now to illustrate – you see that big fly on my nose? A good many wicked men would get angry at that fly, but I don't. I never lose my temper. I simply say, 'Go away, fly, go away.'"

And then suddenly he jumped and said, "Jesus Christ! It's a bee, the son-of-a-bitch!"

The layer of consciousness is so thin. Our pretensions, our promises are not more than just skin-deep. He forgot all about the great sermon he was giving; he acted exactly how he was trying to tell others not to do, not to act.

Shantideva, it will be good not to be only curious about distinctions between things. Become more of a meditator, then the answer will arise within you yourself. And only your answer can make you truly wise. You can accumulate the answers from others but you will still remain "other-wise."

> Osho,
> Every answer you give, not questioned by me, I still take very personally. Is that possible?

Again it is Anand Shantideva. In a way whatever I am saying applies to you all, more or less, because I am talking about the very structure of human consciousness and being. People are not much different, so the question may be coming from anyone but it is also your question too. So there is a possibility – and in fact it always should be the case – that the question is perhaps not yours but the answer is for you. Somebody else has asked your question.

My experience is that it is always good to let somebody else ask your question. Then you can listen more attentively, more peacefully, more at ease because it is poor Shantideva's!

Shantideva cannot listen so peacefully and so silently. He will be tense, worried because nobody knows what I am going to say. Most probably he will get a few hits, so he is sitting in a defensive posture. Everybody else is enjoying, at the cost of poor Shantideva.

But Shantideva, there is no problem. You will have your chance when somebody else asks; you can relax and you can listen and laugh. But remember one thing: any question that any human being can ask will be relevant to you too because we are all in the same boat. Maybe quantitatively somebody may be more involved in the question, somebody less; but it is impossible, unless you are enlightened, unless there is no question left in you, but only the answer...

This is one of the miracles of existence: when there are questions you don't have the answer, and when the answer comes, the questions disappear – just like when you bring the light in the room and the darkness disappears. The questions and the answers never meet. They cannot face each other because the question is only a shadow, a darkness, an absence of light.

But my answer cannot become your answer. Your answer is hidden in your own being at the deepest center. You will have to search for it. I can give you indications, I can give you devices, I can show you the path, but you will have to walk alone. I cannot come along with you because it is an inner journey.

On his ninth birthday, little Hymie walked into the local pub and yelled to the barmaid to bring him a scotch on the rocks. "What do you want to do?" exclaimed the pretty barmaid. "Get me into trouble?"

"Maybe later," replied little Hymie, "But right now I want the drink."

Very few people get beyond the age of thirteen or fourteen as far as mind is concerned. That creates a strange situation. Physically they look older and you start expecting something wise from them, but you don't know their mental age is still thirteen or fourteen, and they will behave according to their mental age, not according to their physical age.

At the annual gathering of the MacTavish clan, Hamish MacTavish suddenly raced to the microphone, interrupted the singing of "Blue Bells of Scotland," and cried, "Hoots! Hear this all ye fine and loyal MacTavishes! My money purse is lost! There is a hundred pounds in that purse and I will give a reward of fifteen pounds to whoever brings it up here, now!"

From the back of the crowd came a voice, "I will give twenty-five."

In real situations you are bound to behave according to your actual mental state. Ordinarily you can pretend to be a wise old man, but your wisest old men are still as retarded as anybody else.

Mulla Nasruddin was sitting on his balcony and suddenly he shouted to his servant, "Bring my glasses, quick."

The servant brought the glasses, but he said, "What is the hurry?"

Mulla said, "What is the hurry? You idiot! A beautiful woman was passing and I could not figure out whether she was a woman or a man. I needed glasses quickly. But you came a little late and that beautiful woman is no longer on the street. She turned the corner into a smaller lane."

One day Mulla Nasruddin is walking on the road. All his hair has become absolutely white. He finds a beautiful young girl and he pinches the girl's backside. The girl shrieks and says, "You are an old man, the age of my grandfather, all your hair is white – and what are you doing?"

Mulla Nasruddin said, "It is true that my hair is white, but my heart is still black – and I follow my heart, not my hair."

Shantideva, it is perfectly good that you take my answers to questions not asked by you very personally. That's the right attitude. It doesn't matter who has asked; what matters is that the question is also yours, lurking somewhere in your unconsciousness. Because the other has asked, it has surfaced. My answer is as much for you as for the man who has asked the question.

I am talking to you all almost as if you were one individuality. I am not answering questions for different people because my understanding is that all questions are human, and those who are understanding enough will take as much out of the answer for themselves as they can without thinking whose question it was.

And it is easier, I repeat again, to understand the answer when it is not your question because you are relaxed. It has nothing to do with you, it is somebody else's problem; you can listen more attentively, more totally. The person who has taken the trouble to ask the question cannot relax while I am answering.

You can feel it, Shantideva, right now. You will be tense because I am not a reliable man. Sometimes I am good, sometimes I am not; sometimes I can be absolutely mad. If you can provoke me by your question, then I can behave just like a bull in a china shop.

The third question is also from Shantideva, so I am not going to answer it today. It is enough. We will take his question another time. Three questions in one morning session – he will get dengue fever!

12

Surrender to Existence

Osho,

How can I leave my ego outside the front gate? It follows me like a shadow and even hides behind my back and then I am not able to see it.

Anand Shantideva, the question shows you have not understood the meaning of the ego. It is not something visible or tangible; it is not even a shadow that follows you. It is something that sits upon your head – that's why you cannot see it. It is all that you know about yourself: your name, your respectability, your power... Whatever you have, it is your ego.

The ego is simply a mind formation. To understand it is a very subtle process. The society you have been brought up in does not want you to know yourself. But it will be very dangerous not to allow you to know yourself and to leave you in a state of chaos. The danger is that in that chaos you may start looking for yourself.

One cannot live in a chaos. One has to find the center of the cyclone; it is an absolute necessity for survival. The society creates the mind as a substitute for your being. And for its own part, the mind creates the idea of "I," the ego. That substitute is absolutely necessary to keep you away from yourself because once you believe that this is you, the very question of any search for yourself does not arise. That has happened to millions of people who have lived on this earth and that is happening even today to the millions of people that are on the earth.

Today we have more ignorance in the world than ever, just because of the population. Now there are five billion idiots on the earth. It has never happened before; it is absolutely unique. You are living in a world that is very special – five billion people knowing nothing about themselves. The ignorance was never so thick and the night was never so long.

But whatever the case with the world, each individual is capable of coming out of this darkness. The first thing he has to realize is that he does not know himself. And whatever he knows about himself is just opinions imposed on him by others.

Somebody has said to you, "You are so intelligent," and it was so satisfying to believe it that you believed it. It needs tremendous courage to disassociate yourself from all that you have been believing you are.

Shantideva, you are the ego; hence you find it difficult to leave it outside the gate. If you leave it outside you will be leaving yourself outside because you don't know anything else about yourself, except the ego. It can be left outside the gate only if you understand its very structure. It is a false substitute to keep you engaged and busy so that you don't have time, you don't have the energy and you don't have any need to look for your authentic self.

In short, you are completely false. I don't believe in compromises. Either you are real or you are unreal; it is not possible that half of you is real and half of you is unreal. The real and the unreal cannot meet. It cannot be that a certain percentage in you is real and the remainder is unreal. It is impossible. It is not allowable by the universal law of consciousness. The real and the unreal never meet.

Have you ever seen light and darkness meeting? Either it is light or it is dark; you cannot have both together in your room – one sitting on this side of you, the other sitting on the other side of you so that you can enjoy both the light and darkness.

A meditator enters into his mind and starts watching how the mind functions. Just the very fact of watching the mind makes him aware that he is not the mind, and he is not anything that belongs to the mind. He is a faraway entity, qualitatively different, just a pure watching. In other words, just a pure mirror which only reflects the reality but is not imprinted by any reality.

If the ugly face comes in front of it, without any judgment, without any condemnation, it shows the ugly face in its full detail. And when the beautiful face appears there is no appreciation, no evaluation either. It shows the ugly face and the beautiful face with the same detached, faraway, reflective witnessing.

The moment you become a witness there will be no need to leave your ego outside the gate. In fact, the ego will have left you; even if you run after it you cannot catch hold of it.

So the right process has to be understood. The ego is not something like your umbrella and your shoes and your raincoat that you leave outside the gate. The ego is hidden inside your mind. Of course you cannot leave your head outside, and the ego comes along wherever you go.

The ego has to be understood. In that understanding it disappears. Only a witness knows that the ego is a false entity and you need not fight with any false entity.

Do you ever fight with darkness? When you find darkness in your room, do you struggle with it to throw it out? Do you wrestle with it? Do you start taking out your sword to cut off the head of darkness? If you do any of these stupid things, you will simply show your unintelligence. You will not be able even to touch the darkness that is in your room. You cannot put it into bags and take out the bags and throw them into the neighbor's house.

With the negative nothing can be done directly. If you want to do anything with the negative, do something for the positive. When you don't want darkness in the room you bring the light. You don't bother about darkness. Your whole approach is totally different. You bring the light in, and the moment the light is in you don't find any darkness.

The same is true about your ego. It has no existence of its own; it is a false substitute that has been given to you so that you can go on playing with it and completely forget the search for the real self. And the demands of this false ego are immense, never fulfilled. It will demand money, it will demand respect, it will demand power – and you go on fulfilling it but it will always remain empty.

You cannot make an egoist contented. The ego is always like an open wound; it goes on growing bigger. The more you try to fill it the more you find it is empty and the more demanding it becomes. You become almost a slave to a false entity. Your whole life is wasted in ambitions created by the ego.

The ego is the most dangerous invention that society has managed to create. When you want to drop it, don't think in terms of dropping it – because even the word *drop* gives you the idea that it is something. It is nothing. You cannot drop it, you cannot put it out of doors. You have to look into the reality of it.

In deep meditations you have to become a witness of all the functionings of the mind because the ego is the combined by-product of your mind's functioning. Its thoughts, its desires, its ideologies, its prejudices, its politics, its philosophy, its religion – everything contributes in some way to create a certain ego in you.

I had a professor, Doctor Das, a very famous philosopher not only in India but in almost every country. He had been teaching around the world; he had come back to India, to his home, just to retire. He was my teacher for only three months; after those three months he went into retirement. But those three months were a great revelation to me and to him.

The first day when he entered the classroom I was sitting in his chair. He looked so embarrassed standing by my side and I was so relaxed in the chair. The students started laughing and he said, "What is going on?"

I said, "Nothing is going on. I find this chair more comfortable than the other chairs; and I am not a stupid person, I can choose what is right for me."

He said, "You seem to be a very strange person. This chair is for the teacher."

I said, "Then there is no problem. I will teach! What is the problem? If this chair is for the teacher, then the teacher is sitting in it. You can find some other chair and sit down."

He was an old man, a world-famous philosopher, and his ego was immensely hurt. He said, "You don't understand with whom you are talking."

I said, "I understand perfectly well. *You* don't understand with whom *you* are talking." But I did not leave the chair. I told him he can do whatever he wants to do. He can go to the vice-chancellor, he can bring the vice-chancellor... "I am going to remain in this chair."

He said, "What is the purpose of all this mess?"

I said, "The purpose is to show you that it is not my sitting in the chair that is hurting you, it is your ego. If you accept it I will leave the chair. If you don't accept it then you can bring anybody to help you, but as far as I know the students, nobody is going to help."

He waited a minute. There was utter silence in the class. Everybody was afraid that if the vice-chancellor came and the proctor came, there was going to be trouble for me. They would immediately expel me. I had already been expelled from so many places, but I always continued to do strange things. What was the need to sit in his chair?

But Doctor Das was certainly an intelligent man. He did not go out. He said, "Perhaps you are right. It is my ego that is hurting, it is not a question of the chair."

I said, "Then I can leave it. But remember, before you retire you have only three months more in this university. It will be good if you retire but don't take your ego away with you. Leave it here in this chair for somebody else to use."

I left the chair, and he was in such confusion that he told the students, "Today it will not be possible for me to teach." And to me he said, "I would like you to come with me to my home. I want to discuss some important matters with you."

He was an unmarried man. He had written many beautiful books, and before encountering him I had read everything that he had written. He took me in his car to his home. On the way he said, "I am sorry that I did not understand your purpose. You are the first man in my life who has pointed at my ego. I certainly have a very big ego and it has gone on becoming bigger and bigger as I have become more and more respected in the world of philosophy. You will have to help me to get rid of it. I am also feeling the torture of it, I am also feeling the burden of it, but I don't know what to do with it."

He had never thought about meditation. Philosophers never meditate; their whole approach to life is intellectual. They think about everything, but never become a witness of any experience, particularly the experience of their inner thought processes.

Shantideva, if you really want to get rid of the ego, you will have to go so deep into your meditations that you can create a distance between you and your mind – and immediately you will see the phoniness of your ego. And the moment you have seen it, it is dropped. Not that you can drop it, but your seeing it, your understanding it, your witnessing it and it drops on its own accord.

Little Elmer was in the toy section of the huge department store checking out the latest electronic kids' toys. Over the loudspeaker came an announcement, "Mrs. Ethel Evan is missing her son, Elmer Evan. Will little Elmer please come to the manager's office immediately."

Little Elmer was visibly depressed. "Damn it," he grumbled, "I am lost again."

But in fact everybody is lost – lost because you don't know who you are, lost because you have not encountered your being, lost because you are not a real, integrated individual but only a phony personality.

An Englishman was marooned on a desert island where he was looked after by a beautiful native girl. On the first night she gave him the most exotic drinks. On the second night she fed him the most delicious food imaginable. On the third night she said to him, "Would you like to play games with me now?"

"Don't tell me," replied the passionately-excited Englishman, "that you have got a football here as well!"

An Englishman is just an Englishman!

Everybody has grown a certain ego, and the ego goes on dominating you in every sphere of life. It dictates to you the style in which you should live. It dictates to you what is right and what is wrong. And if you look deeply, the day you will be able to see your ego as a false entity you are bound to feel so sorry for yourself: you have been dictated to by a false entity your whole life. Now you will be able to see that whatever was told to you as right, is nothing but nourishment for the ego; and whatever was told to you as wrong, is nothing but deprivation of nourishment to the ego.

All your right and wrong, all your moral and immoral acts, all your good and evil can be demarcated with a single thing; a definition that you may have never thought about. All that fulfills your ego is moral, virtuous, spiritual, religious, and all that goes against your ego is a sinner's life, a criminal way of living, immoral, unspiritual, condemnable. All honor is for the ego, all dignity is for the ego and all dishonor is for the person who is not fulfilling the demands of the ego.

But once you become a witness, you can see this subtle strategy, this whole psychology of destroying you and keeping you away from yourself and the very center of existence.

Your ego is your hell, your ego is your misery. Your ego is the cancer of your soul. The only way out of it is to become a witness of your mind processes.

Osho,

The other night during discourse I realized that I am so stubborn and pigheaded. I always have this "but" inside me, and I don't know how to jump over it. Osho, how can I surrender to you totally?

Your question is tremendously interesting. You say, "The other night during discourse I realized that I am so stubborn and pigheaded." The moment anybody realizes that he is pigheaded, he no longer is. No pig can ever realize that he is pigheaded; that's an impossibility. If you have realized that you are pigheaded, one thing is absolutely certain: you are not a pig.

And you have also realized that you are "so stubborn." I would like humbly to say to you that you are not because a really stubborn person will jump any "but," howsoever big it is. It will become a challenge to his stubbornness.

You are asking, "I always have this 'but' inside me and I don't know how to jump over it." Just be pigheaded and stubborn and jump!

Moreover, I have never asked you to drop your "buts" and "ifs". You cannot. Your mind is always schizophrenic; it is always split in diametrically opposite directions. So one part of the mind says one thing and the other part immediately contradicts it. That is the "but." One part wants to complete the sentence but the other part comes in.

But I have never asked you to drop it or jump over it! You have misunderstood me. I only want you to understand whatever is the case within you. Just the understanding is enough to dispel all darkness. This is the language of the ego: How can I jump? How can I drop? Every "how" is born out of the ego.

The man of understanding simply wonders: Where is the ego? Where are all those "buts" and "ifs"? They have simply disappeared. In the intense light of your awareness all these things cannot exist.

And finally you say, "Osho, how can I surrender to you totally?" From where did you get the idea that you have to surrender to me?

You have to surrender to existence, not to me. That's my continuous fight with all the religions: they all want you to surrender to them.

A few months ago the Catholic pope even declared that you are not allowed to confess to God directly; he has called it one of the greatest sins. You have to go via the right channel. First you have to confess to the priest, who has a direct line with God. Then he will persuade God on your behalf – but you cannot do it directly.

Even God is not allowed to you; you have to surrender to the priest, to the Pope, to the Shankaracharya, to the imam, to the Prophet. And who are all these people? Most probably they are highly egoistic personalities who are enjoying the ego of being a prophet, who are enjoying the idea that they have come to save the world – that they are the saviors – who are enjoying the idea they are the only begotten son of God. They don't have any evidence, not even a birth certificate. These people seem to be very pious egoists, and their piousness hides their ego.

I am not a savior. Surrendering to me is absolutely futile. I am not a prophet; I am not even a faraway cousin of any god. I am just simply myself.

And do you understand the responsibility? When you surrender yourself to anybody, you are also surrendering your freedom. You are becoming a slave in the name of religion and spirituality. And this slavery goes far deeper than the ordinary slavery when your body is enslaved. This is spiritual slavery.

You can revolt against physical slavery because it has been imposed on you by others. You have accepted this spiritual slavery on your own. You have surrendered to someone – a Jesus Christ, a Gautam Buddha, a Mahavira. How can you revolt? Not a single Christian has revolted against Jesus Christ in two thousand years. Not a single Buddhist has revolted against Gautam Buddha in twenty-five centuries. The simple fact is: it is your own surrender, you never think of it in terms of slavery.

I have never asked you to surrender to me even partially, what to say about totally.

Surrender to existence, surrender to the stars and the ocean and the mountains, and they will not become a bondage to you. They will give you freedom and they will give you tremendous blessings. The whole existence will become your home. Surrender to the whole. In that surrender there is some significance because in that surrender your ego will disappear.

And surrender can only be total; it cannot be partial. You cannot say: "I surrender to existence twenty percent, thirty percent." It is not a business deal. It is not in any way a negotiation. Either one hundred percent or zero percent – these are the only two simple alternatives.

But remember never to surrender to any man. Howsoever the man may be bragging, all men are just made of the same flesh and the same bones and the same marrow as you are. Just a few cunning people, pretenders, hypocrites take advantage of your innocence and start calling you "the sheep" and they become the shepherds. And you enjoy being called "the sheep" and you don't feel the humiliation in it and you don't see that you are being spiritually insulted. On the contrary, you think that it is something to rejoice about – the shepherd, the only begotten son of God has accepted you.

In the first place there is no evidence of God. In the second place there is no evidence that he has any wife. In the third place there is no evidence that he has ever produced a son, and he is described as omnipotent in the scriptures, and he is finished by giving birth to only one son in eternity! I don't think he knows anything about birth control methods because they were not in existence in the beginning when he was creating the world. He himself never created them.

Neither does God exist, nor are there messengers of God, nor are there prophets of God, nor are there only begotten sons of God. All these people have only one thing more than you: their egos are very big – so big that they can convince themselves because of any illusion, for any hallucination. The best way to get convinced of any illusion is to spread it to people, and when a few people start believing in you... There are always people ready to believe in anything: interplanetary visitors only six inches in height, colored forest green, who come and meet people...

Just the other day I received a letter from a sannyasin couple: "We both have been visited by these green visitors from faraway planets. And now we are feeling very much afraid because they have promised they will be coming again and again and they want to know more and more about human life. What do you say? What are we supposed to do? Should we meet them or avoid them or escape from this place?"

And whenever such cuckoo letters come to me I have only one answer: Send these fellows to Kaveesha. That is her department because I am tired of answering such things.

People are ready to believe any stupid thing because they are so hollow anything seems to fill them. It is said that to a drowning man even a straw seems to be a saving device; he clings to the straw, knowing perfectly well that a straw cannot save him. On the contrary, he will also take the straw with him down the river. All your beliefs are nothing but straws you are clinging to because you know you are drowning.

I don't want you to surrender to me. It is against my whole conscience. You are my fellow-travelers; I cannot degrade you and I cannot humiliate you. If anything, I can give you more dignity and more self-respect. To me, that is the authentic function of a master. Only the fake, so-called masters demand surrender.

Yes, I also preach surrender, but the surrender is to be not to me, but to the whole. And it will be easier for you to surrender to this infinite beautiful cosmos. Your "buts" will disappear.

But never surrender to anything less than the whole. That kind of surrender is going to be your slavery. That has been the slavery of the whole of mankind for thousands of years.

I teach you freedom, not surrender. I teach you totality in your living, and I teach you tremendous respect and love and gratitude for the whole.

You must have got this idea from all kinds of bogus scriptures that are continuously being written by ignorant people, but they are so ignorant that they cannot be aware of their ignorance. And out of their ignorance they go on saying all kinds of things because those things have been repeated so often they have become almost true.

Beware of crowd psychology and beware of the human past. It has been ugly, utterly ugly. Unfortunately we inherit it, but fortunately there is a possibility to disinherit it. You can cut yourself off from the whole past and you can start a totally new approach and a new style of life that is in tune with existence – not in tune with the Holy Bible, not in tune with the holy Koran, not in tune with me, but in tune with the whole of existence.

Unless you fall in tune with the universal heartbeat, I cannot call whatever you do spiritual. It will be some kind of slavery – maybe some new kind, but slavery is slavery whether it is old or new.

Bridget and Maureen were returning from church, where the priest had just preached a sermon on married life.

"What did you think of the sermon?" Bridget asked.

"I wish," said Maureen, "that I knew as little about marriage as he did."

It is a very strange world. Here, people who are not married, who have taken the vow of being celibate for their whole life, teach people about marriage, and these idiots are called "Father" by others: father to whom? All your religious scriptures that teach you how to live are written by people who have renounced life. They don't even know the *ABC* of life. And they are cowards because they have escaped from life and its struggle and its challenges, and now they are trying to preach the essential meaning of life, the fundamentals of life to people.

People who have never loved anybody write treatises on love. Because of these strange people it is a very strange world: they never think for a moment that they don't have any authority to talk about something that they have not experienced. But it is so ego-fulfilling to preach, to advise – whether you know anything or not.

It happened once that I was invited to a religious conference and a Jaina monk spoke before me. He was saying beautiful things, but I could feel the vibe of the person, whatever he was saying was just like a parrot: he knew nothing. It was not in his eyes, it was not in his face, it was not in his gestures, it was not in his words, even though they were from the scriptures, they were so hollow, so empty.

I had to speak after him. I was very new in that city and the monk who had spoken before me was a very famous man in those parts, so people had really come to hear him. I was too young and absolutely unknown in that part. I was visiting that city for the first time, so as he stepped down, people started leaving.

I had to shout on the microphone, "Everybody should stop, wherever he is!" Naturally, they had never heard such a man. I told them, "Sit back down in your seats. You don't know me. Just give me five minutes and then I will order you to go out. After five minutes I will pause and anybody who wants to go should go immediately. But five minutes is absolutely my right. You have invited me and you are misbehaving with me."

So they all sat down feeling, "This is a strange man. Perhaps there may be something." And in those five minutes I criticized the monk who had spoken before me.

I said, "The first thing is, he knows nothing about what he was saying." There was a wave of shock because they had all respected that old man – he was almost seventy-five. And I said, "Although he is seventy-five, he is utterly retarded because he does not know how to interpret the scriptures he has been quoting. All his interpretations are misinterpretations, and I am going to contradict him point by point."

And then I told the people, "Now five minutes are over. Anybody who wants to leave should leave immediately." Out of almost ten thousand people, not a single person left. It was too difficult now to leave; they wanted to know exactly what I was going to say against the monk.

I contradicted the monk completely, in absolute detail, not leaving anything to be improved upon. The monk must have been a sincere man. There are still a few people who must have been present in that meeting. One I particularly remember is Ishwarbhai from Mumbai and his wife Guna.

I remember them because after that day they became my people, and Ishwarbhai's wife Guna told me, "When you were in the middle of destroying that Jaina monk so completely, I told my husband, 'It is time we got out of the crowd. There is going to be a riot without any doubt. After this man has finished there is going to be immense fighting.'"

Ishwarbhai was also willing: "It seems dangerous, but to move is also dangerous because that man is strange." They were sitting in the front row. "He will immediately stop and he will say, 'Sit down!' And I cannot stand up; I am feeling so shaky. We have been hearing that old monk for years. We thought he knew, and he is sitting there with his head down. It seems that perhaps this young man is right."

After the meeting that old monk sent two messengers to me. "I would like to meet you because it is the first time in my life that anybody has been so sincere and so honest, so fearless to expose me. It is true: I don't know anything, and all that I was quoting was practiced and rehearsed. I have been preaching for years so it has become almost my profession. But nothing was spontaneous and nothing was supported by my own experience because I don't know what consciousness is, what meditation is.

"Just one thing you will have to grant me, because I am the head of my whole community and they won't allow me to go to the place where you are staying. They are already angry with you. Their longstanding teacher has been completely contradicted. Although they are angry, they cannot do anything because I am not supporting them, I am saying you were right. But one thing they will certainly do: they have made it clear to me that, 'You cannot go to see that man at his place. If you want to see him, invite him to your own place. It is a question of the prestige of our community.'"

So when those two strangers came to me, I said, "There is no problem. I don't have any community and I don't have any chains on me. I am a free man. I can go anywhere; nobody can prevent me. I am ready to come with you."

They were thinking that it would not be so easy. I went, and there was a big crowd; great sensation, apprehension in the air that there might be some trouble. But when they saw me coming alone they could not believe it because I had been informed that they were violently angry against me.

Their teacher, their master, the man to whom they had surrendered, had been utterly humiliated, although I had not humiliated the man. This was my way of giving respect to him, to bring him to his reality, to wake him up. It is not humiliating. And as I reached the temple where the man was staying, he asked me, "I would like to talk to you in aloneness, so please, everybody should go out and close the door."

And as the door was closed, that old man simply started crying like a child. I can still see his face and his tears.

I said, "You don't have to feel so desperate. There is still time."

He said, "But seventy-five years are lost, and not a single man ever told me that what I am talking is parrot talk. For a moment, in the beginning, I felt a certain anger arising in me. My ego hurt. But then I thought it was better to listen to the whole thing. And as I listened to you, slowly, slowly it became clear that you are right: I don't know myself. And without knowing myself, I have been preaching things. It is really not only criminal but absolutely a sin to tell people something that you don't know yourself."

Sharon was supporting Paddy at the altar at their wedding, when the priest announced that he would not perform the ceremony so long as Paddy was drunk.

"Take him away from here," he told Sharon, "and bring him back when he is sober."

"But Father," wailed Sharon, "he won't come when he is sober."

Who will get married when he is sober? A certain kind of drunkenness is needed, a certain unconsciousness. In your unconsciousness you are repeating about surrender, about totality. You have heard these words – and perhaps you have heard these words from me – but you have managed the meaning that you wanted to.

Surrendering to me is giving your responsibility to me. There is no way that any individual can perform your spiritual journey on your behalf. So one day you will be frustrated, then you will be angry, then you will start condemning me: "I have wasted ten years and I have not reached anywhere."

It is such great stupidity, but you won't recognize that from the very beginning you have chosen a wrong way. You have not listened exactly to what I am saying. You are managing to listen to what you want to listen to. If you surrender to the whole, you won't feel that you can condemn the whole one day if nothing happens. Then people will laugh and they will say, "What do you mean by 'the whole'? The stars, the sun, the moon, the sky, the mountains, the rivers – do you think these are going to transform you?" You will be laughed at. But I want to tell you that only such a surrender can bring a transformation to you.

But transformation is not brought by the stars, neither is it brought by the mountains, nor by the whole. The transformation is brought by your surrender and your totality – but remember the meaning of surrender and totality. Ten years or ten lives, you cannot go back if surrender is total. You cannot take back your surrender one day and say, "Now I am no longer surrendered."

If you do that, that means that all the time you thought you were surrendered, you were not. Surrender is absolute, unconditional, and there is no way to take it back. That's why I insist on totality. Don't hold back anything. Just give up all to the whole to which it belongs.

You have come out of the whole. You belong to the whole. Your life is nourished every moment by the whole. Just allow the whole to take over your being completely, entirely.

And in the right moment, in the right season, the spring comes and the flowers start blossoming.

13

Only Change Never Changes

Osho,

Why am I forcing situations according to my will, instead of accepting them and letting them just happen? I have a feeling that my body makes me aware of it, reacting with a high fever.

The upbringing of man is so poisonous, so crippling, that it destroys all that is significant and valuable in you and replaces it with cruelty, violence, a desire to dominate. The whole of society from all sides supports this destruction of your innocence; it is favorable to these.

Forcing anything simply means you are forcing against yourself. This creates the schizophrenia, the split personality that is fighting with itself. This is the most ugly and destructive device that has been used by the vested interests for thousands of years. They found a simple clue to how to destroy the individual because the individual is a danger – a danger against exploitation, a danger against slavery, a danger against any kind of enforcement. An individual would rather like to die than submit.

Individuality has a dignity, but man has been taken away from his individuality by a simple device: put the individual in conflict. And you know the ancient proverb: A house divided cannot stand for long.

You are continuously fighting with yourself because you have been given such stupid ideas about yourself that you have to either choose between your nature, your relaxedness with nature; or you have to choose thousands of years of conditioning. And conditionings go deeper and deeper every day. Pleasure has been condemned, non-seriousness has been condemned, playfulness has been condemned. The whole of humanity has been turned into utter seriousness – and seriousness is a psychological sickness. It can seep deeper and can even make your soul sick.

There is nothing to be serious about in the world. There are only three things that happen in your life. One has already happened – your birth. You could not do anything about it. Another is death. Again, although it has not happened yet, you cannot do anything about it. So drop these two things completely, they are beyond your grasp. Between these two remain life, love, rejoicing.

A man who is alive cannot be suppressed so easily. A man who loves has a clarity of vision and cannot be befooled by any politician. And a man who knows how to be playful will not be found in any church, any temple, any mosque, any synagogue. Those are the places where people who have died before their death go; people who have taken a standpoint against life, against love, against playfulness, against joy, against the whole universe.

But if you become blinded by these conditionings, then you will start repressing within yourself any possibility that can make you livelier, more loving, more blissful, more ecstatic. It is a struggle between you and your whole past. The past is long; it has gone to your very roots. But if you are alert enough there is still time to get out of the net, out of the chains of the past.

A man who is free from the past is the only man who is free to live in the present. And a strange thing to be remembered: the man who is free from the past – as if he is absolutely new and fresh on this beautiful planet – will also be automatically free from the future.

The future is a projection of the past. The past no longer exists, the future does not exist yet, but the past gives you ambitions and desires and all kinds of stupid ideas of greed and desire. Automatically you start looking at the future as a refuge.

And the reality consists only of now – the present. It has nothing to do with the past and nothing to do with the future. It is so concentrated in this moment that if you can be in this moment, all that you are seeking and searching will be fulfilled.

This moment is the door to the divine.

My whole effort here is to pull all my people away from the past and from the future and just make them available to the intense beauty of the present.

Live moment to moment, dropping the past continuously as dust gathered on the mirror. A man who is contented in the present will never bother about the future. You think about the future because your present is misery; you are in utter agony. To avoid it, not to look at it, you focus on faraway goals. Those goals are never to be fulfilled. You will become addicted to ambitions and goals; but remember, wherever you will be, it will always be the present, never the future.

Once you have forgotten to live the present you have already died. It is another matter that it may take sixty, seventy or eighty years for you to be buried or burned on a funeral pyre. You have died long before. The moment you have lost contact with the present your death has happened. But if you can regain the contact, resurrection is possible.

Only the present can give you the space to relax and not to force anything. It is the past that gives you ideals, moralities against nature. You cannot win against nature. It is so big and so huge and you are simply a small dewdrop in the ocean of nature. The dewdrop cannot fight with the ocean. It just has to relax and become one with the ocean.

According to me, an authentic sannyasin, a seeker of truth, is a seeker of the present.

You are asking, "Why am I forcing situations according to my will?" These are stupid ideas that have been given to you. You don't have any will. The very idea of willpower is an absolute fallacy. The will belongs to existence. You can participate in that will. If you drop your personality, your separation, you will have the universal will within you. You don't have individual wills. But it is ego-satisfying when people tell you that you are a man of great will.

What is man? – just a fistful of dust. Yes, something is also present within that dust, but it doesn't belong to you. It belongs to the total.

Secondly, why are you forcing situations? Haven't you seen a river coming from the mountains' high peaks where the snow has never melted; passing through valleys, passing through unknown territory? Where is the river going? It is utterly relaxed – no goal to be tense about, nowhere to reach. Each moment it is enjoying the trees it is passing by, the mountains it is descending. And one day every river, without exception, reaches the ocean.

But every man is not so fortunate. Most of them get lost in a desert and evaporate on a funeral pyre. Only a few fortunate ones, the blessed ones, reach the ocean. The secret is so simple and so obvious. That's why it misses you.

Who are you to force situations? What power have you got to force situations? Situations are coming from existence itself. The wiser course will be to be in accord with them, not in discord. When you are in accord, you can ride on those situations, but the moment you start fighting, you are so tiny and the universe is so vast. There is no possibility of any victory. Then frustration sets in; then misery, agony, suffering follow.

Be just like a white cloud passing in the sky without any desire to reach anywhere. There is no need; you are already there. What more do you want? If the winds are blowing toward the south, the white cloud goes toward the south. Each moment of floating high above, on the air, in the sky, is such an ecstasy – who cares whether the direction is south or north or east or west? And if suddenly the winds change and they start moving again toward the north, the cloud does not complain; it does not say that this is illogical. "We were going toward the south and suddenly for no reason at all you started moving toward the north again." Without any resistance the cloud simply starts moving with the winds, wherever they are going. There is no conflict between the cloud and the wind.

That should be the right standpoint for all seekers of truth: no conflict with nature, no conflict with existence, and all your misery, all your tension, all your anguish and angst will disappear on their own accord. They are your creation. Of course you are not totally responsible; they are the heritage of a long, ugly, unnatural past.

What kind of situations do you try to change? Love arises in your heart, but the society says, "Love is blind: beware of it! It is infatuation; it is a kind of slavery and you will repent for it, so it is better from the very beginning not to allow such things." The head is full of all this kind of morality, puritanism, and you start fighting with your heart.

Your head and your heart are not together, that is the problem. Your head is full of all kinds of nonsense, and that nonsense does not belong to you. It has been given to you by your parents, by your society, by your teachers, by your professors, by your priests, by your politicians. You have a head full of all kinds of bullshit. And this head tries to dominate the heart, which is still beyond the capacity of anybody to distort, to contaminate.

That is the only hope for man: to listen to your heart and go along with it. Then your life will become a blissful pilgrimage. All the methods of meditation I teach you are nothing but... In short, it can be said they are bringing you from the head to the heart, from logic to love, from ego to egolessness, from your separation to a deep merging and melting with the whole.

The whole knows better. The whole knows nothing of your ideals, the whole knows nothing about your moralities and conceptions of right and wrong. But the miracle is, the moment you merge with the whole, everything is right and everything is good and everything is beautiful. *Satyam shivam sundaram*: it is true, it is divine, and it has a beauty that is not of this earth.

You are also stating... The thing I said just yesterday to Shantideva, "Don't ask so many questions otherwise you will get dengue fever." You have got dengue fever! You are saying, "I have a feeling that my body makes me aware of it, reacting with a high fever." It is not a high fever, it is simply dengue fever. It will go within two days, so don't be worried. It is bound to happen in this city of Pune, where there must be at least twenty times more mosquitoes than people – and not small mosquitoes. Maharashtrian mosquitoes are very stubborn!

I am reminded...

I was staying with one of the Buddhist monks, one of the most learned in India, Bhikkshu Jagdish Kashyap, in Sarnath. There were so many mosquitoes that even in the daytime we would sit inside the mosquito net. He would sit in his mosquito net, I would sit in my mosquito net.

I asked him, "Jagdish Kashyap, do you know why Buddha never came again to Sarnath?" Because it is a strange thing that Sarnath is the only place that Buddha visited only once and stayed only one day. He visited Vaishali twenty times and he visited hundreds of towns dozens of times – because in forty-two years of continuous preaching he was always on the move. But in the whole of history no one has ever wondered why he did not come to Sarnath again.

Jagdish Kashyap told me, "I am a great scholar of Buddhist scriptures, but I cannot answer your question. How can you find such strange questions?"

I said, "Write down in your scriptures that Buddha never came back to Sarnath because he had no mosquito net!"

And when I came to Pune, I realized the mosquito net is far more necessary in this religious city, this cultured city. You can see all around – even

in such a hall you have to put up a mosquito net. I have looked at the mosquitoes. They are bigger than the mosquitoes of Sarnath.

Don't be worried about the dengue fever. It will go.

Osho,
What is religion?

Religion is not what people understand it to be. It is not Christianity, it is not Hinduism, it is not Mohammedanism. Religion is a dead rock. I teach you not religion, but religiousness – a flowing river, continuously changing its course, but ultimately reaching to the ocean. A rock may be very ancient, far more experienced, far older than any Rig Veda, but a rock is a rock, and it is dead. It does not move with the seasons, it does not move with existence; it is simply lying there. And have you seen any rock with any song, with any dance?

To me religion is a quality, not an organization.

All the religions that exist in the world – and they are not a small number, there are three hundred religions in the world – are dead rocks. They don't flow, they don't change, they don't move with the times. And anything that is dead is not going to help you – unless you want to make your grave. Then perhaps the rock may be helpful.

All the so-called religions have been making graves for you – destroying your life, your love, your joy and filling your heads with fantasies, illusions, hallucinations about God, about heaven and hell, about reincarnation, and all kinds of crap.

I trust the flowing, changing, moving because that is the nature of life. It knows only one thing is permanent, and that is change. Only change never changes; otherwise, everything changes. Sometimes it is fall and the trees become naked. All the leaves fall down with no complaint. Silently, peacefully they merge back into the earth from where they have come. The naked trees against the sky have a beauty of their own, and there must be a tremendous trust in their hearts because they know that if the old leaves are gone, the new will be coming. And soon new leaves, fresh, younger, more delicate, start coming out.

A religion should be not a dead organization but a kind of religiousness; a quality which includes truthfulness, sincerity, naturalness, a deep let-go with the cosmos, a loving heart, a friendliness toward the whole. For these no holy scriptures are needed.

In fact, there are no holy scriptures anywhere. The so-called holy scriptures do not even prove that they are good literature. It is good that nobody reads them because they are full of ugly pornography.

When I said this, one of my friends started working on the Holy Bible, and now he has found five hundred solid pages of pornography. If any book has to be banned from the world, it is the Holy Bible. But that friend does not know that the Holy Bible is just nothing. If you look into the Hindu *puranas*, you will be surprised. They are the most ancient editions of *Playboy*! Not only the human beings but even the gods described there are such ugly, dirty old people. It is strange, and they are still worshipped as gods.

For example, the moon is worshipped as a god by the Hindus and by the Jain. But the story is that the moon was very much sexually interested in a beautiful woman who was the wife of a saint. In India the saints go to take a bath early in the morning before the sun rises, and that was the time when the moon would come – in disguise, of course, because gods can do anything. He would knock on the door and the wife would think her husband was back. The moon would make love to somebody else's wife and then disappear.

Almost all the so-called Hindu gods are rapists. And they are not satisfied that in heaven they have the most beautiful women – not covered with skin, of course, but covered with plastic. In those days it seems they had no word for plastic, so they say that these heavenly girls – the word is *apsara*, which you can translate very accurately as a call girl, not ordinary prostitutes, but very high class – don't perspire.

When I came to know that they don't perspire, I started thinking: How is it possible for a man or woman with skin not to perspire? Plastic seems to be the only alternative. And they remain stuck at the age of sixteen; they never grow up. For centuries they are only sixteen. And how many saints have enjoyed them? I don't think they can even remember the number over millions of years.

An authentic religiousness needs no prophets, no saviors, no holy books, no churches, no popes, no priests because religiousness is the flowering of your heart. It is reaching to the very center of your being. And the moment you reach to the very center of your being, there is an explosion of beauty, of blissfulness, of silence, of light. You start becoming a totally different person. All that was dark in your life disappears, and all that was wrong in your life disappears too. Whatever you do is done with utter totality and absolute awareness.

I know of only one virtue, and that is awareness.

And if religiousness spreads all over the world, religions will fade away. It will be a tremendous blessing to humanity when man is simply man: neither Christian nor Mohammedan nor Hindu. These demarcations, these divisions have been the cause of thousands of wars all through history. If you look back at the history of man, you cannot resist the temptation to say that we have lived in the past in an insane way. In the name of God, in the name of church, in the name of ideologies that have no evidence at all, people have been killing each other. Religion has not happened to the world yet.

Unless religiousness becomes the very climate of humanity there will be no religion at all. But I insist on calling it religiousness so that it does not become organized. You cannot organize love. Have you ever heard of churches of love, temples of love, mosques of love? Love is an individual affair with another individual. And religiousness is a greater love affair with the individual directed toward the whole cosmos.

When a man falls in love with the whole cosmos, the trees, the mountains, the rivers, the oceans, the stars, he knows what prayerfulness is – it is wordless. He knows a deep dance in his heart and a music that has no sounds. For the first time he experiences the eternal, the immortal; that which always remains. In every change it renews its life afresh. And anyone who becomes a religious person and drops Christianity, Hinduism, Mohammedanism, Jainism, Buddhism, declares his individuality for the first time.

Religiousness is an individual affair. It is a message of love from you to the whole cosmos. Only then will there be a peace that passeth all misunderstanding. Otherwise these religions have been parasites exploiting people, enslaving people, forcing people to believe. And all beliefs are against intelligence, forcing people to pray with words without any meaning because they are not coming from your heart, but only from your memory.

I have often told the beautiful story of Leo Tolstoy. The story is about three uneducated, uncultured villagers who lived on a small island in a big lake. Millions of people were coming to them and worshipping them, and the archbishop of the old Russia – before the revolution – became concerned.

The churches are empty, nobody is coming to the archbishop, and the Russian church is the oldest church in the world, very orthodox. People are going to those three persons who are not even initiated into the secrets of Christianity.

How had they become saints? In India it is easy to become a saint, but in Christianity it is not so easy. The English word saint comes from a root, *sanctus*. It means that unless you are sanctioned, certified by the pope or the archbishop, you cannot be accepted as a saint. But people were saying, "Those three people are so saintly."

One day, in anger, the archbishop took a boat and went to those three people who were sitting under a tree. He looked at them and he could not believe it. What kind of saints are these?

From the very beginning he declared and introduced himself: "I am the archbishop." The three saints all touched his feet. Then he felt relaxed: "These are fools, and things have not yet gone too far so that they cannot be managed."

He asked them, "Are you saints?"

They looked at each other, and they said, "We have never heard the word. We are uneducated, uncultured. Don't talk Greek to us; just simply say what you mean."

"My God!" said the archbishop, "you don't know what a saint means?

Do you know the Christian prayer?"

Again they looked at each other, and nudged each other as if to say, "You tell him."

The archbishop now became really powerful. He said, "Tell me what your prayer is."

They said, "We are very uneducated. We don't know what Christian prayer is. We have made a prayer of our own."

The archbishop laughed. He said, "Nobody makes his own prayer. Prayer has to be authorized by the church. What is your prayer, anyway?"

They felt very embarrassed, very shy, and finally one said, "Because you are asking, we cannot refuse, but our prayer is not much of a prayer. We have heard that God has three forms – God, the Holy Ghost, and the Son – so we thought to make a prayer of our own. Our prayer is: You are three, we are three, have mercy on us."

The archbishop said, "You idiots! Do you think this is a prayer? I will teach you the prayer authorized by the church."

But the prayer was too long, and all three said together: "We cannot remember such a long prayer. We will try our best, but please repeat it one time more." And they asked him to repeat it a third time because it was too big. "If we remember the beginning, we forget the end. If we remember the end, we forget the beginning. If we remember the beginning and the end, we forget the middle."

The archbishop said, "You need education." But they said, "We cannot write, otherwise we could have written your prayer. Just one time more and we will try our best."

The archbishop was very happy that he had converted three idiots who were being worshipped by millions of people. He said the prayer a third time, they touched his feet, and he went back into his boat.

Just as he was in the middle of the lake he saw a huge something coming toward him. He could not believe it. What could it be? He started praying. As they came close, he understood that it was those three idiots walking on the water. He said, "My God! Only Jesus has ever walked on water."

And they came with folded hands saying, "We forgot the prayer, so we thought – one more time."

The archbishop, seeing them standing on the water, realized the fact. He said, "You don't need my prayer. Your prayer is perfect. I have been praying my whole life, I have reached the highest post in the Orthodox Church of Russia, but I cannot walk on water. God seems to be with you. You just go and do your old prayer."

They were very happy. They said, "We are so grateful because that long prayer would have killed us!"

Here is a beautiful story saying that the traditional, the orthodox religion becomes dead. Religiousness has to arise within your heart as an individual offering of love and fragrance to the cosmos.

Even God is not necessary for a religious person because God is an unproved hypothesis, and a religious person cannot accept anything unproved. He can accept only that which he feels.

What do you feel? – the breathing, the heartbeat... Existence breathes in and out, existence goes on giving you your life every moment. But you have never looked at the trees, you have never looked at the flowers and their beauty, and you have never thought that they are divine. They are really the only God that exists.

This whole existence is full of godliness. If you are full of religiousness, the whole existence simultaneously becomes full of godliness. To me, this is what religion is.

Osho,

Why do I get so sensitive? Where does it come from and is it possible to share sensitivity?

Every child is born sensitive, utterly sensitive. But the society does not want so many sensitive people in the world. It wants people with thick skins. It needs laborers, it needs soldiers, it needs all kinds of hard people who have bypassed their hearts. It needs professors, intellectuals; it needs scientists. They are the people who don't know anything about their own hearts, about their own sensitivity.

It is absolutely blissful that you are feeling sensitive. Perhaps a woman is more capable of being sensitive than a man because she is not going to be a soldier, she is not expected to kill people. A woman is more sensitive than a man because the society has rejected the woman for any important work.

It has been a blessing in disguise. The woman has remained still human, while man has become a monster. His whole work seems to be either to kill or to be killed. His whole life is devoted to accumulating more and more war weapons. It seems the Second World War has not satisfied him; he is preparing for the third. And remember, whenever a soldier dies on the front, a father dies, a son dies, a husband dies. Men fight and kill each other and women suffer.

And because women have suffered for centuries, they have become more and more sensitive to subtle nuances of joy, of suffering, of pain, of pleasure. Don't ask, "Why do I get so sensitive?" You are born sensitive; it is your birthright. When you don't feel sensitive you can ask the question, "Why I am not feeling sensitive?" Sensitivity is one of the great qualities of being religious.

It is told of one of the great men of this century, George Bernard Shaw, that a man had come to meet him, a creative artist, a novelist. He saw so many beautiful flowers in George Bernard Shaw's garden that he could not believe it. And when he went into George Bernard Shaw's room there was not even a single flower there. He asked him, "This is strange. You have so many beautiful flowers in your garden, an abundance. Can't you pick a few flowers for a flower vase in your room?"

George Bernard Shaw said, "I love children too. They are as beautiful as any flower, but I don't cut their heads to decorate my sitting room. The flowers will blossom, they will dance in the rain, in the sun, in the wind. There, they are alive. I am not a butcher; I cannot cut a flower from its life source, and I don't like corpses in my room."

He was right. He was a sensitive man, very sensitive.

You are asking, "Where does it come from?" It comes from your very being. Don't look for any outside source; it is your nature. "... and is it possible to share sensitivity?" Of course.

You may have observed that when shaking hands with a few people, you feel as if you are shaking hands with a dead branch of a tree – no life, no warmth, no energy. And you will have also experienced shaking hands with someone else, and you feel something is being transferred, something has transpired between your energies – a warmth, a loving friendliness. These are the people that you will feel nourished by if you sit with them. And those others, like dead branches of a tree – if you sit with them you will feel strangely as if you are drained.

Sensitivity can be shared in a thousand and one ways. The most fundamental is a lovingness – not a love relationship but just pure lovingness, without any conditions. Not asking anything in return; just pouring your heart on people, even on strangers because it is overflowing with sensitivity.

Now the scientists say you can shake hands with a tree, and if you are friendly you will feel tremendous sensitivity in the tree itself. There are old stories, unbelievable ones, which cannot be factual – but one never knows, maybe they are factual. It is said that whenever Gautam Buddha passed, trees that had been without leaves suddenly grew leaves to give him shade. Whenever he sat under a tree, suddenly thousands of flowers blossomed and started falling over him. It may be simply symbolic, but there is a possibility of its being real too. And modern scientific research about trees supports what I am saying.

It was the first Indian Nobel prizewinner, Jagdish Chandra Bose, who proved to the scientific world that trees are not dead. But since

Jagdish Chandra Bose much has happened. He would be tremendously happy if he could come and see what scientists have managed.

Now they can have something like a cardiogram attached to the tree. A man comes to the tree, a friend with love in his heart, and the tree starts dancing even without any wind and the cardiogram becomes very symmetrical. The graph on the paper almost has a harmonious beauty.

When another man comes with an axe, with the idea of cutting the tree, even if he has not come close, the graph of the cardiogram goes berserk. It loses all symmetry, all harmony. It simply goes insane: something is going to harm the tree. It is strange because the tree has not been harmed; it is just an idea in the woodcutter's mind. The tree is so sensitive that it even catches your ideas. And the same man comes with the ax, not desiring to cut the tree, and the graph remains sane. There is no fear, nervousness in the tree.

And another thing they became aware of, that they had not thought about before, was that if one tree was trembling with fear and a scientist just put a few cardiograms on other trees surrounding it, when the tree started trembling with fear, the other trees also participated. They must have been old friends. Growing in the same grove, they must have shared their love with each other, they must have been friendly. They also reacted immediately.

The whole of existence is full of sensitivity – and man is the highest product of this existence. Naturally, your heart, your being, is ready to overflow. You have been hiding it, repressing it because your parents and your teachers have told you to be hard, to be strong because it is a world full of struggle. If you cannot fight and compete you will be nobody.

So only a few people like poets, painters, musicians, sculptors – who are no longer in the competitive world, who are not hoping to accumulate billions of dollars – are the only people who have some trace of sensitivity left.

But a meditator is on the way of the mystic; he will become more and more sensitive. And the more you share your sensitivity, your love, your friendliness, your compassion, the closer you will come to the goal of being a mystic.

Even small children, particularly male children, are deprived from the very beginning and are told, "You are not supposed even to cry." It is something condemnatory. Women can weep and cry because they have never been accepted up to now as equal human beings. They are somewhat subhuman; so it is allowed for them – "these women are weak." Sensitivity has been thought to be weak. The strong person should not have any sensitivity. When he cuts off people's heads he will not think twice.

The day President Truman ordered the first atom bombs to be dropped on Hiroshima and Nagasaki – which killed more than two hundred thousand people – he remained awake till he received the message that the atom bombs had been dropped. According to the calculations they had functioned perfectly well. Then he went to sleep.

In the morning he was surrounded by the news media and their first question was, "After killing two hundred thousand innocent people" – because they were just citizens, they were not soldiers – "could you sleep in the night?"

And President Truman said, "Of course! I slept as deeply as possible for the first time in a few months. The work is done perfectly. Now Japan is bound to surrender. When I received the news, I was so contented that I slept the whole night without waking up even once."

These are the insensitive people – and his name is "True Man!" Since that day I have started calling him President *Untrueman*.

But from our very childhood, the head is trained and the heart is left absolutely untrained.

Ernie was talking to Ronnie, the little boy from next door.

"How old are you?" asked Ernie.

"I don't know," replied little Ronnie.

"Do women bother you?" inquired Ernie.

"No," said Ronnie.

"Then," said Ernie knowingly, "You are four."

My final suggestion to you is, keep climbing upwards. You may never reach the top, but it is definitely the right direction. Sensitivity is the beginning of a new opening in your being. Don't be afraid; just go on climbing higher and higher. Become more and more sensitive. Hopefully, it will bring you the ultimate flowering of humanity – the mystic rose.

It was a very special day in Paddy's household and Maureen came down to breakfast with an air of expectancy.

"This is our tenth wedding anniversary," she whispered to Paddy, who was reading the newspaper, "so let's have a chicken from our own farm and celebrate."

Paddy looked up and said, "Why kill an innocent bird for what happened ten years ago?"

"Some young man is trying to get into my room through the window," screamed old Mrs. Kleinman into the telephone.

"Sorry, lady," came back the answer, "you've got the fire department. What you want is the police department."

"No, no," she pleaded, "I want the *fire* department. What he needs is a longer ladder!"

"My poor husband," said Mrs. Ginsberg to her psychoanalyst, dragging her husband behind her. "He's convinced he's a parking meter."

The analyst looked at the silent, morbid fellow and asked, "Why doesn't he say something for himself? Can't he talk?"

"How can he," said Mrs. Ginsberg, "with all those coins in his mouth?"

You are living in a very insane, pathetic world. If you don't take yourself out of the mob psychology and manifest your authentic reality, you will be drowned in the mess of the whole world.

In my vision, a sannyasin is one who is making every effort to get rid of the insanity that he has been conditioned for.

Sensitivity will help immensely to make you sane, sensible. And if you go on moving in the right direction it will become your meditation, and finally your mystic experience of enlightenment.

14

Politicians: The Biggest Lies in the Loudest Voice

Osho,
The United States government proudly proclaims itself "the land of the free and the home of the brave" and points to its constitutional protections of fundamental rights. At the same time it twists and breaks its own laws to persecute you who embody freedom and truth. It seems the politicians always tell the biggest lies in the loudest voice. The worst tyrants talk most about peace and freedom. Could you please comment?

Prem Niren, there are many questions in your question, many implications of tremendous importance. I would like to go step by step, giving you the total view of the situation that exists in the United States of America. And what I am going to say is not only true about the United States of America; it is more or less true about every nation dominated by the cunning, clever and crooked politicians.

The first thing you say is, "The United States government proudly proclaims itself 'the land of the free and the home of the brave' and points to its constitutional protections of fundamental rights."

The first thing to be noted about the United States of America is that the land does not belong to the so-called Americans; the land belongs to the natives, the Red Indians. And America is, in fact, one of the strangest places to talk about freedom and democracy. If they really mean what they say, then all Americans are foreigners except the Red Indians – simple hearted, innocent people who have been forced to live in forests, in special reservations. The whole land is theirs, but they don't rule it. Those who rule it are from either Britain or France or Italy or Switzerland or Sweden or Belgium or Greece. They all come from European countries. If they are really sincere, they should pack their luggage and go back home.

It is a strange kind of democracy in which the people of the land, the real owners of the land have no participation at all. And the foreigners – the invaders – who have mercilessly killed the innocent people of America are proudly proclaiming freedom, democracy, basic human rights, freedom of expression and all kinds of nonsense. At least Americans should not use these words at all. It is the greatest slavery that is still in existence, and there seems to be no possibility that the Red Indians will ever again be rulers of their own land because they are poor, they don't have modern war technology.

That is what has irritated the Americans the most: when I said to them, "You are just as much foreigners as I am here. The only difference is that I am new and you are old tourists. I have come with a valid visa, and you entered America with your guns, not with your visas. In what way have you become citizens of America? Who accepted you? You destroyed the poor people, peaceful people, at the point of a gun and proclaimed yourselves the Americans. And you call the real Americans "Red Indians" – giving the sense that America belongs to the Americans. It creates an illusion."

The Americans are all invaders, and if they have any self-respect and dignity they should leave America and go back home.

They deported me. This is strange – foreigners deporting another foreigner. At least I had a valid visa and I was not an invader. They are invaders and entered America with force and violence – and now they have become the proclaimers of freedom and democracy.

America will be free the day it is in the hands of Red Indians. It is the greatest land of slavery today.

As far as their constitution is concerned, Americans have been very proud, proclaiming that they have one of the best constitutions. The latest research has just been published. Just two or three days ago I received the information that all that is beautiful in the American constitution is borrowed from the Red Indians and their old, ancient books of wisdom. So the so-called "great American fathers," the founders of America, were simply thieves and nothing else. They have not mentioned, not even once, that they have borrowed the whole constitution from the poor Red Indians and their books of wisdom.

And you are saying, "At the same time it twists and breaks its own laws to persecute you." It has been persecuting the Red Indians; if it has decided to persecute me, there are valid reasons for this persecution.

One of the most shocking things to the fundamentalist Christians of America – and Ronald Reagan belongs to that group... They have always been sending missionaries to the East, to the poor countries of the East. There are thousands of missionaries all over India, converting the beggars into Christians, the orphans into Christians, the prostitutes into Christians, the aboriginals into Christians, the uneducated, uncultured. But they have not been able to convert a single cultured, educated, high-class brahmin, or a Jaina or a Buddhist.

Their shock was that I was there and the most cultured and educated people of their country – doctors, surgeons, scientists, engineers – were dropping Christianity and becoming sannyasins. And I am not a missionary; I have never told them, promised them any salvation or any heavenly pleasures. I have not told them, "I will be your protector against hell." I was simply telling them what is true and what is divine and what is beautiful. *Satyam shivam sundaram.*

Christianity has nothing to offer to the educated and the cultured. The shock was tremendous. Before me also there have been many people from the East – but they were all cunning, clever and the

Christians were not annoyed with them. For example, Vivekananda: he was the first Indian who was very much appreciated by the Christians because he proclaimed that Christianity is teaching essentially what all religions are teaching. This was very ego-fulfilling.

When I said that Christianity comes lowest as far as the hierarchy of religions is concerned – it has nothing that can be compared with Zen or Sufism or Hassidism; it has not even known the word *meditation*. All that it consists of is hypothetical. In fact, it prevents people from experiencing the truth. Its emphasis is on believing in God and believing in Jesus Christ.

Whenever a religion emphasizes belief, it is against wisdom, it is against enlightenment. It does not want you to become high peaks of consciousness and freedom. It simply wants you to become just a sheep and the shepherd, Jesus Christ, will take care of you. It takes away your responsibility, and you think, "This is very good. We are unburdened." But with your responsibility, your freedom automatically disappears. A Christian is the poorest religious person in the world.

Before me there was Ramateertha, but he praised Christianity just as Vivekananda did. These are not authentically enlightened people; their whole interest is in how to get more admirers. And it is very easy to get admirers in a Christian country if you admire Christianity. If you admire Mohammedanism in a Mohammedan country, you will have thousands of admirers. It is a very mutual conspiracy: they fulfill your ego, you fulfill their egos.

I am a simple person and I simply say whatever is the truth. Whether it hurts you, shocks you, does not matter. To me truth is what matters – and certainly only the very cultured cream of the society has been attracted toward me. I cannot attract the beggars, I cannot attract the orphans, and I cannot attract the aboriginals because they will not even be able to understand what I am saying. Everybody is not capable of understanding the music of Mozart or Wagner. You will need very trained ears to understand those great masters.

And as far as spirituality is concerned, it is the highest point of intelligence. Unless you have that intelligence you are bound to misunderstand. Authentic religion is only for very few people because it requires a tremendous preparation beforehand.

The American Christians were tremendously puzzled how to protect, to prevent their educated and cultured people from moving toward me, because that will ultimately become a movement where even less cultured people will start following the more cultured. That is human nature. When people see that all the geniuses, scientists, engineers, doctors, surgeons are moving toward a certain magnetic force, a certain charisma, the others – without even understanding – also start following. That was the danger.

And the politician was also in difficulty. His difficulty was that I had created a commune of five thousand people according to my ideas, which go essentially against a Christian society, or a Hindu society, or a Mohammedan society. I am against any organized religion because to me truth can never be organized. It is an individual affair, just between one individual and the cosmos.

This was appealing to all those who had the intelligence. The commune became an alternative society in the eyes of the politicians. They could see the great success of the commune – it was the highest quality of communism – and they could not believe that five thousand people are living there, and there is no murder, no theft, no rape. Women could move alone in the middle of the night without any fear. And because my concepts about marriage, about family, about education, are absolutely against the traditional concepts, their fear was: "If this commune goes on succeeding, more communes will arise." And I am absolutely anti- political. Deep down I am an anarchist. My ultimate goal finally is that there should be a humanity without any government.

Government is a condemnation of every one of us. The very existence of the government and the police and the army shows that we are still not civilized. Otherwise there is no need for courts, judges, police officers – what is the need of them?

If man is really man, if people become meditators and their criminal mind disappears, then the politician is naturally alerted. It is dangerous. If this commune succeeds, then there will be more communes arising in the country, and the politician will be in danger.

I have been condemning the politicians and the priests together because they are two sides of one coin. They are conspiring against humanity together. They have made a division: the politician will rule the body of man, and the priest will rule his soul. And they will support each other because their interest is the same – domination over humanity.

My effort to make life absolutely based on freedom and to destroy all possibilities of domination by anybody naturally brought the politicians and the Christian priests together.

This persecution was not the simple persecution that every religion does against any competitive religion. This was a very unprecedented persecution. All religions, all societies, all nations were against a single man who had no organization, but only friends and lovers and fellow travelers.

It is a strange fact that Christians are against Hindus, Hindus are against Jain, Jain are against Buddhists, Buddhists are against Mohammedans – but as far as I am concerned they are all together. On one point at least I have created a unity: they are all my enemies because I am hammering on the basic roots of every religion, which are the same.

You are saying, Niren, "At the same time, it twists and breaks its own laws to persecute you who embody freedom and truth." That is my crime: freedom and truth. Politicians are very happy if you simply talk about it. But if you start creating a certain group of people who start living truth, who start living in freedom, then the danger immediately arises in the hearts of the priests and politicians. They are perfectly at ease if you are only talking. I was not only talking.

My effort is that I want to see whatever I am saying as a realized experience for all those who have come in some deep loving commitment with me. This was the danger.

You say, "It seems that politicians always tell the biggest lies in the loudest voice. The worst tyrants talk most about peace and freedom." There is some hidden psychology behind it.

First, the worst tyrants talk most about peace and freedom. They have to, just to create a facade around them, so that you cannot see their reality in the smoke of their talk of peace and freedom. They have to make much fuss around themselves just to hide behind it. And the biggest lies come in the loudest voice from the politicians.

One of my vice-chancellors was one of the greatest legal experts of his time. He had three offices: one in London, one in New Delhi and one in Peking. He was continually running from China to India, from India to England, and he was fighting the greatest cases. I was not his student, but even though he was a vice-chancellor, he loved law so much that he used to teach law in the university, and I used to go to his class. I had a certain friendship with him that arose by accident.

I used to go for an early morning walk at three o'clock in the morning, and by chance he was also a lover of going at three o'clock. We met every day on a lonely place by the side of a lake. I have never seen such a beautiful lake with so many lotus flowers; it was almost covered with flowers. And just by the side there was a huge forest and mountain, and a small path going around the lake.

We were the only two persons every day, so naturally we started talking to each other, we became friendly. He told me that he would be very happy if I sometimes turned up to his class, although I was not a student of law. I said, "What will be the point?"

He said, "At least you will be a challenge to me. I have lived my whole life challenging the greatest legal experts all around the world, and I feel sorry... Why have you joined the philosophy department? You should have been in the department of law because your logic is so sharp and so clear."

So I started going to his class, and I started arguing with him. I had no idea about law – but logic I understand, and law is simply a by-product of logic, just logic applied. But if you understand logic in its purity, you can understand law without any difficulty.

One day it was the final day before the examinations and he was saying in the class to his students, "My last advice to you: if you have facts in your hands and you also have the support of the law, be calm and quiet. Lay out your facts, lay out your laws. There is no need for you to be excited, angry or in a fighting mood; that will spoil the whole thing. Just be utterly silent. Evidence and law is enough.

"But if you don't have any evidence for your case and you have only the law, then bring all the law books in your car to the court and make as much fuss as possible about laws, ancient precedents, ancient decisions by other courts. Create a jungle of laws. Because you don't have any evidence for your case, it all depends how much you can enforce on the mind of the judge that your position is logical and legal.

"But sometimes there are situations when you don't have evidence for your case and neither do you have any support of the law. Don't be worried. Shout as loudly as you can. Go on hitting on the judge's table. Let everybody present shake and be afraid, and make it a point that you must have all the evidence and the laws, otherwise you could not be roaring like a lion. It all depends on how much louder you are and how many times you hit the judge's table."

Whenever you see politicians telling the biggest lies in the loudest voice, you should know that lies can only be told in loud voices. The loudness of the voice hides the lies. Truth can be whispered, but lies can only be loudly declared. Their strength lies in your voice.

Truth is self-evident. Just whispering it is enough.

Prem Niren, what happened with me in America and with my people has to become a historical fact, exposing both the religions and the politicians, and all their bogus talk about great words.

Niren himself was one of my attorneys. In fact he was my chief attorney because he was my sannyasin. All the other attorneys were chosen by him. He was the coordinator. The others were paid, only he was working for love. You cannot depend on the paid people because their interest is money. They don't care what is true and what is not true.

Secondly, you can never be sure of their own prejudices, which I became aware of sitting silently for three days in North Carolina. They were all insistent that I should not say a single word. They were afraid that if I said anything the case would become too long, complicated, and that I might say things that may become contempt of court and it would complicate things.

Their insistence was that I should remain completely silent. So I enjoyed complete silence for three days, watching, witnessing what those attorneys were doing. And the first thing that came to my vision was that although they were fighting for me, their hearts were with the American government. Although they were fighting for me, their conditioning was for the Christian church – so deep down they were not for me. Except for Niren, I could not feel any of the attorneys – and they were the best attorneys in America.

A man may be an attorney or a judge, but it doesn't matter; he is still a human being with the whole unconscious conditioning. Even they – being Christians, being Americans – could not accept my approach toward life's problems. And, moreover, I was a non-American, a non-white, against whom they have deep prejudices. Because they were paid so much money, they were ready. But they were simply paid people, servants, and I could see that their arguments were halfhearted – as if deep down they wanted that I should be persecuted, that I should be fined, that I should be jailed. Except Niren, I could not feel the sincerity and honesty in any of those attorneys.

There came a situation when one of the best experts, Peter Schey, who is head of the department of law in a Californian university – Niren must have been his student, so he had employed him. He was one of the best experts, there is no doubt about it, but at a certain point Niren came running to me in the jail and said, "Peter Schey seems to be shaky. He is not willing to say a few things under the oath of truth, so what should we do?"

I said, "There is no problem. You simply go to the witness stand instead of Peter Schey. Only you can overcome the prejudices of Christians."

Niren did a beautiful job. And in a roundabout way he brought Peter Schey into his witnessing: "Peter Schey told me..." and then he repeated the whole thing that was supposed to have been told by Peter Schey.

I was sitting by the side of Peter Schey and I could see his head down – afraid that this man, Niren, was bringing him in. And I could see these lawyers' split personalities: they cannot say no to money, but just for money they cannot go against their prejudices either. It was a strange experience.

One of our attorneys, Jack Ransom, told Niren, and he informed me, "We are fighting a losing battle because the people we depend on..." A man like Jack Ransom, a topmost attorney, said to Niren, "We cannot fight as totally as we could have fought for any American because Osho will go to India. But we have to live in America and we cannot annoy these magistrates and judges because we have to be continually in the courts in front of them. This is not our last case."

Niren again became very shaken that our attorneys were saying that they would only go so far, not more than that; that they couldn't annoy the magistrate; they couldn't annoy the judge – even if he ruled illegally, against the constitution.

And that's what finally happened. They did everything against their own constitution, against their own law.

Just the other day I was informed by Barkha – she was an important sannyasin in the commune; she was the head of the commune police. The government wanted the city to have a magistrate and a police department because the commune had become a city, had been incorporated as a city. We did not want non-sannyasins to be in the commune because they would feel strange and our people would feel strange. So the only way was to train our own people as the police, to train one of our own people as the magistrate. So one woman was the magistrate. Sangeet is here, she was the city attorney; and Barkha is here, she was the city's police chief.

The day I was arrested and I was shown on all the television stations of America, the chief of police of Oregon phoned Barkha because Barkha was working under him as chief of police of the city of Rajneeshpuram. He phoned to tell her that this was absolutely illegal; you cannot arrest anybody without an arrest warrant. And even in special cases when the warrant has not arrived yet, but you have to take somebody into custody – you have been told to do so – then you cannot put handcuffs and chains on the person because he is not yet confirmed as a criminal by the magistrate.

But that's what was done. And the police chief said, "I am feeling so sad and sorry that they arrested Osho with twelve loaded guns, and they did not show any arrest warrant, they did not even show verbally what was the cause of arrest."

And the second day when he saw that I had been taken to another jail and I was descending the staircase of the airplane with handcuffs, chains on my feet, and with another chain around my waist to which the handcuffs were joined – a fly was sitting on my head and I could not even scratch my head – he said, "It is absolutely unprecedented: a man for whom they have no warrant, a man who has done no wrong."

In three days the government attorney could not prove a single thing against me, and he accepted it in his summarizing statement: "We have been unable to prove anything against Osho." Still, the way they were behaving was simply to humiliate.

But you cannot humiliate me, and they felt it. Even the jailers said to me, "Everything is being done to humiliate you, but it is strange, we don't see any humiliation. You are taking it so coolly and so silently and so peacefully as if this has been your whole life's practice."

I said, "Who knows? It may be in the future. So I am training myself because one never knows about tomorrow. This may be my whole lifestyle in the future, and I never miss a single moment of learning."

According to every psychoanalytic school, politicians suffer from an inferiority complex. In fact, if a man does not suffer from an inferiority complex he will not try to dominate anyone. The very effort to dominate is just to convince oneself that "I am not inferior, I am superior to those whom I rule, whom I dominate." It is strange that your presidents, your prime ministers are all psychologically sick people. They are full of jealousy, competition.

They became jealous of the commune because the commune was living according to my ideology. I am against poverty; hence in the commune there was nobody poor and nobody was rich either. There was not a single beggar, and the commune itself was comfortably rich. It had its own airport, its own four airplanes, its own hundreds of cars, its own one hundred buses – particularly for the celebration days when people used to come from all over the world and the population of the commune, which was only five thousand, used to rise to twenty thousand.

We had every arrangement for twenty thousand people. We created new kinds of tents which can be air-conditioned, which can be centrally heated, which can be used around the year, whether it is hot or cold or snow is falling. These were our own invention. They could be folded in ten minutes and could be put back again in ten minutes. We were keeping those tents for the fifteen thousand people coming for the festivals.

And the festivals were exactly what festivals should be – twenty thousand people eating together under one roof, and while people were eating, somebody was playing guitar and somebody was dancing and somebody was playing on the flute. That was my idea always, that people should live as festively as possible. Their lives should be one long celebration.

Happy people can never be forgiven, and the commune was one of the happiest collections of people that has ever happened on the earth. You could not find a single person who was miserable. Misery was simply sent away to other American cities.

In five years there was not a single fight between two sannyasins. The whole of America, and particularly the politicians, became jealous: "This is dangerous because if people came to know more and more about it..." And they were going to know because every day planes were landing in the commune – television stations, reporters, all kinds of news media.

For a time it looked as if Rajneeshpuram had become the capital of America. I was on the television more than the president of America. Naturally, jealousy arises.

I was not even a tourist because my tourist visa expired in three months. I asked for an extension. That expired again in three months, and then I applied for permanent residency and the immigration department was in trouble. The trouble was that they could not say yes to me because the government was pressurizing them, the church was pressurizing them: "This man should not be allowed in America."

They could not say yes and they could not say no either, because if they had said no I could have gone to the court. On what grounds could they say no to me? They have six categories of people who can be allowed to stay in America as permanent residents; I fulfilled five categories. I could not fulfill only one category, and that was marriage. But if the worst had come to the worst I could have fulfilled that too. There was no problem in it.

They could not say no, they could not say yes, so for five years I was there without any visa, without any permission. A man without a visa who is getting more attention than the president of a country is naturally going to create a great violence in these inferior, psychologically sick and almost retarded beings – then they will forget all the constitutions and all the laws that they have themselves made.

Paddy was showing...

[*There is an outburst of sudden and surprised laughter as Osho, after all this serious talk, begins reading a joke.*]

I will have to begin it again.

Paddy was showing Sean his pet turtle. "Wow," said Sean, "that certainly is a magnificent turtle."

"Maybe," replied Paddy, "but he is very shortsighted."

"Shortsighted?" asked Sean in surprise. "How can you tell?"

Paddy smiled and said, "He has fallen in love with my old army helmet."

Politicians are almost like Paddy's turtle – very shortsighted. The day America deported me, I told a few of my friends who had come to send me off at the airport, "This is the beginning of their downfall."

Existence functions in its own way, not according to human stupidities. After Socrates, what happened to Greece? It was at the highest peak of consciousness, but the day they poisoned Socrates, they poisoned themselves. Never again in these twenty-five centuries could they rise back to being a world power. What happened to Judea that crucified Jesus? It has disappeared from the map completely.

The day they fined me without my having committed any crime, and forced me to leave America immediately, they were not aware that existence is more just than any human court or any human constitution can be. I told my friends, "My leaving America – you will soon see it falling from being a world power." And it has come true. Now every day America is falling into a ditch, and I declare that it will never again be the world's greatest economic power, as it has been.

Existence supports even a single innocent man against a whole country, against a whole government because existence has no fear of your atomic missiles, your nuclear weapons. It does not care about anything except innocence. The only value in the eyes of existence is the eyes of a sage, so utterly innocent and mystified and wondrous that for a single sage like Socrates or Jesus, the whole country can be removed, erased from history.

Sean and Paddy were having a drink at the pub when Sean said, "I heard you having a great argument with Maureen, your wife, last night. How did you make out?"

"Ah," said Paddy, "she came crawling to me on her hands and knees."

"Is that so?" said Sean. "What did she say?"

"She said," replied Paddy sipping his beer, "come out from under the bed, you coward."

America behaved with me and my people like utter cowards. If they had had any guts, they could have called me to their senate and I was ready to answer all their questions and I was ready to defend all my ideas. That would have been dignified, rather than forcing me into a jail under loaded guns and then trying to poison me. And because they failed to send me to jail for twenty or thirty years, they managed to have a bomb planted under my seat.

Just today I received the whole investigation report. I had asked them whether they had investigated how the bomb had entered the jail with all their security, and how it managed just to be under my seat. Now comes a long report with so many contradictions and stupidities.

The report says that at four o'clock, just after the judgment was given by Federal Judge Leavy against me, an anonymous phone call came to the police station, to the jail, and to a television station – that a bomb had been placed under a certain seat in the visitors' room. And the report from the police department of Portland says: "We searched the whole place, we evacuated the whole ground floor. But it was only a threat. No bomb was found."

I have asked my legal secretary to write to them, "If you had evacuated the whole ground floor, why did you take me there? You evacuated everybody from the ground floor and immediately you took me there." The first thing I noticed was that there was nobody on the ground floor, where there used to be hundreds of people working. I asked the man who had taken me there, "What has happened to all the people – some kind of holiday?" If it was a bomb threat, then certainly they should not have taken me to the ground floor.

But it was not a bomb threat, and the ground floor was not evacuated because of the bomb threat. It was evacuated in case the bomb under my seat exploded. Then nobody else would be hurt. When I asked that man, he said, "I don't know. Perhaps it is a shift change."

I said, "I do understand a little bit about shift changes. The second shift people should be here; only then can the first shift people go. This gap cannot be left between the two."

He became shaky and he said, "I don't know anything at all about what has happened." And he left me inside the waiting room, exactly the same waiting room that the anonymous call had indicated: that under a certain seat there was a bomb that was going to explode at five minutes to six.

That was their calculation: that the case would take at least that much time, that the court would not decide before five. And after the court's decision my fine would have to be paid and only after my fine was given to the court would I be allowed to be taken to the jail. So they had calculated perfectly – at nearabout six I may come back to take my clothes.

But because there was no trial... The government was not ready to go for a trial, knowing perfectly well that they didn't have any evidence against me. For three days they had seen the same government attorney general fighting in the court of North Carolina and concluding in his speech, "We don't have any evidence against him." Now, what more could they do?

It was absolutely clear that if they went for a trial they would be defeated. And they told my attorneys, "You should remember one thing: you can win the case, but it may take ten years or twenty years. We can go on postponing it. And the second thing you should remember is that the government of the United States of America is not going to be defeated by a single individual. If you are interested in saving Osho's life, it is better not to go for a trial."

That's why the case was finished within two minutes. I reached the jail too early. In the waiting room where they were going to deliver me my clothes, there was only one man, and he was shaky.

The form in his hand showed that his whole being was shaking. I asked him, "Is something wrong with your hand, or is something wrong with the form?"

He said, "Sit on this seat, and just wait. It will take ten or fifteen minutes for me to get my boss's signature on the form – which was an absolute lie because there was no place on the form where anybody else's signature was needed. It was a simple form saying that I had received my clothes back. Only my signature was needed.

When he went out, locking the door from the outside, he indicated the chair on which I had to sit. That was the same chair under which the bomb was found. Perhaps he had gone to ask what had to be done now because he may not have been aware what the decision in the court had been. If I was released, then there was no need to explode the bomb; if I was going for trial, then it was better to finish it on the first day. Why wait unnecessarily for years of trial and millions of dollars to be wasted?

Looking at the police department's report, it is absolutely clear that now they are trying to make it simply a rumor. But if it was a rumor, why did they evacuate the prison? And if they believed in the rumor and evacuated the prison, they should not have taken me in there. It is so clear. So what they have been doing for an investigation is finding out who phoned. They found out the locality where the call had come from, but in that locality there are many people and many phones. That is the end of the street. The investigation has stopped. Where to go from there?

Even a certain belief in an anonymous phone call was stupid because the jail was so secure and safe; it was perhaps the most modern jail in America. It had opened only three months before I entered it. It has all the latest security equipment: doors that only open with remote control buttons; nobody can open them by hand. And there were doors beyond doors. As far as I remember, there were three doors through which they took me in.

Just inside the car they had the remote control, and then the first gate would open. The gate was a solid steel rock, rising up to give just enough space for the car to move in. Then there was the second gate, and the second gate would open only when the first gate had come down. And then there was a third gate, and the third would open only when the second had come down. It was all automatic.

It was absolutely impossible for any individual who was not an insider to reach inside and plant a bomb.

The American government may have the nuclear weapons, but it has a very cowardly soul. They could not encounter a single individual. That very day I thought, "How are these people going to manage in the Third World War with the Soviet Union?" And now their situation is becoming worse every day.

It will be good for you to be reminded that it was not Columbus who first discovered America. It has been discovered many times, and then it was found that it was not worth discovering. Then it was hushed up.

In Turkey there exists a map eight hundred years old that has America on it, exactly as you have it on any modern map. That was four hundred years before Columbus discovered America – but that also is not very old.

In Mahabharata, a great war happened five thousand years ago in India. The hero of the war was Arjuna, perhaps the greatest archer of all time. He married many wives from different countries, and one of his wives was Mexican.

Of course America was known, but it has been hushed up again and again. Perhaps the time has come again to hush it up.

15

Attention Is Nourishment

Osho,

From what I heard you say, I understood that for enlightenment to happen, meditation is a preparation, but also an intense urge is required, a realization that nothing else really matters. I see myself being interested in all kinds of things, all kinds of mind-stories, music, women, sense perceptions. Will these interests prevent enlightenment?

A very ancient story is that an old man came to his master and said, "I have been to see a great number of teachers and I have given up a great number of pleasures. I have fasted, been celibate, and stayed awake all night seeking enlightenment. I have given up everything I was asked to give up and I have suffered, but I have not been enlightened. What should I do?"

The master replied, "Give up suffering."

Neither music can prevent your enlightenment, nor sense perceptions, nor women. Only one thing can prevent your enlightenment, and that is suffering. Enlightenment is the ultimate celebration, so any small celebrations that you are having will become just like steps toward it. But suffering cannot become a step toward enlightenment.

You are asking, "I see myself being interested in all kinds of things, all kinds of mind-stories..." They will disappear as your meditation grows, just as when you bring the light in, the darkness disappears. The darkness can never be a hindrance. You cannot say that the darkness is so thick and so old that whenever I bring the light in, the light goes out. Darkness cannot put the light out.

Your mind-stories are just soap bubbles. Once you have touched even a glimpse of meditation – what to say about stories, mind itself disappears.

Music will be deepened as your meditation grows; your music will have new flavors, new flowers, new fragrances. Your music will become more and more in tune with your meditation. Ultimately the music comes to a point of perfection when no instrument is needed – but pure silence, without any sounds. In fact, what you call music is a play between sound and silence. Those who emphasize the sound miss the deeper meaning of music. The deeper meaning is between two sounds, in the gaps.

Meditation is not against music. On the contrary, music has been born out of meditative consciousness. For the first time it was used to express something about meditation. But the gestalt has to change; from sound the emphasis should change to the silence. And meditation will do that miracle automatically.

As far as women are concerned, it is impossible to become enlightened without women. They are the real driving force! People say that behind every great man there is a woman. That may be right, may not be right, but behind every enlightened man there are many women – torturing him, harassing him until finally he decides it is better to become enlightened. If there is no woman to harass you, why should you try to become enlightened in the first place? Women have not become enlightened for the simple reason that no man is harassing them. So don't be afraid of women; they are an immense help, absolutely necessary.

Sense perceptions are not a hindrance. Your sensitivity, your perceptivity will become deeper as your meditation deepens. So, finally, the old man in the story was given the right answer by the master. That's my answer also to you.

Just get rid of suffering. Nothing else in the world can prevent your meditation.

> Osho,
> Sometimes, sitting with you is pure delight. My whole body is flooded with a strange and lovely feeling, like a silent orgasm that has no top or bottom. But more often I feel so busy with my aches and pains and thoughts that I can't be here, I can't seem to relax into myself, or let anything be. Then I get really worried that there is some unconscious resistance. Can you tell me if I am fighting or what? And if I am fighting – what for?

What is happening "sometimes" will start happening more and more. Your emphasis, your attention should be on what is happening, not on what is not happening. You have to understand a fundamental law: attention is nourishment.

Your question is: "Sometimes, sitting with you is pure delight." Why sometimes? If it can be even once a delight to sit with me, then pour your whole attention into what is happening that is making you so delight-full, so peaceful, so relaxed. Once in a while you will find that the mind is "...so busy with my aches and pains and thoughts that I can't be here." It is natural. Old habits, long friendships, drop slowly. These aches and pains and thoughts are your old habit.

It is a miracle that sometimes you come out of your old structure, out into the open sky. Just pay more attention to these moments. Nourish them, relish them. And when it does not happen, don't be worried. Just remember one thing: it is an old habit. But don't give it any attention, don't be bothered. It is absolutely human. For centuries, for many lives, we have not known anything other than misery, pain, agony. Naturally they have gone deep into our unconscious.

No fight at all is happening within you. It is just that an old habit takes possession of you. You should remember that it is just a habit and "I am not to be concerned with it, not to be bothered with it. Let it be there." And soon those old habits will start falling like dead leaves from the trees.

In fact, there seems to be no problem; it is just that you are not aware of your habits, unconscious accumulations. It is good that they are coming up because that is the only way to get rid of them. Don't repress them, otherwise they will go on coming up. And don't give them attention, otherwise you are giving nourishment to things that should be starved and allowed to die.

Your whole focus should be on those beautiful moments that happen to you, those orgasmic spaces. Fill them with all your energy and slowly, slowly it is an absolute inevitability that that which is blissful is going to win over the suffering, that which is ecstatic is going to win over the agony – unless you decide to pay more attention to the agony and take the ecstasy just for granted. Then there will be trouble.

So the only thing to remember is: pour your attention and love, and rejoice and feel grateful for those moments which give you orgasmic blissfulness. The others are not to be even talked about. Let them come, it is good that they are surfacing.

Now there are three things you can do. You can repress them: then you will not get rid of them, they will come again. Or you can give nourishment to them. That will make them stronger and your orgasmic moments will become shorter, fewer. And the third thing is: don't repress them and don't give attention to them. Just accept them. It is your past; it is dead. It will go away by itself. Don't even fight with them because fighting is another name for suppression, and fighting is also giving attention to them.

Sandy MacTavish, a young Scotsman, went down to London for a holiday. When he returned, his friend Hamish asked how it was. "All right," said Sandy, "but they are funny folk down there."

"Why is that?" asked Hamish.

"Well," said Sandy, "one night, very late, it must have been about two in the morning, a man came banging on the door. He screamed and shouted and was in a really nasty temper – at two o'clock, man."

"And what did you do?" asked Hamish.

"I didn't do anything," replied Sandy, "I just went on quietly playing my bagpipes."

Just a little awareness, and all problems can be solved so easily!

But the mind's tendency is negative. And it is not only for you, it is for all to remember that mind tends to be negative because the negative balance of the mind is big. Your suffering has been long, your pains have been too many, your agonies too much, your failures innumerable.

If you count the moments of joy, you will be surprised that in the whole life of a man he may not be able to find even ten moments of joy to be counted on ten fingers. But if you want to listen to his miseries, the story is so long! It is his whole life: a seventy-year-long story of misery. And if you think of many other past lives, the same is true about them.

Naturally, the negative is too heavy on you. It is such a mountainous load, it is a vast dark night around you. And what are your pleasures? – just a few fireflies here and there in the deep darkness. Naturally you tend unknowingly, unconsciously, to pay more attention to the negative. You don't pay attention to the positive. The positive has been so small that it has not made even a dent in you.

Because of this negative habit a small thing becomes so big that it prevents your energy from flowing toward the positive. I want you to pay all your attention to the positive and ignore what is negative. That's what Gautam Buddha's advice has been.

Buddha's word for ignoring the negative was *upeksha*. It is a very beautiful word. Ignoring is a literal translation of *upeksha*, but it misses something immensely valuable which I will have to explain to you. *Upeksha* is ignoring, plus. When you ignore something, there is a possibility that even in ignoring you are paying attention. Even though you are ignoring, you are paying attention. You may not look at somebody, but you are holding yourself back from looking. You may not be speaking to somebody, but you are holding back. It is the same – whether you are speaking or you are holding it back.

Upeksha means: as if the negative does not exist, as if it is just a shadow which will disappear on its own; no attention at all. You don't pay attention to your shadow, or do you? The whole day it follows you and you don't take any note of it. That is *upeksha*.

Ebenezer MacTavish was known to be the grumpiest farmer in the neighborhood. One year when MacTavish's apple crop was exceptionally good, a neighbor was confident that he would not complain.

"I'll bet you are happy with your apple crop," said the neighbor, "just about every one of them is a perfect apple."

"I suppose they are all right," replied MacTavish grudgingly, "but what am I going to do? I have got no rotten ones to feed to my pigs."

That is the tendency of the negative mind. Even in paradise you will find so many things wrong that paradise will not be a paradise with the negative mind; it will become a hell. Psychologically, the negative mind is hell and the positive mind is heaven.

I have told you the story of Edmund Burke, one of the great English philosophers. He was very friendly with the Archbishop of Canterbury, the archbishop of England. They had graduated together and they loved each other very much. And the archbishop was waiting, that some day Edmund Burke would come to listen to him. But he never came, although the archbishop was always going to any meetings that were addressed by Edmund Burke. This was very strange.

Finally, he invited him specially: "This Sunday you have to come. You have not heard me even once and I have heard you each time you speak."

Very reluctantly, Edmund Burke said, "If you invite me, I will come."

He came and sat in the front. The archbishop had prepared his sermon as perfectly as he could because Edmund Burke was there and he wanted to impress him. But all the time he was becoming more and more nervous because Edmund Burke was sitting there with the same face, with no movement of any emotions, no encouragement in his eyes, no joy in listening to what was being said. The archbishop thought, "This is strange. He is sitting just like a dead man. And I am trying my best. It is the best sermon that I have ever delivered."

Coming back home there was a long silence. Finally, as they were parting, the archbishop could not resist the temptation. He asked, "What is the matter with you? Are you sick or something? – because I did not see a single emotion on your face. If the sermon was not good, then there should have been some emotion; if it was good, then too some emotion. But you remained almost like a stone statue. When people were laughing you did not even smile; when people were crying I did not see that your eyes were wet with tears. You behaved strangely, and I had prepared the best sermon of my life."

Edmund Burke said, "You created such contradictory statements that it is enough that I did not hit you then and there. I was holding myself back. That's why I looked like a stone statue. If I had been relaxed I would have come near you and given you a good hit!"

The archbishop said, "But what was so bad that you wanted to hit me?"

Edmund Burke said, "You made two statements without realizing that they are contradictory. First you said, those who believe in Jesus will enter into paradise. Secondly, you said, those who are living a moral life will enter into heaven."

The archbishop said, "But what is the contradiction?"

Edmund Burke said, "You studied philosophy with me, but you don't understand philosophy at all. What about a man who is living an immoral life but believes in Jesus Christ? And what about the man who is living a moral life and does not believe in Jesus Christ? That's where the contradiction is. It is not apparent to you or to your listeners, but you cannot deceive me."

The archbishop thought about it. Certainly it was a contradiction.

Edmund Burke said, "You can answer me now. A man who has been moral and good his whole life, but does not believe in Jesus Christ – what is going to happen to him? What happened to Socrates? – because Jesus Christ was born five hundred years later; he had no idea of Jesus Christ, and he never believed in anyone else, but he was one of the most pious, most moral, and one of the greatest human beings that the earth has produced.

"What about Gautam Buddha, who did not believe in any Jesus Christ, who did not believe in any Hindu gods, who did not believe even in the existence of God, but who lived one of the greatest lives you can conceive of? You cannot find a single fault in his life.

"Have they gone to hell? And if the law of your God sends Socrates, Gautam Buddha, Lao Tzu to hell, your God cannot be said to be just, cannot to be said to be compassionate. He seems to be absolutely ugly and cruel. All that he wants is belief in him. And I know millions of people who believe in Jesus Christ, who come to your churches, who believe in your God, who believe in your Holy Bible, and who live an utterly ugly and immoral life, doing all kinds of crimes and committing all kinds of sins. What is your answer?"

The archbishop was taken aback. He had never thought about the implications. Very few people think about implications. He said, "Right now I am not able to answer, but next Sunday... Give me seven days to think because you have raised a very fundamental question and I am caught in a dilemma. If I say yes, a moral man will enter heaven even if he does not believe in Jesus, then naturally the question arises: What is the need to believe in Jesus? And if I say a man who believes in Jesus is bound to go to heaven, then the question arises: If that is enough, then why bother about living a moral life? Why not enjoy all kinds of sins and crimes? So just give me seven days to figure out how I can come out of the dilemma."

Edmund Burke said, "Granted. I will come again next Sunday. Be ready with the answer!"

Those seven days were the most torturous days for the archbishop. However he tried, he was always caught in the dilemma. Utterly tired, he could not sleep. The whole night he was thinking, but no answer seemed to be arising.

On Sunday he got to the church earlier than ever before, just to pray to Christ in silence and ask him, "Now help me. I cannot manage to find the answer. *You* give me the answer" – because he had not slept for seven days.

Utterly tired, he fell asleep while he was praying at the feet of Jesus Christ, and he saw a dream. He was in a train, a very fast train, and he inquired, "Where are we going?" Somebody said, "You don't know where we are going? We are going to heaven." He felt very relaxed because this was a great chance to see whether Gautam Buddha, Socrates, Chuang Tzu – people like that – were in heaven or not. He was immensely happy.

When the train stopped at the railway station of heaven, he looked out of the window and he could not believe his eyes. It was just a desert – no greenery, no flowers, dead trees without leaves, and under those dead trees were sitting even more dead saints, with no juice. The dust had gathered on them because they had been sitting there for centuries. He said, "My God, if this is heaven, what will be the situation in hell?"

He asked a saint, who could hardly open his eyes, and who said, "We have never heard of these people here." He inquired of another man who said, "Gautam Buddha? Socrates? Lao Tzu? From where did you get these names? These fellows are not here." He was shocked because even though he was an archbishop – a fanatical Christian – still, to put Gautam Buddha in hell seemed to be too cruel.

He rushed to the railway station to inquire, "Is there any train going to hell?" The train was ready, so he jumped in. As they started coming closer to hell, strangely, the air became cooler, there was beautiful greenery all around, beautiful lakes and so many flowers, and everybody looked so happy. People were playing on their musical instruments; a few people were dancing.

He said, "This is hell?" He got down, inquired of the stationmaster, "Are you certain this is hell?" The stationmaster said, "Absolutely certain. What is your problem?" The archbishop said, "My problem is, I want to know whether Gautam Buddha, Socrates, Lao Tzu, Chuang Tzu, all these people who never believed in God, who never believed in Jesus – are they here?"

The stationmaster said, "You see all this greenery and all these flowers and all these crops and you see all this singing and dancing? It started when Gautam Buddha, Socrates, Lao Tzu and people like that started coming into hell. They transformed the whole face of it. Now there is nobody in hell who wants to go to heaven."

This was even more shocking, and the very shock of it woke him up. The early members of the congregation had started coming. Edmund Burke had arrived. The archbishop must have been a very sincere man. That day he did not deliver any sermon, he simply told his whole dream. And he said, "I don't have to conclude. You can draw the conclusion yourself.

"My own simple understanding now is that wherever there are good people, there is heaven. I used to think that heaven was a certain place; now I think heaven is a certain spirituality, a certain flowering of your being. Wherever these people are, whether they believe in Jesus or not, whether they believe in the Bible or not is irrelevant because I have seen both. I have seen the believers, and heaven seems to be a complete graveyard. And hell seems to be such an oasis that even I am wondering what to do – to continue to believe in Jesus Christ, or to start living like a Gautam Buddha."

It all depends whether you are paying too much attention and allowing your consciousness to go to the negative. All your saints are negative; condemning everything is their whole profession. There are millions of people who are not sensitive but continuously negative. They cannot see anything good anywhere. If by chance they come across something good, they pass it by with absolute indifference. They don't count the roses, they only count the thorns. They are so accustomed to viewing things negatively that it is almost impossible for them to see any beauty anywhere: all is wrong. Naturally, a person who thinks all is wrong is going to live in a world which is all wrong, in suffering, in misery, in pain, in agony.

A sannyasin has to change his gestalt. Try to find the positive, the beautiful, and you will be surrounded with the positive, the beautiful, and the blissful.

I am not saying that there are no wrong things in the world. I am not saying that there are no thorns in the rosebush. It is a question of your emphasis. If you look at the roses you will be so ecstatic that who cares about the thorns? But if you look only at the thorns – and not only look, but count them – you are going to have bloody fingers, and in that pain you will forget all about roses.

Life is absolutely balanced between the positive and the negative. Now it is your choice which side you want to be, in heaven or in hell. Wherever you want to be, try to find it in your life, every moment. And whenever you have found something positive, pour all your attention and all your love on it. That will make it grow; that will make it more and more important in your life, more and more taking the space of your being.

Remain absolutely indifferent about the negative. I am not saying it is not there. It is there because a few people need it. A few people are so much in love with the negative that if there is no negative they will die out of sheer agony: "Now there are roses and no thorns, what am I going to do? Everybody looks so beautiful, nothing ugly, everything seems to be so right, nothing is wrong." They will lose all interest in existence. Their only interest was in the negative.

But they are both there. There are positivist thinkers in the world, particularly in America, who say, "Go on thinking about the positive because the negative does not exist. It is always the positive; the negative is your imagination." I don't agree with them.

The negative is not your imagination, neither is the positive your imagination. They both are there, absolutely balanced. It is up to you to choose.

I have heard about a young man meeting an old lady. That old lady belonged to a positivist group that was very prominent fifty years ago in America – the Christian Scientists. They believe there is no negative. Everything is divine. There is nothing wrong; everything is right. They forget completely that if there is nothing wrong, how are you going to define right? If there is nothing negative, how are you going to define positive? If there is no darkness, how are you going to define light? But it was a very interesting, attractive philosophy.

The old woman asked the young man, "I have not seen your father coming to our weekly meetings."

The young man said, "He is very sick."

The old woman said, "All nonsense! Has he forgotten our philosophy? Sickness is your imagination. Just go home and tell him, 'Sickness is your imagination.' There is no sickness, no death, nothing wrong in the world. It is God who created the world. How can there be wrong?"

The young man said, "I will convey your message."

Three weeks passed and the old man still did not turn up. Again the woman encountered the young boy and asked him, "Did you convey my message?"

He said, "I did."

The old woman said, "But he has not turned up to the meeting."

The young man said, "I am sorry to tell you that now he imagines he is dead!"

He could not say that he is dead because that woman will immediately bounce on him with all kinds of positive philosophy – how can he be dead? So he managed to say that now he imagines himself to be dead.

"What can we do? We had to put him in a grave. He is so certain of it that he does not speak, he does not breathe. He believes so much that he is dead that his pulse has gone, his heartbeat has gone. We tried hard your way. I told him, I whispered in his ear, 'It is all imagination; remember your positivist philosophy.' But his imagination is so strong."

You live in a world, in an existence that has both. Out of sheer necessity it needs balance in opposite polarities. But you need not be worried about that which makes you miserable.

Choose the flowers and leave the thorns.

> Osho,
> I see that I am eager to drop my jealousy, judgments, greed, anger – all the baddies. Yet at the same time I am reluctantly clinging to the parts of my personality I still enjoy indulging in – my passion, my clown, my gypsy adventurer. Why am I so afraid that just to be the watcher will be boring?

Deva Dwabha, I can see you must be in a great conflict. You say, "I see that I am eager to drop my jealousy, judgments, greed, anger – all the baddies. Yet at the same time I am reluctantly clinging to the parts of my personality I still enjoy indulging in – my passion, my clown, my gypsy adventurer. Why am I so afraid that just to be the watcher will be boring?"

It seems you are not experienced enough. You have just heard these great things, that if you drop your jealousy, judgments, greed, anger and all the baddies, you will have all the pleasures and blissfulness of paradise showering on you.

In fact, you are not really interested in dropping them. If you can get all the pleasures and ecstasies of enlightenment and can still keep your jealousy, judgments, greed and anger, I think you will be immensely happy.

The trouble is you will have to choose. How can you drop your greed and jealousy and judgments and anger, if you enjoy your passion, your clown, your gypsy adventurer?

My suggestion is, first enjoy your gypsy adventurer, your passion, your clown as much as you can. Be completely fed up with them. Don't get in a split. This happens to many people, hearing great words they create a split within themselves. I don't want you to be schizophrenic; I want you to be psychologically and spiritually healthy.

My suggestion is, first indulge in your passions as much as you can till you get really bored. This has to be the first step. Only then can you take the second step very easily. It is the first step that is preventing you from taking the second step. When you are utterly finished, you are bound to drop all greed, jealousy, judgments, anger. What are you going to do with these things? It is one complete package. But begin with your passion because I have never heard that there has ever been a single person in the world who did not become fed up with his passion.

Yes, if you live a lukewarm life you may not get fed up. But live totally, pour your whole energy into your passion, into your clown, into your gypsy adventurer, and soon you will see that what you were thinking was going to bring great blessings to you has only destroyed your energies and has left you like a spent cartridge.

Only then will you be able to drop jealousy. There will be no need to drop it. They will all drop on their own accord. And then at the third step you will not be able to ask: "Will being the watcher be boring?"

Do you think I am bored? I am not even bored with you! Every day, in the morning, every day in the evening, I come with such joy to see you. I never remember that you are the same people I have seen the night before. I am absolutely fresh every moment.

The watcher is not boring. The watcher is such an utter silence, such tremendous peace – and such a joy arising within yourself, not coming from outside. And the watcher brings you experiences that you have not even dreamed about.

You have heard the word *ecstasy* but you don't know what it is. You have heard the word *truth* but you don't know what it is. You have heard the word *beauty* but if somebody asks you what it is you will not be able to answer.

The watcher brings *satyam shivam sundaram* to you. It opens the door of truth, of godliness, of immense beauty and eternal life. It gives you new eyes, new perception. The trees look greener than they are looking now, and even a small wild flower gives you so much joy, so much wonder. The whole world becomes such a mystery. There is no question of being bored.

And for the watcher the world goes on changing so quickly. It is only for the people who are blind – and I call all those people who don't have their watcher awake, blind. That is the only spiritual blindness. That's why you think these are the same trees, these are the same birds, this is the same sun, this is the same ocean. You can't see that existence goes on renewing itself every moment.

I love to quote Heraclitus, who says, "You cannot step in the same river twice." Finally I have improved upon Heraclitus. I say you cannot step in the same river even once because the river is constantly flowing.

But to the blind it seems it is the same river. You are becoming different each moment; otherwise from your childhood, how did you become a young person? If your first photograph, taken the day you became part of your mother's body, is shown to you, you will have to see it with a magnifying glass, and it will be nothing but a full stop. You will not be able to recognize where your nose is, where your ears are, where your eyes are. "Is this me?" But once it was, and since then things have been changing continuously.

Do you remember the date when from a child you suddenly became a young man or a young woman? It doesn't happen suddenly. It goes so gradually that unless you are a watcher you will not be able to see the subtle changes that are happening every moment all around. It is the same world for the blind.

You are asking, "Why am I so afraid that just to be the watcher will be boring?"

You are afraid not because you know that the experience of being a watcher will be boring – because there is not a single exception in the whole history of mankind that any watcher, any meditator has said that the inner experience is boring. That is not the fear because you don't know what the inner explosion from the watcher arising is going to be.

Your fear is that the watcher will not arise unless you drop your passion, your clown, your gypsy adventurer. Your fear is of change. You don't know anything about the watcher. In fact, as far as I can see you must be utterly bored right now because only a bored person becomes a gypsy adventurer. You can see all these tourists running from one place to another...

This is a different class of humanity and a different category: the tourist. They are utterly insane people, loaded with cameras, and always in a hurry. Even if they come to the Taj Mahal, they don't have much time. They immediately take a few photographs and the taxi moves on. They have not seen the Taj Mahal; they were adjusting their cameras. By that time the taxi-driver has started honking that it is time to go, there are many other places to see. And finally they decide, back at home, relaxed, "We will look at the album and we will appreciate the beauty of the Taj Mahal and the Himalayas and Kashmir."

This seems to be such a stupidity. You could have purchased all those photographs in your own town. They are available, and you cannot have better photographs than those that are available because they are taken by great, professional photographers. Your photographs will be just amateurish. Did you go around the world just to collect photographs? What was the fear of remaining with the Taj Mahal for at least for twenty-four hours?

Those who know the Taj Mahal the way I know it remain there exactly fifteen days. When the moon starts rising, the first day of the moon, you have a beautiful Taj Mahal, just a glimpse for a moment and then there is darkness. Then the second day more light, the third day more light... As the light grows, the Taj Mahal also becomes more and more clear, as if a dream is becoming a reality.

And on the full moon night exactly nearabout nine o'clock, the Taj Mahal is the most beautiful. The combination of the full moon and the Taj Mahal has been made not by ordinary architects; it has been made by Sufi mystics. It has been made to create gratitude and prayerfulness in you. It is not a place for tourists. It is a place for seekers.

Seekers are not in a hurry. They will wait, they will look at the Taj Mahal from every side in different lights: in the day, in the night, in the morning. When the sky is full of stars, the Taj Mahal has a different beauty. The beauty goes on changing. That is the grandeur of this Taj Mahal – and this is the grandeur of this whole existence. The Taj Mahal is just a representative.

The adventurer, the gypsy is really a bored person. He is trying to get rid of boredom, so he goes on running from one place to another place, from one woman to another woman. He gets bored quickly with everything, runs after another thing, thinking perhaps he will not be bored there. But he forgets completely that *things* are not boring, *you* are bored. Wherever you are, you will be bored.

If you come to meet God himself, you will take a few photographs – what else to do? – and will start getting fed up. The same God, eternally ancient, how many pictures can you take? You can finish your whole roll of film and then you are stuck with this old dull and dead God. You will start running, even if it is to hell, and you will enter into it. Maybe there is some adventure there. But you will get bored in every place because boredom is your approach and attitude; it is not a quality of things. What is your passion? How long does it take you to get fed up with one passionate relationship? Perhaps one night, or perhaps that is too much.

There is a Sufi story...

A king was very angry because he wanted a beautiful woman, a poor woman in the city, to be his lover. But the most shocking thing was that she was in love with one of his servants. That was too much, too humiliating and insulting. When the king wants her, the girl refuses and she is interested in a poor servant of the same king.

He asked his council of wise men what should be done. The oldest of them suggested both should be brought to the court, stripped naked, tied together embracing each other, and "...let them stand in your garden for twenty-four hours surrounded by guns so they cannot escape."

The king said, "What? Allow them to embrace naked in my garden?

What kind of advice are you giving me?"

The old man said, "I am old enough, and I know how much it takes for one to be bored. Just do it, and in the morning you will see the result."

This young man and young woman had been hankering and dreaming about when they will get married and when they will go for a honeymoon and how beautiful it is going to be. Perhaps there has never been such a beautiful honeymoon ever because nobody has ever loved so much. Every lover thinks that way. Every lover thinks, "I am the first, the foremost lover in the world."

But when they were brought and made naked and told to embrace each other, it looked very awkward, surrounded by a gang of people with loaded guns – and the whole court was watching. But the order had to be followed, so they embraced each other and then they were tied so that they could not separate from each other.

And you can see what happened. In twelve hours they pissed on each other, they had to defecate, and it became such a stinking phenomenon. That was really the greatest honeymoon: it was a hot night in New Delhi, and they were perspiring and stinking and just hoping when the morning comes...

They started hating each other that night – in just twelve hours. Everything became very condensed. In your life it is spread in a thin layer, so it takes a little time, fifteen days. They were experiencing it really totally and intensely. That is passion.

In the morning they were released, and the story is that they ran away from each other, never to see each other again. They had seen enough, more than enough. They never met again in their lives. They both left New Delhi, just for the simple reason not to see that ugly man again, not to see that ugly woman, that bitch, who was pissing on him.

What is your passion? Make it total and intense, and within twenty-four hours you will be finished with it. And then a few more experiences perhaps, it depends on your intelligence. If you are intelligent one affair is enough. If you are an idiot, then you may go on hoping for your whole life that perhaps another affair will be the right one.

The more intelligent a man or a woman is, the sooner comes the realization that all these lusts, passions are sheer stupidity. And if you can understand the reason for your being an adventurer, that deep down it is your bored life that goes on seeking for new avenues – perhaps somewhere, someplace you will not feel bored. You go on running, just simply wasting your life.

And the day your passions are gone, how can you be jealous? Jealousy is a by-product of your passions. And when you are no longer interested in anybody, except the exploration of your own being, judgments will fall away. When you discover your treasure, the hidden splendor within you, your greed will disappear. And when you are feeling so fulfilled, how can you be angry? – because that anger will destroy your contentment and your fulfillment.

But the secret of all this transformation is watching. No meditator in the whole of history has ever felt bored. In fact, the meditators are the only people who destroy boredom completely. They are so thrilled by existence, they are so thrilled just by their consciousness, they are so thrilled by falling in tune with the heartbeat of the universe that it is impossible to be bored. And it is changing every moment: it is every moment a new universe, and it is every moment a new dance, a new song, a new music, which you have never heard before.

Moishe Finkelstein had just entered the parlor of a familiar whorehouse when to his great surprise he saw his father coming down the stairs. Moishe reeled back in surprise. "Dad!" he exclaimed, "what are you doing in a place like this?"

Old man Finkelstein was equally stunned, but recovered quickly. "Now Moishe," he said nonchalantly, brushing off his suit, "for twenty lousy dollars would you want me to bother your dear, hard working mother?"

People go on finding strange excuses, but the real thing is they get bored.

Hymie Goldberg had been having lunch in the same restaurant for twenty years and every day he ordered chicken soup with never a change. But one day Hymie called the waiter back after receiving his soup. "Yes, Mr. Goldberg?" inquired the waiter.

"Waiter," said Hymie, "please taste this soup."

The waiter was shocked: "What do you mean, taste the soup? For twenty years you have been eating the same chicken soup every day. Has it ever been different?"

Hymie ignored the waiter's comments. "Please taste this soup," he repeated.

"Mr. Goldberg," cried the waiter, "what is the matter with you? I know what the chicken soup tastes like."

"Taste the soup!" Hymie demanded.

"Okay, okay," said the waiter. "I will taste it. Where is the spoon?"

"Aha!" cried Hymie.

He is not bored with the soup – the spoon is missing.

First be finished with your passions. It is too early to be a watcher. And as you are finished with your passions and your adventures, you will find your anger and jealousy and greed disappearing. Then will be the right time, the right moment to start the ultimate adventure of being a witness, a meditator, a watcher.

First, play around with the toys you are playing with. In each child's life a moment comes when he throws his toys away and forgets all about them. In each intelligent man or woman's life also comes the time when he is finished with the toys of ordinary life, which are available even to the animals. Then comes an urgent urge to go beyond the animals, to go beyond this so-called human society, to inquire into the very life source – one's consciousness. Then you have entered a mystery that is unending.

You will never be bored. I say this to you with absolute authority because I am not talking about it, I am within it, part of it. I have never felt a single moment of boredom.

But I will not tell you to believe in what I say. I can only tell you to proceed step by step, so that one day you can also experience this immense benediction. It is your birthright.

16

The Miracle of Meditation

Osho,

Why am I always running so fast? Is there something that I don't want to see?

It is not only you; almost everybody is running as fast as he can from himself. And the problem is, you cannot run away from yourself. Wherever you go you will be yourself.

The fear is of knowing oneself. It is the greatest fear in the world. It is because you have been so immensely condemned by everybody for the smallest things, for the smallest mistakes – which are absolutely human – that you have become afraid of yourself. You know that you are not worthy.

That idea has sunk very deep into your unconscious – that you are not deserving, that you are utterly worthless. Naturally, the best way is to get away from yourself. Everybody is doing it in different ways: somebody is running for money, somebody is running for power, somebody is running for respectability, somebody is running for virtue, saintliness.

But if you look deep down, they are not running *for* anything, they are running *from*. That somebody is running after money madly is just an excuse; he is deceiving himself and the whole world.

The reality is that money gives him a good excuse to run, and hides the fact that he is running from himself. That's why when he accumulates money, he comes to a point of tremendous despair and anguish. What has happened? That was his goal; he has achieved it – he should be the happiest man in the world.

But the people who succeed are not the happiest people in the world. They are the most miserable. What is their anguish? Their anguish is that their whole effort has failed. Now there is nothing more to run after, and suddenly they are encountering themselves. At the highest peak of their success they meet nobody else but themselves. Strangely enough, this is the fellow they have been running from.

You cannot run from yourself. On the contrary, you have to come closer to yourself, deeper into your being, and to drop all the condemnatory tones that have been handed over to you by everybody you have known in your life. The parents, the husband, the wife, the neighbors, the teachers, the friends, the enemies – everybody is pointing to something that is wrong in you. From no source comes any appreciation.

Humanity has created a very strange situation for itself in which nobody is at ease, nobody can relax because the moment you relax you face yourself. Relaxation becomes almost a mirror, and you don't want to see your face because you are so much impressed by the condemnatory opinions of others.

You have not been allowed even the smallest pleasures by your church, by your priests, by your religion, by your culture. Only misery is acceptable, not pleasure. In this situation when from every source, from every direction comes only condemnation, it is very natural for you to feel that you are a sinner. Every religion has been shouting for centuries that you are born in sin, that suffering is your destiny – from so many sources without exception – that it is very natural for any individual to be impressed by this vast conspiracy. Everybody is caught in it.

And if you try to understand it you will be very much surprised. Just as others have condemned you, you are condemning others. It is a very mutual conspiracy. Just as your parents have never accepted you as being of any worth, you are doing the same with your children – without ever becoming aware that everybody is what he is, he cannot be otherwise. He can pretend to be otherwise, he can be a hypocrite, but in truth he will always remain himself.

Your running away is nothing but creating more hypocrisy, more masks so that you can hide yourself completely from the eyes of everyone. You may succeed in hiding yourself from others, but how can you succeed in hiding yourself from yourself? You can go to the moon; you will find yourself there. You can go to Everest; you may be alone but you are with yourself. Perhaps in that aloneness on Everest you will become more alert and aware of yourself.

That is one of the reasons why people are also afraid of aloneness; they want a crowd, they want always to have people surrounding them, they want friends. It is very difficult for people to remain silent and peaceful in aloneness. The reason is that in aloneness you are left with yourself – and you have accepted the stupid ideas that you are ugly, that you are sensuous, that you are lustful, that you are greedy, that you are violent, that there is nothing that can be appreciated in you.

Prem Amita, you are asking, "Why am I always running so fast?" Because you are afraid you may be overtaken by yourself. And the implications of running so fast have many dimensions. This running fast from yourself has created a craziness about speed. Everybody wants to reach somewhere with as much speed as possible.

It happened once...

I was coming from a place called Nagpur, back to Jabalpur. I was traveling with the vice-chancellor of Nagpur University, and the car broke down on the road. I have never seen anybody become so miserable.

I told him, "There is no hurry. Nobody is waiting for you there, and the conference which you are going to is going to begin in twenty-four hours. And Jabalpur is only three hours away. There is no problem. Either we will get the car repaired, or we will call for another car to come from Jabalpur, or we may get a lift, or buses are continually passing by. There is no problem. You need not be so miserable."

He sat in the car and I went looking for somebody. It was a small village, but maybe some mechanic or some help was possible. Perhaps the landlord of the village had a car. When I came back from the village, that man was almost in tears. I said, "What is the matter?"

He said, "I cannot afford to be alone. It exposes me so deeply, it makes me utterly naked before myself. It makes me aware that I have wasted my whole life – and I don't want to know it."

I said, "Your not knowing it is not going to help you in any way. It is better to know it, and it is better to go deeper into yourself. Why this misery and aloneness?"

Aloneness should be one of the greatest joys.

People are running. It does not matter where they are going; what matters is whether they are going at full speed or not.

You are asking, "Is there something that I don't want to see?" There are many things. Fundamentally, it is *you* that you don't want to see – and it is because of a wrong conditioning.

My whole approach of inner transformation is that you will have to drop your conditionings. Whatever has been said about you by others – simply drop it. It is absolutely crap. They don't know about themselves; what can they say about you that can be truthful?

And the opinions that you have collected from others – just try to watch from whom you are collecting your opinions. They are not from a Gautam Buddha, or from a Jesus, or from a Socrates. They are from people who are as ignorant as you are. They are simply passing on others' opinions that have been given to them.

There is a beautiful story. Whether it is factual or not does not matter; its beauty is in its meaning. One of the greatest emperors India has known was the Mogul emperor, Akbar. He can be compared only to one man in the West, and that is Marcus Aurelius. Emperors are very rarely wise people, but these two names are certainly exceptions.

One day he was in his court talking with his courtiers. He had collected the best people in the country – the best painter, the best musician, the best philosopher, the best poet. He had a small, special committee of nine members who were known as "the nine jewels of Akbar's court."

The most important of them was a man called Birbal. Immensely intelligent and a man with a great sense of humor, he did something which was improper to do in front of the emperor. Every emperor has his own rules, his word is the law, and Birbal's behavior was against something about which Akbar was very stubborn. Akbar immediately slapped Birbal. He respected Birbal, he loved Birbal, he was his most intimate friend, but as far as the rules of the court were concerned, he could not forgive him.

But what Birbal did is the real story. He did not wait for a single moment; he immediately slapped the man who was standing on his other side. The other man was shocked, and even Akbar was shocked. He had thought that this man was very wise. "Is he mad, or what? I have slapped him. This is strange; absolutely absurd and illogical."

And the other man was standing there, shocked, and Birbal said, "Don't stand there like a fool! Just pass it on." So that man slapped somebody else who was standing by his side – and now the game became clear: you have to pass it on.

In the night, when Akbar went to sleep with his wife, his wife slapped him. He said, "What is the matter?"

She said, "It has been going on around the city, and finally it has reached to its original source. Somebody else slapped me, and when I asked, 'What is the matter?' I was told that this is the game that Akbar started. I thought it is better to finish it, to complete the circle."

And the next day, the first thing, Birbal asked was, "Have you received my slap back or not?"

Akbar said, "I had never thought that this would happen!"

Birbal said, "I was absolutely certain because where will it finally go? It will go around the city. You cannot escape; it is bound to come to you."

Everything goes on being transferred for centuries; being passed on from one hand to another, from one generation to another generation – and the game continues. This is the game that you have to come out of. The only way to come out of it is to rediscover your self-respect, to again attain your dignity – which you had when you were a child, when you were still not contaminated, when you were still not conditioned and poisoned by the society and by the people around you.

Be a child again and you will not be running away from yourself, you will be running within yourself. That is the way of the meditator. The worldly man runs away from himself, and the seeker runs within himself, to find the source of this life, this consciousness. And when he discovers the source, he has discovered not only his life source, he has discovered the life source of the universe, of the whole cosmos.

A tremendous celebration arises in him. Life becomes moment to moment just a song, a dance. One becomes absolutely free from all the jargon that the society has handed down. One simply throws away all conditionings, all traditions – the whole past.

I say unto you, only one thing you have to renounce, and that is the past and nothing else.

If you can renounce the past you will be absolutely fresh, just born. And to be in that freshness is such a blessing, such an ecstasy, you cannot even think of going away even for a single moment. The man who knows himself never takes any holiday. But most people go on behaving stupidly.

An American was driving along a small country lane in Ireland when he was horrified to see a cartload of hay coming out of the field into the narrow road. He jumped on the brakes but couldn't stop in time, and ended up driving through the fence into the field where the car burst into flames.

"Bejabers!" exclaimed Paddy to his friend Seamus, who was driving the hay cart, "Some of these tourists are terrible drivers. We only just got out of that field in time."

The old farmer, plowing his fields with a pair of bulls, was asked by a neighbor why he did not use oxen.

"I don't want to use oxen," replied the farmer, "I want to use bulls."

"Well," continued the neighbor, "If you don't want to use oxen, why don't you use horses?"

"I don't want to use horses!" retorted the farmer, "I want to use bulls!"

"Well, perhaps," tried the neighbor, "you could try using that new tractor your son has just bought."

"I don't want to use tractors, either, I want to use bulls." reaffirmed the farmer.

"Why do you only want to use bulls?" asked the neighbor at a loss.

"Because," said the old boy, "I don't want them to think that life is all romance."

This is simply the situation in which you are born, in which you have been conditioned. Nobody wants you to know that life is simply romance. And that is my crime because that is my whole teaching, that life is nothing but romance.

The newlywed couple flew to Miami and checked into the honeymoon hotel. For days nothing was seen of them, until the morning of the sixth day, when they came to the dining room for breakfast. As the waiter approached their table, the bride turned to her husband and said, "Honey, do you know what I would like?"

"Yes, I know," he replied wearily, "but we have to eat sometime."

So once in a while it is good to have breakfast; otherwise life is a continuous romance. And I teach you not only the romance of the body, which is very ordinary. I teach you the romance of the spirit, which is eternal, which begins but never ends. But this is possible only if you start going inwards.

Going inwards is going godwards. Going inwards is the whole secret of all alchemical transformation of being.

Running away is simply wasting tremendously valuable time, and a life that could have been a great song, a great creativity, a tremendous festival of lights. The farther away you are from yourself, the darker your life will become, the more miserable, the more anxiety ridden, the more wounded, condemned, rejected by yourself.

And the farther away you are, the more difficult it becomes to find the way back home. You have been going away from yourself for many, many lives. But if you move in a right, meditative path you have not gone very far away.

Meditation is the short cut from where you are to where you should be. And meditation is such a simple method that anybody, even a small child, can enter into its wonderland.

Rather than running away, run withinwards. Come closer to yourself to have a better look – because nobody else can see your inner reality, only you can see that splendor and that glory. And because nobody else can see your inner beauty, they go on condemning you. Only you can assert your blissfulness, only you can ultimately assert your enlightenment.

Even then people will be suspicious. They were suspicious about Socrates, they were suspicious about Gautam Buddha, they were suspicious about Jesus. In fact, their suspicion is rooted in their own unawareness of their inner being.

How can they believe Gautam Buddha: that in the inner silences of the heart is the ultimate ecstasy? They don't know anything of the inner, not even the *ABC*. They don't know anything about ecstasy. They may listen to a Gautam Buddha – just because of his presence, his charismatic eyes, his magnetic vibration – but when they go home, they will start suspecting, doubting.

And this is happening even here. I receive many letters saying that, "When we listen to you everything seems to be absolutely right. As we reach home doubts start arising; the mind starts saying that we have been hypnotized." There are millions of people who want to come close to me but are afraid – for the simple reason that they may be hypnotized.

It is something far deeper than hypnosis. You are not hypnotized, you are simply taken into a different vision of your own self. It is not something like magic; you are not being befooled. You are being awakened.

The word *hypnosis* means sleep, and my whole work is to awaken you.

You are already asleep and you have been asleep for lives together. It is time to wake up.

You have wasted too much valuable time, energy, opportunity already. But still there is time – and the moment you wake up, for you the night ends and the dawn begins.

> Osho,
> I am becoming more and more conscious of the barriers I have built up in myself over the years against being a joyful self-loving open being. It feels like the wall in me is getting stronger and stronger the more I am aware of it, and I can't come through. Do I first need more courage? Could you please help me with your understanding?

It is the same question again. I have been answering Amita, but I have also answered you – although you have phrased your question in a different way. A few small details are different; otherwise it is the same problem. I will discuss those small differences in detail.

You say, "I am becoming more and more conscious of the barriers that have built up in myself over the years against being a joyful, self-loving, open being. It feels like the wall in me is getting stronger and stronger the more I am aware of it, and I can't come through."

The first thing to understand is that the wall is not becoming stronger; it is only that your awareness is becoming clear. There is no reason at all why the wall should become stronger when you are becoming more aware. It is simply when you bring the light into your dark house, you start seeing the cobwebs and the spiders. Not that they have suddenly started growing because you have brought the light in; they have always been there. It is just that you are becoming aware, alert.

But don't think that they are growing. Your light has nothing to do with their growth. Yes, it reveals their presence. Your growing awareness is revealing the presence of your prison walls.

And you say, "I am aware of it and I can't come through." Because these walls are not true walls, they cannot prevent you. They are not made of bricks or stone; they are only made of thoughts. You just have to know the secret of how to come through them. If you start struggling with your thought processes, which constitute the prison walls, then you will get into a tremendous mess. One can even go insane.

That's how people go insane: they are surrounded by so many thoughts and they are trying hard to come out of the crowd and they go on getting deeper and deeper into the crowd. And then naturally a breakdown follows. Their nervous system cannot sustain so much pressure and so much tension. They have opened Pandora's box. It was all hidden there, but they were blissfully unaware of it. Now they have brought a meditative awareness and suddenly they see a great crowd, so thick that the more they try, the more they feel their impotence against the walls that are surrounding them.

If you start fighting with them then there is no way. Sooner or later – tired, tattered – you will find yourself slipping from your sanity. But if you use a right method, instead of a breakdown you will have a breakthrough. The right method to deal with all that you feel you are surrounded with is to be just a witness: not to fight, not to judge, not to condemn. Just remain silent and still, purely witnessing whatever is there.

This is almost a miracle. I have not come across any miracle other than the miracle of meditation, the miracle of witnessing. Because if you can witness, you will be surprised that the strong wall is becoming thinner, the crowd is dispersing. Slowly, slowly you see doors and gaps through which you can get out.

But there is no need to get out. Remain where you are. Just go on witnessing. As your witnessing becomes stronger, the wall that surrounds you will become weaker. The day your witnessing is perfect, you will find there has been no wall, nothing is surrounding you, the whole sky is available to you.

Rather than fighting with thoughts, fighting against wrong conditionings, just become a pure witness. Fighting, you cannot win. Without fighting victory is yours. Victory belongs only to those who can witness.

Hymie Goldberg was having trouble getting Becky, his wife, to make love to him anymore. So one night just before bedtime, he offered her a glass of water and two aspirins.

"What are you giving me these for?" Becky asked. "I have not got a headache."

"Great," said Hymie. "Let us get started."

This headache was the problem. Every day, whenever poor Goldberg would ask, the wife had a great headache. This time he worked through a different methodology. Becky could not understand that now he is using a very wise strategy – offering aspirins even before she has said she has a headache.

So just be a little wise...

Doctor Klein finished the examination of his patient and then said, "You are in perfect health, Mr. Levinsky, your heart, lungs, blood pressure, cholesterol level – everything is fine."

"Splendid," said Mr. Levinsky.

"I will see you next year," said Doctor Klein.

They shook hands, but as soon as the patient had left the room, Doctor Klein heard a loud crash. He opened the door and there, flat on his face, lay Mr. Levinsky. The nurse cried, "Doctor, he just collapsed. He fell down like a rock."

The doctor felt his heart and said, "My God, he is dead." He then put his hands under the corpse's arms.

"Quick," said the doctor, "take his feet!"

"What?" cried the nurse.

"For God's sake," said the doctor, "let us turn him round. We have to make it look like he was coming in!"

Just be a little intelligent.

It is said that intelligence is not of much use unless you are intelligent enough to know how to use it.

Just the other day I came across a tremendously great discovery. It says that every idiot you meet in the world is the end product of millions of years of evolution.

Intelligence is certainly rare but the people who have gathered around me, just the fact that they had the courage to be here is enough proof of their intelligence. Now you have to put your intelligence into action.

"My God," sighed Paddy, "I had everything a man could want – the love of a gorgeous woman, a beautiful house, plenty of money, fine clothes."

"What happened?" asked Seamus.

"What happened? Out of the blue without any hint of warning, my wife walked in."

Just be alert. There are dangers on every step. A man who decides to be a meditator has to be very cautious.

Lao Tzu's statement is that a man of meditation always walks as if he is passing through an ice-cold stream in winter, very careful, very alert.

Unless you are very careful and very alert, the millions-of-years-old mind and its functioning is going to be difficult to transcend. Although the strategy is simple, sometimes the simple seems to be the most difficult– and particularly when you are absolutely unacquainted with it.

Meditation is only a word to you. It has not become a taste, it has not been a nourishment, it has not been an experience for you; hence I can understand your difficulty. But you also have to understand my difficulty. Your diseases may be many, but I have only one medicine – and my difficulty is to go on selling the same medicine for different patients, different diseases.

I don't care what your disease is because I know I have got only one medicine. Whatever your disease is I will discuss it, but finally you have to accept the same medicine. It never changes. As far as I know, in these thirty-five years it has never changed.

I have seen millions of people, millions of different questions, and even before I hear their question I know the answer. Because it does not matter what their question is, what matters is how to manage to bring their question to my answer.

The math teacher turned to little Ernie and said, "Ernest, if your father borrowed three hundred dollars and promised to pay back fifteen dollars a week, how much would he owe at the end of ten weeks?"

"Three hundred dollars," Ernie quickly replied.

"I am afraid," said the teacher, "that you don't know your math very well."

"I am afraid," said Ernie, "that you don't know my father."

17

Yes Is Your Soul

Osho,
I've had a glimpse of what it could be to just be, but so much fear comes up about doing nothing. I have this sense that I am stuck. What is this fear?

Deva Tarshita, the first glimpse of one's own being is inevitably unbelievable. First, because you have never known it before so you cannot recognize what it is. It is so much vaster than what you have been thinking of as yourself. It is just like a dewdrop coming in contact with the ocean.

The fear is necessary. The dewdrop cannot think in other ways except that slipping into the ocean is death, although it is not true. But we have to be compassionate toward the dewdrop too. It is beyond its comprehension. The ocean is so vast; it is almost a necessity to think, "I will disappear and be lost" – and naturally one becomes tremendously afraid.

Only one thing can be done, and that is to have courage and take a jump. That's the fundamental function of the master, to tell you, "I was also a dewdrop one day. I was also afraid when I came closer to the ocean. I was also in deep trembling as much as you are, but there was no way of going back. I have known being a dewdrop for millions of lives and it has been nothing but misery and darkness and anxiety. Why not take a chance and see?"

It is risky; one never knows what is going to happen when the dewdrop simply disappears in the ocean. But I can say to you that the dewdrop does not disappear in the ocean. On the contrary, the ocean disappears in the dewdrop. The dewdrop becomes the whole ocean. It is not death, so that you have to be afraid. It is eternal life, for which you have been searching.

I have given you the name Tarshita. Tarshita means "one who is thirsty." Now that you have come so close to the glimpse of what it means just to be, don't turn back. Turning back is only for the cowards. This is the most precious moment. Allow it to happen.

The whole of history is a witness that those who have allowed themselves to disappear into the vastness of existence have not really disappeared. On the contrary, for the first time they have found themselves so huge: without any limits, without any boundaries, without any bondages. This is freedom: to be oceanic. To be a dewdrop is to be imprisoned in a small boundary.

Your self is only a dewdrop. The ocean is a no-self.

Gautam Buddha has the right word for it. The language he used was the people's language of those days, Pali. In Pali "the self" has much more meaning than in the English language. The Pali word for self is *atta*. The very word is not synonymous only with self, but also contains ego, arrogance. And the word for when the *atta* disappears into the oceanic existence is *anatta*. The ego is lost, the arrogance is lost, the anxiety is lost; death disappears, and for the first time you are really and totally alive in a cosmic sense. For the first time you have touched the eternal.

This fear grips everybody. When the river comes traveling thousands of miles from the mountains and the valleys and the plains to the ocean, for a moment it trembles. Those who can understand even the language of mountains and trees, those who are so sensitive they can feel... There are many references from enlightened people that when the river comes to the ocean, for a moment it trembles.

Great anxiety grips it. A moment of decision, a decision of tremendous importance – to go back?

But there is no way to go back. You cannot travel backward in time. You have only one possibility: to go ahead. If the river cannot go back, at least it certainly looks back to all those beautiful mountains it descended, to all those beautiful primeval forests it passed, to all those beautiful people. All the memories – just a moment of looking back. But it cannot stay long; it has to take a plunge into the ocean, knowing perfectly well that "this is going to be my death."

But it is not a death. The river itself becomes the ocean. It is the expansion of your consciousness, of your being. You are becoming synonymous with the universe.

You have to put aside your fear. If you don't put aside your fear and you cling to it, there is danger because once you start clinging to your tiny self there is no way to persuade you to take the jump.

That's why I said, this is one of the fundamental functions of the master – to persuade you and show you that I have jumped and I am more alive than I have ever been. I have not lost anything; I have conquered the whole existence. Hence, the master can say to you, "Come, follow me."

There are complications in things. Unless you have a deep love for the master and an absolute trust, he will not be of any help in this moment of fear. Your trust and your love give nothing to the master, remember. They simply give you the opportunity to be courageous.

Just the other day a sannyasin asked me a question: "If I can say only yes and not no, then what kind of freedom is this?" You can say no, but remember that this freedom of saying no is the freedom of the tiny dewdrop that is saying no to the ocean.

Before you became a sannyasin the freedom was yours: you could have said no, you could have said yes. Once you have said yes, then your yes has to be total. There has not to be any space for no. Otherwise, when you need the yes, the more the no will arise in you. It will support your fear, it will support your ego, it will support your self.

I have no objection because I am not going to lose anything. You can say no as loudly as you want. But remember, you have come here for a transformation, and only after the transformation will you know the real taste of freedom. What freedom can you have by just saying no or yes? Your yes is as stupid as your no. You are stupid!

And when you say such things and you ask questions like this, I am amazed. Why did you become a sannyasin in the first place? – because sannyas is a commitment, it is a dedication, it is a declaration of your love, your trust. It is a declaration to the skies that: "Now I am dropping the no from my being. It has tortured me enough. It has been a disease. I am entering into the world of yes, into life-affirmation."

And the yes to the master is not only to the master, because the master is only a window to the universe. You are saying yes to the universe. Only in that yes will you expand and know tremendous freedom. Your yes and no are just stupid games of the mind.

But if you are still feeling to enjoy the no you can enjoy, but then sannyas is not for you – perhaps a few lives more. And if you can meet somebody like me again, which is not necessarily...

The day Gautam Buddha died, Ananda burst into tears. Gautam Buddha said, "Ananda, you have been with me for forty-two years. It is more than enough. Whatever I had to give to you, I have given. You don't need me. Why are you crying?"

Ananda said, "I am crying because even while you were alive and I was with you, day in, day out twenty-four hours a day for forty-two years..." He even used to sleep in the night in the same room where Buddha was sleeping – who knows what he may need in the night? He served him almost like a shadow and followed him almost like a shadow.

He said to Buddha, "I am crying because I have not become enlightened yet, and you are leaving the body. I cannot conceive that again, in the future, there will be this immense opportunity; that I may again be so close and so intimate with a man like you. What will happen to me?"

Buddha said, "Don't be worried. Your 'yes' was mixed with 'no.'"

And there was a reason for it. Ananda was an elder cousin-brother of Gautam Buddha. So just the ego saying, "I am the elder brother of Gautam the Buddha..." And when he took sannyas he told Gautam Buddha, "Listen. Once I have become a sannyasin I don't have any right to go against your will. Your will, will be my will. But I am still not initiated, so before initiation I am still your elder brother and you have to listen to me. I have three conditions. Promise me that you will never go against those conditions."

Buddha said laughingly, "What are those conditions?"

The conditions were not great – but a condition is a condition whether it is great or small. The condition carries an undercurrent of "no." He is making it clear from the very beginning that Buddha cannot touch these three things. One was, "You cannot send me away from you. I will always remain with you. You cannot find any excuse like, 'Go and propagate the word.' That is not possible. I will remain with you. Wherever you go, I will go.

"The second condition is that I will even sleep in your room. And the third condition is that even in the middle of the night, if I want to ask a question or one of my friends wants to ask a question, I will bring the friend in and you will have to answer. You cannot say, 'I am tired. The whole day's journey on foot and then the whole day hundreds of people coming to meet me... and their questions. At least in the middle of the night, don't disturb me.' You cannot say that."

Buddha said, "You are my elder brother and I cannot deny you. So I promise, all these three things will always be fulfilled."

Then Ananda took initiation.

The last day, after forty-two years, Buddha said, "Those three conditions have been the barrier. Many came after you and became enlightened, and you had the first opportunity. But when a dewdrop starts making conditions on the ocean it is creating barriers. Although you have been thinking that you had made those conditions when you were not a sannyasin, the consciousness and its current are the same. You may not be aware, but I have been aware that deep down in you, you still carry that ego that says, 'I am the elder brother; I have a particularly special place.' Nobody else has made any conditions."

Initiations cannot be conditional. You are a sannyasin; you should have thought before that you are going on the path of yes. And this path of yes will end up in freedom. If you think you also need the no, then the whole world is free – everybody has the no, the yes, everybody has his mind.

The effort on the path of sannyas is to drop your mind, and your mind can be dropped only if your no is dropped.

Let me say it in other words: "no" is mind and "yes" is your soul.

You can choose and still there is no problem. But remaining a sannyasin you cannot continue to have the no. Freedom will come, but it will come from the door of yes – and that will be real freedom.

But many sannyasins go on writing me strange questions that surprise me. Just the other day in the newspapers, one sannyasin has given an interview. In the interview he was asked, "When Osho was in the jails of America, were you disturbed?"

He said, "One day Osho is going to leave the body. He cannot be eternally in the body, so we have to accept it. It was a good opportunity to accept his absence."

On the surface the answer looks perfectly right. It is true: I am not going to be in the body forever. But are you going to live in the body forever? The sannyasin has completely forgotten that. There is every possibility you may pop off before me. You are becoming accustomed to my absence, and sannyas is becoming accustomed to my presence. Underlying it, the invisible writing is that you are saying, "No. I am enough unto myself."

But I would like to remind you that even if I leave the body, I am not going to leave you. I will haunt you in your dreams, I will harass you as much as I can. And remember, when I am in the body the harassment is not so much. When I am without the body, I will simply touch you and you will freak out!

So pray that the longer I live in the body, the better for you. And if you become so accustomed to my presence, so deeply accustomed… My life source is eternal, just as your life source is. Body or no body, I will be here. I have been here always.

Those who are open to me, and that opening means those who will still be ready to say yes to me, will be able to be blessed far more in the silence of my bodiless presence than they are benefited while I am in the body. But to say that it was a good opportunity for you to become accustomed to my absence means that somewhere deep down the no is floating.

The relationship between the master and the disciple is not an ordinary relationship. There is no other relationship that can be compared to it. Even love falls far below. Even in love you remain two: struggling, fighting, trying to dominate each other. Only in the relationship between master and disciple you are no longer two. There is no fight, no struggle.

The master is already an absolute yes. Slowly, slowly you also become an absolute yes. Only then is the meeting, the merger, the dewdrop slipping into the ocean.

Tarshita, if you are too much afraid, stuck, there is every possibility you will always remain thirsty because when you come close to the water you become afraid.

The water is not going to come to you.

An old farmer went to the circus for the first time. Before he went into the big tent he saw a camel in a cage and stopped in amazement to look at it. He had never seen such wobbly legs, such dozy eyes, such floppy lips and such a huge hump for a back.

Soon everyone was inside the tent and the circus began, but the old man was still staring in disbelief at the camel. Finally, after about half an hour, he turned away in disgust, "Darn it!" he cried, "there ain't no such animal."

He tried hard to figure out how such an animal is possible. Now the only way is to deny it, to get unburdened – otherwise that camel will trouble him.

If you become afraid of the ocean, of the very isness of life, the only way to be away from it is to say, "It was just a hallucination, an illusion, a dream. It was not a reality." You can protect your small ego, but that is the cause of all your troubles.

You have to be very watchful about your ego because the language of the ego is "no" and the language of your being is "yes". The language of the ego is doubt and the language of the being is trust. And only from trust can you grow into *satyam shivam sundaram* – into the ultimate truth, into the ultimate godliness, into ultimate beauty.

Your no will make you more and more small and ugly. Have you ever watched? Whenever you say no, something in you shrinks and whenever you say yes, something in you expands. Whenever you say yes, you are in tune with the universe, and whenever you say no, you declare your ego as separate from life, from existence.

It is up to you. In love you will find yourself filled with yes; in hate you will find yourself filled with no. In blissfulness there is no space for no; in misery there is nothing else but no.

So it is not as simple as you think. These simple words *yes* and *no* belong to two different planes of life: *no* to the lowest and *yes* to the highest.

Osho,
Suddenly, sitting with you again, I tingle inside. Your beat inside the tablas – a magic moment. Is that the quality of non-doing?

The question you have asked is immensely significant. You say, "Suddenly, sitting with you again, I tingle inside. Your beat inside the tablas – a magic moment. Is that the quality of non-doing?" Yes, but only a beginning. There is much more to non-doing, but it is a good beginning, a small taste, just a small glimpse. But if you can go on growing in that direction, it has shown you the way.

When you are just sitting silently, then even the noises of the birds and the silent trees and a faraway cuckoo – they are no longer separate from you. You suddenly expand; you are not just hearing them, you become them.

And it will be particularly helpful for others too that you have used the word *again*. "Suddenly, sitting with you again..."

Mind's tendency is to take things for granted; then it falls asleep. There has been a gap, and you have come after that gap, after waiting long. You cannot take me for granted. That is giving you a deep communion. You can keep this communion alive every day; you can make it deeper. Your arrow is pointing in the right direction.

You say, "I tingle inside. Your beat inside the tablas – a magic moment." It all depends on you. You can turn every moment of your life into a magic moment. I am only just helping you to have a few glimpses and to learn the knack of how to transform your life into a constant flow of magical moments – each moment bringing more and more wonder, each moment opening new mysteries.

Yes, this is the first experience of non-doing. You are not doing anything, you are just being here. The highest peaks of consciousness are when you are just a being – not doing anything, unmoving, utterly silent, as if you are no more. And suddenly the whole existence starts showering flowers on you.

Man is trained for doing because society needs him as laborers in different directions, for production, for the greedy, for the cunning, for the powerful. He has to be turned into a slave whose whole life is nothing but doing from morning till night. He is not even rejuvenated by sleep and again he has to go to work on the roads, to work in the fields, to work in the orchards.

Out of this vested interest, society has made doing very prominent and respectable. It has completely forgotten that there is another dimension to life. I am not saying you should not do anything. You have to eat, you have to clothe yourself, you need a shelter; so some kind of doing will be needed. But doing should be only utilitarian; it will not give you the great experiences for which life is an opportunity. Your doing will give you survival.

But just to survive is not to be alive. To be alive means to have a dance in the heart. To be alive means to have each fiber of your being full of the celestial music. To be alive means to experience the eternal flow of life force within your veins. That is possible not by doing; that is possible only by non-doing. So non-doing is the ultimate value. Doing is just mundane: out of necessity you have to do something.

But there is enough time – twenty-four hours. You can devote five or six hours to ordinary necessities and still there are eighteen hours left. If you can find even two hours for non-doing, you will be enriched so much that you cannot conceive beforehand because when you are not doing anything, you are not.

Then what is? This whole silence of existence, this whole beauty of all the flowers, this infinitude of the sky surrounding you – all become part of you. And the touch of the eternal and the infinite and the deathless brings so much joy that even when you are doing, slowly, slowly you will find that even in your doing those joys, those ecstasies are entering into your work.

Then the work is no longer work. Doing is no longer doing. It becomes your creativity. Whatever you do now, you do with your totality. And the whole of existence supports you, goes on filling you with more juice so you can pour that juice into your actions, into your doings. Suddenly you yourself become a magician. Whatever you touch becomes gold. Wherever you move, existence goes on welcoming you, and whatever you do, howsoever small, becomes part of your meditation.

I don't want you to follow the old pattern, which was basically faulty: to meditate for one hour and then for twenty-three hours destroy whatever you have meditated. There are even Sunday religions like Christianity: just one day, for one hour, go to the church for a good morning's sleep – that's enough! Then for six days you can do everything that goes against all divine values, but there is no fear because one day you can again sleep in the church and you will feel very refreshed, all sin gone. Then you are again ready to sin and commit all kinds of crimes and ugly things – anger and hatred and rage – because the church is there and on Sunday everything will be settled again.

In Catholic Christianity they have developed really very sophisticated cunningness. They call it confession. You have to go to confess to the priest; he gives you a punishment and he prays for you and persuades God that you should be forgiven. Then you are free again for one week to do whatsoever you want because you have a means to get out of all stupidities.

It happened once...

A bishop and a rabbi were very good friends, and they decided to go to the golf course. But strangely enough, on that day there were so many confessors that they were standing in a queue. The bishop was finishing them quickly, but still the line was long.

Finally the rabbi came into the cabin where the bishop had only a small window to hear the confession from the other side. The bishop said, "I am sorry but the line is too long."

The rabbi said, "Don't be worried. Just get ready; I will finish the line."

He had seen the bishop; just when he came in a man was saying, "I have raped a woman." The bishop had said, "Ten dollars in the donation box." Finished. The rape is finished with ten dollars. It seems the rate for rape is ten dollars.

The bishop went away and the rabbi took a seat. Another man came and said, "Forgive me, Father, I have committed three rapes."

The rabbi said, "My son, don't be worried – forty dollars in the donation box."

The man said, "It seems the rate has increased. I have committed rapes before, too, but it was always ten dollars. For three it comes to thirty. What do you mean by forty?"

The rabbi said, "Don't be worried, those ten are an advance. You can commit one more."

Rabbis understand business far better than anybody else. The man was also happy: "This is new. We have never heard of paying in advance for our sins, so we need not come to bother you again." These are strategies, these are not religious. This is psychological exploitation.

The only religion is the religion that teaches you non-doing.

Only when you start coming in communion with the universe, a tremendous change happens in you. Even your doing starts becoming just an expression of your non-doing. The day your doing also becomes an expression of non-doing, you have come back home. You have touched the ultimate beauty and the blessing of existence.

It is good, but don't get stuck. It is only a beginning. On the path, it is always a beginning. Yes, the end also comes, but even the beginnings are so beautiful that you have to be reminded of two things: don't lose the track, and secondly, don't feel that you have arrived.

The day you arrive there will not be any need for anyone to say anything, not even for you to say anything. The arrival is so tremendous that it brings its own self-evident certainty.

The distance between the beginning and the end is not something fixed; it is relative. One can move from the beginning to the end in a single moment. It is only a question of totality and intensity. Someone can go on moving for years if he is partial, just partly involved. If spiritual evolution is not the only focus of all his energies, then there is a danger he may get stuck somewhere because he has so many things to do.

Spirituality needs a certain kind of concentrated effort. It demands your total being. You cannot hold anything back. The more you hold back, the longer the journey becomes. I would like your journey to be as short as possible.

Humanity has almost forgotten what it means to feel the heartbeat of the universe, what it means to be filled with an absolute silence which is not the silence of the graveyards, which is the silence that music creates, which is the silence that is created by the wind passing through the pine trees.

Judge Jeffreys leaned forward and said, "Are you trying to tell this court that the defendant actually strangled his wife in a disco, in front of three hundred people?"

"Yes, sir."

"But didn't anyone try to stop him?" Judge Jeffreys asked in amazement.

"No, sir. Everyone thought they were dancing."

We have even forgotten what dancing is. The woman is being killed and three hundred idiots think they are dancing. Our so-called modern musicians and dancers are all cuckoos, but they have tremendous influence on other cuckoos. From the Beatles to the skinheads: all these people need psychiatric treatment, but instead of psychiatric treatment they became heroes.

You just have to be a cuckoo who is a little articulate and then all cuckoos immediately start rushing toward you.

Old Sammy Moskowitz was walking home late one night when he was stopped by a man with a gun who hissed, "Your money or your life." There was a long silence while old Sammy just stood there. The robber became restless, looking around in case anyone was coming. He waited a bit longer and then hissed again: "Come on, your money or your life."

"Okay, okay." old Sammy replied. "Just a minute, I'm thinking, I'm thinking."

We have made mundane things so important that even life has lost all its value. We have made ourselves laughingstocks – but we are all in the same boat, and nobody reminds us. A man who does not know the silences of the heart, a man who does not know a merger and melting with the universe, a man who has never felt what William James used to call oceanic experience – such a man has never been born. He was a miscarriage. He lived, he breathed, he walked around, but he was just a somnambulist – and he died, too.

It is a strange fact that people who have never lived, die. Life needs immense centering and deep meditativeness. Only very few people in the trillions of people who have been around this planet have really lived.

One day it happened, Gautam Buddha was visited by one of the emperors of those days, Prasenjita. Naturally, nobody interfered because the emperor was talking to Gautam Buddha, although everybody wanted to be close to hear what was transpiring. But one man, a *bhikkhu*, a sannyasin, had to interrupt. He asked forgiveness from both because he had to leave before sunset to spread Gautam Buddha's message to the people. But he could not leave without touching the feet of Gautam Buddha.

He was to be gone for many months, and the sun was just going to set, so he said to Prasenjita, "Forgive me, I don't want to interrupt you. Just a single moment, I want to touch the feet and I will be gone. I have to leave, but I can leave only before sunset."

He touched the feet, he was an old man nearabout seventy-five, and Gautam Buddha asked him, "Bhante" – that was Gautam Buddha's word of deep respect for sannyasins – "Bhante, how old are you?"

The old man said, "I feel ashamed to say it, but I am only four years old."

Prasenjita could not believe it. A seventy-five-year-old man? It is absolutely impossible that he is only four years old. And when Gautam Buddha accepted it, it was even more amazing.

He said to Gautam Buddha, "This man does not look four-years old."

Buddha said, "Perhaps you are not aware. The way we count life, unless one enters into deep meditation and realizes the light that radiates from his center, he is not thought to have been born. This man experienced his first glimpse of himself four years ago. Those seventy-one years that passed before were of deep sleep. They cannot be counted as his age."

Prasenjita was very much puzzled – but it was true. And he touched Gautam Buddha's feet and said, "Help me also to be born again. Up to now I was thinking I am alive. You have made me dead."

Gautam Buddha said, "Just the realization that up to now you have been dead is a great beginning."

Now, I have been teaching continuously for meditation, and you have been listening to me for years. It is time to start it. Only listening only won't help. And that will be your first birthday – when you realize who you are.

It happened only in Gautam Buddha's commune that life was counted from the day you touched your innermost core. Otherwise only corpses are walking, moving around, doing all kinds of nasty things, creating wars, nuclear weapons, destroying beautiful cities like Hiroshima and Nagasaki. These are the works of the dead people.

The whole history that you are being taught in the colleges, in the universities, is not the history of the living; it is the history of dead people. Living people have been so few that if you make a history of them, every child is going to be very happy.

A teacher was asking Ernie, "Why do you hate the past?" Ernie said, "Because past creates history and I hate history."

In fact, the history that is being taught has to be burned completely. It is better that humanity forgets its nightmares – Genghis Khan, Tamerlane, Alexander the Great, Ivan the Terrible, Napoleon Bonaparte, Adolf Hitler, Joseph Stalin, Benito Mussolini – and the combination of them all, Ronald Reagan.

18

The Secret of the Mystic Rose

Osho,

What is the secret of the magic rose?

Milarepa, it is not a question suitable to you, but I will answer anyway.

The mystic rose is an ancient symbol of tremendous importance.

Charles Darwin propounded a theory of evolution. Most of it is relevant, but he has missed something very basic. He only thought of the evolution of the human skeleton. He was continually comparing the skeletons of other animals with human skeletons. The ape, the chimpanzee, certain species of monkeys, have an almost similar skeleton; that's why he finally concluded that man has come either from apes or from chimpanzees or from monkeys.

Of course, he was laughed at all over the world, particularly by the Christians because Christianity has a very stubborn, fanatic, attitude which was never so clear before Charles Darwin's proposing the theory of evolution. Even today, most people are not clear what the problem is, why Christians are so much against Charles Darwin.

Christians believe that God created the world in six days in its completion. Obviously, when God creates something it is bound to be complete and perfect, hence the question of evolution does not arise. Evolution means things are evolving, becoming better, more perfect, reaching to higher levels. This was against the idea of a fixed creation; hence Charles Darwin was criticized, condemned.

I remember... There was a small school and the teacher was explaining to the students how God created the world. One small boy, whose father was a scientist and had been teaching him about the theory of evolution, stood up and said, "But my father says something else. He says we are born out of the monkeys."

And the Christian teacher said, "As far as your family is concerned, he may be right. We are not discussing your family here. You can see me later after the class."

But that was the attitude all over the world, not only of Christians but of Hindus and of Mohammedans. They thought that Charles Darwin had taken away their dignity as the greatest and the most superior creation of God. He has destroyed their ego: that God created man in his own image. Now this fellow is saying that God created man in the image of a monkey! Nobody was ready to accept it.

I am also not ready to accept it, but my grounds are different. It is not a question of comparing skeletons; the evolution is in the consciousness, not in the body. Man has a body, monkeys have their own bodies, chimpanzees have their own bodies.

Even Charles Darwin was very much puzzled: How can a monkey suddenly become a man? As far as we know, for at least ten thousand years, there has not been a single case when suddenly a monkey jumps out of a tree and becomes a man. If it has not happened in ten thousand years, it is inconceivable that it could ever have happened.

His whole life he was looking for some missing links. The gap between the monkey and man seemed to be too big. He wanted to find a few missing links so he could make smaller gaps: the monkey becomes something else, then something else becomes something else, and then finally a small difference and the animal becomes man.

But he could not find any missing link because he was born in the West and had the attitude of a materialist. That caused the whole trouble. Otherwise he was saying something of immense importance.

When evolution is not of the body but of consciousness; then it becomes a spiritual progress. But Darwin had no idea of any spirit in man. To him, man was just the body and nothing more.

I propound a theory of spiritual evolution, and that has been the basis of all mysticism in the world.

Man is born as a seed. To accept the seed as your life is the greatest mistake one can commit. Millions of people are born as seeds; fresh, young, with tremendous potential for growth. But because they accept the seed as their very life, they die as a rotten seed. Nothing happens in their life.

The symbol of the mystic rose is that if man takes care of the seed that he is born with, gives it the right soil, gives it the right atmosphere and the right vibrations, moves on a right path where the seed can start growing, then the ultimate growth is symbolized as the mystic rose – when your being blossoms and opens all its petals and releases the beautiful fragrance.

Unless you blossom into a mystic rose, your life is nothing but an exercise in utter futility. You are born unnecessarily, you are living unnecessarily, and you will die unnecessarily. Your whole biography can be reduced to a single word: *unnecessary*.

But if you can blossom and release that which is hidden in you, you have fulfilled the longing of existence. You have given back to existence the fragrance that was hidden in your seed. You have come to fulfill your destiny.

The mystics have never accepted man as the ultimate product. Man is only a beginning and one should not die as a beginning. That is ugly, insulting, damaging to your dignity. Man should reach to the absolute fulfillment – not only to his own contentment, but to the contentment of the cosmos. That is the secret of the mystic rose.

Yes, in a few traditions the mystic rose is also called the magic rose. Both words are meaningful. It is certainly magic when you see the blossoming of the rose within yourself, the beauty of it, and the divinity of it, and the truth of it: *Satyam shivam sundaram*.

You cannot believe your own eyes. You have never dreamed that you contain so much, that your potential is so valuable, that your interiority is an inexhaustible treasure, that you need not be in debt to existence forever. You can return to existence in a millionfold way what existence has given to you. That moment is of great joy, not only on your side but on the side of the whole cosmos.

The experience is such a mystery that there is no way to demystify it. You can experience it but you cannot explain it. That is the meaning of the word *mystic*. You can have it, but you become almost dumb. You cannot utter a single word that may carry something of that rose, its beauty, its fragrance, its dance, its music; nothing can be carried through any word.

The word *magic* is also meaningful. Things like this only happen in magic – unbelievable. You see with your own eyes things which should not be happening but they are happening.

One of the greatest losses to India happened when India became divided from Pakistan, and it was the last thing the politicians ever thought about. In my childhood I encountered it almost every day because all over the country the streets were full of magicians.

With my own eyes I have seen things which even today I cannot figure out how they were managing. Of course there were tricks behind them; there was no miracle, neither were they claiming that they were performing miracles. They were simple people, poor people – not arrogant – but what they were doing was almost a miracle.

In my childhood I have seen magicians planting a small mango tree, just six inches high at the most. In front of everybody they would dig the hole, put the plant in, cover the plant and then chant in gibberish. You cannot understand what they are saying but the pretension is that there is some communication between them and the hidden plant.

The moment they removed the cover, that six-inch mango plant would have ripe mangoes. And they would invite people – you could come close, you could see that those mangoes were not in any way tied on. People would come and see and they would say that they are growing, not attached.

The magician would offer those mangoes to a few people so that they could taste that they were not false or illusory – and people would taste them and they would say, "We have never tasted such sweet mangoes in our whole life!" And there was no claim for any miracle.

I have seen magicians bringing from their bellies big round balls of solid steel. They would be so big it was difficult to take them out of their mouths – people were needed to pull them out of their mouths – and they were so heavy that when they were thrown on the earth they would make a dent.

The magician would go on bringing bigger and bigger balls... It was a trick – but how were they managing it? And they would throw those big balls, almost the size of a football – they would throw them in the air and they would fall and create such a big dent in the earth. They would tell people, "You can try" – and people would try, but they were so heavy that it was difficult to pick them up. And they all have come – a dozen or more, all around – from the belly of the magician.

He would show, half naked, the upper part of his body naked – he would show that the ball was moving upwards. You could see that the ball was moving upwards, that it was stuck in his throat, and you could see and you could go and touch and feel that the ball was inside. Then, with great difficulty, he would bring it into his mouth and he would cry, tears coming, and ask people to take it out somehow, because he is not able. It would destroy all his teeth so help him – and the miracle was that as they were taking it out, the ball was becoming bigger. By the time it was completely out, it was so big that that man's belly could not contain even a single ball, to say nothing of one dozen balls.

But all these magicians were Mohammedans: it was not a very creditable job. These were street people. Because of the division of Pakistan, all those Mohammedan magicians have moved to Pakistan. They were coming from faraway Pakhtunistan, Afghanistan. But now the roads are closed. Now you don't see the magicians anywhere.

Otherwise it was almost an everyday affair: in this marketplace, in that street, near the school; anywhere where they thought they could gather a crowd.

With my own eyes I have seen something, and I sometimes wonder whether I have seen it or I have dreamed it. I have not dreamed for thirty- five years, but this thing is such that it is absolutely unbelievable that it really happened...

A magician came to our school. The school was a very big school, with almost one thousand students and nearabout fifty teachers. Even the principal of the school, who was a postgraduate in science, first rejected the man: "We don't want any nonsense here."

But I had seen that man doing impossible things, and I told him, "Wait!" I went into the principal's office and said, "You are missing a tremendous opportunity. You are a scientist. I know this man; I have seen him performing things. I can ask him to do the best that he can. And what is the harm? After school time, those who want to see can stay." And those magicians were so poor that if you could give them five rupees, it was too much.

I told the magician that I had convinced the principal, he was ready to allow it after school – "but you have to do the greatest trick that you know. On your behalf I have promised – and he is a man with a scientific mind, so be careful. There will be fifty graduates, postgraduates, so you have to be very alert. You should not be caught because it is also a question of my prestige."

He said, "My boy, don't be worried!"

And he did something so that my principal called me and said, "You should not associate with such people. It is dangerous."

I said, "Have you any idea what he did?"

He said, "I don't have any idea, and I can't even believe that this has happened."

Because the magician threw up a rope which stood in the air just like a pillar – a rope which has no bones, nothing. It was just coiled and he had carried it on his shoulder; an ordinary rope. He went on uncoiling it and throwing it out, and soon we could not see the other end. What happened to the other end?

All magicians used to have a child who was their helper. He called the boy, "Are you ready to go up the rope?"

The boy said, "Yes, master" – and he started climbing the rope. And just as the other end of the rope had disappeared, at a certain point the boy also disappeared. Then the magician said to the crowd, "I will bring the boy down, piece by piece."

I was sitting by the side of the principal. He said, "Are you going to create some trouble for me? If the police come here and see that a boy is cut into pieces..."

I said, "Don't be worried, he is just performing a magic trick. Nothing is going to be wrong. I have been watching him in many shows, but this I have never seen."

The magician threw a knife up and one leg of the boy came down, and everybody was almost breathless. He went on throwing knives... another leg... one hand... another hand... and they were lying there on the ground in front of us, not bleeding at all, as if the boy was made of plastic or something. But he was speaking, he was doing all the things the magician was saying. Finally his body came, and just the head remained.

My principal said, "Don't cut his head!"

I said, "Don't be worried. If he has cut him, what does it mean? If the police come, you will be caught."

He said, "I was saying from the very beginning, 'No nonsense here' and now you are talking about police. I have always been suspicious of you. Perhaps you have informed the police beforehand to come at the right time."

I said, "Don't be worried."

And then the magician shouted into the sky, "Boy, only your head is there; let it drop." The head came rolling down, and he started putting the boy together again. He joined him perfectly well, and the boy started collecting his things and said, "What about the rope? Should I start pulling it back?" The magician said, "Yes" and the boy started pulling the rope back and coiling it.

I had only heard about the rope trick, which is world famous. Akbar mentions in his *Akbarnama*, his autobiography. Since Akbar it has been a rumor in the air that there are magicians who can perform it, but no authoritative account is available. One British viceroy, Curzon, mentions in his memoirs that he saw the rope trick in New Delhi before his whole court.

I was making every effort to find some magician – so many magicians were passing through my village, and I would ask them, "Can you perform the rope trick?"

They said, "It is the ultimate, and only very rare masters in magic can do it."

But this man – I had not asked him particularly for the rope trick, but he did it. Even today I cannot believe it. I can see the whole scene, I can see the principal freaking out – and all the magician got was five rupees.

Magic simply means something unbelievable, so absurd, so irrational that you cannot find a way to figure it out. That's why both the words have been used, the mystic rose or the magic rose. But even the rope trick is nothing compared to your inner flowering – because you don't think you have anything inner, just hollowness. But in that hollowness is the possibility and the potentiality of a rose blossoming.

And this is no ordinary rose. It does not die. It is not that it blossoms in the morning, dances the whole day, sings songs, plays with the wind and the rain and the sun – and by the evening all the petals have fallen to the ground and tomorrow you will not find even a trace of it.

This inner rose is eternal. Once you have found it, it will be always within you.

But, Milarepa, I repeat again, these are not the questions that are suitable to you! What is suitable to you... I will tell you this small joke.

Rubin Moscowitz went crazy and was committed to the local lunatic asylum. Immediately he started causing trouble there because he demanded kosher Jewish meals. So the staff hired a chef to prepare this special food for Rubin. One Friday night after a delicious dinner, Rubin leaned back in his chair and lit up a large Havana cigar. This was too much for the director of the asylum, and Rubin was summoned to the office.

"Now, look here, Moscowitz, you get the best meals of anyone here because you claim you only eat kosher food. And now, on your Sabbath night, you flout your religion and smoke cigars!"

Rubin shrugged his shoulders and said, "Why are you arguing with me? I'm crazy, aren't I?"

What is the point of arguing with a crazy man? He can do anything, any time, any day. He can ask for special Jewish food, kosher food, and he can flout his religion. On Friday nights the traditional Jewish community stops everything; nothing must be done on the Sabbath. From the night, as the sun sets on Friday, nothing should be done. And to smoke a Havana cigar... But Rubin is perfectly right: "Why are you arguing with me? Don't you know I am crazy?"

So is Milarepa. When he asks crazy questions that look very perfect; they have the quality of his being in them. But asking such questions as, "What is a mystic rose?" is not for you, Milarepa. It is for Kaveesha, the head of the cuckoo department.

Osho,
You say we don't know what love is. What is it I feel for you? It caresses my heart, it makes me laugh and cry, it makes me feel ecstatic, it takes me deep inside. Beloved master, what is it?

It must be the beginning of a great love affair.

But remember the difference between ordinary love affairs and the great love affair. The great love affair is qualitatively different from what you call love affairs. Your love affairs are just soap bubbles. One day you are in deep love and another day – or perhaps the same day – the soap bubble is gone and with it your love affair too. It is momentary.

The great love affair is not really with the master, but with the universe through the master. The master is at the most only a window through which you can see the whole sky with all its stars. You don't fall in love with the window frame.

There are many who have fallen in love with the window frames too. What is being worshipped in temples, in mosques, in churches, in synagogues? – just windows, and those windows also are not present there. Once they used to be: two thousand years ago, three thousand years ago, four thousand years ago there used to be a window.

Those who were contemporaries of the window must have condemned it because it takes them away from their mundane activities. It disturbs them – their peace, their life, their business, their job. Why was Jesus crucified? Why was Socrates poisoned? Why were many attempts made on Gautam Buddha's life?

The simple reason is that these people were disturbing everybody: Whatever you are doing is wrong; wherever you are is not the right place; your greed is wrong, your anger is wrong, your jealousy is wrong, your lust is wrong, your desire is wrong.

They were not telling you something that was not right; they were absolutely right, but their right was disturbing your life. Then they became almost a harassment to everybody. People like Jesus going around a small country, Judea, harassing people: "This is not the real world; these parents and these children are not your real relatives... Your real father is in heaven, and unless you believe in me, there is no way to find your real father."

People were distracted. They could not figure out what was right. These people were creating confusion. Jesus was saying, "Blessed are the poor because they shall inherit the kingdom of God." It was disturbing to the rich and it was also disturbing in a certain sense to the poor, because every poor man is trying to be rich. Now this man is saying that you are blessed as you are, so don't try to become rich.

The rich were very angry because Jesus was saying, "Even a camel can pass through the eye of a needle, but a rich man cannot pass through the gates of heaven." Whoever heard him was disturbed. People could not sleep easily. People could not do their work.

And if you don't listen to him and don't believe him, at the last day of judgment he will choose his people and the remaining ones will be thrown into utter darkness, into hell for eternity. Then there is no possibility of your liberation.

Naturally, such things are bound to disturb people. And finally they could not bear to be disturbed anymore. They had to crucify Jesus just to have peace in the land, just to have a certain relaxedness in life.

Contemporaries have always been condemnatory to people who could have led them to the ultimate. But there is something strange: nobody wants to go to the ultimate. And there are a few people like me whose whole business is that it does not matter whether you want it or not, they are bent on taking you to the ultimate. They are ready to sacrifice themselves, but they will not leave you. They will haunt you for centuries. Now Moses is still haunting people, Jesus is still haunting people.

Gautam Buddha is still nagging, but once these people die, you start feeling a little guilt that you did not listen. Perhaps the man was right. Your own experiences in life teach you that jealousy is not right, anger is not right, greed is not right, and what these people were teaching perhaps was right – and you killed them. Now that guilt takes revenge.

Once I was asked, "Why does Jesus have more followers in the world than anybody else?" I said, "The simple reason is the crucifixion."

Mahavira was never crucified, so there was no guilt. But because Jesus was crucified, people started feeling guilty, started thinking about it. Perhaps that innocent man, he had not done any crime and we killed him. They found the blood on their hands; now how to wash it?

Guilt turns into worship. This is a strange psychology. The moment you start feeling guilty, the only way to get rid of the guilt is to worship the man whom you have crucified. The worship will help you to feel good. Even though you crucified him, now you recognize that you committed something wrong, and you are ready to do everything. You will worship, you will pray, you will read the Holy Bible, you will follow him for centuries. You will become a fanatic – just as fanatical as the contemporaries of Jesus who crucified him were. They were fanatically against him and their descendants are fanatically for him. This is a very strange psychological change that happens again and again.

If while I am alive and if you can behave with me just humanly, there is a possibility of a window opening for you. And if you can love and if you can trust, then nothing is impossible. Only very few will be able to do it, but only those very few will be able to attain something – not the millions of Christians who are worshipping someone whom they crucified. Their worship is only a compensation, it is not love. It is a consolation, not love.

Love has a totally different quality. It is a rejoicing, it is feeling blessed in the presence of the person with whom the great love affair is happening.

Your question is, "You say we don't know what love is." Even if you start loving you will not know what love is. You will experience it, you will be full of it, you will be overflowing with it, you will be able to share it, but you will not be able to understand what it is because love is one of the ultimate mysteries of life.

You are asking, "What is it I feel for you? It caresses my heart, it makes me laugh and cry, it makes me feel ecstatic, it takes me deep inside. What is it?"

Don't seek for any explanation. Every explanation becomes a disturbance in the growth of the mysterious. Never ask what it is. If you are rejoicing in it, it must be right. If you are celebrating it, it must be right. If you are dancing it, you are on the right path.

But never ask what it is because the moment you start asking what it is, you start making it something intellectual. It is something of the heart which knows experience but does not know any explanation. Something tremendously beautiful is happening to you, but don't give it a name. Words are dangerous beyond a certain stage. If you give it a name, you may think you have come to the end.

Don't call it love. You are on the right path, you are in the right direction, but don't give it any name. If you call it love you will become satisfied and you will stop growing – "What more can there be?" You have arrived at the final stage: it is love. Please avoid giving names; just remember that you are on the right path.

One day the mystic rose will open within you and the fragrance will be released. Even then, don't give it a name. Existence is so eternal, there are no boundaries to growth. There are skies beyond skies, and there are peaks beyond peaks.

That's the beauty of existence, that it ends nowhere. It is always an adventure; it is always a pilgrimage; it is always a searching, searching for more, searching for deeper realities. But you never come to an end so that you can say, "I have passed the final examination." There is no final examination as such.

Hymie Goldberg went to see a fortune-teller. After he had sat down in the darkened room, the fortune-teller said, "I will read your palm for fifty dollars, and that entitles you to ask three questions."

"Questions about what?" asked Hymie.

"About anything," replied the psychic.

"But isn't fifty dollars an awful lot to charge for that?" complained Hymie.

"Maybe," said the palmist, "and what is your last question?"

In life the last question comes very soon; but in real existence, even the first question never arises. One goes on becoming more and more silent. In that silence questions don't grow, and when there are no questions, the possibility of any answer becomes impossible.

Those who know, they don't know the answer. We call them the awakened ones, the enlightened ones because they have dropped all their questions; now they don't have any questions in them. If you want to call this absence of questions the answer, you can call it that – but there is no answer either.

A man is stretched out on his back across four seats in a theater. The usher comes down and says, "Mister, you will have to get out of those four seats. You are only entitled to one."

The man only grunts and does not move. The manager comes down and says to the man, "Mister, you will have to get up. All you are entitled to is one seat." The man grunts and does not move.

Finally a policeman is called in. He walks down the aisle and says to the man who is still on the four seats, "Get out of those seats!"

The man grunts, and policeman says, "Okay, wise guy, where are you from?"

The man moans and says, "The balcony."

You love to laugh. Everybody should love to laugh because in my vision of religiousness laughter is far more valuable than any prayer. Prayer is just intellectual. Laughter is total; your body, your mind, your heart, everything joins in it. You laugh as a single unitary whole.

Three famous surgeons were bragging together over their morning coffee.

The first said, "I grafted an arm onto a man and now he is a professional golfer."

"That's nothing," said the second, "I grafted a leg onto a man and now he's one of the world's best long distance runners."

"So what?" said the third, "I grafted a smile onto a donkey and now he is the president of America."

19

If Sex Drops, It Is a Festive Moment

Osho,

Sometimes I have the feeling that sex has dropped me. But it seems I have not got it yet, or I just don't want to accept the fact of it. Can you help me to understand what is going on?

Sarjano, the Western mind has completely forgotten that sex is not life, hence everyone born in the West carries in his unconscious the idea that the moment sex is finished, all is finished. This is not true. On the contrary, the moment sex falls away from you, real life begins. On the graveyard of sex grows the mystic rose. It is not only happening to you, it is going to happen to every sannyasin who is honestly and sincerely seeking the truth.

Sex is so childish, so stupid that if you take a photograph of yourself making love, you will be surprised to note a few things. The woman you are making love to has closed her eyes because she cannot see you in such a stupid activity. The only way is to keep the eyes closed and let this ugly moment pass. People have chosen the night to make love – except a few idiots. And you will see yourself doing such gymnastics, huffing and puffing and perspiring over the poor woman – and you are not even ashamed that the fragile woman is under you and you are on top!

But you are so much engaged in the futile activity that you are not aware of it. In fact, in a few cities in Europe and America there are restaurants, hotels, which have a very special attraction...

I have heard about one man who asked, "What is this special attraction?"

And the manager said, "The fee is high, but if you are interested and you have the money, you will get one of the most gorgeous women to make love to."

He could not resist the temptation, so he paid the money and he was led into a room. The woman was certainly gorgeous, and as he started making love, he started hearing a few giggles from this side, a few giggles from that side. He could not understand what was happening. He has made love many times, but giggles, and from all sides?

When the lights came on, he could see that those people had made a great arrangement. There were holes around the room – it was a round room – and people were watching him through magnifying glasses. That's why those giggles were coming. He said, "My God, these restaurant people are cheating!"

He went back and he said, "What is all this? You never told me."

The manager said, "The fee for watching the show is much more. There is no harm done. Tomorrow you can watch the show. And what is a show if there is no watcher?"

He paid the money because he felt that the people who had been giggling were enjoying more than he had been. And the next day he was sitting by a magnifying hole and he enjoyed it so much he started giggling himself.

The person who was watching the show by his side said, "What are you giggling at? This is nothing, you should have come yesterday, the man was absolutely nuts!"

Sex has been kept hidden for centuries, in the darkness of the night, with the woman's eyes closed. One day, at nearabout thirteen or fourteen years of age, it begins. It is a biological device for reproduction; it has nothing to do with you. You are just being used by the blind forces of biology. And if you are understanding enough, my own calculation is that by the time you are forty-two you will start feeling that sex is dropping.

Not that you have to drop it, let me insist again and again, you should never drop it because that is the only way to keep it alive to the very last breath of your life. And what you will do by dropping it is what has been done by Hindu, Christian and Buddhist monks all over the world. They call it celibacy: a beautiful name for an ugly fact. In the name of celibacy they are repressing their sex, and sex is a vital energy because it reproduces life. You cannot repress it. It will find perverted ways to come out – in homosexuality, in sodomy. And the ultimate perversion of all the religious teaching is the disease AIDS. It is the outcome of your so-called celibacy.

But nobody is condemning the Vatican, nobody is condemning the *shankaracharyas* saying, "You are responsible that at least ten million people in the world today are AIDS positive sufferers." These are the data from only the Western world because the East has not yet the facilities, the processes, the experts to find the AIDS virus. So these ten million people belong to the Western part of the world.

Hundreds of people are dying every day because AIDS has no cure; it is slow death. For between six months and two years, you will be dying slowly. Dying quickly has a beauty about it: you don't suffer. But hanging in limbo, knowing perfectly that there is no cure, for two years your life becomes a horrible nightmare. You don't think about anything except death.

If you repress sex, you are not going to transform the immense energy contained in it. But if it drops through your meditations and through your understanding – by itself, with no effort on your part – it will release such a tremendous beauty and openness to your being that all you have been always dreaming and thinking will become a reality.

And Sarjano, just as I said, it is going to happen to every sannyasin. I call it celibacy only when sex drops, not before it. If you force it before it drops by itself, you are simply becoming perverted. This is a fundamental law of life: you can change the natural flow of life energy, but once it gets perverted, then it becomes very complicated. First you have to bring it back to the natural state and then only transformation is possible. Perversion cannot be transformed.

It is not only you; your ancient girlfriend has also written to me. Her name is Prem Premal. She says:

> Osho,
> Is it possible that sex has dropped me and I did not realize it?

It seems it is very hard for the Western conditioning to realize the disappearance of sex with joy and as a blessing from the beyond because they only believe in the material body. So then sex becomes the only possibility of having any moments of orgasmic joy – if you are fortunate enough, which millions are not. Only once in a while somebody will get a little glimpse of orgasmic joy. Your conditioning prohibits it.

In the East, if sex drops by itself it is a celebration. We have taken life in a totally different way: we have not made it synonymous with sex. On the contrary, while sex continues you are not mature. When sex drops a great maturity and centering comes to you, and a true celibacy, an authentic *brahmacharya*. And now because you are free from the chains of biology, which are the only chains that are making you a prisoner of blind forces, you open your eyes and you can see the beauty of the whole of existence. You will laugh in your days of celibacy about your own stupidity: that you once thought that is all that life has to offer.

I have heard about an old drunkard who was sitting early in the morning on the sea beach, and he saw a young man doing push-ups. The drunkard could not believe it. He went around the young man; he looked from this side, he looked from that side.

Finally he could not contain his curiosity, and he said, "My poor boy. Why are you unnecessarily perspiring and doing these push-ups? Your girlfriend is not here" – because he knew only the push-ups which people go on doing in the name of love.

Sarjano and Premal, it is perfectly okay, not *just* okay, that sex is disappearing. As sex disappears you will find authentic love growing in you. Sex is not love: it is just a fallacy, a blindness. You are tricked by biology into believing that this is love. But once sex has disappeared your whole life energy is redeemed from its animal past. And just as sex was reproducing more and more children, sex-freed energy starts giving you every moment a new birth. Your whole life becomes fresh, growing in a new direction.

Sex is horizontal; love is vertical. It takes you upwards to higher realms of being, and the higher you are in your love, the closer you are to the ultimate truth. The day your love has reached to its climax, you will experience what I have been defining as *satyam shivam sundaram* – the truth, the godliness and the beauty. And these experiences are not momentary glimpses any more. They become part of you; you become part of them. They become just like the heartbeat – they are with you for eternity.

But I can understand your problem: up to now you have known only one joy and that was sex. You are absolutely unaware that there are skies beyond skies and you are just creeping on the earth. You are not aware that you have wings and you can fly just like an eagle across the sun into the faraway sky. The whole sky becomes your kingdom.

Because of this fact, a misunderstanding arose. Down the ages mystics have experienced it, and because they experienced that sex is functioning as a blinding force, as something imprisoning you, they started condemning sex. And the misunderstanding was that people started thinking that if sex can be repressed, they will also become part of the mystical world and its experiences. Nobody has had the courage to say that this is not a true understanding of the fact.

Celibacy is not something to be practiced, it is not something to be rehearsed, it is not something to be imposed on you by any method, any effort, any doing. Celibacy comes when sex disappears of its own accord. Certainly the word *celibacy* has tremendous meaning in my sense. But the misunderstanding was that seeing the mystical people rejoicing and dancing and singing, and their eyes and their faces and their charismatic pull, people started repressing sex – thinking that it is sex that is preventing them from knowing higher realms of being. And there lies a great misunderstanding.

My effort has been to destroy this misunderstanding. It has brought me condemnation from all over the world, from all the religions because they are all living in this misunderstanding. I am not for sex, but I am not against sex either. It has a time, its season, its climate – and that time should be given to it. It is absolutely a natural phenomenon, but it should not spread beyond its limits.

Just as at the age of fourteen it appears, if you live it totally, intensely, without any guilt created by religions, you will be out of the imprisonment by the age of nearabout forty-two. This is an average: those who are more intelligent may get out of it sooner. Those who are a little dull-witted will take a little more time. But misunderstandings are everywhere.

Just before the operation, the high-powered surgeon was explaining all the new recovery techniques to his patient. "Now, you should begin walking as soon as possible," explained the doctor. "On the first day, you must walk around for five minutes; on the second day ten minutes, and on the third day you walk for at least an hour. Do you understand?"

"Yes, doctor," answered the apprehensive patient, "but is it all right if I lie down during the operation?"

Things were not going so well for Gilroy and Loretta when they went to bed together for the first time. Gilroy was working away hard, but Loretta was not responding at all. Finally in exasperation he asked her, "What is the matter?"

"It's your organ," Loretta replied, "I don't think it is big enough."

"Well," Gilroy replied indignantly, "I did not think I would be playing in a cathedral."

Misunderstanding – there is so much in the world. It creates confusion, it creates chaos, and when everybody has misunderstood something and you stand alone to make them understand, they feel offended. Not a single religious leader has logically condemned, refuted whatever I am saying because they don't have any logic. But they have been condemning me without refutation, and because they are all together in the same boat, naturally it seems that I am alone against the whole world. But what I am saying is a simple truth to understand.

You cannot bring sex in forcibly. Can you make a seven-year-old child potent enough to reproduce children? The very idea looks absurd. Sex comes on its own accord. It is a certain maturity of your body, of your chemistry, of your physiology that brings it at the age of twelve.

If the coming is not in your hands, the going is also not going to be in your hands. It will go at the age of forty-two without any problem. Just one thing has to be remembered: don't be corrupted by your religions, don't be corrupted by your scriptures, don't be corrupted by your so-called saints. They are the most poisonous people on the earth. They have destroyed man in so many ways that their crimes are uncountable.

The greatest crime is to create a guilt against sex because it keeps sex alive beyond its natural boundary. So even a person of seventy is still thinking of sex. In fact, there is nothing else for him to think about. Retired, what can you do? You simply have to think about it and talk about it. Sex, which used to be a part of the physical body, has moved and become just cerebral, just in the mind. Even at the time of death, most people die with some sexual image floating in their minds. This is ugly, and the responsibility is on your so-called saints. Neither do they understand the psychology and the science of the transformation, nor do they care that what they are teaching is going to destroy people's lives.

I teach you that when the sex energy is starting to function, allow it full support. At the age of nearabout eighteen or nineteen, man has his greatest sexual energy; that is the peak point. But your society prevents you: you have to go to college, you have to go to university, you have to come back after university – maybe twenty-five years old – and then you will have to be married.

But at twenty-five years old, you are already six years downhill! This is absolutely unscientific. Boys and girls in the colleges and in the universities should live together, not in separate hostels, and they should be given all that the scientific approach has found out about sex. In the past, of course it was a little difficult because of the problem of the girl becoming pregnant, but now there is no problem at all. The pill has been the greatest revolution in the world – even greater than the Russian Revolution!

And now two more pills have come into existence, which have made sex simply fun, nothing to worry about. The first pill was to be taken by the woman for a certain period of time; only then was it possible to prevent pregnancy – and that too was not a hundred percent safe. And it used to happen that you were not expecting your lover and he suddenly comes and you have not taken your pill. And the human mind is so stupid that it goes on thinking that nobody gets pregnant every time; it is very rare, so there is nothing to worry about, you can take the chance. But that chance has always proved very dangerous.

I have heard about a man traveling with a busload of children. Somewhere he stopped for the children to take some drinks, tea or something. The manager of the small hotel asked him, "My God! Are all these children yours?"

He said, "They are not my own. I am a salesman for birth control methods. These are my failures! I am going to take them to the factory to show the owner that something is wrong with his birth control methods. Just count these children! And every parent is sitting with a loaded gun wanting to kill me because I promised them a one hundred percent guarantee."

The first pill was not a hundred percent guaranteed. The second pill is tremendously important. The second pill has to be taken after you have made love – so there is no problem, no risk. And the third pill is even more important because it brings about the equality of men and women.

Why should only the woman take the pill? The third pill can be taken by the man.

If one looks in a scientific way without any prejudice, then every young man and young woman who is sexually potent – at their highest peak – should be allowed to make love without any guilt. But we force them to remain repressed about sex, and by the time they are declining in their energies we allow them to get married.

Two problems arise out of this. Firstly: for twenty-five years you have been telling them that sex is wrong, to prevent them from getting into any sexual relationship. Twenty-five years is one third of your life! It is a long time to create a great prejudice against sex. And then suddenly, in one day, everything changes. You allow them to get married. This is idiotic because what will happen to twenty-five years' propaganda against sex? And those who are getting married are also idiots; they don't ask the priest and their parents, "What will happen to that twenty-five years' conditioning? Now you are giving us license to make love, but what about those twenty-five years that you prevented us?"

So the first problem is that man is the only animal in the whole world – he is the most intelligent animal, but absolutely unintelligent as far as sex is concerned. There are no sex classes for deer and lions and horses and donkeys. They don't need to be taught about sex at all. It comes naturally. But because of twenty-five years' constant insistence from the religion, from the society, from the university, from the parents, man gets confused. On the honeymoon he does not know what to do.

I have heard about a young man who got married and went to the honeymoon hotel in a holiday resort. It was a full-moon night. The woman immediately undressed and lay down on the bed, but the young man was sitting at the window looking at the full moon. Minutes passed, hours were passing, and the woman said, "What is the matter with you? What are you doing there? It is our honeymoon."

The man said, "Shut up! When I was coming here, I asked my mother, 'Any advice?' She said, 'This is the greatest night of your life. Don't miss a single moment.' So I am waiting and watching the night, the greatest night. Don't distract me!"

But this is bound to happen. And then the second thing that happens is a deep guilt feeling about sex: that it is sin. If you are carrying the idea that something is sin you cannot really enjoy it. Your sin will be holding you back; your guilt will be making you feel ashamed of yourself: "What are you doing?"

So no man, no woman is prepared to make love in deep joy, in freedom. On the contrary, everybody is prepared against love. This is the reason why people don't get rid of their sexuality at the age of forty-two. They will continue even if they live eighty years. Society spoils people in such a way – and perhaps they are also doing it absolutely unconsciously. They are taking away your home: the experience that was possible for you, but which happens only when sex drops on its own accord.

Then freedom has a totally different meaning. You have not achieved it; it has been bestowed upon you from the beyond. Existence has accepted that now you are ready for greater mysteries, you are no longer clinging to your teddy bears; you can move on into ecstatic lands, into experiences of bliss that know only a beginning but no end. You can move toward finding the truth of your being and the truth of existence.

It seems very strange that I am condemned for teaching sex to people. In fact, I am teaching them natural celibacy, but to bring about natural celibacy the sex also has to be natural. Sex is not the goal, but only a staircase. If it can be natural, without any guilt, without any poison, you will reach beyond it and you will be immensely surprised that only now you have become mature. Now the bodily pleasures don't have any meaning because in comparison to your spiritual blessings, blissfulness, they all fade away.

Sarjano, what is happening is perfectly good, but particularly for an Italian it is a little difficult to accept. But the moment you became my sannyasin, you dropped all boundaries and discriminations that make men different from each other. My sannyasins are simply the first world citizens. They don't belong to any nation and they don't belong to any church.

The other day I received a letter from Australia. Just like other lands and other continents, Australia also has an Osho International Foundation, and we have thousands of sannyasins in Australia. The Theosophical Society of Australia was selling my books up to now, and those books were their best-sellers. This time, when the representative of the Australian Osho International Foundation went to the Theosophical Society, they said, "We have been ordered by our world headquarters that your books should not be sold."

The sannyasin saw that books that were written against me were being sold. He asked about it and the man said, "I love Osho myself, and his books were our best-sellers. I even wrote a letter saying that this is not right, but they overruled my letter and they said, 'You have to do what you have been told. Books against Osho can be sold, but literature by Osho or any literature written in his favor is banned.'"

It was not a surprise to me but it is very inconsistent with the Theosophical Society's own philosophy. They pretend that they are synthesizing all religions, all philosophies, all approaches – just my standpoint is excluded! They are exposing themselves because this letter banning my books must have gone not only to Australia; it must have gone to Japan, it must have gone to America, it must have gone to other countries in Europe.

What is their fear? Their fear is that they cannot manage my approach with all the other religions' approaches. It stands aloof and apart and alone in its own majesty. And they cannot answer, and they are not ready to confront me publicly. So from the back door they try to destroy whatever I'm trying to do – to help humanity come out of the garbage that has been accumulating in you for centuries behind very good names.

Sarjano, it is a festive moment if sex has dropped from you. And it must have dropped because the certificate is there from Prem Premal. Now you can move from ordinary animal life into authentic transformation. It is the same energy that is involved in sex. If sex drops you have so much energy for meditation, you have so much energy for friendliness, you have so much energy to be creative – and you are a creative person.

Now with all this energy released you can manage so much creativity in your work that you may not have even dreamed about. And this creativity will bring to you your self-realization.

> Osho,
> I want so much to give you nothing in return, but I haven't found it yet. And the something I want to give you is already in your eyes. Thank you for singing my heart-song.

The question you have asked is not just a question from your mind; it is the very heartbeat of your inner being. You are saying, "I want so much to give you nothing in return, but I have not found it yet. And the something I want to give you is already in your eyes. Thank you for singing my heart-song."

First, you will never find anything to give me in return because here we are not in a marketplace, here we are not selling God or selling love. Here we are simply rejoicing in and relishing what has happened to me and what is going to happen to you. It is not a business; it is authentic religiousness. But I can understand the desire: one feels like giving something, and the sadness that you can't find anything to give. Just that you feel to give is enough. You have given it.

And you say, "And the something I want to give you is already in your eyes." From where has it come into my eyes? Without knowing, you all have given your love, your trust, which you see in my eyes. My eyes are more your eyes than mine. And a gift that is given without knowing is the real gift. What you see in my eyes is just the joy and the blissfulness of you all growing, of you all expanding in consciousness, of you all coming closer to *satyam shivam sundaram.*

Just as a gardener becomes immensely happy when he sees thousands of flowers blossoming in his garden, I am also a gardener. You are my garden, and I would like every one of you to become a mystic rose, fully grown, utterly blissful. What you see in my eyes is your future.

And you say, "Thank you for singing my heart-song." There is no need to thank me. It is simply my joy to bring song and dance into your heart. It is not that I am doing it for any return. In fact, I should be thankful toward you, that you were courageous enough to open your heart and allow my dance and song and music to fill it. You could have remained closed.

Nobody's heart can be opened forcefully. It opens only when you are totally in love and relaxed, without any fear you allow me in. I should be thankful because I am the guest and you are the host.

A great Zen master entered the hall where all the disciples had gathered for the evening meditation. "There is good news and bad news tonight," he said. "First, the bad news: there is no good news. Now the good news: you don't have to listen to the bad news."

Hamish MacTavish, the old Scottish gamekeeper, returned from taking the new minister on a grouse-shooting trip over the highland moors.

As he sank wearily into his chair beside the fire, his wife Margaret approached with a cup of tea.

"Here's a cup of tea for you, Hamish," said Maggie. "And is the new minister a good shot?"

Hamish puffed on his pipe, staring into the fire and replied, "Aye, a fine shot he is. But it is marvelous indeed how the Lord protects the birds when he's shooting."

I am not an archer, nor a shooter. But strangely enough my arrows reach to your heart and because God is dead, nobody can protect you.

Just a joke for you. You need a good laugh. Last night you did great because I went on hearing your laughter for almost half an hour. I loved it so much that my people are starting to learn how to pray. Don't be miserly as far as laughter is concerned. That is the only miserliness I hate.

Solomon and Deborah won a contest. The first prize was a week's stay at the Watergate Hotel in Washington.

When they got to their suite, Debbie was acting nervously.

"What is the matter, darling?" asked Solly.

"This is the Watergate Hotel," replied Debbie, "maybe the place is still bugged."

Solly looks behind the curtains, behind the light shade, picks up the carpet and sees a brass disc with four screws. He unscrews the disc and puts it in his pocket.

The next morning, the manager knocks on the door.

"Good morning," he says, "how do you like the suite?"

"Fantastic," replies Solly.

"How did you like the champagne and caviar we sent you? And the flowers?"

"Just great," replies Solly, "But why are you asking so many questions?"

"Well," replied the manager nervously, "we had a terrible accident last night in the honeymoon suite downstairs. The young couple were trapped together on their bed all night long after the chandelier fell on them."

20

Become a Luminous Being

Osho,
The other day you were telling us the effects of radioactive matter on the body. But I am feeling and experiencing the radiation of a buddha – an enormous energy radiating from you which not only rejuvenates body-mind continuously, but makes us laugh, dance and celebrate. Please comment.

The question that you have asked has been asked for centuries. Perhaps it is one of the oldest questions mankind has raised whenever there was a man who has come to know himself. It has been felt around Gautam Buddha, it has been felt around Lao Tzu, it has been felt around Mahavira and thousands of others who were more blessed than ordinary humanity.

But it has only been felt by those who were receptive, by those who were in deep love. It has not been felt by those who were closed. It has not been felt by those who had come just like spectators, by the curious; but only by the disciples, and more clearly by the devotees.

So two things are involved in it. A man who has come to know himself – certainly all his darkness that was within him is no longer there. He has become purely a luminous phenomenon, and his luminosity is very delicate and very subtle. It is not like the radiation that comes from an atomic explosion. The radiation from an atomic explosion will affect all – whether you are open or closed doesn't matter. The radiation from an atomic explosion is a violent aggression against anyone who comes across it. But the radiation of one who is awakened is a very delicate phenomenon. It is just like a fragrance. Only if you have the understanding and the courage to receive it will you be able to know it; otherwise, thousands of people passed by Gautam Buddha realizing nothing. They were puzzled: "Why are others feeling so much, why are others in tears of joy?"

The radiation of the awakened, of the enlightened, is nonaggressive. That is one of the most significant things to be understood. In no way is it going to transgress your individuality unless you invite it, unless you are in a state of welcome, unless you are waiting for it. Unless you are ready to be a host it won't knock on your doors.

And naturally, if it does not knock on your doors you will feel that all these people who are experiencing radiation, light, joy, seem to be a little strange because the majority of humanity has not felt it. The majority of humanity is completely closed – not even a single window of the heart is open. It is almost the same as a blind man denying that there is sun and there is light. As far as he is concerned, he is right. He has never seen the sun and he has never seen the light.

I have told you the most illuminating story about Gautam Buddha and a blind man. It contains so much that if you can comprehend it in its totality, it may help you to open your eyes, to open your heart.

A blind man was brought to Gautam Buddha, and the people who had brought him told Buddha, "This man is not only blind, he is a genius in logic, in argumentation. We all know there is light. We all know there is the sun, there is the moon, there are the stars, but we cannot convince this man. He lives in our village and he argues so well against all of us that sometimes we start thinking that perhaps we are deluded.

"His arguments are very strong. He says, 'I am absolutely willing to accept your sun, your moon, your stars, your light, but just let me touch your light. I want to feel it. If touching it is difficult, let me smell it. If that too is difficult, beat it like a drum so I can hear the sound of your light. Or I am ready even to swallow it, to have some taste of it. But unless out of my four senses at least one sense is convinced, I can only say to you that you are in an illusion. And moreover, I feel that you want to humiliate me by declaring this stupid idea about light, so that you can claim you have eyes and I don't have eyes. You simply want to insult me.'

"Hearing that Gautam Buddha was passing by the nearby village, we rushed here. We thought that perhaps this would be the only moment, the only chance and opportunity to take this blind man to a man who is ultimately awakened and may be able to convince him about light. If he fails, then there is no hope."

Gautam Buddha laughed and he said, "As far as I am concerned, I absolutely agree with the blind man, because he confirms my attitude about truth. Unless you experience it, don't believe it. And because he cannot experience light, it does not matter whether light exists or not. He is absolutely correct not to believe in it because every belief is far more dangerous than blindness because every belief is spiritual blindness."

The blind man could not believe that for the first time somebody of the status of Gautam Buddha would support him. Tears came from his blind eyes. Gautam Buddha said, "Don't be worried. I have the best physician of the land with me." A great king, Prasenjita, had offered Gautam Buddha his own personal physician because he was fragile, old, and he needed somebody to look after him.

So Gautam Buddha said, "Don't be worried. I will call the physician, he is just in another camp. Let him treat you. You don't need an awakened man, you need a talented physician, a genius – because no other argument can convince you, and you should not be convinced by any other argument."

The blind man was taken to the physician, and Gautam Buddha said, "Stay in this village till you have cured his eyes."

It was not a difficult job. Within six months the man's eyes were cured, and the moment he saw the light he rushed to the other village, far away, where Buddha was. Dancing, in utter joy, he fell at Gautam Buddha's feet and told him, "If you had not met me I would have remained blind. In fact, with all my arguments I was defending my blindness. But you are a man of tremendous discrimination. You did not argue with me; you simply said, 'I am not a physician and your problem can be solved only by a physician.'"

This is the situation with the majority of humanity. That's why it was so easy to crucify Jesus. The day he was crucified thousands of people had gathered to see the miracle of his resurrection, but none of them was seeing the man who was the real miracle. They were utterly blind and closed to the radiation of Jesus.

There is certainly a radiation that is of the highest quality, but it is only available to those who can also raise their consciousness to that height – if not their consciousness at least their longing, their thirst, their openness. Then even a faraway star can be seen. But if you are standing with closed eyes and you insist on your eyes being closed, then it becomes almost impossible to help you.

You are your greatest enemy. You can be your greatest friend too. You are your greatest friend when you make yourself available to higher realities, to higher layers of consciousness, to farther away stars.

With the opening of your heart, your wings also start opening. With the understanding of the light radiating from the awakened one, a synchronicity happens. In the beginning, your heart starts trembling, then the trembling changes into a dancing, and a moment comes when the master's heartbeat and your heartbeat become one. All division, all separation is dissolved.

Perhaps science will never be able to understand this radiation of the illumined being because science needs something material that can be experimented upon. This is not something material; it is as immaterial as love, it is as immaterial as gratitude, it is as immaterial as poetry, as music. In life, all that is great is immaterial, and this is the greatest experience of immateriality.

It all depends on you. There are people who may stand on the bank of a river and remain thirsty because they are keeping their back toward the river and they are adamant and stubborn. They may die of thirst, but they will not change their position. Man's ego is such a barrier that it prevents everything that is a nourishment to his being and a push toward the heights.

In one of his beautiful poems, an Indian mystic Kabir says: "Unless you bow down and make a cup of your hands to fill it with the water of the river, you are going to remain thirsty. You may be standing in the river, but if you are not ready to bow down a little, the river is helpless. It cannot jump to your lips, it cannot jump to quench your thirst."

The ego does not allow you the opening. The ego is very much afraid of anything of the beyond. Just a ray from the beyond and it is enough to kill your ego forever. So the ego lives in a dark cell; no light should enter in it. And the radiation of the enlightened one is so delicate and so respectful of your individuality and your dignity that it will not interfere. It will not enter without your invitation, without your receptivity.

Even here, sometimes spectators arrive. Sometimes people who are just curious arrive: knowing nothing, not knowing that this is not the place for the curious, and this is not the place for the egoist. This is a place only for those who come with an open heart, who come with deep love and trust. The purpose of this place is not to convey more information and knowledge to you. The purpose is to raise your being to the heights that are its birthright.

Just three days ago, one man wrote a letter. Because I said that these space visitors are just hallucinations, illusory, he must have become freaked out. Perhaps he has met some faraway visitor from another planet. He wrote a very angry letter. His handwriting and his spelling show that he must be an American because he has not signed his name – an utterly cowardly person. I never answer any question unless it is signed because the person should take the responsibility for asking it. To whom am I going to address my answer? I cannot say, "To whomsoever it may concern!"

And his anger – which is just the other side of cowardliness – is so much that he has threatened that if I don't answer his question, he will stand up and make trouble in the gathering of seekers. I have waited for three days, but the guy has not stood up. He is afraid that if sometime in the future it is discovered that life exists on other planets and visitors have been coming to the earth, then I will be proved wrong.

His point is: can an enlightened man commit a mistake? As far as I am concerned, my first mistake was becoming enlightened! And my second mistake was to make people aware about my enlightenment; otherwise I would not have been tortured by all kinds of idiots and such fools.

Remember one thing, I am the first enlightened man in the whole of history who accepts that there is every possibility of his committing mistakes. I don't say I am infallible like the pope; I don't say I am omniscient, omnipotent, omnipresent like Gautam Buddha, Mahavira, Krishna because that creates problems. Christians claim these same qualities for God, and Mohammedans also for their God. But their God is in constant difficulty, and Krishna and Buddha and Mahavira are all in constant difficulty because they claim something that is not right.

For example, there was no reason for Christianity, for the pope, to force Galileo to change in his book where he has written: "The common understanding is not right. People think that the sun goes around the earth, but my whole discovery, my whole life's effort has made me aware that the situation is just vice versa. It is the earth that goes around the sun."

Now, the problem was that in the Bible it says that the sun goes around the earth. Galileo was sick, almost on his deathbed, in his old age – he was seventy-seven – and he was dragged to the court of the pope and the pope forced him to change the statement.

Galileo, even at that age, must have had an immense sense of humor. He said, "There is no problem. Why are you so worried? You could have just sent me the message. But can I ask what is hurting you?"

The pope said, "It is a question of God's prestige. In the Bible it says that the sun goes around the earth, and if you contradict it, you are telling us that God and God's son are not omniscient: they don't know the future, what is going to happen, they don't even know what is already happening. And God made the earth and God made the sun – and he does not know. You will spoil our whole religion."

Now, religion is not at all concerned with whether the earth goes around the sun or the sun goes around the earth, or both go anywhere! What concern is it for the religious? – let them go! But the problem is omniscience: the all-knowing God becomes fallible.

Galileo said, "I will change it without making any difficulty, but one thing I want you to know: whether I change it or not, the earth will still continue to go around the sun. It is not in my hands. What can I do? I can change it in my book, but in the footnote I will make it clear that I cannot help it; it is simply beyond my capacity. I can write anything you want me to write, but in the footnote am I allowed to state the fact?"

And in fact in his book he changed the statement, but in the footnote he said, "Whatever I say, don't be bothered. It does not make any difference: the earth still continues to go around the sun. They don't listen to me, what can I do?"

In Jainism Mahavira is number one, because Jainism does not believe in any God so naturally the number two becomes number one. In Christianity, Jesus is only number two. In Jainism, because there is no God, Mahavira is number one – so he has the highest position and he says that the moon is the place where virtuous people go. This means that up to now only one or two Americans have been virtuous!

For Mahavira it was good to say that the moon is paradise: it looks like paradise, so beautiful, and nobody could criticize him because nobody had gone there. But now the situation is different. Two virtuous people have visited the moon and they have not found anyone there, not even Mahavira. It is just absolute desert, unlivable because the oxygen is eight times less than on the earth so you cannot survive; you have to continuously keep yourself going with artificial oxygen.

You cannot grow anything because there are no rains; the earth is absolutely dry. You cannot dig a well; there has never been any water. And because there is no water, that's why there are no clouds. For the clouds to form, water is needed so that in the hot sun the water evaporates and becomes clouds. And when it becomes cool the vapor again turns into water and rains. There is no water; hence there is no possibility of clouds, no rain, and nothing grows on the whole moon. The moon has never known a single roseflower. But now Jainism and its followers are in difficulty...

I was traveling in Gujarat and a Jaina monk was collecting millions of dollars to create a scientific lab to prove that all these people, Russians and Americans, are deceiving the world. They have not reached the moon; all that they are sending are simply photographic tricks.

I asked him, "Why are you worried and why are you collecting so much money? What is your concern if they are sending photographic tricks? It is good entertainment for the whole world."

He said, "It is a question of Mahavira's omniscience. Our whole religion is at stake. If these people are right, then Mahavira is wrong. And if he can be wrong in one thing, what is the certainty that he is not wrong in other things?"

This is the fear, and this is why science has been continuously fighting against religion for progress and religion has been creating hindrances of all kinds – because every progress in science will prove the Bible wrong, and finally it proves God wrong. All these saviors and prophets and messengers have claimed the same three qualities: that they are all- powerful, omnipotent; all-knowing, omniscient; and present everywhere.

I don't belong to these people's category. And whenever I see something that shows utter stupidity, I don't care about the consequences. I say unto you, even the enlightened man has the right to commit mistakes because his enlightenment is concerned only with one thing: knowing oneself. It does not mean that he knows everything in the world: past, present, future. Knowing oneself does not mean that whatever I say about other things is bound to be right forever.

But you don't understand the ways of a master. I am perfectly aware that there are a few scientists who guess – it is not certain – that there may be life on other planets. But it is only a scientific guess. And I know that many people have seen flying saucers and six-inch-tall green people descending from these saucers. But one thing is very strange: all the people who have seen these things are either cuckoos, lunatics, whimsical, schizophrenic – not even a single intelligent person has come across any flying saucer. It is very strange. It seems that the people who are coming in flying saucers have a certain communication with the cuckoos.

If the man who wrote the letter to me has some connection with these flying saucers and these green people, just tell them to land here and I will be the first to accept their existence. But I cannot trust lunatics. Not even a single person on the whole earth who has some credibility has encountered these things. Faraway farmers, drunks, people who have escaped from lunatic asylums – only they see them. They even communicate with them – in what language?

If these people from other planets want to communicate with the earth, they should descend in Oxford, in Cambridge, in Harvard: somewhere where the geniuses, the intelligent, the cultured people are – with whom some connection can be created, and their acceptance will become the acceptance of the whole world. They should meet some scientists.

What I was saying was that at this moment it is simply a cuckoo phenomenon. I am not saying that in the future there may not be some connection with other planets – who am I to predict about the future? And if the future finds my statements incorrect, that's perfectly all right; that's how humanity progresses. If I am entitled to find incorrect statements in Jesus, Buddha and Socrates, how can I be so illogical and irrational as to not allow the future to find incorrect statements from me? That is how humanity progresses.

If everything has been written once and for all five thousand years ago in Rig Veda, then there is no possibility of progress. And all these people have been very insistent. For example, Jesus said, "I am the only begotten son of God." Why this emphasis on only begotten son? There can be other cuckoos who can declare, "I am a cousin to Jesus," "I am Jesus' younger brother," "I am his..." Neither does Jesus have any certificate, nor do these people have any certificate. What is the problem? How are you going to decide?

Evolution means nobody is infallible. It is a misunderstanding that the enlightened man cannot commit mistakes because the enlightened man is not a chemist, is not a druggist, is not a doctor, is not a tailor, is not a shoemaker.

What do you want the enlightened man to be – all knowing? I cannot even make a cup of tea! In my whole life I have never made one, just out of fear that it may prove I have committed a mistake! I don't do anything, out of the consideration that if you don't do anything, at least one thing is certain – you are infallible! The moment you do something, there is every possibility to commit a mistake because self-knowledge does not mean omniscience. To know oneself does not mean you know all the stars – the whole of astronomy – it does not mean you know the whole of physics, it does not mean you know nuclear weapons.

I am the first man in the whole of history who is accepting authentically and sincerely that self-realization, or awakening, or enlightenment, or buddhahood, is confined to a certain sphere. It is confined to one's own consciousness. All darkness disappears: one becomes a luminous being. One is utterly blissful, ecstatic; one's life becomes a living poetry. And if people approach such a person with joy, with love, with openness... certainly enlightenment is contagious and there is no cure for it.

Just to make you a little less serious because I hate seriousness... All these talks about enlightenment and awakened people are so desert-like that I have to plant some oases in a few places.

Two rival poets met in a tea shop, and over a pot of tea each started boasting about the progress they had made in their careers.

"You have no idea," bragged one, "how many people read my poetry now. Why, my readers have doubled."

"Wonderful! Congratulations!" cried the other poet, enthusiastically, pumping his hand. "I had no idea you got married!"

A playboy with a permanent leer on his face got into a crowded lift in the hotel where he was staying. The lift was operated by a very pretty young girl and as she let people off at each floor she was finally alone with the playboy. He came up close to her and said, "Sweetheart, I imagine you must be tired after a day of all these stops and starts?"

"The stops and starts," she replied, "don't bother me. What I can't stand is the jerks."

Osho,
Why am I not in the front row?

Before I answer your question, there is another question also which will make your question complete.

Osho,
Why am I sitting in the front row?

A Lufthansa airliner had to make an emergency landing at sea. The captain assured the passengers that they would be picked up shortly and that the plane would remain afloat for at least thirty minutes.

After twenty minutes had passed no rescue boats had arrived, and the captain announced, "Everybody who can swim, get on the left wing. And everybody who can't swim get on the right wing. Now for the people on the left wing – when the water gets to your knees, start swimming. And for the people on the right wing – thank you for flying Lufthansa."

Those who are in the front row are the people who cannot swim, and those who are not in the front row are the people who can swim. Okay?

Osho,
Oftentimes, when I close my eyes and look inside, I get in touch with a deep longing in my heart, for nothing in particular, just a longing. Beloved master is this a hindrance on the path, or is this the fire that keeps me going?

Prem Amiyo, it is one of the most beautiful experiences to have a pure longing, not knowing for what. The moment you know what the longing is for, the longing becomes a desire, and a desire is a hindrance, a bondage. But a pure longing, a heartache, not knowing at all for what; with no objective in the vision, no goal to reach, but just a pure fire – it burns all the hindrances, it burns all the rubbish that centuries have put around you.

This is the fire that Zarathustra taught his disciples to worship. But as it has happened with every great master, the followers of Zarathustra are still worshipping fire. You will be surprised to know that even here in India, when the followers of Zarathustra escaped from Iran against the Mohammedan invasion and against the Mohammedans' forceful conversion of people into their religion – because Mohammedanism knows only one argument, and that is the sword. Either be a Mohammedan or they will cut off your head. They don't allow any other alternative.

So now there are only very few people, but at one time the whole of Iran was full of the followers of Zarathustra. Now there are not any followers of Zarathustra; they have all been converted into Mohammedanism, but a few escaped and they landed in India. So a great religion has become confined to a small space, Mumbai.

But they have not forgotten one thing: the fire. Still, after twenty-five centuries, that ancient fire continues to be burned in Zarathustran temples. They never allow it to go out. They go on putting new fuel, watching twenty-four hours that the fire should not go out because Zarathustra taught them that once the fire goes out you are dead.

But Zarathustra was talking about the fire that Prem Amiyo is asking about. It is the fire of pure longing that burns in your heart and that burns everything that is not you. And out of this fire comes your twenty-four carat gold character: you in your authenticity.

Don't be puzzled about it. It is natural when for the first time you feel something like a longing but with no object; it is puzzling to the mind. Mind knows longing for money, longing for sex, longing for power, the longing for prestige. But longing without any object? It goes beyond mind.

But it is the most beautiful experience to go through this fire. It is not hot. It is cool, it is calm, it is something magnificent. It makes you a temple. It will burn everything false and unauthentic in you. It will kill your hypocrite, it will destroy your divisions of being, your schizophrenic structure of mind. It will bring you into your utter purity and innocence. You will blossom in this fire: your mystic rose.

So be happy, sing and dance. You are on the right path.

Two old English gentlemen were sitting in their London club when one said, "Ah yes, my late wife was a most remarkable person, a very religious woman. She never missed a day in church and at home it was prayers and psalm singing from morning to night."

"Remarkable, "said his friend, "how did she come to die?"

The first man puffed on his cigar and said, "I strangled her."

Prem Amiyo, don't let others know about your fire. Don't let others know the transformation that is going on within you because people become more antagonistic about your inner transformation than anything else. They can tolerate your having great power as a president, as a prime minister, or being the richest man in the world. This they can tolerate. But they cannot tolerate it if your essential being in its crystal-clear purity starts showing. This is a great insult to them because they feel that this was possible for them too, but they have been wasting their time in stupid games. Now you remind them of what they have missed. The only way to forget is to destroy you.

All the great, illumined people have been killed, destroyed, poisoned – for the simple reason that the crowd could not tolerate it; it was too much. They were flying so high, it was hurting millions of people: "They belonged to us, they have been amongst us, and it is humiliating that they have attained such height and such flight and we are still crawling on the earth." The only way to forget their humiliation is to destroy them. They don't think of the other possibility.

A few think of it, and those few go through the transformation. Those few are very blessed. Those few start looking at those who have reached to the height as their pioneers, as glimpses of their own future and their potentiality. They start also moving in the same direction.

But these people are very few. The majority take the easiest course and that is to destroy those who create unnecessary disturbance: disturbance in your business, disturbance in your love affairs, disturbance in everything.

The greatest wound is in the ego: that you cannot reach to that height and somebody else has reached.

And the last thing, for everybody:

The US Navy was looking for recruits to fight in its latest war against Iran. Due to lack of interest, the draft was reintroduced and an unfortunate young student was called up. During his physical examination he pretended to have poor eyesight in order to be judged unfit to fight.

But the doctor did not believe him, so he sent for a gorgeous young nurse and told her to take off her clothes. "Describe what you see, young man," the doctor demanded.

"All I see is a blur, doctor," the student replied.

"Well," said the doctor, "your eyes may not be as good as they should be – but your missile is pointing straight at the gulf."

21

Even Death Will Disappear

Osho,
For about six months I have been waking up every morning with a deep fear of death. I must be missing the most important experiences in my meditation to be so afraid of death in my sleep. Years ago, I woke up every morning with a smile and deep happiness that I had found you. Osho, I am still smiling, and the happiness to be with you has deepened even more – it's just that the mornings are a bit different. Can you please shine some light on them?

There are a few important things to be understood. They will become the background and you will be able to understand your question.

My work is not to answer you, but to help you to solve your questions. This is a totally different kind of work.

Our whole education system is based on giving ready-made answers. Because of those ready-made answers you never develop your intelligence. There is no need – you ask the question and a computer- teacher answers them.

I cannot do that tremendous harm to your intelligence, so my answers have to be looked at in a totally different way. I will give you the background, all the implications, and the question will be solved by you, not answered by me.

Unless a question is solved by you yourself, your intelligence never becomes sharp, your consciousness never becomes alert. You go on accumulating ready-made answers in your mind, in your memory, which is simply a load, of no use. In any situation which is fresh and new you will be at a loss what to do because you don't have the ready- made answer.

I am working from a totally different angle. I want you to be capable, conscious, alert, intelligent, so whenever a new situation arises – and every day you are going to face a new situation – you are capable of responding with certainty on your own. It is a joy when you find an answer to any question yourself.

This should be the fundamental of all educational systems. It is not. They have chosen the cheapest way, the shortcut: you ask the question and they will give you the answer.

I don't give you an answer while I am answering you; I am trying to put your whole situation before you. If you can become aware of the whole situation the answer will arise on its own, in your own intelligence. It will become a flame within you. And because it is yours, you will have a certainty, an indubitability, a tremendous trust in it.

You can believe any answer given from outside, but you cannot trust it. You can manage, you can force yourself to believe it because the person who has given it seems to be the right person. But all these are guesses, and a belief is not a trust. Belief is always in somebody else; trust is something that arises in you as a fragrance of your being – as your intelligence sharpening, as your consciousness growing.

The question is, "For about six months I have been waking up every morning with a deep fear of death. I must be missing the most important experiences in my meditation to be so afraid of death in myself."

The situation is just the contrary: because your meditation is deepening, that's why your morning is filled with the fear of death, not vice versa.

You say you used to wake up every morning "...with a smile and deep happiness that I had found you. Osho, I am still smiling, and the happiness to be with you has deepened even more – it is just that the mornings are a bit different."

Because your joyfulness, your blissfulness has deepened, because your meditation is going perfectly well, that's why in the morning when you wake up there is a fear of death. It is not a bad sign. It is tremendously important for you to understand that it is absolutely beautiful.

Why does it happen? – because meditation and death are almost synonymous. On the one hand, meditation brings you the realization of your being, on the other hand it kills your ego – and you have been attached, identified with the ego, not with the being. So the first experiences of deepening meditation feel like you are dying.

And why only in the morning? – because as meditation deepens your sleep deepens. Your sleep becomes more silent, thoughtless; a tremendous serenity. While you are doing meditation with effort, the very effort does not allow it to go deeper, but once you have tasted something of meditation your sleep automatically moves in the direction of meditation. It is so delicious that when there is nothing to do you are relaxed, your consciousness starts slipping into deeper layers of meditation.

In the morning when you wake up a fear arises of death because meditation is death of the ego. But the death of the ego is the beginning of your authentic life. Once this is understood, slowly, slowly the fear of death will disappear.

Secondly, your being a woman, the fear of death is deeper than it is in man. These are the uniquenesses and differences between man and woman. The woman always wants to remain young, particularly the modern woman. Once she is thirty-five, to reach thirty-six takes almost six years! She does not want to grow older because she knows unconsciously that every growth is going to end up in death. Particularly for a woman, her youth is her life. And the modern stupidity has given it more emphasis – that a woman's life is just while she is young; the moment she is old, she is a used cartridge, she is of no use.

A young couple was sitting on the beach on a full-moon night and the woman as usual was insisting on getting married...

Why are women so insistent on getting married? – because they know unconsciously that this beauty, this youth is very momentary, and after it is gone it will be very difficult to find anyone to be married to. It is even difficult when you are young and beautiful to get someone intelligent to marry you.

The man looked at the woman and he said, "I will marry you sweetheart, just wait."

The woman said, "I cannot wait anymore. You have been telling me this for almost two years."

The man said, "If you insist we can get married today."

The woman asked one question, which perhaps is inside every woman: "You love me so much. Will you also love me when I am old?"

The man was shocked with the very idea of her being old. He said, "You are putting me in a dilemma. Just one thing you have to tell me: when you are old will you look like your mother? If so, then I am finished. I don't want to get married!"

But every woman is naturally afraid when she becomes old. Man has reduced woman into a commodity. Fresh, young, juicy, she has a market value. As all these phenomenal, momentary things pass by, her price in the marketplace goes down. In her old age, unless she has attained some insight into her consciousness, which is always young and fresh and which need not be dependent on anybody else, death is really a great horror. The very word *death* is associated with something terrible.

You need not be worried about death. Meditation is the cure, the cure from the fallacy that one dies.

Nobody has ever died, *ever*. Death is simply the greatest fiction, which we go on believing because we always see somebody else dying; we never see ourselves dying. So knowingly or unknowingly we go on believing that it is always the other who dies.

Obviously, when you die you will die to others. And in this continuous flow of millions of years, everybody has only seen somebody else dying. Nobody has seen himself dying except very exceptional people whose meditation has gone so deep that the moment they are separated from their body they know that the body was always dead, that it consisted of dead materials: the life that was showing in the body was just the inflow of eternal life that was reflected in the body.

The constant river of eternal life flowing within you also makes your body look alive. The moment the eternal flow has moved, has changed its course, your body comes to its reality. But you never die. And the whole art of meditation is to make you aware and alert that you are not the body.

This is a good symptom, very significant, that as your meditation is deepening, your joy is deepening, your happiness is deepening, a strange thing happens... Because logically you must have thought that when meditation deepens, happiness deepens, joy becomes greater; then every morning getting up with the fear of death seems to be absolutely illogical, irrelevant – because even before your meditations, before coming to me, you were getting up without the fear of death. There are millions of people who will get up every day, but they will not be at all afraid of death because their consciousness never goes to that depth where they can feel in their sleep that the ego is dying. But being a woman, naturally you are more afraid.

Meditation will take that fear away and meditation will also take away the idea that one is man and one is woman because those things belong to the body. Consciousness is transcendental; it is neither male nor female.

"There is only one thing I want," she told him. "All I want is a solid gold boy scout knife."

He offered her yachts, cars, mink coats – but she insisted on a solid gold boy scout knife. The stunned suitor went away and had one especially made.

A week later he brought it, and asked her, "Is this all you want to make you happy? What are you going to do with it?"

She opened a huge chest and put the knife in amongst hundreds of other gold knives.

"Why?" he asked.

The girl replied, "Well right now I am very young and beautiful and everyone wants me. But some day I'm going to be old and ugly – and can you imagine what a boy scout will do for one of these?"

This is the way people live – so unconsciously! The greatest unconsciousness is that which makes you believe that you are your appearance, your body. It does not allow you to know it is not your appearance that constitutes your inner witness. That witness can see the body as separate from itself, it can see the mind as separate from itself, it can see the ego and everything separate from itself.

The moment the witness awakens in you – and meditation is nothing but nagging the witness to wake up. Meditation is a woman! She goes on nagging and finally the poor fellow, the witness, has to wake up!

Once the witness has awakened you have come to a point of transformation. Now you will not be identified anymore with all that is mortal. Now you will know from your inner sources with absolute unconditional certainty your eternity, your immortality. And unless a man knows that he is deathless, the fear somehow lurks in his mind.

You can try to forget it. It is easier to forget it when you are young because you can go on doing all kinds of foolish things when you are young. But when you are old and left alone – because the young fools are doing their own things, nobody takes care of you, nobody even bothers whether you exist or not – then one finds oneself in a deep depression.

Except death, there is no future. Life has passed away; one cannot go back, and ahead, ahead is only death.

Ronald Reagan was addressing a mass gathering of American farmers. He began by telling a couple of jokes to try and get the men of the land on his side.

Realizing that this was not working he tried another approach. He drew himself up to his full height and began. "Fellow pioneers! I want you to know that when I became president, the country's economy stood on the edge of an abyss. I am proud to tell you that since then we have made a brave step forward!"

When you are old, there is no step forward, just an abyss, abysmal. Only the meditator knows there is no death. His certainty that there is no death is not based on scriptures, borrowed knowledge because such things cannot be based on scriptures and borrowed knowledge.

Nothing helps except your own realization. And the old woman particularly becomes very frustrated. She was so much loved, so much appreciated. Now nobody looks at her; hence her fear of death becomes many times greater than man's.

Frank was talking to his wife Alice, while the little old lady sat in the living room, knitting.

"Now look, Alice," he whispered, "I don't want to sound harsh, but your mother has been living with us for twenty years now. Isn't it about time she got an apartment of her own?"

"*My* mother?" gasped Alice. "I thought she was *your* mother."

They have not even bothered to inquire whose mother she is, and for twenty-five years... This shows a deep ignoring, tolerating.

But this is not going to happen to you. You are already on the right path and the symptom of death arising in the morning is very indicative that your meditation is going deeper and making you aware that the ego is not you. Your sleep is perfectly good, your day is perfectly good – so why is it happening only in the morning?

It is because the whole night you are enjoying a silent, meditative state, but as you wake up the old habit of getting identified with the ego grips you. A silent knowledge that this ego is going to die and "I am this ego" makes you afraid, worried, anxious.

But the situation is very clear: If you understand what I am saying, you should rejoice that this fear of death is coming at the right moment. The morning is the right moment.

In India for centuries we have a word *sandhya*, for prayer. *Sandhya* means twilight. In the evening when the day turns into night and in the morning, when the night turns into day, there is such a tremendous change that these are the two points chosen by India to be alert, conscious – because if you can be conscious in these two moments your meditation will become perfect very easily. Because of the shifting gears as the day moves into night, in the night you are no longer an ego.

That's why the night is so relaxing, that's why it is so rejuvenating, that's why you feel after a beautiful sleep that you have become again young and fresh. All tiredness is gone and you are again ready to work – because the ego was left when the sun was setting you were simply pure consciousness. And in the morning the reverse happens: from simple consciousness you again jump into the old bullock cart of your ego and for a moment, the fear.

The modern, contemporary society is very confused because people go to sleep in the middle of the night, wake up at eleven o'clock in the morning. They have disturbed the whole harmony with nature. When there was no light, no electricity, no kerosene oil, as the sun was setting people were preparing their beds. There was nothing else to do. It was in a deep synchronicity with nature – nature is going to sleep, the trees are going to sleep, the birds are returning back to their trees and they are preparing to go to sleep. Everything is going to sleep, except man.

There are a few men whose real life begins in the night but they are upsetting their balance with nature. Particularly the rich people who can afford to sleep the whole day and drink and eat and listen to music or see a dancer – their whole night is an Arabian night. Day seems to be a little stale. It is better to pass it by sleeping. But even those who are not very rich have forgotten that when the whole of nature is going to sleep it is better to follow it.

Don't be left out of nature's harmony. And when the whole of nature is waking up, wake up. With the sunrise you should also rise up: with the birds singing and flowers opening and bees buzzing around the flowers and butterflies opening their wings and the birds moving again into the sunlight to distant places – this is the time for you too to wake up!

These two moments... *Sandhya* means evening, and *sandhya* also means the meeting of day and night. So there are two *sandhyas*: one in the evening, one in the morning when the day and night separate. In those gaps you can enter very deeply into meditation, and it is meditation alone which can help your witnessing self to be completely unidentified with all that is ephemeral, dreamlike. One day it is there, another day it is gone. Only fools can go on playing with the ephemeral.

A little intelligence is enough to make you aware that the real search is not for the ephemeral but for the eternal. And unless you have found the eternal your life was a wastage. It was a tremendous opportunity given by existence to you, but you did not use it.

Your symptom is perfectly good, so rejoice in it. Go deeper in meditation, go deeper in your happiness, go deeper in your dance and the fear of death will disappear.

And not only the fear – even death will disappear because death does not exist.

Osho,
Since I have been able to trust more and more in existence, everything is going so easily, so softly, so beautifully. I get everything I need, and even when something goes wrong, after a while I can see its sense. I feel so thankful that I can see that existence is always providing the right thing for me. It gives me so much trust. Would you please talk about it?

The phenomenon of trust has to be understood a little more clearly. Then I can discuss your question.

First, trust has to be unconditional – not that nature goes on fulfilling your needs, existence goes on giving you help, supports you. What about if it doesn't support you? What about if it creates hindrances on your path? Your trust will disappear. This trust is not very authentic.

And another thing to remember: the trust in existence can only be real if you trust in yourself because you are the closest experience of existence. Otherwise, when things are going right you will trust; when things are not going right the trust will start disappearing.

Once a man came to me and he said, "I trust in God absolutely."

I said, "How have you found absolute trust in God? I have not even found God yet!"

He said, "I have been married for seven years and no child was coming our way. Finally somebody suggested to me, "It is your irreligiousness. Trust God and you will have a child.'" And the man said, "I was suspicious, but I said what is the harm in trying? At the worst there may not be any child – and anyway it is not coming. So I started worshipping the elephant god, Ganesha, whose temple was just close to my house. Strangely enough, after nine months my wife gave birth to a beautiful child. I trust in God absolutely, particularly the elephant god."

I said, "As far as I know, you are a lecturer of science in a college."

He said, "That's true."

I said, "Then a simple thing has to be understood: no scientific experiment is thought to be conclusive unless you make many experiments and always come to the same conclusion, without exception."

He said, "That's true."

So I said, "Now start a few other things with your elephant god." He was a little afraid. I said, "Don't be afraid; absolute trust knows no fear! Now start asking the elephant god for a girl. You have got a boy; you need a girl too."

He said, "My wife also insists for a girl."

So I said, "Try it! It is only a question of nine months, and then I will give you another experiment."

Nine months passed, ten months passed, and the man did not turn up, so I had to go to his home. I knocked on his door saying, "What happened? What happened to your elephant god?"

He said, "Forget all about this god. That was just accidental, just a coincidence because I have been praying and praying, morning and evening and ten months have passed, and my wife is not even pregnant!"

I said, "Just one failure and your trust has disappeared?"

When everything is going smoothly and beautifully, you can trust. But you are trusting somebody else: God, God's only begotten son, any messenger of God, a prophet, a *tirthankara* or a Gautam Buddha. It does not matter. You are trusting somebody else and things can go wrong any moment. The basic trust has not to be in existence, it has to be within you.

You should learn to become more conscious and alert to trust yourself. Do you trust yourself? If you trust yourself that will be unconditional trust because it cannot be for any particular reason. And out of that unconditional trust will grow many branches: you will become a huge tree with great foliage. You will trust love, you will trust the truth, you will trust godliness, you will trust beauty; you will simply trust because your heart is full of trust and there is not even a shadow of distrust. Even if you want to distrust, you cannot.

Only when you cannot distrust, even if you want to, have you come to the very center of your being, from where arises the trust in existence, in life, in people, in trees.

And that is not because of any conditions. Trust itself is such a blessing, such an ecstasy in itself. Once you have tasted it within yourself you would like to taste it in the whole cosmos. If it is so great just within you, how much greater it will be when you trust everything. It does not depend on any condition being fulfilled.

You say, "Since I have been able to trust more and more in existence..." How do you manage to trust more and more in existence – on what grounds? Existence gives you birth, which is a pain; existence gives you a life, which is nothing but misery; existence gives you hopes which are never fulfilled; existence gives you promises and the goods are never delivered; and finally the existence makes you old, and then one step more – Ronald Reagan's step forward – and you are finished!

What has been able to create in you more and more trust in existence? And remember there are things that either you have or you don't have. You cannot have them more or less.

Love is another dimension of trust. Have you ever thought about it? People go on saying, "I love you more and more." But love does not know any quantities. It is a quality; you cannot measure it less or more – one kilo or two kilos or three kilos. It is good that people don't use that, that: "I love you two kilos, and it is growing. Don't be worried! Soon you will see – I will be loving you three kilos."

It is not a quantity, it is not part of the world of quantities, it is not matter that it can be measured into more or less. Trust is the highest fragrance of love. You cannot say, "I have been able to trust more and more." You are saying it because existence – perhaps just by coincidence – has been a great support to you, or perhaps you are imaginative enough that whatever existence brings to you, you start imagining, "This is what I always wanted."

In either case it is not trust. So first I would like you to see that trust is not a quantity but a quality. Either you have it in total or you don't have it in total; either it is nil or it is one hundred percent. You cannot divide it into slices. It is indivisibly one, organically one.

But I can understand why you say "more and more," because every day you find everything is going so easily. But everything is not going so easily in Ethiopia. Everything is not going so easily for the millions of poor on the earth. Everything is not going so easily for the millions who are sick and ill and just on the waiting list of death.

What is going easily? You cannot find a more insane world than that which surrounds you. There are millions of people behind bars in the jails – things are not going easily for them – and there are millions of people who cannot manage even a single meal in a day. Things are not going easily. And don't be so egocentric: if they are going easily for you then you can trust existence – but what about the whole world? How many people are committing suicide? How many people are murdering each other? How many people are insane? Things are not going easily. If that is your criterion of trust, soon it will disappear. A small accident, a car crash, and things are no longer going easily.

One of my old sannyasins and a man who has reached very close to enlightenment – any day he will explode into luminosity – is sitting here, Pungalia. He was the man who invited me to Pune twenty-five years ago. In these twenty-five years many have come and gone, but he has remained unwavering and is going deeper and deeper into meditation. Such a man can say that he trusts in himself because every moment and every day he is reaching closer to the light that has been searched for by all the seekers of the world.

Because of his inner experience and the blissfulness and the peace and the silence, he can spread his wings toward existence, toward people, and can find trust. But it will not be more and more: it will come on its own accord the day the small distance that has remained is crossed.

It often happens when the caravan reaches its destination after crossing miles and miles of desert and sand, tired and tattered, but with the hope of reaching the goal... But just as they come close to the goal, everybody wants to relax a little. Now that they have reached there is no hurry. They suddenly feel tired because now there is no question of hope keeping them together. The destiny has arrived. So just before they take the last few steps and enter into the temple, they sit outside the temple. They are so tired.

This happens to every traveler in the inner world. Those few steps when you have reached seem to be the longest steps. But as you get relaxed and as you see the light radiating from the temple, as you hear the celestial music, as you hear some beautiful dance going inside, you cannot remain outside long. You will have to stand up and enter into the temple.

The moment somebody enters in his own temple of being he knows there is no death, he knows there is no disease, he knows there is no problem. Then the trust arises: then the trust in the master who has helped for no other reason than simply that he loved and loved abundantly. Then love arises toward all those who have helped: the friends and the enemies both. And then a trust arises in the whole existence because it is the whole existence that has brought you in different ways to the highest peak of consciousness. There is nothing other than gratitude.

You say, "Everything is going so easily, so softly, so beautifully." It is good, but don't depend on this. What is beautiful today may become ugly tomorrow, and what is smooth today may become very tough tomorrow, and what is so soft may become the greatest hindrance. One never knows about tomorrow.

Rather than focusing your eyes on the trust in existence, first find your center because that is the only guarantee that the trust in existence will be unconditional: whatever happens, there is not going to be any change in your trust.

You are saying, "I get everything I need. And even when something goes wrong, after a while I can see its sense. I feel so thankful that I can see that existence is always providing the right thing for me. It gives me so much trust. Would you please talk about it?"

You are living in an illusion. You don't mention any trust in yourself, and a man who has not experienced it in his own being can only imagine. And you have a tremendous capacity for imagination. If things are going well naturally anybody, howsoever stupid, will trust. When things go wrong your trust must be wavering a little but you wait: perhaps finally, in the end, what looked wrong is not wrong. Then again the trust settles more deeply, but this trust is not going to transform your being because this is a secondary trust, it is not the primary trust.

You are making a castle of sand. Everything is going right; the castle is going up and you trust in existence that no disturbance... But you never know: just a strong wind may disturb your castle, destroy it; or just a small child, out of joy, may come and jump on your castle and it will be finished. There are a thousand and one possibilities of the castle being destroyed. Perhaps you will console yourself with "There must be something good for me in the destruction of the castle. Perhaps it is time to go back home. I'm feeling so hungry – that's why existence destroyed the castle. 'Go back home and eat something.' Existence is taking so much care..."

In this sense your trust is not very trustworthy. It may give you a few beautiful moments, but they are like a dream. I would like you to have a trust so solid that whatever changes it will remain with you without any change. But the beginning has to be from within. From within you can reach to the without, but not vice versa.

It is good that you have been thinking of trust. It is good that the very idea of trust has been surrounding your mind and its atmosphere. Don't feel hurt if I say to you that this is the time when you should turn your trust, the arrow, toward yourself. Do you trust in yourself? And you are the closest to existence. Existence penetrates you to your very being. You should begin from *ABC*, not from somewhere in the middle or somewhere at the end. You are beginning almost at the end: *XYZ*. This is not a right way of progression. There is danger because the whole alphabet is missing. Start from *ABC* and let it grow spontaneously to *XYZ*.

It will grow, it certainly grows. Your being is an immense potential for growth but start from the being.

All the religions of the world have been distracting man from himself. They say, "Pray to God, believe in God, trust in God. He will take care." And we know that for thousands of years nobody has taken care of this world. If God was taking care then there would have been no need for Genghis Khan and Tamerlane and Nadirshah and Adolf Hitler and Joseph Stalin and Ronald Reagan – no need at all. If this is what you think of as caring about existence then there would have been no Hiroshima, no Nagasaki.

In three thousand years man has fought five thousand wars: certainly nobody is taking care. All kinds of diseases go on growing. When I was a child tuberculosis was the greatest disease; now it is just like the common cold. Nobody has much fear if you have tuberculosis – there are medicines available. But those medicines have not been given by any God; they have been given by science, they are man-made.

Then came cancer, and now has come an utterly ugly disease, AIDS. Right now on the earth there are ten million people who are suffering from AIDS. And this is not the total survey of the whole earth; it is the survey only of the Western countries.

Just to give you a total view, I can say that if the Eastern countries are also surveyed, where homosexuality has existed longer than in the West, then there may be at least twenty million people suffering from AIDS – which has no cure. Is existence taking care? Is God taking care? And these twenty million people are the courageous people who have allowed themselves to be examined. There may be many more who are hiding out of fear because the moment a man is found AIDS positive he becomes dangerous to everybody. Friends turn into enemies, lovers forget all about love, his own family closes their doors. He becomes an outcast. This is a double calamity: a certain death between six months and two years, and the people for whom he has lived – even his own children, his wife, his parents, his friends – have thrown him away: "Even to touch you is dangerous."

The AIDS virus can come from any liquid coming out of the body – even perspiration, saliva, tears. Anything coming out of the body can carry the virus. And the virus seems to be immortal; no medicine kills it. It becomes immune to all kinds of treatment. Who is caring for this existence?

So don't just feel that if your life is going goody-goody you can trust existence. I'm not against trust, but it should grow roots within your being, and then it should spread its branches all around. Then perhaps you will have the perceptivity that existence is taking care. Even in a calamity like the disease AIDS perhaps existence is taking care to make man aware that no sexual perversion should be permitted. Existence is telling all the religions, "You are responsible for creating homosexuality." Homosexuality was born in monasteries, in monks, in nuns because men and women were separated. That was unnatural.

You may have the perception that existence is not against; it is simply trying to clean. So much crap has gathered in the human mind, in human beings, that it has to be taken out.

But to have that perception you need a trust in yourself. And how will you find this trust? It is not a belief; it is not just a Christian sermon from any stupid missionary who knows nothing about religion at all, but has crammed beautiful phrases from the Bible and is telling you things that have created all the troubles in the world. More people have been killed by religious wars than by political wars. In the name of God, in the name of religion there have been so many crusades, jihads, religious wars, that one cannot believe that these people are going to bring a better humanity, a loving earth.

If you have the perceptivity that arises out of trust within yourself, it is not a belief. The Christian missionary and all other missionaries of other religions only create belief. Belief is a fake trust.

Trust cannot be created in you by anyone. You will have to dig deep through meditation to find the pure waters of trust within your being. It is going to be your own work on yourself. It is going to be your own creative exploration, adventure.

Yes, buddhas can show you the path, but they cannot help you in any other way. I can tell you about meditations, but I cannot do meditations for you. Without meditation you will not be able to find trust in yourself. And the day of finding the trust in yourself is the greatest day in your eternal life. It changes all the vision, all perception, all judgment about existence and about other people.

The trust goes on growing and spreading all around you. Only then will you have unconditional trust in existence.

You are groping for the right thing, but in the wrong direction. Change your direction. Grope within. You will find it. If your longing and your thirst are strong enough, there is no reason why you cannot find it. It is just there, within your being, not far away.

You don't have to climb Everest; you have just to settle into your own center – unwavering, undistracted, in utter silence and peace – and the trust will grow out of it without any of your effort. Only that trust is trustworthy. Then no changes in the world, no changes in people are going to make even a dent in your trust. Otherwise just a small thing and all your so-called believing, trusting disappears.

I remember the attorney-general in Madhya Pradesh came running to me one day and he said, "You are needed immediately. My father had a heart attack and he loves you so much." His father was an all-India figure, Dada Dharmadhikari – a very intelligent person who had been in deep contact for almost forty years with J. Krishnamurti.

Whenever he used to come to visit his son he would always come to me, and I would tell him, "All your J. Krishnamurti jargon is only intellectual. It won't help you at the right time."

He said, "No, in forty years it has reached to my bones, to my blood, to my marrow. There is no question that it can be shaken by anything."

I went to his home. They had arranged for him to relax in a dark room. I entered without making any noise because I heard somebody saying, "Hare Krishna, Hare Rama."

I said, "Dada Dharmadhikari cannot say that, and there is nobody else." As my eyes became accustomed to the dark room I went close, without making any noise. Very silently he was whispering, "Hare Krishna, Hare Rama."

I shook him and I said, "Dada, what are you doing? This goes against your J. Krishnamurti completely. Have you joined the Hare

Krishna, Hare Rama movement so suddenly? I saw you yesterday and you were a Krishnamurti-ite."

He said, "Don't harass me at this moment. I *know* there is no God and I know this Hare Krishna, Hare Rama is just foolish. But in case – who knows if God exists? And what is the harm? I'm lying down and just repeating my childhood mantra that has been given to me by my traditional guru who said, 'In any difficulty, repeat it and you will be helped.' I'm dying. This is not the moment to discuss it."

I said, "This *is* the moment to discuss it because I have been telling you for almost twenty years that all your Krishnamurti jargon is intellectual. At the right moment it will disappear. Now this is the moment! Now say to me, 'There is no God!'"

He said, "At this moment I cannot say that. It is too risky. Just leave me alone because only a few minutes are left – and perhaps maybe not even a few minutes. Let me repeat my mantra. If he is, I will tell him, 'I repeated the mantra. Forgive me for all my stupidity when I used to tell people that there is no God and things like that.' If he is not, there is no problem. But I can't take a chance."

But he didn't die; it was only the first heart attack. People almost always die when the heart attack comes for the third time. He survived, and after four or five days I went to see him. He was sitting in the garden, in the sun.

I said, "What about Hare Krishna, Hare Rama?"

He said, "All that is nonsense."

I said, "Have you forgotten?"

He said, "No, I have not forgotten, but in weakness, in helplessness one starts looking for some help from the beyond."

I said, "Then all your intellectual, philosophical argumentation is only superficial. If it can't help you in your helplessness then it is of no use."

You can trust existence as an intellectual effort, and you can go on managing your intellectual effort, but in any helpless moment you will start forgetting about it all and you will come to your reality that you have been hiding. I would not like to put you in a mess such as Krishnamurti has put millions of people. I have come across many of them. Just their intellect is full of the answers that Krishnamurti has been repeating continuously almost for seventy years.

Krishnamurti lived long, ninety years, and he started speaking when he was twenty. I think nobody else has ever conditioned people's minds for seventy years – and he was against conditioning people's minds. He conditioned them so much. And he was a great intellectual, a great rationalist: he could convince people very easily, and he convinced them. But all that conviction melted immediately when a person was dying. Dada Dharmadhikari was one of his very close friends.

Never start from the secondary. Always remember as a fundamental rule to start from the primary. And the primary reality and existence is you.

Hidden within you is *satyam shivam sundaram* – the truth, the godliness and the utter beauty of it. That is the seed. Take care of it, and you will soon have a vast tree arising in you, spreading its branches in all directions with millions of flowers.

But the beginning is you, and unless you begin right from the interior of your being, all your beginnings are wrong.

22

Come Closer to Life

Osho,

Sex seems to be dropping me. Is music next?

Milarepa, sex is dropping so many people that the problem is not that sex is dropping you also, the problem is that many others may start picking it up! Dropping is okay. Avoid picking up.

And I can understand your worry. You are asking, "Sex seems to be dropping me. Is music next?"

Music is not something biological, it is not something concerned with your chemistry or physiology. Music is not even of the mind. Music is something – a space between mind and meditation. It is one of the most mysterious phenomena. To conceive it is almost impossible in intellectual terms, for the simple reason that it is beyond mind, but not yet meditation.

It can become meditation. It has both possibilities. It can come down and become mind – then you are only a technician, not a musician. You may be playing perfectly on the instruments, without any faults, but still you are only a technician. You know the technique perfectly and entirely, but it is not your heart and it is not your being. It is just your knowledge.

Music can go higher and further away from mind, and then it starts becoming closer and closer to peace and silence. One is a musician only when he understands the sound of silence, and one who understands the sound of silence is capable of creating sounds which are synonymous with silence. And that is the most miraculous thing. Then the musician has come to his full flowering. Beyond this music starts the world of meditation.

In fact, as far as the East is concerned, the ancient-most sources about music say one thing definitively, and that is that it has been born out of meditation. People who went deep into meditation enjoyed the silence of it, loved the peace that seems to be unfathomable. They wanted to convey that you are far more than you think you are, far bigger than you think you are. You are as big as the whole universe – but how to say it? Words are very poor philosophical concepts – almost like beggars.

The ancient meditators tried to find some way to convey their peace, their silence, their joy, and those were the people who discovered music. Music is a by-product of meditation.

But you can go both ways: either from meditation you can come to music as an expression, a creative expression of your experience; or you can go from music to meditation – because music brings you closer and closer to meditation as music becomes immense silence, sounds merging into silence, sounds creating deeper silences than you have ever known. Then you are very close to the boundary of meditation.

You need not be worried about music. Music is not in the same category as sex – although in the West the modern music has fallen so low that it has come very close to the category of sex. In the West only that music which provokes sexuality in you is appreciated. Sex is the lowest point of your life energy, and if music is used to provoke sexuality, then naturally it has to fall to the same category.

Super-consciousness is the highest point of your life energy. When music reaches super-consciousness, it provokes unknown territories within you, unexplored skies. It can become a door to the divine. Just as it can become a door to the animal at the lowest, at the highest it can become the door to the divine.

Man is only a bridge to be passed. Man is only a bridge between the animal and the divine. You should not make your house on the bridge. Bridges are not for making houses on. You have to pass on, from this shore to that further shore.

Your fear that perhaps music is going to be the next to be dropped comes from your Western conditioning because in the West only music which is sexual is appreciated. The West has completely forgotten its own great musicians who have almost touched the super-conscious. But even the greatest musicians in the West could not go beyond life energies. They could not reach to the cosmic energies.

I am reminded of two stories – both historical, both factual. One is about a man who wanted the emperor of China to declare him the greatest archer of the empire. Certainly he was, and the emperor was absolutely willing to send a message around the empire: "If there is anybody who thinks of being a competitor, he should reach to the capital by a certain date. If nobody comes, then this man is going to be declared the greatest archer in the whole empire."

Just then his old servant who was not just a servant because the emperor's father had died when he was just a child and the father, before dying, gave the child to his very devoted servant and told him, "Now you take care of him. It is your responsibility to see that the empire is not taken over by anybody thinking that now only a child is left. As soon as he is of age, immediately declare him to be crowned as emperor."

The servant had served so well, so wisely, so cleverly, that he had saved the empire for the child for almost fifteen years. So he was not just a servant, he was almost a stepfather, and the emperor had great respect for him. That old man said to the emperor, "Wait! This man is a good technician as far as archery is concerned – I have seen him working – but he does not know what ultimate archery is. He is a good technician; his targets are never missed – one hundred percent perfect."

The emperor said, "If he never misses the target, if his archery is one hundred percent perfect, then why are you telling me that he is not a great archer?"

The old man said, "I know an archer and I can compare. You don't know... In the high mountains there lives an old man, older than me. Nobody knows how old he is. He himself has never bothered to count his years, but certainly he must be more than a hundred years old. And I have seen what archery can be at the highest.

"So I would like to suggest to this young archer to go to the mountains. I will give him an introductory letter. He should be with the old man for a few days and he will forget all about being the greatest archer."

The archer could not believe it: "Who can be greater than me? What can be better than my art?"

But the emperor said, "I cannot do what you are asking me to do. You will have to do what the old man has said. Go to the mountains with this letter and be with this old archer and watch and see the difference between the technician and the real master."

The archer also became interested, although he could not figure it out intellectually: "What can be better? He cannot be more than what I am." But he had no idea.

It took many days for him to reach the old man, who lived on a high mountain. He was so aged, his back was bent down and he could not stand straight. The archer could not see anything in the old man's small cave which gave any indication of archery – not even a bow, no arrows. He said, "You are sure you are the man for whom I have come?"

The old man said, "I am absolutely sure because except me nobody lives on this mountain. Looking at your letter – you think that you are a great archer. If you are a great archer then why are you carrying this bow with you and these arrows? These are good for the beginners, the learners, but not for the masters."

The archer said, "But without arrows, without a bow, what kind of archer will I be?"

The old man came out. He took him to a cliff that went far away above the valley – a very thin cliff and underneath was a valley thousands of feet deep. Although his back was bent and he could not stand straight he went without any trembling, without any wobbling. He simply went to the very edge of the cliff. Half of his feet were off the cliff; and he was standing on only half of his feet, and he called the archer, "Come on!"

The archer said, "My God! Just a little strong wind and you are gone; just a small mistake and you are gone – gone forever! Not even bits and pieces of your body will be found; the valley is so deep and so dangerous." The old man was standing there as if he were standing in his own home.

The archer tried, but he could go only one or two feet, and then out of fear he was trembling so much that he sat down. But that was not enough; then he lay down on the stone, clinging to the cliff and he said, "Help me!" and the old man was at least five or six feet further away.

The old man said, "What kind of archer are you? If the archer cannot stand on this small cliff without trembling, how can he be called an archer? If your hands are trembling, people may not be able to know it – but you cannot deceive a master. Practice for a few days on this cliff: just coming to the very edge and standing there without any fear, without any nervousness."

The man said, "Even trying that is dangerous. Even the rehearsal may finish me. Is there not some other way to learn archery?"

The old man said, "Then the other way is..." And the old man raised his head. Seven cranes were flying overhead and he looked at each crane and the crane fell immediately to the earth – seven cranes without any arrows. He said, "Unless your eyes become arrows you are not a master. So go home, learn to be a master. If I am alive, I will come myself when I think you may be ready. Or if I am not alive – look, my son is coming. I will give him all the instructions and send him. If he approves you, the emperor can declare you, without any contest, the greatest archer of the empire."

The man went home trembling. Even when he reached home the trembling was there. He had never thought that a man, just by looking at a bird, could shoot the bird. He had never thought that just eyes can function like arrows. Just the idea is enough, it needs the support of an absolutely steady, fearless heart, then just the idea "Come down!" is enough and the bird will come down.

He started trying. Twenty years passed, and one day a young man came. He had completely forgotten. The young man asked him, "I don't see your bow and arrows that I saw last time when you came to see my father. He is dead, but he has left instructions for me. The first question is: Where is your bow and where are your arrows?"

The man remained silent for a moment and then he said, "I have heard these words. I remember there was a time when perhaps I used to have a bow and arrows. But since I saw your father, for the first time I understood the old Chinese proverb that when an archer becomes perfect, he throws away his bow and arrows. And when a musician becomes perfect, he forgets all about his instruments. He himself is music; his very being is music. I don't know any more. But your father gave me, in a very strange way, the whole teaching."

He took the young man out, looked at a bird and the bird fell down. The young man said, "Now you can go with this letter that my father has left for you to the emperor."

He said, "Now who cares to be declared the master of archery by the emperor? I am! Forget all about it. Who can declare it? Who has the authority to examine me? If your father were alive – perhaps he had the authority to declare me, but nobody else. It has nothing to do with the emperor, it has nothing to do with the empire.

"But you are the son of my master. Although he has only taught me very little, that little has grown into a huge mastery within me. The old man is not alive; I touch your feet instead because you come from his own blood. And when you go back, take these roses from my garden on my behalf and put them on the grave of your father. Although he will not be able to hear, tell him, 'Your teaching has not gone in vain. The man has really become a master and he has no longer any desire to be declared the champion of the empire.' All longing has disappeared, all desire has disappeared. I am feeling so fulfilled and so complete that I cannot conceive that anything more can be added in my being, and I owe everything to your old father."

Milarepa, when music becomes perfect it does not drop. You become music itself: your every gesture, your eyes, your hands, your feet, your whole being starts throbbing into a music which is in tune with the universal music. Don't be worried about it.

London fog was swirling over the River Thames as a young tramp settled himself for a night on the embankment. Suddenly he was awakened by the sound of a beautiful woman alighting from her Rolls Royce. "You poor man," she said, "you must be terribly cold and wet. Let me drive you to my home and put you up for the night."

Of course the tramp climbed into the car beside her. After a short drive they came to her mansion. The door was opened by the butler. She instructed him to give the tramp a meal, a hot bath and a comfortable bed in the servant's quarters.

Some while later the woman slipped on her negligee and hurried along to the servants' wing. Knocking on the door she entered the room and seeing that the light was on, asked the young man why he was not sleeping.

"Surely you are not hungry?" she asked innocently.

"No, your butler fed me royally," he answered.

"Then perhaps your bed is not comfortable?" she continued.

"But it is," he said, "it is soft and warm."

"Then you must need company," she said, "move over a little."

The young man was overjoyed. He moved over and fell in the River Thames.

So don't be worried, Milarepa. All that is dream will drop, all that is real will remain.

Osho,
The other day I visited Sitama. I looked into her eyes and felt almost as if time had stopped and exploded. Completely overwhelmed, and with much reluctance, I came away laughing and crying. Can you talk about the moment when time stops: when I feel as if everything is rushing at me and at the same time away from me; all in a split second which also seems like a lifetime and leaves me feeling like a small child?

The question about time and its stopping is immensely complex. For centuries philosophy has been trying to figure out what time is. And there have been many different standpoints, but none of them seems to be supported by logic and rationality.

The ordinary idea of time is that it is like a river that is flowing by your side. That which has passed is the past; that which is passing is the present; that which is going to pass is the future – as if time is a flux, a movement, and you are standing and time goes on moving.

But it is not true that you are standing still because once you were a child, now you are young, now you are old, now you are dead. You are not standing still; you are continuously changing. Because of this fact there have been philosophers who propounded a second theory: that time is static, it is always the same, what changes is you. You are the flux: from childhood to youth, from youth to old age, from old age to beyond. Because you cannot conceive your own changing process – it is so subtle and so quick – you project it on time.

Nobody knows what time is, where time is. Nobody has ever seen it. Nobody has ever touched it. Nobody has ever come to grips with time and its existence.

Then three hundred years ago science became interested in what time is because philosophy had not given any satisfactory answer. Science came to a point where it needed an answer about time. Without it, its many hypotheses remain simply hypotheses. It was a gap that had to be filled.

Albert Einstein proposed something that has been temporarily accepted. In science, nothing is accepted permanently because one never knows, tomorrow somebody else may bring a better hypothesis. So science is always hypothetical. That is the beauty of science and that is the ugliness of religion – because religion goes on insisting that whatever is written in the holy scriptures is true, and true forever; no change is possible. How can there be any change when the holy scriptures of all the religions are written by God?

Science has a more significant attitude. Everything is, at the moment, hypothetically right. Nobody can say anything about what will happen the next moment. That is the meaning of relativity: when we say something is true, it simply means that relatively it is true. In comparison to other hypotheses, this hypothesis is relatively true. But tomorrow somebody may introduce some new hypotheses, and in comparison to them it may no longer be true. Something new may become true, but that too will remain only hypothetically true. Science is very honest.

Albert Einstein stated something very great about time: that it is only a dimension of space. We have always known that space has three dimensions; Einstein added the fourth dimension to space, and it fits very well with his physics and it fits very well with all that has been discovered, taking it as a hypothetical truth. So many things, so many discoveries, so many inventions and they all prove reflectively the truth of the hypothesis.

If time is only a dimension of space... You never ask about space: whether it is moving or static. Nobody ever asks. Space is always there, the same. It is the same sky, it is the same space: things in it may change but space remains unchanging. And if time is also a dimension of space that means it does not change at all.

You are saying that you felt in a moment as if time had stopped. Those moments when you experience that time has stopped are great, tremendously great. In fact, time is always in a state of being the same. It is not a flux; it is not a river – the old idea.

Time is always present – never past, never future. Things go on passing, disappearing, new things go on coming, but time itself is only a dimension of space, absolutely static. So when time stops for you it is not time that stops. What stops is your mind.

Your mind is in a constant flux: so many thoughts, so many ideas, so many imaginations and dreams and projections – and they have all stopped. Because your mind stops, suddenly you realize time has stopped.

But in fact the stopping of the mind only reveals to you the reality of time: it is never moving, it is unmoving, it is just here, it is just now. It has never changed, and it will never change. Everything in it changes, but time itself remains absolutely unchanging.

The moment your mind stops moving, suddenly you realize that time has stopped. So it is significant to understand that it is your mind that has stopped, not time.

J. Krishnamurti used to say, again and again, that "Mind is time." This is a strange statement, particularly for those who do not understand the state of no-mind because when the mind disappears, time also disappears – the time that you used to think of as a flux. The mind stopping is a revelation that appears to you as a stopping of time.

But as you grow more and more meditative and your mind becomes more and more silent, you will become aware that as your silence, your peace, your mindlessness is growing, time is disappearing.

When the mind is absolutely still, there is no time. That means there is nothing that you can think of as changing, nothing visible that you can conceive of as time. Hence, the ancient-most treatise on meditation says that those moments when time stops are the moments when you experience meditation. And those are the moments that have given an inclination, a vision, a glimpse of something beyond the mind. Looking at a sunset, you are so absorbed that the mind stops at the beauty of the sunset. Suddenly there is no time.

Time is a reflection of your mind. You can watch it in many ways. When you are miserable, time passes very slowly. Strange – why should the time pass so slowly? And when you are happy and joyous, time passes fast.

There is a statement in the Bible that those who are thrown in the darkness of hell will remain there forever. One of the great agnostic thinkers of our times, Bertrand Russell, has written a book, *Why I Am Not A Christian*, and he insists on that point very much. And logically – and he was a logician and a mathematician – you will be convinced when you look at his argument.

Bertrand Russell accumulated all the facts that made him decide not to be a Christian. He was born a Christian, he belonged to a large family, and he himself had the title of earl – a very respectable man, a Nobel Prize winner. One of the points is that this is absolutely unjustified. Because Christians believe in only one life, in seventy years, how many sins can you commit? If you commit sins from the very first day you are born, without sleeping, without eating, without doing anything else – just committing sins and sins and sins to the very last breath – still, how many sins can you commit?

In the first place it is not possible. You will need sleep – even sinners need sleep – you will have to eat food, you will have to earn your bread, you will have to take time for your bath, for changing your clothes, for shaving your beard. If you count, very little time is left in a seventy-year life when you can commit sins.

Bertrand Russell himself says, "I have noted down how many sins I have committed, and I have also included the sins that I wanted to commit, but could not. Even if I am punished for those sins which I never committed but only thought about, then too the hardest and cruelest judge cannot send me to jail for more than four and a half years."

For such a small sentence an eternity of hellfire? God seems to be insane. There should be some judgment. And he has omitted the point that the same is true for virtue. How much virtue can you do? Eternal paradise for that small amount of virtue that you do? There has to be some limit – and neither are there sinners who need to be eternally in hellfire.

Do you understand what is meant by eternity, unending, forever? Just think what it means – *forever* – and your mind will feel tired. Wherever you go: go on, go on! It never comes to an end. Hellfire just for the few small sins: that you eloped with somebody's wife, that you picked somebody's pocket – eternal hellfire? And just because you donated to Mother Teresa's orphanage and you made a hospital for the poor and opened a school for the poor, you will have eternity in paradise of all pleasures, joys unending! Is there some measure? Is there some justification?

The book was published nearabout seventy years ago, and in seventy years not a single Christian theologian has been able to answer Bertrand Russell. On all other points I agree with him; he is perfectly right. In fact not only he, nobody should be a Christian – but on this point I have a disagreement because it involves the concept of time.

Perhaps he was not aware that he was talking about time, and he should take note about time. I think the Bible is right and closer to Albert Einstein than Bertrand Russell, particularly on this point because the fire in hell will appear as if it is eternal. Pain seems to make time longer. Time seems to be something like elastic, and very cunning. When you are in pain it goes on stretching longer and longer; and when you are blissful and happy, the moment you realize you are blissful it is gone.

But this happens not because of time; this happens because of the mind. When the mind is feeling blissful, time stops. And because time stops you cannot count how many minutes, how many hours, how many days. But when you are in misery your mind is running – so many thoughts, so many worries, so many anguishes. Time becomes very long. In a certain way this means that miserable people live longer lives and happy people die sooner.

Meditation is the way to stop the very idea of time as flux. Meditation is a total stillness. Nothing moves. That's why you felt for a moment that time had stopped. It was just something else that had stopped – it was your mind.

But this is our way of looking at things. You don't even know your own face unless you look at it in a mirror.

When you see that time has stopped, watch immediately what is happening within you. Has the mind stopped? I am giving you a clue: whenever time stops, immediately find out if your mind has stopped. In fact the mind stops first; then only do you discover that time has stopped.

Now you have a key in your hands. Let your mind stop completely and time stops completely. You start living in a timelessness.

For example, I don't know what date today is. When Anando or Neelam come for some signature from me, they immediately tell me the date because I don't know what date it is. What do I have to do with dates? I use my watch only when I come to talk to you because I am afraid I may continue for eternity! The whole day I don't look at the watch. I don't need to.

I don't know exactly... In the morning when I wake up it often happens that I forget whether it is morning because I have cut every day into two days. In the afternoon I sleep for three hours so when I wake up the problem arises again: is it morning or is it afternoon? From my inside no answer comes.

For almost thirty-five years I have lived in absolute timelessness. I don't know when the new year begins and ends. To me, the day my ego disappeared, my mind became silent, the whole existence has become silent and still, unmoving.

And you are saying, "At the same time... it seems like a lifetime and leaves me feeling like a small child."

There are two things to be remembered about the experience of being a child. One is to be childlike, which is immensely beautiful. Jesus says, "Unless you are born again just like a child..."

But remember, he is not exactly saying a child, but *just like* a child – something similar to the child's consciousness. But that does not mean that you are as ignorant as a child. You are just innocent as a child, but not ignorant as a child.

So childhood has two dimensions: one is ignorance, one is innocence. Both are mixed, but we have to make a clear-cut division. And we have two different words. When we say, "You should be born again like a child," it is one thing, and when we want to condemn somebody then we say, "Don't behave in a childish way." That childish way is not the way of "just like a child"; that childish way takes only the ignorant part of the child, and "just like a child" takes only the innocent part of the child. We are dividing the child into two different dimensions.

Always remember – because one can forget, listening again and again to "be just like a child." You may start being childish. That is not the meaning.

The little boy was putting his shoes on by himself for the first time, but he put his right shoe on his left foot and vice versa. When he had finished, he ran to his mother: "Look Mummy," he said proudly, "I put them on all by myself."

"That's very good," said his mother, "but I am afraid you have put them on the wrong feet."

The little boy looked down, and then said confidently, "No, Mummy, these are definitely my feet."

A reporter asked Ronald Reagan, "Mr. President, with all the problems in the world today, how do you manage to sleep at night?"

"I sleep like a baby," replies Reagan. "I cry a little and I wet the bed."

I don't want you to be that childish.

Osho,
I have always heard you say, "Stop doing. Watch." Several times lately I've heard you say that the mind should be the servant instead of our master. It feels that there is nothing to do except watch. But the question still arises: Is there anything to do with this unruly servant but to watch?

There is nothing else to do with this unruly servant but just to watch. Apparently it appears too simple a solution for too complex a problem, but these are part of the mysteries of existence. The problem may be too complex; the solution can be very simple.

Watching, witnessing, being aware seem to be small words to solve the whole complexity of mind. Millions of years of heritage, tradition, conditioning, prejudice – how will they disappear just by watching?

But they disappear because as Gautam Buddha used to say, "If the lights of the house are on, thieves don't come close to that house knowing that the master is awake." Because the light is showing from the windows, from the doors, you can see that the light is on. It is not the time to enter into the house. When the lights are off, thieves are attracted to the house. Darkness becomes an invitation. As Gautam Buddha used to say, the same is the situation about your thoughts, imaginations, dreams, anxieties – your whole mind.

If the witness is there, the witness is almost like the light: these thieves start dispersing. And if these thieves find there is no witness, they start calling their brothers and cousins and everybody, "Come on!"

It is as simple a phenomenon as the light. The moment you bring the light in, the darkness disappears. You don't ask, "Is just light enough for darkness to disappear?" or, "When we have brought the light, will we have to do something more for the darkness to disappear?"

No, just the presence of the light is the absence of the darkness, and the absence of the light is the presence of darkness. The presence of the witness is the absence of the mind, and the absence of the witness is the presence of the mind.

The moment you start watching, slowly, slowly as your watcher becomes stronger your mind will become weaker. The moment it realizes that the watcher has come to maturity, the mind immediately submits as a beautiful servant. It is a mechanism. If the master has arrived, then the machine can be used. If the master is not there or is fast asleep, then the machine goes on working things – whatsoever it can – on its own. There is nobody to give orders; there is nobody to say, "No, stop! That thing has not to be done."

Then the mind is slowly convinced that it itself is the master. And for thousands of years it has remained your master, so when you try to be a witness it fights because it is a question of it having completely forgotten that it is only a servant. You have been so long absent that it does not recognize you; hence the struggle between the witness and the thoughts.

But the final victory is going to be yours because both nature and existence want you to be the master and the mind to be the servant. Then things are in harmony. Then the mind cannot go wrong. Then everything is existentially relaxed, silent, flowing toward its destiny.

You don't have to do anything else but to watch.

Paddy bought a parrot at an auction. He asked the auctioneer, "I have spent a great deal of money on this parrot – are you sure he can talk?"

The auctioneer replied, "Of course I am sure. He was bidding against you."

Such is the unawareness of the mind, and such are the stupidities of the mind.

I have heard that the Irish atheists, seeing that the theists have started a dial-a-prayer service, have also started one – although they are atheists. But the competitive mind... They have also started a dial-a-prayer service. When you phone them up, nobody answers.

Two tramps were sitting by a campfire one night. One of them was very depressed. "You know Jim," he mused, "the life of a tramp is not as great as it is made out to be. Nights on park benches – or in a cold barn – traveling on foot and always dodging the police, being kicked from one town to another, wondering where your next meal is coming from, being sneered at by your fellow man..." His voice trailed off and he sighed heavily.

"Well," said the other tramp, "if that is how you feel about it, why don't you go and find yourself a job?"

"What!" said the first tramp in amazement, "and admit that I'm a failure?"

Mind has become accustomed to being a master. It will take a little time to bring it to its senses. Witnessing is enough. It is a very silent process, but the consequences are tremendously great. There is no other method that can be better than witnessing as far as dispersing the darkness of the mind is concerned.

In fact, there are one hundred and twelve methods of meditation. I have gone through all those methods – and not intellectually. It took me years to go through each method and to find out its very essence. And after going through one hundred and twelve methods I was amazed that the essence is witnessing. The methods' non-essentials are different, but the center of each method is witnessing.

Hence I can say to you, there is only one meditation in the whole world and that is the art of witnessing. It will do everything – the whole transformation of your being and it will open the doors of *satyam shivam sundaram*: the truth, the godliness and the beauty of it all.

23

Life Is a Blessing

Osho,

Why such an enormous fear of allowing myself to be really alive?

The fear of allowing oneself to be really alive is not the fear of life; it is a very camouflaged fear about death. If you are alive you will die. Death is the culmination of life. The fear of life is not basically fear of life; it is basically fear of what life will bring ultimately to you, and that is death.

But mind is very clever at camouflaging things and giving you directions that are not right. They take you away from the actuality of your inner subjective experience. How can one be afraid of life? For what?

All that we have got is life. All the music, all the dance and all the songs and all the beauty and all the search for truth belong to a man who is fully alive. What fear can there be about life?

Life has to be lived so totally and so intensely that you can squeeze each minute's juice without leaving a single drop behind. Only such a life is authentic, great. Only such a life does not come to an end in death. Such a life comes to the door of the divine at the moment of death.

Death is a complex experience – just as life is. Perhaps more complex because life is spread over seventy or eighty years and death is condensed into a single moment, a split second. Because of its condensed nature, it is a miracle that those who have not lived only experience death and those who have lived fully experience an eternal release into the universal consciousness. For them death becomes a friend.

But begin with life because life is the beginning, and death is the end. If you are afraid from the very beginning you will not give nourishment to the rosebush, you will not give water, you will not care about it, you will not come close to it, you will not shower your love on it. The rosebush is going to shrink, and without roses it is going to die without ever having experienced any beautiful moment of blissfulness or ecstasy. It will simply shrink; it will never know that it had the possibility of tremendous beauty and the fragrance of roses. Naturally the state of such a rosebush is very depressive. It will die in anguish without knowing what life was. It will know only death.

This is a simple logic to be remembered. If you don't live life fully you will have to experience death, which is just a fiction, but you will feel it almost more than your actual life – because you have never lived life, it has been just a faint, faraway echo. At the most it consists of the same stuff that dreams are made of – but you have never lived actually, you have never loved actually, you have never danced actually, you have always remained apart. Wherever there was a life source to rejuvenate you, you did not allow yourself the rejuvenation. You did not allow life to visit you and to be your guest, although you seemed to be alive. But that life was only medical.

You were breathing, you were talking, you were sleeping, you were waking up, you were working... These are the symptoms for medical science of a man who is alive, but the mystics know much, much more than medical science. They know that these are only symptoms, but they are not life – and that life can exist without the symptoms, or the symptoms can exist without life.

I am reminded of one Indian mystic, Brahma Yogi. For almost thirty years he was learning a single thing, because he himself was a doctor and he wanted to prove to medical science that your symptoms are not synonymous with life. It is a strange world. He exhibited it in Oxford, in Cambridge, in Harvard, in Tokyo, in Kolkata.

What he used to do was sit in deep meditation and slowly his breathing would stop, the pulse would go away, the heartbeat would not be there and the doctors would check – the best doctors of those universities – and a dozen doctors would write a death certificate for him. All the symptoms that medical science thinks of as death were totally fulfilled in the man. There was no possibility of his being alive.

And this was his condition: that when they found him dead they should immediately sign the death certificate. After ten minutes, slowly he would start breathing again, the pulse would come back, the heartbeat would come back, and slowly he would open his eyes and smile at the doctors. He collected these death certificates so many times, in so many medical colleges, in so many universities that it became a great puzzle. The doctors could not believe it. All the symptoms were absolutely clear. What was his secret?

His secret has been known for centuries in the East. Even you can feel it on a smaller basis because I don't want you to waste thirty years just to prove it. That is useless. But on a smaller basis you can experience it while you meditate. As meditation deepens, your breathing becomes slower, silent.

You know perfectly well that when you are angry, humiliated, your breathing becomes faster; your heartbeat becomes faster. When suddenly you hear some good news, that you have won a lottery, your heart beats so loudly that even the neighbors can hear it!

You know your heartbeat, your breathing changes with your emotions. In meditation you are going beyond emotions, beyond thoughts. Naturally, breathing becomes so silent that unless you try to hear it very closely, it is very difficult.

In Zen, when a meditator goes very deep, the only way to find whether he is alive or dead is to bring a mirror in front of his nose. You cannot hear his breathing, but on the mirror the breathing leaves a little vapor. That remains the only sign that he is alive.

The heart starts going into a subtler rhythm, the pulse becomes so slow... almost invisible. Before quartz watches with batteries came into existence, I was in difficulty. Automatic watches function perfectly, but they depend on your pulse. Your pulse goes on giving them movement, and the movement of your hands. The moment you put them away, within two or three hours they stop.

I have tried almost all the best watches in the world that are automatic, but on my hand they don't go even for three hours. From the moment I put them on my hand, within five or ten minutes they stop because everything is so silent. And unless I have to move my hands – and that is only when I am speaking to you – otherwise my hands are in complete relaxation with my body.

Finally they said that no automatic watch is going to work on me so I have to use either a winding watch, which is an older version, or a quartz watch which runs on a battery.

Brahma Yogi proved beyond doubt to almost all the experts of the world that symptoms of life are only outer. The life source can remain so still inside that you don't have any way to find it from the outside. Only the person who is alive knows its beauty, its luminosity, its blissfulness. But those are not the things that any stethoscope will be able to catch – blessings, blissfulness, ecstasy. There is no instrument to find them.

If life can be dissociated from symptoms – Brahma Yogi never said this, I am saying it – then the other possibility also becomes a reality. It may be that millions of people are only suffering from symptoms of life; inside there is nothing. Just like a robot, they have a physiology, a biology, a chemistry, a brain which has an inbuilt program to go on running for seventy years. It will go on running.

You will be surprised to know that even in the grave, hair goes on growing, nails go on growing because their inbuilt process is such that it does not need life at all. If you dig up a grave, you are going to be amazed: the man's hair has become very long, his nails have become very long. You may freak out: "Is this man really dead or has he befooled us?"

But the world is full of corpses going all around – corpses because they are afraid of life. And why are they afraid of life? They are afraid because if they enter the stream of life, finally they will have to face death. But their logic is absolutely absurd.

The experience of all those in the whole history of mankind who have lived totally and intensely, who have burned their life's torch from both the ends together, is that they never came across death. They were so alive that a great transformation happens at the moment of death. They don't die, they don't become unconscious. They simply move either in a new form of life, or if they have become so awakened that there is no need for any other form, they move into the formless universe. The whole universe becomes their body and their being. That is the ultimate peak that you are capable of. But if you are afraid of life, then it is very difficult.

In India there is a plant, a very beautiful plant. Its name is also very beautiful; its name is *chhuimui*. It means "very touchy." Just touch one leaf of the plant and the whole plant immediately closes. All its leaves close; the whole plant looks as if it is completely dead. Just one leaf! It has a small number of leaves, two leaves, and if you just touch one leaf both leaves will close and the whole plant will immediately go into an emergency situation – some danger! And it takes at least fifteen minutes for it to wait and see whether the danger is gone. Then slowly, slowly it opens its leaves again.

If you are *chhuimui* – so touchy that the moment life comes close to you, you immediately close up – then for what are you living? You are already dead. People are dead to different degrees: a few are a hundred percent dead, a few are fifty percent, a few are thirty percent. The more religious, the more virtuous, the more moralistic, the more puritan – they don't have more than five percent life, or even less. The great saints have even shrunk more. They live only one percent because they can still breathe. Except for that, there is no sign of life.

The fear of death takes you away from life but the reality is that unless you live a hundred percent – or if you can manage it, a little more too – then death is not going to happen to you. You will never experience any death, but only a change of house. Everybody will know that you are dead, but what have you to do with everybody else? You will know that you are alive, and more alive than you ever were because the body is a hindrance, a cage, an imprisonment.

Mind is so heavy and loaded with garbage. You don't see that your consciousness is carrying almost a Himalayan load of thousands of years; its back is bent. The moment your consciousness is freed from the body, it comes into the open, into the clearance, under the sky, under the stars. And this freedom is the freedom from all past because all the past is carried in the body, in the brain. Consciousness is always new.

But because you are identified with the body, you think that some time you are young, and then you are old and then one day you die. It is your identification with the body that is creating the trouble.

You will have to learn from *ABC* about life, love, laughter. You have got such a small time span; don't waste it in fear. Jump into life's deepest waters. Only life can redeem you from death. What ordinarily seems to be the end of life is not the end of life for those who are awakened. It is the beginning of a totally new life, far greater, far bigger, far more luminous.

Start falling in love: at least you may become ten percent alive. Start enjoying food: you will become a little more alive. Start enjoying the beauty that surrounds the world and you will become more alive.

Keep yourself free from all bondages such as marriage because I don't know anything else which comes so very close to death as marriage. Two persons, both are alive, and both are sitting by each other's side, dead – completely dead. I can say from far away, seeing a couple walking, whether they are husband and wife. If you see their faces, long, saintly, they are husband and wife. If you see them laughing, enjoying, joking, then the wife belongs to someone else – or it may be vice versa: the husband belongs to somebody else.

If you really want to be more and more alive, then come closer in every area of life with intensity and totality.

Life is a blessing it is not a sin. Life is a gift it is not guilt. Life is the greatest thing that existence has given to you – for nothing! Just because you have not paid for it, you don't recognize its value. Don't lose a single moment. When there is a chance to dance, don't sit in the corner and be just an onlooker. Participate. When people are laughing, don't participate just not to look stupid.

Laugh with your whole heart. Don't be worried whether anybody else is laughing or not. You should always look at my sannyasin, Sardar. He does not care whether anybody else is laughing or not. When he feels like laughing, he laughs. He is always there at the beginning. Then others follow, slowly, slowly, thinking that everybody is laughing so it is okay, there is nothing wrong here.

Meditation will help you to come closer to life. Love will help to bring you closer to life. Creativity will bring you closer to life. Enjoying small things that have been condemned by your stupid so-called saints will bring you closer to life.

In Mahatma Gandhi's ashram, even tea was banned. Now, tea is not much of a sin: just a little caffeine in it, but no sin at all. No religious scripture says that tea is a sin. And to destroy people's taste, Gandhi invented a new chutney, a new sauce. You have seen the neem trees here? Just taste one of the leaves and you will never forget it! It is the bitterest tree in the world. And he used to make everybody in the ashram... he used to sit with everybody to eat and he checked whether the neem chutney was given to everybody or not. That was a strategy to destroy your taste.

One American writer was preparing to write his biography, and he was allowed to stay in Mahatma Gandhi's ashram for a few weeks. He remembers that the most difficult thing was that neem chutney, twice a day: "The first day I could not believe it – am I being poisoned or what? Then he explained to me the greatness of this chutney..."

In ayurveda, neem is thought to be the most valuable plant in the world. It has great qualities, it purifies the blood. Just its taste is hell.

So when Mahatma Gandhi explained it to him, being a newcomer he took a small taste and said, "My God!" So he thought it was better not to destroy the whole meal: "I should gulp it all at one time and drink water so that I can enjoy the food."

When he gulped it, Gandhi called the cook and said, "I told you he would love it. Bring him another chutney!"

The biographer said, "My God, so now I cannot even gulp it!"

Neem chutney was virtuous because one of the fundamentals in his ashram was taken from Jainism; that is, tastelessness. Now these are the people who are against life. You should not taste food, you should not enjoy beautiful clothes, you should not enjoy the ordinary things of life – a good comfortable bed, a small beautiful house with a beautiful garden and flowers.

Do you know that in Gandhi's ashram all the flowerpots used to grow only wheat? He was against roses: roses are very luxurious and they represent the capitalists, and what India needs is wheat! And how much wheat will he give? Nine hundred million people and his two or three pots are growing wheat.

But it was symbolic of his mind and it was symbolic of the mind of all so-called saints – self-torture. And the only way to torture yourself is to deprive yourself of anything living, loving, beautiful.

Just try to understand that my whole approach is life-affirmative. To me, anything that denies life is irreligious; and up to now all the religions have been irreligious in that sense. They have been denying life any affirmation, and naturally, the more you shrink away from life, the more you already feel dead. You drag yourself from your cradle to the grave.

The only thing that you can enjoy is an ego-fulfillment because people think you are a saint.

Farmer Giles decided to write his will. He called his three sons and gave each one a duck, with the instructions that whoever sold their duck for the most would inherit the farm.

The first son went to market and sold his duck for ten dollars.

The second son sold his duck to the neighboring farmer for fifteen dollars.

The third son, who was a bit of a dreamer, was carrying his duck to town when a village girl approached him and offered to make love with him if he gave her the duck.

It turned out that they had such a good time together, she wanted to give him back the duck if he would make love with her again.

Weak at the knees from his experience, and wandering along the country lane with his duck, the young man was knocked over by a car and the duck was killed.

The motorist jumped from his car and pushed a twenty dollar note into the young man's hand, apologizing all the while for his careless driving. The young man dusted himself off and arrived home, tired and tattered.

Farmer Giles asked him how he had got on.

"Well," said the boy, "I got fucked for a duck, I got a duck for a fuck, and twenty dollars for a fucked up duck."

Just look at the lighter side of life and enjoy it to its fullest, and all fear will disappear. Only experience of life and love and laughter will dispel the darkness of fear.

I have offered to the Jews in Israel... They have been deceived by the American and British politicians who gave them the land of Israel. Perhaps it was the most cunning thing that has happened in this century. The Jews thought it was great, but they could not understand the conspiracy.

The conspiracy was that Israel is a small place and the Jews are surrounded on all sides by Mohammedans, bloodthirsty Mohammedans. And the land that is now Israel had been in their hands for centuries. The Mohammedans used to live there and they cannot accept the idea that their land should go back to the Jews who had lost it centuries ago. For centuries the Jews have been homeless, with no land.

The Jews could not see that with an ocean of Mohammedans all around they would be tortured continuously, terrorized, bombed. Their life is not going to be a life, but a continuous struggle to survive, and finally they will either have to disappear or to leave Israel again.

And when I say this, both England and America are Christian countries. If their intentions were really good, then the Vatican pope should have given recognition to Israel. He has not given recognition to Israel. For him, Israel does not exist as a sovereign country. That shows the reality of the Christian mind.

And on the other hand, after the Second World War, American and British politicians happened to possess the land. It should have been given to Palestine – which has been a Mohammedan country for centuries – but America and Britain forced things because they had great armies there and the land was occupied. They gave the land to the Jews. This is the ugliest thing that anybody could have done.

The Jews have been tortured for two thousand years because they crucified Jesus, and now this is a crucifixion for all the Jews – Israel. They have poured their money into it, they have come from faraway lands, they have been working hard because it is a desert; and alongside there is continuous harassment from the Mohammedans who are not going to accept that Israel is not theirs. On their maps they still show Palestine, not Israel.

And the trouble has increased more and more just now – in a way in which the Jews were not even aware would happen. There are outside enemies all around, and now there are inside enemies.

Firstly, the Mohammedans who have been living in the land for centuries are still there. They function as informers to the Mohammedans because their devotion is to Mohammedanism. And something new, inconceivable, is happening because some Jews have come from Europe, and a few Jews have been living in Palestine for centuries. They are the most orthodox; because they have not seen the world, they don't know what is contemporary. The Jews from Europe are far more advanced, and then the Jews from America are almost not Jews. Now they are fighting; now these three sections of Jews are fighting continuously because the orthodox want to rule over all the Jews. The Americans have enjoyed freedom; they don't follow the old orthodox concepts. And the same to a lesser degree is true about the European Jews – so now they are killing each other.

I said that since America has illegally and criminally taken over the commune land, I offer it to the Jews of Jerusalem to make it a new Jerusalem, a new Israel. And ask the American government – if they are so helpful, then why not give them the whole state of Oregon? Anyway, half the land of Oregon belongs to the federal government of America; it is very easy to give Oregon.

As a beginning, as a token of my love and my understanding, I give my commune's land where we have wasted three hundred million dollars. And it is not a small place; it is one hundred and twenty-six square miles. My idea was to make the commune at least one hundred thousand sannyasins – and they would not have been crowded, it was so big, vast.

Just now I have received the latest joke about Jews moving to Rancho Rajneesh.

Finally, the very last Jew moved with all his belongings to the former Rancho Rajneesh.

With all their energy the new inhabitants threw themselves into working on the fields and the creeks, on reopening the shops and hotel, and on making a kosher kitchen from the former "Magdalena."

Since they had to leave their mourning wall in Jerusalem... They have a long ancient wall in Jerusalem, just to mourn, cry, weep. The louder you cry, the more tears come from your eyes, the more religious you are. Every day you can see this circus: hundreds of people standing by the old wall, crying, weeping. I cannot conceive what kind of religiousness this is.

So the only problem in Rancho Rajneesh was that since they had to leave their mourning wall in Jerusalem, the rabbis decided to build a huge new one at the east side of Rajneesh Mandir.

When the wall was finally built, all the Jews went there to mourn and to pray to God. When one of the rabbis returned to the synagogue, the rabbi who had stayed behind asked him how it was at the new mourning wall.

"Not very good," the other replied. "I could not stop them from dancing and singing."

Naturally, in my place mourning is not possible. I may not be present there, but I have left enough of my vibration there. My people have left enough dance and enough music there in the air. The rabbi was very much shocked that instead of mourning, they were dancing and singing.

To me, dancing and singing can be an intrinsic part of a religious life, but not mourning. Mourning you should leave to the dead; it does not suit the living.

Osho,
Since you have come out again, I'm melting away in the discourses. It feels as if fighting has stopped or become less. Is it awareness that will help me stay in that melting space of yes, trust and acceptance; or is it natural to move through all different kinds of cycles? If I fall back into fighting, "no" and tension, is it due to unawareness?

The more awareness you have, the more you will find your heart filled with "yes". The less awareness and you will find your heart filled with "no". "Yes" brings joy, love, blissfulness. "No" makes you a desert where nothing grows, but only despair, anguish, angst.

You are asking me: should you remain alert and aware to keep your peace, your silence, your trust, or go in circles – sometimes yes, sometimes no?

The question arises from your old habit. This "yes" is so new to you, although it is blissful, the old friends, misery and fighting and "no" and anguish, suffering, will try in every way to pull you back into their company. And to come out of this vicious circle is one of the absolute necessities of being a sannyasin. Unless your "yes" is so pure that there is no shadow of "no" in it, you will not be able to progress on the path of enlightenment. The old friends will pull you backward.

Be courageous and be strong and don't be impressed and influenced by the old gang which has always been around you. But if you like tension, if you like suffering, if you like miserableness, then it is a different matter. I don't want to interfere in your freedom of choice.

There are people who love their misery; in fact they magnify it, exaggerate it. They only talk about misery, nothing else, and if you don't listen to their misery they become antagonistic to you. The psychology behind these miserable people, who are in the majority in the world, is that when they are miserable people give sympathy to them. It is obviously a very subtle human ego. When you see somebody in misery you sympathize because deep down you are feeling happy that you are not in this stupid fellow's position. And secondly, to sympathize makes you higher: you are not in a position that somebody else should sympathize with you.

The miserable person misunderstands your sympathy as love. Sympathy is not love; it is just a poor plastic substitute. Love is a real authentic living phenomenon. Misery is just asking for love – but nobody loves a miserable person; at the most you can manage to sympathize and run away.

What are you going to gain by being tense and unaware? You are only going to lose. For the first time you are out of the clouds and the sun is clear and you are asking me, "Should I go again behind the black clouds?" I cannot suggest that, but I cannot impose on you any order that you should not.

If you want to move in circles and if it is your joy, you can do it. But remember, those who move in circles never progress. Progress has to be on a straight line, not in circles.

There is one spider in Africa – a certain species of spider. They are very religious people in the old sense of the word: they always follow the leader. Wherever he goes, they go behind. One scientist was working on these spiders and their strange behavior. Thousands of spiders will be going, they don't know who is ahead of them, who is the leader. But somebody must be.

He managed a small experiment that will be helpful to you. He brought a big round plate and put the spiders on that round plate. They started moving, but because the plate was round, they soon made a circle. Everybody found somebody else was ahead, so that must be the leader. Even the leader thought, "Somebody is ahead, so there must be a bigger leader than me."

You will not believe the result of the experiment. For three days continuously they moved on. They were not going anywhere, but they could not stop either. Somebody was ahead, somebody was behind. They only stopped when they started dying. By and by, other spiders threw those who died in the middle of the plate and continued their journey, their great pilgrimage. Finally they all died, but even the last one remained true to the tradition. Without eating anything, without drinking anything, the poor fellow just following an old ritual.

But you are not a species of spider. You are human beings with intelligence. There is no need to go in circles of "yes" and "no". It will never lead you anywhere. Whatever you gain with "yes", "no" will cancel. Whatever misery, tension, suffering you gain with "no", "yes" will destroy. But nothing will be in your hands – ever.

Unless you learn to move in a straight line like an arrow toward the goal, you will never reach anywhere. Don't be stupid, that's all I can say to you.

You are a beautiful person because I hear Milarepa has fallen in love with you, and Milarepa is a very choosy fellow! Why not be beautiful inside also? – because the inside beauty is a thousandfold deeper than the outer beauty, and the outer beauty fades one day. And whether it fades or not, Milarepa is going to fade away because he is not a monogamist. He does not believe in monotony. He believes in new pastures, adventures – it does not matter with whom!

But only your inner beauty can only bring you close to me. Just beware of your mind dragging you into unawareness.

Yussel Rabinowitz and his wife Bessie were hiding from the Nazis in a secluded Berlin basement. One day Yussel decided to get a breath of fresh air, but while out walking he came face to face with Adolf Hitler himself. The German leader pulled out a gun and pointed to a pile of horseshit in the street. "All right, Jew!" he shouted, "Eat that or I'll kill you."

Trembling, Yussel did as he was ordered. Hitler began laughing so hard that he dropped his gun. Yussel grabbed it and said, "Now you eat, or I will shoot!"

The Fuhrer got down on his hands and knees and began eating. While he was occupied, Yussel sneaked away and ran back to his basement. He slammed the door shut, bolted and locked it securely.

"Bessie, Bessie!" he shouted. "Guess who I had lunch with today!"

24

The Fragrance of Enlightenment

Osho,
When I hear you say that you are only here for us, I feel such an urgency arising in me, such an urge to move deep inside beyond all my little piddly trips and limitations. And yet inside, realizing such a deep helplessness... Is there any secret or short cut, so I don't miss?

The path that leads to your innermost being makes you feel more and more a tremendous urgency as you come closer to the center of your being. The farther away you are from yourself, the less is the magnetic pull of your being. It is a simple scientific fact.

As you come closer to the magnetic field, you become more and more aware of a tremendous urgency. Something is going to happen, something that is going to transform you completely, something for which you have been waiting for many, many lives, something that... you are not even aware what to call it. This is one part of the feeling of urgency.

The second part is that the closer you are to realization... a deep fear arises: will you be able to make it? When you were far away there was no question of missing. You were certain that you had missed it, there was a certain certainty. But as you come closer to the peak, a human fear arises: are you going to make it in such a short time, with this such small energy of yours?

And as you see the peak, you also can see that your problems are so trivial, your pleasures are also very trivial, your whole life is childish.

Your fights, your friendships, your love affairs seem to be so small and so stupid that you want to get out of them as quickly as possible.

Before, you were never in such an urgency to get out of them because you had never realized what your potential is, to what heights you are entitled, so you went on playing with toys. But now that a vision has arisen and is becoming more and more clear, you can see all your involvements, commitments, relationships – everything is so small compared to your inner consciousness.

And those small things have been clinging to you for many lives. They are parasites; they are not going to leave you easily because to leave you means certain death. It is your blood they thrive on. And the moment you realize that these small things are preventing you – such small things that I am reminded of a beautiful story that Gautam Buddha used to tell his disciples. It is a strange story and perhaps no Buddhist has ever commented on it because only a buddha can comment on it, not a Buddhist; only a man of absolute awareness can see what Buddha was trying to say through this small story.

He said that a man who is blind is lost in a big palace that has one thousand doors, but nine hundred and ninety-nine are closed; only one door is open. The man is blind: he has to grope and find the door. Nine hundred and ninety-nine doors, he goes on searching; some door may be open. And finally he comes to the door that is open – but then suddenly he feels a strong desire to scratch his head. He starts scratching his head and passes the door. Again nine hundred and ninety-nine doors, and who knows what will happen next time when he comes to the one thousandth door? Just a stupid desire to scratch the head...

What Buddha was trying to say is that your problems are not very big. You are far bigger than your problems! Your intrinsic capacities are immense, incalculable. Your problems are utter trivia, but you are so much involved in those small problems that you cannot see beyond them.

But when you come closer to yourself you stand between two things. On one side is your whole past, which is nothing but a long, long history of stupidities; and your future, which is so close, so luminous, such a splendor that naturally a great urgency arises: how to get rid of this whole past? How to get rid of this mind? How to get rid of all these problems that have been torturing you, all these nightmares that you have been suffering, and take a quantum leap to reach to your very center, where no problem has ever entered, where no thought has ever arisen, where nothing is small and trivial, where everything is *satyam shivam sundaram*, where everything is nothing but pure truth and pure divineness and pure beauty.

And when you see it so close, another urgency also arises. Hearing me say that I am here only for you, there is a trembling fear. On the one hand, perhaps you may not be able to make it before I have to leave my body, and on the other hand, the feeling of urgency is not only for you, but for the whole of humanity too: are we going to spread the fragrance of enlightenment? Have we the capacity? Have we the courage to fight against the enormous ignorance all around?

You have as much power and as much capacity as any Jesus, any Socrates, any Gautam Buddha because essentially we come from the same source, essentially we have the same potential.

But I can understand your feeling of urgency. My only suggestion is to avoid making this urgency a problem, otherwise this will be another trivia. Just be absolutely contented that you have come so close. Be contented that you can see what is trivia and what is significant. Be content that I am still with you and the phenomenon of transformation can happen in a split second.

Be content that if I can stand alone against the world, with all kinds of prejudices, you are also capable. You have to stand alone just to represent me. The day you will be able to stand alone against superstitions, prejudices, religions, politicians – that day will be a day of celebration for you because you have represented me with your total being.

It is perfectly good to feel the urgency, but don't try to find any shortcut or any secret because there is none. If there were some secrets I would have given them to you. I am in a deeper urgency than you are. If there were any shortcuts, do you think I am miserly – that I would not give them to you and that I will unnecessarily torture you on long, arduous paths when a shortcut is available?

I have heard about a man who was driving. He stopped his car and asked an old farmer who was smoking, sitting by the side of a tree, very relaxed, "How far is New Delhi?"

The farmer asked, "Are you going the way your car is facing?"

The man said, "You are strange. I am asking how far Delhi is."

The farmer said, "Without knowing, I cannot answer. First answer my question: Are you going in the direction your car is facing? Then Delhi is really too far. I don't think you will be able to make it."

The man said, "I thought you were a simple farmer, but you seem to be a philosopher."

He said, "I am a simple farmer. You have left Delhi almost fifty miles behind. If you turn your car back, Delhi is very close, but if you go in this direction then you will have to go around the whole earth, and then too there is no certainty that you will reach Delhi. There are a thousand and one ways one can go astray."

Gautam Buddha is passing through a forest. It is fall and the whole forest is full of dry leaves and naked trees are standing against the evening sun looking so beautiful.

Ananda, his close disciple, asked him, "I wanted to ask it many times, but other people were present. Now fortunately a few disciples have gone ahead, a few are coming behind, and this is a moment I am alone with you and I can ask a question." And his question was: "Have you told us everything that you know or are there some secrets that you are holding back?"

Gautam Buddha bent down, filled his hand with dry leaves, showed him those dry leaves in his hand and said, "Whatever I have told you is just like these few dry leaves. What I have not told you is just like the whole forest full of dry leaves; but it is not because I am a miser, it is not because I wanted to hold it back from you. Even to say these few leaves has been such a difficult task. I have wasted my whole life in conveying something about these few leaves, but these few leaves are enough as far as understanding all the leaves of the forest are concerned. If you can understand these few leaves – just a handful – you have understood all the leaves of all the forests."

It is a question of understanding. You do not have to know all the oceans to come to the conclusion that ocean water is salty. From anywhere, just a little taste of the ocean will give you the taste of all the oceans – which you may never visit.

Whatever was necessary, whatever was essential I have been telling you. Whatever is left untold is left untold because there is no way to tell it. If you can understand what I have told you, you will come to a situation, a position, a consciousness, a perceptivity, where you can know all that which I have not been able to tell you. But I am not holding anything back from you.

This is a moment that you should be contented that you have come so close. Your urgency must not turn into a discontent; otherwise you will be thrown back far away.

Your urgency should be transformed into a deep contentment and a rejoicing that you have been able to be a fellow-traveler of one who is fully awakened, and you have been a fellow traveler of many who are also searching and seeking with tremendous intensity – something which the whole world is unaware of. If this contentment settles in you, perhaps the quantum leap will happen on its own accord.

Nathan Nussbaum met his old friend, Benjamin Rosenblatt, in the street one day.

"How are things?" asked Benjamin.

"Good," replied Nathan.

"Good?" says Benjamin. "You seem to have plenty of troubles."

"No, no" said Nathan nonchalantly, "it is always good. In summer I am good and hot. In winter I am good and cold. My roof leaks, so when it rains I get good and wet. Also that nag of a wife always makes me good and mad. And when I am at home, I feel good and worried. Believe me, I am good and tired of it all!"

I am not asking for such contentment. Your contentment should be a song, a dance, a rejoicing, a love, a sharing. Your contentment should not be dead. It should be alive and dancing.

Osho,
Being here and meditating, I feel I am drowning inside myself more and more, and although I relate with people, they seem far away on my periphery. At the same time, I am receiving so much: you keep pouring and pouring your love over me. Why am I so miserly in giving to others, when I am receiving so much from you?

I am happy to know that your meditation is going deeper, becoming more alive, and you are feeling as if you are drowning inside yourself more and more. It is one of the great blessings that happen to all meditators.

The meditator is the most blessed person in the whole universe. He is the very cream of the universal evolution.

And I can also understand your problem. You say, "...and although I relate with people, they seem far away on my periphery." They don't seem, they *are*. The moment you are at your center, everything is on the periphery. You had not realized it before because you were also on the periphery, so people looked very close. You were in the crowd. But as you move inwards, nobody can go with you. You have to go alone.

The moment you are drowning within yourself you are going farther and farther away from your own periphery and everybody else is out of that periphery; they are not even on that periphery.

This is the beauty that existence has bestowed upon you as individuals: nobody can enter your individuality; nobody can interfere. You can be killed, you can be crucified, but your freedom, your soul, your consciousness remains untouched even by your death.

Alexander the Great was going back from India, and at the very frontiers of India he remembered that his teacher, Aristotle, the father of Western logic, had asked him, "When you come back from India bring just one thing as a gift for me – you will be bringing gifts for everybody."

Alexander said, "Just say, and it will be brought to you."

He said, "I want to see a sannyasin. I have heard so much from travelers about sannyasins. It seems they are a different species of humanity; it seems they are far above us. If you can bring a sannyasin I will be immensely happy."

Alexander said, "This is a small thing. If you had asked me to bring the Himalayas I could have dragged it back to Greece. A sannyasin? – no problem."

He remembered. He had collected so much garbage but at the last moment he remembered, "My God, I have forgotten a sannyasin!" But he was still on the frontiers of India, so he inquired of people, "Can I find a sannyasin nearby?"

They said, "It is a little difficult if you really want an authentic sannyasin; otherwise, this country is full of sannyasins."

Alexander said, "I want an absolutely authentic sannyasin because I cannot offer to my teacher a phony fellow. Wherever you tell us I will go."

They said, "You don't have to go too far. Just a few miles back you may have passed by the side of a river where an old sage lives. He lives naked, and as far as we know in this part of the country there is no one who has a higher consciousness, more blissfulness, than this old sage."

Alexander sent two of his generals first because he thought it was below his dignity to go and ask the sannyasin. Those two generals went, and the sannyasin was standing naked by the side of the river. They told him, "Alexander the Great wants you to be the royal guest. Everything you need, all the luxuries possible will be made available to you for your whole life, but you have to come with us to Greece."

The sannyasin looked at them and said, "You seem to be utter idiots! A man who calls himself Alexander the Great must be just an egoist, and a sannyasin cannot accept the invitation of any egoist. I can come running to somebody who is humble, even without invitation. Just go back and tell your Alexander the Great what I have told you."

Although they were great generals of Alexander, they started shaking, became nervous. The old man was so strong; his voice just pierced like arrows in their hearts. They came back and they told Alexander that that man was difficult.

Alexander said, "How difficult? I have never met any difficulty in my life. I am the world conqueror. I will see for myself. I am coming – just lead the way!"

On the way those two generals persuaded him: "It is better to leave this man. He seems to be very strange. He says that the person who calls himself "the great" is simply ignorant, does not know anything, and he says, 'I would have come to anyone uninvited if there was simplicity, innocence, love, humbleness – but power cannot move me a single inch.'"

Alexander said, "Don't be worried. He does not know me and he does not know my sword." He pulled out his sword as he reached the sannyasin, just to make him afraid. He was thinking the sannyasin will become afraid, but he started laughing.

Alexander looked very embarrassed. What to do? The sannyasin said, "Yes, that's perfectly okay. You can cut off my head. Cut it! I am ordering you!"

Alexander said, "Nobody orders me!"

The old man said, "You are strange. What do you want of me?"

Alexander said, "I want you to come with me to Greece. You will be my royal guest."

He said, "I used to be a king myself. I dropped my kingdom, I dropped all my possessions in search of something that is immortal, and I have found it. That's why I ordered you to cut off my head. Why are you feeling so shaky? You are a world conqueror; I am a poor sannyasin with nothing."

Alexander said, "Don't make me mad by your statements. I am a dangerous man! I can really cut off your head."

He said, "I am more dangerous than you. When the head falls on the ground, you will be seeing it from the outside. I will be seeing it from the inside. You cannot kill me. I have reached the point where there is no birth and no death. That's why I say you cannot move me a single inch. All your power is just impotent."

Against a single sannyasin the power of a world conqueror is absolutely impotent, for the simple reason that the man of meditation knows that he is not the body. And everything else that he used to be identified with – the wife, the children, the money, the power, the prestige – are all left far away. Just a pure consciousness, just a flame of light has remained within him, which is indestructible.

Krishna says, in one of his beautiful statements: *Nainam chhindanti shastrani* – "you cannot cut me with weapons" *nainam dahati pavakah* – "and you cannot burn me with fire. You are absolutely powerless as far as I am concerned."

Your experience is perfectly right: just a little change, which will come automatically. As you are drowning more and more into yourself, a moment is bound to come when you will see it does not just appear that people are appearing on the faraway periphery – they really are there. From your very innermost center you cannot call them, you cannot communicate with them. Your innermost center is so transcendental to their ordinary, ignorant, unconscious selves that there is no bridge possible.

You are also saying, "At the same time, I am receiving so much: you keep pouring and pouring your love over me. Why am I so miserly in giving to others?" Just wait a little more. Soon you will be overflowing, all miserliness will be gone.

Why are people miserly? You have to understand their psychology. What is the psychology of miserliness. It is strange that even the greatest psychoanalysts, psychologists, don't think of fundamental problems. Now, miserliness is one of the fundamental problems. Nobody wants to give; everybody wants to get.

The psychology is simple. The miserliness arises because you are empty and you want to fill it with something – anything. You are always a beggar waiting for somebody to give something to you.

But your inner emptiness is vast. It cannot be filled by money, power, prestige, respectability. You may have all and still you will feel the same emptiness. In fact, the more you have the more you will become aware of the emptiness, and then arises a tremendous anguish: "I have done everything to fill the emptiness and that has all disappeared into the dark hole and I am as empty as ever. My whole life has been a sheer wastage."

But if your meditation is going deep and you are feeling my love showering on you... It can shower only on a meditator. It is not in my hands. I go on overflowing to everybody, but the non-meditators are keeping their umbrellas open. From wherever I want to reach them they move their umbrellas. They are hiding behind their umbrellas. They think this love is something like rain – you have to protect yourself.

But because you are not keeping your umbrella open to protect yourself, soon you will be overfilled. Only love in a meditative consciousness gives you the feeling of fullness, and after fullness comes overflowing, and that overflowing takes away all your miserliness.

It is the emptiness that creates miserliness; it is overflowing love that takes it away. The miserliness is only a symptom of emptiness. It won't last much longer because you are aware of receiving and you are grateful for receiving; you are opening up and becoming more and more available. You need not be worried about miserliness. Soon you will find you are overflowing, sharing yourself with others.

The only real sharing is the sharing of your being: not your money, not your house, not anything else, but only of your being because only that belongs to you. Everything else is not authentically yours.

You were born only with your being: that is yours. And then you accumulate many things, but they are never yours and the day you die you cannot take them with you. You lived in an illusion that they are your possessions. The fact is that they possessed you; they were not your possessions.

Your only possession is your being, and when the being radiates, those radiations are your love, your compassion, your fragrance, your celebration. Out of sheer necessity you are bound to share them because the more you share them, the bigger your bliss becomes.

So sharing is not an economic loss; sharing is the way of getting more and more from your innermost core. Deep down at the very bottom you are joined with the universal energy. You cannot exhaust it.

You are just like a well: go on taking the water out and new water goes on running in. If you stop – and that's what the miserly person does. He is afraid that if this water is taken by all the neighbors, "Who knows? The rains may come late, or may not come, and I will be suffering from water loss." He covers and locks his well. That is the mind of the miserly person. But he does not know that his well's water will die, it will become poisonous. The longer it is kept locked, the deadlier it will be. This is not wisdom. This is utter ignorance.

The wise man invites the neighbors to take as much water as they can because the more water is taken out – your small well is joined with the vast oceans underneath the ground. It has its currents that go on bringing fresh water.

If you want yourself to remain continuously fresh – share. That is the only way of remaining continuously fresh, continuously alive, continuously young. Even in your old age your eyes will show that you are young or even perhaps that you are just like a child.

But our minds are managed according to all kinds of wrong psychologies. Somebody is a Hindu, somebody is a Mohammedan, somebody is a Christian; it is very difficult to find somebody who is simply a man. Other than my sannyasins, you cannot find simple human beings.

I have not voted in my whole life for the simple reason that on the form that has to be filled at the census time, there is a column to be filled in asking your religion. The officers used to come around and I told them that I have come without a religion: "As far as I remember I have not brought any certificate saying to which religion I belong."

They looked at each other and said, "You must be born to some family..."

I said, "Yes, the family has its religion, but that is not my religion. If my father is a doctor, do you think I will be a doctor? If my father is a murderer, do think I will be a murderer? And if he is a Catholic, why should I be a Catholic? There seems to be no connection."

They said, "Then it is very difficult because our officers ask us that every piece of information should be filled in."

I said, "I am not much interested in being counted. You can take your form. And neither am I interested in voting because it will be such a trouble to choose who is the bigger idiot between two idiots. I don't want to get into unnecessary trouble. There are enough troubles already."

I am not on the census list of India. And I don't want any of my sannyasins to be Hindu or Mohammedan or Christian; to be German or to be American or to be Japanese or to be Indian. These are small cages that don't allow you to grow into your fullest capacity. They keep you starved as far as consciousness is concerned; they keep you starved as far as love is concerned. They keep you empty, and then necessarily miserliness is bound to be there.

I want you to be full. But the only way to be full is to be meditative – there is no other way. If by chance you can meet a master, then don't protect yourself, don't defend yourself. Just open yourself completely.

Perhaps the master functions almost like a rain cloud. He showers on you and everything becomes green in you and flowers start blossoming in you, and then you cannot prevent the fragrance of the flowers going into all directions, sharing the joy and the dance that have happened to your being.

But our minds are made really in such primitive, unintelligent, inhuman ways that it is unbelievable that even in the twentieth century we are not living in the twentieth century. Everybody is living in different centuries! I have never come across contemporaries. Somebody is still hanging on to ten thousand years ago, somebody five thousand years ago, somebody two thousand years ago. It is very rare, at least I have not come across a single human being who is my contemporary – and perhaps in this life I can't hope to meet anyone.

And this is my last life, you can understand my trouble. I will never meet a single contemporary. I am trying hard to make you my contemporaries, and perhaps it may happen. It all depends on you: how intelligently you can get rid of past conditionings.

Moishe Finkelstein, having been shipwrecked on a desert island for three years, is finally reached by rescuers. Proudly he shows them around the island pointing out the irrigation system, the pastures and orchards, the barn, the house and all his other constructions.

At the end of the island are two small buildings.

"And those," he announces "are the synagogues."

"Two of them?" he is asked. "But you are alone here."

"Well," he says, "this is the one I go to and this is the one I would not even be seen dead in."

Two different sects of Jews: one belongs to him and the other belongs to the enemies – but he has built both because without the enemy, without any fighting and quarreling, there is no joy. Although he is alone, even this much is enough consolation: that no one goes in that synagogue. He has made it, but looking at that synagogue, it brings tremendous contentment to him that nobody goes there. Such is the situation of almost all human beings.

In India there are the Jain: a small minority religion but with tremendous literature and great heritage. Philosophically, religiously, they have penetrated very deeply into human psychology. But on the surface that does not matter. Who looks into the scriptures? Who has the time? They have two major sects, there are smaller sects also, but two major sects that worship the same masters, that believe in the same scriptures. But they make their temples separately.

The only difference, and you will not be able to believe it, is that one sect – the Digambaras – believe that Mahavira, their great master, meditated with closed eyes. The Svetambaras, the second great sect, believe that Mahavira meditated with open eyes. This is the only difference, but it is enough for them to fight with each other. Riots happen, they burn each other's temples, without even bothering that the other temple also is the temple of Mahavira.

I was passing once through a small city in Madhya Pradesh and I saw a Jaina temple. I stopped my car because I saw three locks on the temple's door. Those three locks made me stop and inquire what was the matter. One lock is perfectly okay – but even one lock is not needed because a stone statue cannot escape. One lock can be allowed, but why three locks?

People gathered around my car and I inquired about it. They said, "It is a very sad story. The Jain to whom this temple belongs are very few in this village. We are so few that we could not manage to have two temples. Finally we decided that we should make one temple because after all we are all followers of Mahavira. The only difference is of open and closed eyes. So we would use a device: half the day it will belong to one sect – the stone statue is made with closed eyes, so half the day, from the middle of the night up to twelve o'clock in the day, it will belong to the Digambaras. They can do whatsoever they want. The other half of the day it will belong to the Svetambaras. And they have made false eyes, open eyes, that they put on the stone statue just like you put on glasses. It looks very idiotic but it fulfills their conditioning, and then they worship..."

But it used to happen often because religious people are more or less fanatical types. I don't see how anybody who is not a fanatical type can be part of any religion. A non-fanatical person is bound to be out of all these stupid ideas because he can see that this is nonsense. He cannot belong to any nonsense. And fanatical people are always ready to fight. They are looking, searching, for any excuse to have a good fight.

Although they had made the temple together, they had purchased the statue of Mahavira together, every day there was trouble and the trouble was created by the most fanatically religious people. For example, the Digambaras will be worshipping and they will go on worshipping after twelve. Now the Svetambaras are waiting outside the door. After twelve they cannot tolerate it, and they will rush in and start putting the eyes on Mahavira. And the Digambaras will take those eyes off saying, "Wait! Don't disturb our worship!" And that worship is prolonged only for the fight.

And they could have waited because there was no hurry. They worship ten or fifteen minutes more – let them worship, there is no harm. You can worship afterward. But they could not tolerate it; it was a question of prestige. It was happening so often: they would beat each other and they would send each other to the hospital with fractures.

Finally, the police were getting reports every day. One day the police came. They drove them out and put the second lock on the door. And they had a police case in the court. Because the case was in the court, the court decided to put a lock on the temple: till the decision, nobody can touch that sealed lock. That's why there were three locks.

And almost twenty years have passed. Now what judgment can the poor magistrate give? On what grounds can he say whether

Mahavira was meditating with open eyes or closed eyes, or whether in the first place Mahavira ever existed or not? Even that is not certain. And he himself, not being a Jaina, was not interested at all, and there was no argument in favor or against.

I had to delay my journey to where I was going. I informed them that I would come one day late: I had to meet the magistrate. I went to see him and I asked him, "This is strange. Many magistrates have changed, and you have not been able to decide a simple thing?"

He said, "You say 'a simple thing'? Now, how to decide? The one party says open eyes, the other party says closed eyes, and both have their scriptures. Now, whom to believe? Who is true?"

I said, "There is no problem. Take my authority! I say to you that he meditated with half-closed eyes."

He said, "My God! I never thought about it."

"In fact, that is easier. If you meditate with closed eyes the possibility is that you may fall asleep. If you meditate with open eyes, you cannot meditate. Some woman passes and everything is disturbed! And you cannot prevent it: you can close your eyes but you cannot prevent it. All kinds of things are moving all around. So to avoid the outside world and to avoid sleep, the real meditator meditates with half-open eyes. Half-open eyes means he looks only four feet ahead; so just find a place where within four feet nobody will move. That's why meditators have been going to the mountains and faraway places."

He said, "That's absolutely right! Tomorrow I am going to give the decision, but how to make the eyes half open?"

I said, "It is easy. If they can make fully open eyes artificially, you can order them to make half open eyes. And only then will those three locks be removed."

That is the only place in the whole of India where Mahavira is sitting with half open eyes. No time to sleep, no time to enjoy women, flowers, rivers, mountains – nothing! Just half open eyes: day in, day out. But both the parties agreed, seeing the point that twenty years had passed. Now it is better to settle, and this seems to be a perfect compromise.

So that is a very unique temple in the whole of India. Otherwise Svetambaras have their temples – they keep the eyes open. There is no need for anything artificial; they just tell the sculptors to make the eyes open. And Digambaras tell the sculptors to keep the eyes closed.

It was a strange case: both together had contributed to the building of the temple – but such is the mind, everywhere. It is not that one person is so illogical; it is the whole of humanity.

This is a lesson in logic...

The professor said, "If the show starts at nine and dinner is at six and my son has the measles and my brother drives a Cadillac, how old am I?"

"You are forty-four," said a student promptly.

"Right!" said the professor. "Now tell the rest of the class how you arrived at the correct answer."

"It was easy," the student said. "I have got an uncle who is twenty-two and he is only half nuts."

25

Just a Little Patience, Just a Little Awareness

Osho,
Inside, there is something that I cannot look at: I can only be it. And then I am at the center of experiencing my mind, my body, and what comes to my senses. This feels ecstatic, yet is very subtle, and easily disappears when I again identify with what is experienced. Is this my mind entering by a back door, or am I going in the right direction?

The experience that you are going through happens to everyone when he first comes into contact with his being. Our whole experience of the past is of identification. When you are full of anger, you don't say, "I see anger in my mind," you say "I am angry". In fact you are not angry; you are just a watcher. The anger is on the screen of the mind.

But identification is the greatest spiritual disease. We get very easily identified because for centuries that has been our habit. So when for the first time you get out of identification, you become centered, naturally you cannot see your being, just as you cannot see your eyes.

To see your eyes you need a mirror and to see your being you need a master, or someone who is already totally centered. In his presence you may be able to see reflected – just as in a mirror things are reflected – your being. But you cannot see your being directly.

I have been telling you many functions of the master. This is one of the most subtle and perhaps the last function. The master is already settled. You are wavering, one moment you are at the center: then you can see your body and your mind and your thoughts and feelings. There is a gap between you and your body-mind system. But the gap is very small and very fresh, and the habit of being identified is very old and very strong.

So one moment you feel you are the being, but the very desire to see the being disturbs the whole thing. You cannot see it. You need a mirror to see it – and no ordinary mirror will do. You need a mirror of consciousness. And then too you will not be seeing your being, just the reflection of it. In a completely settled and silent lake of consciousness,of somebody, you may be able to have a reflection of your being.

But to try to see your being alone is not possible. It is just not in the nature of things. You can be the being – you are the being. You can experience the ecstasy of *there*, at the very center; you can feel immense joy, fulfillment, contentment. But the moment the desire to see it arises, you have already slipped out of it. You have come back into the mind, and because the gap is very small you will not even be aware when you are slipping.

But it is a tremendously significant experience that you are going through. If the gap is small today, tomorrow it may be bigger. If the gap has already happened, the day is not far away when the desire to see yourself will disappear. You will simply be yourself, full of ecstasy. And as you become centered, everything else – your body, your mind, your thoughts – go on becoming farther away from you. Just a little patience, and just a little awareness.

You say, "It is very subtle and easily disappears when I again identify with what is experienced." Being is never experienced. *Experienced* means a memory: it is already past. Being is always a process of experiencing.

Perhaps the word *experiencing* does not exist in the dictionaries, but that's exactly the existential situation. It is always a process that goes on deepening. You can never come to a moment when you can say, "I have experienced." That moment will be that you have fallen out of the flow of experiencing.

"Is this my mind," you are asking, "entering by a back door, or am I going in the right direction?" Both are true. When you are centered within yourself and feeling ecstatic you are going in the right direction. And the moment you start thinking about it – what this experience is, how to see it – the mind is coming from the back door.

You have to avoid the mind completely. Except mind, there is no enemy in the whole world as far as one is concerned. Mind is your enemy for the simple reason that your whole experience of past is accumulated there. And you have always experienced identification. You say, "I am thirsty, I am hungry," without ever thinking what you are saying. Just look at the process: are you really hungry, or are you aware that there is hunger in your body? Are you really thirsty, or can you experience the thirst in your throat, in your body? But because of language, which has been made up by people who are not enlightened...

There exists no enlightened language in the world yet, and perhaps there never will exist – for the simple reason that language is needed for communication.

There are only three possibilities of communication.

Two ignorant persons can communicate very easily: they are in the same boat, they are surrounded by the same darkness, their identifications are same.

The second communication is a little difficult but can happen: it is between an enlightened person and one who is ignorant. The difficulty is created by the ignorant person because he knows the language of ignorance but he does not know the language of enlightenment; so constant misunderstanding. But the enlightened people of the world have tried their hardest somehow to reach you. They have succeeded in reaching only a few people. The task seems to be immensely difficult.

And there is a third possibility: two enlightened people – but they will sit in silence. That is their communication.

So I don't see any possibility that there will ever be an enlightened language. And the language that we have created is basically faulty. For example, when you say "the tree," you make a noun of a process. The tree is not static; it is treeing, it is growing. Even when you see with your own eyes a river flowing, you don't use the word *rivering*, you use the word *river*. River makes it something static. It never is – not even for a single moment. It is constantly flowing. That is its intrinsic nature.

The same is true about everything that we have made static. You are growing, even this very moment. When you came this morning to see me you were younger; now you are a little older. By the time you are going, you will be very much older.

Existence consists not of nouns and pronouns; existence consists only of processes. Hence, we cannot use the word *experience*; we can only use the word *experiencing*. We cannot use the word *love*; we can only use the word *loving*. We cannot use the word *friendship*; we can only use the word *friendliness*.

But then talking with people will become impossible: "I am coming from rivering. On the way I saw many people becoming old." People will think you have gone cuckoo. In fact, you are stating the actual facticity, the very existential nature of things, beings. Everything is always in constant movement. Howsoever slow, the movement is there.

Learn something very basic: in the inward world, please don't use the wrong language. Because the wrong language is not only a mistaken language, it becomes your mind also – and your mind is full of all wrong identifications of the past.

And you are entering into a totally new territory of your being. This territory belongs to no language; it belongs only to silence. So when it happens remain utterly silent and relish it, rejoice in it, feel it, taste it – but don't try to see it, don't try to figure out what is happening, don't bring your logic in and don't bring your old intellectual acumen to understand something which is beyond intellect.

And soon the gaps will become bigger, and a day finally comes when you are settled and nothing can distract you from your being. You will see your mind and you will see your body, but on the periphery. And even when they are taken away, killed and destroyed, you will not be affected because you are no longer identified. It is the identification that has to be understood.

A man had a very beautiful house that even the king wanted to purchase. He had made it with such love. He himself was an architect and the king was jealous because even his palace was not so beautiful. All the rich people had made an offer – whatever money he wanted he could have – but the man always refused. The palace that he had made was a small palace hidden in a thick garden with bushes and roses.

One day he went out. When he came home there was a vast crowd: his house was on fire. It may have been either the conspiracy of the king or the conspiracy of other people who were very jealous of his house. He was an old man but tears started flowing from his eyes. It was not just a house for him; it was his very creativity. He was so identified with it – as if the house was not burning but he was. Such a deep attachment.

And then his son came running and told him, "Father, you need not cry for that house. Last night I sold it to the king. He was offering any price we wanted and there was no question of any negotiation, so I asked for three times the price. We can make a house three times bigger, and then the king will know... It is already old and you have so many new ideas. It is a good opportunity."

The moment he heard that the house was sold, his tears disappeared, in fact he started laughing: "This is a great coincidence!" He started talking with his son and with his neighbors, "Perhaps I may purchase the land back because what is the king going to do with the land? And I will make a palace that is three times more beautiful and big." He already started dreaming about the future, and the palace was burning.

His second son came running and he told him, "Yes, my elder brother is right. We had agreed to sell, but it was only verbal. Neither had the money been given to us, nor had even a sales deed been written. We were waiting for you."

Again the tears came because now the king is not going to purchase it, he is not going to give the money. He forgot all about a palace that will be three times bigger and he was again crying like a small child.

What happened?

The attachment, the identification... The moment you are unidentified with your body, even if the body is on the funeral pyre there will be no problem for you. It is as if somebody else is being burned. You can also stand by the side in the crowd and nobody will see you.

To be in the being one has to learn more and more disidentification with everything. Use everything but don't get attached. I have been telling you to be in the world but don't be of the world. Be in the world, but don't let the world enter in you. I have been saying the same thing in other words: Don't be identified. Use this whole existence, but don't be possessive. Remain aloof, aware and silently watching.

A man had been bitten by a dog, but did not give it much thought until he noticed that the wound was taking a remarkably long time to heal. Finally he consulted a doctor who took one look at the wound and ordered that the dog be brought in.

Just as the doctor suspected, the dog had rabies. Since it was too late to give the patient a serum the doctor felt he had to prepare him for the worst.

The poor man sat down at the doctor's desk and began to write. The physician tried to comfort him.

"Perhaps it won't be so bad," he said. "You needn't make out your will right now."

"I'm not making out my will or anything," replied the man. "I'm just writing out a list of people I'm going to bite."

This is awareness! Even in such a bad situation he is not identified with the body or death or anything. He is calm and cool and writing a list of all the people in the city. Before dying at least he will bite all of them: a very alert mind, a very centered being!

> Osho,
> Relaxation has always been one of the most valuable states of being for me. Watchfulness seems to be possible only then, or at least so much easier. Would you like to comment on how relaxation is connected to awareness?

They are not only connected with each other, they are almost two sides of the same coin. You cannot separate them. Either you can begin with awareness and then you will find yourself relaxing because what is your tension? – your identification with all kinds of thoughts, fears, death, bankruptcy, the dollar going down! All kinds of fears are there. These are your tensions. They also affect your body. Your body also becomes tense because body and mind are not two separate entities. Body-mind is a single system, so when the mind becomes tense, the body becomes tense.

You can start with awareness; then awareness takes you away from the mind and the identifications with the mind. Naturally, the body starts relaxing; you are no longer attached. Tensions cannot exist in the light of awareness.

You can start from the other end also. Just relax, let all tensions drop, and as you relax you will be surprised that a certain awareness is arising in you. They are inseparable. But to start from awareness is easier; to start with relaxation is a little difficult because even the effort to relax creates a certain tension.

There is an American book – and if you want to find all kinds of stupid books, America is the place. The moment I saw the title of the book, I could not believe it. The title is *You Must Relax*. Now if the *must* is there, how can you relax? The must will make you tense; the very word immediately creates tension. *Must* comes like a commandment from God. Perhaps the person who is writing the book knows nothing about relaxation and knows nothing about the complexities of relaxation.

Hence, in the East we have never started meditation from relaxation; we have started meditation from awareness. Then relaxation comes on its own accord, you don't have to bring it – because if you have to bring it there will be a certain tension. It should come on its own; then only will it be pure relaxation. And it comes...

But if you want to try, you can try from relaxation – but not according to American advisors! As far as experiencing the inner world is concerned, America is the most childish place on the earth. Europe is a little older, but the East has lived for thousands of years in search of its inner self.

America is only three hundred years old. In the life of a nation, three hundred years are nothing; hence America is the greatest danger to the world – nuclear weapons in the hands of children. Russia will behave more rationally: it is an old and ancient land and has all the experiences of a long history. In America there is no history. Everybody knows his father's name, forefather's name and that's all. There your family tree ends.

In India, it is very different. One of the scholars of this very city, Lokmanya Tilak, proved – and his proof has not yet been disproved by any argument by other scholars. Now, almost the whole century has passed, but his evidence is such that it cannot be disproved.

The Western scholars used to argue that Rig Veda, the most ancient book in the world, is five thousand years old. There was a difficulty because according to Christianity, God created the world four thousand and four years before Jesus Christ – so now it is only six thousand years old. Now they have to put everything, fit everything into six thousand years. Beyond that they cannot go. Going beyond means going against Christianity, against the Bible, against Jesus Christ – and it is too risky.

Lokmanya Tilak proved with intrinsic logic that in Rig Veda there is a description of a certain constellation of stars, which astronomers are absolutely certain happened ninety thousand years ago. And there is no way to describe it unless these people had been the observers of that constellation, and it has not happened since then.

Lokmanya Tilak proved that Rig Veda may not be older than ninety thousand years old, but it is certainly ninety thousand years old. And one thing brings in another thing. In Rig Veda, the founder of Jainism, Adinatha, is mentioned with great respect. That means that if Hinduism is ninety thousand years old, Jainism must be even older because nobody talks with such respect about contemporaries, particularly contemporaries who are not willing to agree with you.

Adinatha did not agree on any point with Hinduism; that makes it certain that he was not a contemporary. Perhaps by the time the Rig Veda was written, he had been dead for a thousand years. People have a certain tendency to be respectful about the dead, and the longer they are dead, the more respectful they become. So I am giving you a recipe: if you want to become respectable, be dead, and everybody will be respectful to you.

Have you watched that when somebody dies, nobody speaks anything against him? It is simply etiquette and manners.

In one small town a man died. The tradition there was that before a man is lowered down into his grave somebody should say some good things about him. Everybody looked at each other, but because he was such a rascal they could not find a single word. He had tortured almost everybody in the town. He was such a harassment that deep down everybody was very happy that finally he had died: "Now we can relax a little."

So nobody was ready to say something good about the man because everybody knew that people would laugh if they said something good.

Finally one man stood up and said, "Compared to his other four brothers he was an angel. His other four brothers are still alive; you should not forget that fact." And it was true; those other four brothers were even more nasty, more dangerous. But he managed to say something good about the man: "Compared to his other four brothers he was an angel."

Rig Veda mentioning Adinatha with deep respect can mean only one thing: that Adinatha was dead long before. About contemporaries, it is very difficult, it hurts your ego, and particularly for those who are not in agreement with you. Not only that, their arguments are far superior to yours, and you cannot even answer them. Then it becomes very difficult to respect them, and condemnation comes on them from all sides. But Rig Veda has a whole passage just making Adinatha almost a god, with not a single word of criticism.

On this point Jainism can be said to be even older than ninety thousand years. Now, these people have a history. America is just a baby – or not even a baby – just in pregnancy! Compared to ninety thousand years, maybe it has just been conceived. It is dangerous to give these people nuclear weapons.

There are political, there are religious, there are sociological, there are economical problems – all torturing you. To begin with relaxation is difficult; hence in the East we have never started from relaxation. But if you want to, I have a certain idea how you should start because I have been working with my Western sannyasins and I have become aware of the fact that they don't belong to the East and they don't know the Eastern current of consciousness. They are coming from a different tradition which has never known any awareness.

For the Western sannyasins especially, I have created meditations like Dynamic Meditation. While I was taking camps of meditators

I used a gibberish meditation and the Kundalini Meditation. If you want to start from relaxation, then these meditations have to be done first. They will take all tensions out of your mind and body, and then relaxation is very easy. You don't know how much you are holding in, and that is the cause of tension.

When I was allowing gibberish meditation in the camps in the mountains... It is difficult to allow it here because the neighbors start going mad. They start phoning the police and the commissioner, saying, "Our whole life is being destroyed!" And they don't know that if they could participate in their own houses, their lives would come out of the insanity in which they are living. But they are not even aware of their insanity.

The gibberish meditation was that everybody was allowed to say loudly whatever comes into his mind. And it was such a joy to hear what people were saying because I was the only witness. No relevance, absurd... People were doing all kinds of things. There was only one condition: you should not touch anybody else. You could do anything, whatever you wanted. Somebody was standing on his head; somebody had thrown off his clothes and become naked, running all around for the whole hour.

One man used to sit in front me every day – he must have been a broker or something – and as the meditation would begin, first he would smile just at the idea of what he was going to do. And then he would take up his phone, "Hello, hello..." And from the corner of his eyes he would go on looking at me. I would avoid looking at him so as not to disturb his meditation. He was selling his shares, purchasing... the whole hour he was on the phone.

Everybody was doing strange things that they had all been holding back, and when the meditation ended, then there were ten minutes for relaxation. And you could see that in those ten minutes, people fell down... Not with any effort: they were utterly tired. And all the rubbish had been thrown out, so they had a certain cleanliness, and they relaxed. Thousands of people, and you could not even think that there were a thousand people.

People used to come to me and say, "Prolong those ten minutes because in our whole life we have never seen such relaxation, such joy. We had never thought we would ever understand what awareness is, but we felt it was coming." So if you want to start with relaxation, first you have to go through a cathartic process: Dynamic Meditation, latihan, Kundalini or gibberish.

You may not know from where this word *gibberish* comes from. It comes from a Sufi mystic whose name was Jabbar – and that was his only meditation. Whoever would come, he would say, "Sit down and start!" and people knew what he meant. He never talked; he never gave any discourses. He simply taught people gibberish. Once in a while he would give an example: for half an hour he would talk all kinds of nonsense, in nobody knows what language. It was not a language. He would go on and teach people just whatever was coming to his mind. That was his only teaching. And to those who had understood it he would simply say, "Sit down and start!"

But Jabbar helped many people to become utterly silent. How long can you go on? The mind becomes empty: slowly, slowly a deep nothingness, and in that nothingness a flame of awareness. It is always present, surrounded by your gibberish. The gibberish has to be taken out; that is your poison.

The same is true about the body. Your body has tensions. Just start making any movements that the body wants to make. You should not manipulate it. It wants to dance, it wants to jog, it wants to run, it wants to roll down on the ground. You should not do it; you should simply allow it. Tell the body, "You are free, do whatever you want!" And you will be surprised: "My God! The body wanted to do all these things but I was holding, and that was the tension."

So there are two kinds of tension: the body tensions and the mind tensions. Both have to be released before you can start relaxation which will bring you to awareness.

But beginning from awareness is far easier, and particularly for those who can understand the process of awareness, which is very simple. The whole day you are using it about things: cars in the traffic, even in the Pune traffic you survive! It is absolutely mad. Just a few days ago I read about Athens. Athens is even worse than Pune. The government made a special seven-day competition for the taxi drivers and they had put up golden trophies for three people – those who were the best, the second, and the third best at following traffic rules. But they could not find a single person in Athens! The police were getting worried. The days were ending: anyhow on the last day they wanted to find three. They may not be perfect, but those prizes had to be distributed.

They found one man who was following the traffic rules exactly, so they were very happy. They rushed toward him with the trophy, but seeing the police coming toward him the man rushed through a red light. Who wants to get into trouble unnecessarily? The police were shouting, "Wait!" He did not listen, he was immediately gone, against the light. They tried with two other people, but seeing the police nobody would stop.

So after seven days' effort, those three prizes are still sitting in the headquarters of the police, and Athens is going on as rejoicingly as ever.

You can have a little taste in Pune, but still you survive because you remain alert, aware. Perhaps the worst traffic situation is in Italy. That's why I was telling you the other day that the people who sell cars have come to the conclusion that if the man tries to look at the engine of the car first he is a German. If the man looks at the beautiful lines and curves of the car first he is French. But if the man first looks at the horn, whether it works or not, he is an Italian – because the real thing is the horn, otherwise you cannot survive.

You are using awareness without being aware of it, but only about outside things. It is the same awareness that has to be used for the inside traffic. When you close your eyes there is a traffic of thoughts, emotions, dreams, imaginations – all kinds of things start flashing by.

What you have been doing with the outside world, do exactly the same with the inside world and you will become a witness. And once tasted, the joy of being a witness is so great, so otherworldly, that you would like to go more and more in. Whenever you find time you would like to go more and more in.

And it is not a question of any posture; it is not a question of any temple, of any church or synagogue. Sitting in a public bus or in a railway train, when you have nothing to do, just close your eyes. It will save your eyes being tired from looking outside, and it will give you time enough to watch yourself. Those moments will become moments of the most beautiful experiences.

And slowly, slowly, as awareness grows your whole personality starts changing. From unawareness to awareness is the greatest quantum leap.

Hymie Goldberg was on holiday in Ireland, driving his new Mercedes. He came to a small farm where the road went right through a large puddle. Paddy was standing next to it, so Hymie leaned out and asked if the puddle was shallow.

Paddy said, "Yes," so Hymie drove on, only to have his car sink slowly out of sight.

Spluttering with rage and dripping wet, Hymie shouted at Paddy, "You idiot! Why the hell did you tell me it was shallow enough to drive through?"

Paddy scratched his head and said, "I don't understand it. The water only came half way up my ducks."

Just learn to be aware in all situations. Make a point of using every situation for awareness.

A man rushed into "The Pig and Whistle" pub in great agitation.

"Does anyone own a great big black cat with a white collar?" he said in a nervous voice. There was no reply.

"Well, does anyone know of a large black cat with a white collar?" asked the man again, raising his voice above the general noise of the bar. But still there was no answer.

"Oh dear!" muttered the man, "I think I have just run over the priest."

The difference between a politician and an English lady...

When a politician says yes, he means maybe. When he says maybe, he means no. If he says no, he's no politician.

When an English lady says no, she means maybe. When she says maybe, she means yes. If she says yes, she's no lady.

26

Contagious Health

Osho,

This morning the top of my head flew off to greet you. Like a lidless pot I sat drinking you in. Suddenly a question popped up: all the historical rebellions have a huge "no" at their source. Your rebellion of the soul is centered in the mystery of "yes." Will you please speak to us on the alchemy of yes?

There are a few very fundamental things to be understood.

First, there has never been a rebellion in the past, only revolutions. And the distinction between a revolution and a rebellion is so vast that unless you understand the difference you will not be able to figure the way out of the puzzle of your question. Once you understand the difference...

Revolution is a crowd, a mob phenomenon. Revolution is a struggle for power: one class of people who are in power are thrown out by the other class of people who have been oppressed, exploited to such a point that now even death does not matter. They don't have anything. Revolution is a struggle between the haves and the have-nots.

I am reminded of the last statement in *The Communist Manifesto* by Karl Marx. It is tremendously beautiful, and with a little change I can use it for my own purposes.

First, his exact statement: he says, "Proletariat..." his word for have- nots "Proletariat of the world unite" – and don't be afraid because – "you have nothing to lose except your chains."

Moments come in history when a small group of cunning, clever, people start exploiting the whole society. All the money goes on gathering on one side and all the poverty and starvation on the other. Naturally this state cannot be continued forever. Sooner or later those who have nothing are going to overthrow those who have all.

Revolution is a class action; it is a class struggle. It is basically political; it has nothing to do with religion, nothing to do with spirituality. And it is also violent because those who have power are not going to lose their vested interest easily. It is going to be a bloody, violent struggle in which thousands, sometimes millions of people will die.

Thirty million people were killed just in the Russian Revolution. The czar's whole family, he was the king of Russia before the revolution, was killed so brutally by the revolutionaries that it is inconceivable. Even a six-month-old girl was killed. Now, she was absolutely innocent, she had done no harm to anybody; but just because she belonged to the royal family... The whole royal family had to be destroyed completely. Seventeen people were killed, and not just killed but cut into pieces. It is bound to happen in a revolution. Centuries of anger ultimately turn into blind violence.

And the last thing to remember: revolution changes nothing. It is a wheel: one class comes into power, others become powerless, but sooner or later the powerless are going to become the majority because the powerful don't want to share their power; they want to have it in as few hands as possible.

Now, you cannot conceive it: in this country there are nine hundred million people, but half the capital of the country is just in Mumbai. Nine hundred million people in the whole country, and half the capital of the whole country is just in a small city. How long can it be tolerated? Naturally, it comes automatically. Revolution is something blind and mechanical, part of evolution, and when the powerful become the smaller group, the majority throws them away and another power group starts doing the same.

That's why I say revolution has never changed anything, or in other words, all the revolutions of history have failed. They promised much, but nothing came out of it. Even after seventy years, people are still not getting enough nourishment in Russia. Yes, there are no longer the old czars and counts and countesses and princesses and princes, but in a vast ocean of poverty, even if you remove those who have power and riches, it is not going to make the society rich. It is just trying to make the ocean sweet by dropping teaspoonfuls of sugar in it.

All that has happened is a very strange phenomenon that nobody takes any notice of. Only poverty has been distributed equally. Now in Russia everybody is equally poor – but what kind of revolution is this? The hope was that everybody would be equally rich. But you cannot become rich just by hoping.

Richness needs a totally different ideology, of which mankind is absolutely unaware. For centuries it has praised poverty and condemned richness, comfort, luxury. Even if the poor revolt and come into power, they don't have any idea what to do with this power – how to generate energy to create more richness, comfort and luxury for people – because deep down in their minds there is a guilty feeling about richness, about luxury, about comfort.

So they are in a tremendous anguish, although they have come to power and this is the moment they could change the whole structure of the society, its whole productive idea. They could bring more technology, they could drop stupid kinds of wastage.

Every country is wasting almost ten percent of its income on the army. Even the poorest country, even this country, is doing the same idiotic thing. Fifty percent of the people in this country are on the boundary of becoming an Ethiopia any day – a bigger Ethiopia. In Ethiopia one thousand people were dying per day. The day India starts becoming another Ethiopia – and it is not far away – then one thousand will not do; it will be many thousands of people dying every day.

And by the end of this century the population of India will be the biggest in the whole world. It has never been so; it has always been China who was leading, ahead. By the end of the century – and there are not many years left, just within twelve years we will be reaching the end – India will have one billion people. And five hundred million people are bound to die because there is not enough food for so many people.

But still the politicians, those who are in power, are not concerned at all about what happens to humanity. Their concern is whether their power remains in their hands or not. They can sacrifice half of the country to death, but they will go on making efforts to have atomic weapons, nuclear missiles.

It is a very insane kind of society that we have created in thousands of years. Its insanity has now become a high peak. There is no going back. It seems we are all sitting on a volcano that can explode any moment.

Revolutions in the past have happened all around the world but no revolution has succeeded in doing what it promised. It promised equality without understanding the psychology of human individuality: that each human individual is so unique that to force equality is not going to make people happy, but utterly miserable.

I also love the idea of equality but in a totally different way. My idea of equality is equal opportunity to all to be unequal; equal opportunity to all to be unique and themselves. Certainly, they will be different from each other – and a society which does not have variety and differences is a very poor society. Variety brings beauty, richness, color.

But it has not yet dawned on the millions around the world that revolution has not helped, and they still go on thinking in terms of revolution. They have not understood anything from the history of man.

It is said that history repeats itself. I say it is not history that repeats itself. It seems to repeat itself because man is absolutely unconscious: he goes on doing the same thing again and again without learning anything, without becoming mature, alert and aware.

When all the revolutions have failed some new door should be opened. There is no point in changing the powerful into the powerless and the powerless into the powerful again and again. This is a circle that goes on moving.

I don't preach revolution. I am utterly against revolution. I say unto you that my word for the future, and for those who are intelligent enough in the present, is rebellion. What is the difference?

Rebellion is individual action; it has nothing to do with the crowd. Rebellion has nothing to do with politics, power, violence. Rebellion has something to do with changing your consciousness, your silence, your being. It is a spiritual metamorphosis.

And each individual passing through a rebellion is not fighting with anybody else, but is only fighting with his own darkness. Swords are not needed, bombs are not needed. What is needed is more alertness, more meditativeness, more love, more prayerfulness, more gratitude. Surrounded by all these qualities you are born anew.

This new man, this rebellion that can become the womb for the new man, I teach. We have tried collective efforts and they have failed. Now let us try individual efforts. And if one man becomes aflame with consciousness, joy and blissfulness, he will become contagious to many more.

Rebellion is a very silent phenomenon that will go on spreading without making any noise and without even leaving any footprints behind. It will move from heart to heart in deep silences. And the day it has reached to millions of people without any bloodshed... just the understanding of those millions of people will change our old primitive animalistic ways. It will change our greed. And the day greed is gone there is no question of accumulating money.

No revolution has been able to destroy greed, so those who come into power become greedy. We have passed through a revolution just now in this country, and it is a very significant example to understand. The people who were leading the revolution in this country against the British rule were followers of Mahatma Gandhi, who preached poverty, who preached non-possessiveness. And the moment all his disciples came into power, they started living in palaces that were made for viceroys. All his disciples who had been thinking their whole lives that they are servants of the people became masters of the people.

There is more corruption in this country than anywhere else. This is very strange: this is Gandhian corruption, very religious, very pious, and the people who are doing it were trained, disciplined to be servants of the people. But power has a tremendous capacity to change. The moment you have power you are immediately a different person. You start behaving exactly like any of the other powerful people who have gone before.

I was very young when India became independent, so I have been watching this independence for forty years. My whole family was involved in the freedom struggle, and when freedom came there was so much celebration all over the country. But each year the celebration has become less and less, and sadness started settling.

I used to tease my father, my uncles, who had all been to jail, suffered as much as possible. And because all the elders were in jail we suffered too because there was nobody to look after the children. There were only women and children left, and Indian women cannot be of much help. They cannot even come out into the society; they are not capable of earning money.

I know how difficult it was when all the elders of the family were thrown into jail. After the freedom I used to tease them, "Is this the freedom? You destroyed your family, you destroyed yourself, you suffered and you made us suffer. Is this the freedom?"

And my father used to say, "Don't say such things. We know this is not the freedom that we have been fighting for. We were thinking that when the country becomes free, everybody will enjoy freedom."

But nothing has changed. Only the British are gone, and in their place a single party has been ruling for forty years – not a single party, but a single family. It has become a dynasty. And the exploitation continues and the poverty continues. It has grown at least a hundred times more since the British Empire has gone.

Everything has deteriorated: the morality, the character, the integrity. Everything has become a commodity. You can purchase anybody: all that you need is money. There is not a single individual in the whole country who is not a commodity in the marketplace: all that you need is money. Everybody is purchasable. Judges are purchasable, police commissioners are purchasable, politicians are purchasable. Even under British rule this country has never known such corruption.

What has the country gained? The rulers have changed, but what does that signify? Unless there is a rebelliousness spreading from individual to individual; unless we can create an atmosphere of enlightenment around the world where greed will fall down on its own accord, where anger will not be possible, where violence will become impossible, where love will be just the way you live, where life should be respected, where the body should be loved, appreciated, where comfort should not be condemned – it is natural to ask for comfort...

Even the trees... In Africa, trees grow very high. The same trees in India don't grow that high. I was puzzled. What happens? I was trying... they should grow to the same height but they don't, and the reason I found was that unless there is a density of trees, trees won't grow high because even at a smaller height the sun is available, and that is their comfort, that is their life, that is their joy. In Africa the jungles are so thick that every tree tries in every way to grow as high as possible because only then can it have the joy of the sun, the joy of the rain, the joy of the wind. Only then can it dance; otherwise there is nothing but death.

The whole of nature wants comfort, the whole of nature wants all the luxury that is possible. But our religions have been teaching us against luxury, against comfort, against riches.

A man of enlightenment looks with clarity. It is unnatural to demand from people, "You should be content with your poverty, you should be content with your sicknesses, you should be content with all kinds of exploitation, you should be content and you should not try to rise higher, to reach to the sun and the rain and the wind." This is absolutely unnatural conditioning, that we are all carrying. Only a rebellion in your being can bring you to this clarity.

You say that in history all the rebellions were based on "no". Those were not rebellions. Change the word. All the *revolutions* were based on "no". They were negative, they were against something, they were destructive, they were revengeful and violent.

Certainly, *my* rebellion is based on "yes" – yes to existence, yes to nature, yes to yourself. Whatever the religions may be saying and whatever the ancient traditions may be saying, they are all saying no to yourself, no to nature, no to existence. They are all life-negative.

My rebellion is life-affirmative. I want you to dance and sing and love and live as intensely as possible and as totally as possible. In this total affirmation of life, in this absolute yes to nature, we can bring a totally new earth and a totally new humanity into being.

The past was "no". The future has to be "yes".

We have lived enough with the no, we have suffered enough and there has been nothing but misery. I want people to be as joyful as birds singing in the morning, as colorful as flowers, as free as the bird on the wing with no bondages, with no conditioning, with no past – just an open future, an open sky and you can fly to the stars.

Because I am saying yes to life, all the no-sayers all over the world are against me – because my yes-saying goes against all the religions and against all the ideologies that have been forced upon man. My yes is my rebellion. The day you will also be able to say yes it will be your rebellion.

We can have rebellious people functioning together, but each will be an independent individual, not belonging to a political party or to a religious organization. Just out of freedom and out of love and out of the same beautiful "yes" we will meet. Our meeting will not be a contract, our meeting will not be in any way a surrender; our meeting will make every individual more individual. Supported by everybody else, our meeting will not take away freedom, will not enslave you; our freedom will give you more freedom, more support, so that you can be stronger in your freedom. Long has been the slavery, and long has been our burden. We have become weak because of the thousands of years of darkness that have been poured on us.

The people who love to say yes, who understand the meaning of rebellion, will not be alone. They will be individuals, but the people who are on the same path – fellow-travelers, friends – will be supporting each other in their meditativeness, in their joy, in their dance, in their music. They will become a spiritual orchestra, where so many people are playing instruments but creating one music. So many people can be together and yet they may be creating the same consciousness, the same light, the same joy, the same fragrance.

It is a long way: "no" seems to be a shortcut. That's why it has not been tried up to now. Whenever I have discussed it with people, they have said, "Perhaps you are right, but when will it be possible that the whole earth will say yes?"

I say, "Anyway we have been on this earth for millions of years and you have been saying no – and what is your achievement? It is time. Give a chance to 'yes' too."

And my feeling is that "no" is a quality of death. "Yes" is the very center of life. "No" had to fail. Death cannot succeed, cannot be victorious over life. If we give a chance to yes-based rebelliousness, it is bound to become a wildfire because deep down everybody wants it to happen. I have not found a single person in my life who does not want to live a natural, relaxed, peaceful, silent life. But that life is possible only if everybody else is also living the same kind of life.

I can understand the fear of people that individual rebellion may take a long time, but there is no problem in it. In fact, each individual who passes through this rebellious fire becomes a bliss and an ecstasy for himself at least, and there is every possibility that he will sow the seeds around him. But he has not failed: he has conquered, he has reached to the very peak of his potential, he has blossomed, there is nothing more that he can think of. The whole existence is his.

So as far as that individual is concerned the rebellion is complete and he will be able to sow seeds all around. And there is no hurry; eternity is available. Slowly, slowly more and more people will become more and more conscious, more alert. Enlightenment will become a common phenomenon.

It should not be that once in a while there is a Gautam Buddha, once in a while there is a Jesus, once in a while there is a Socrates – the names can be counted on only ten fingers. This is simply unbelievable. It is as if your garden is full of rosebushes, thousands of rosebushes, and once in a while one rosebush blossoms and gives you roses – and the remaining thousands remain without flowers?

Unless a rose bush comes to blossom it cannot dance – for what? It cannot share; it has nothing to share. It remains poor, empty, meaningless. Whether it was or not makes no difference. The only difference is when it blossoms and offers its songs and its flowers and its fragrance to existence and to anybody who is willing to receive. The rose bush is fulfilled. Its life has not been just a meaningless drag; it has become a beautiful dance full of songs; a deep fulfillment that goes to the very roots.

I am not worried about time. If the concept is understood, time is available; enough time is available.

In the East we have a beautiful proverb: "If the man who loses his path in the morning returns home by the evening he should not be called lost."

What does it matter? In the morning he went astray – just little adventures here and there – and by the evening he is back home. A few people may have come a little earlier; he has come a little late, but he is not necessarily poorer than those who have come earlier. It may be just vice versa: he may be more experienced. He has known more because he has wandered more. He has known more because he has committed more mistakes. He is much more mature and experienced because he has gone wandering so far astray. And then coming back again, falling and getting up... he is not necessarily a loser.

So time is not at all a consideration for me.

My rebellion is absolutely individual and it will spread from individual to individual. Sometime this whole planet is bound to become enlightened. Idiots may try to wait and see what happens to others, but they also finally have to join the caravan.

The very idea of enlightenment is so new, although it is nothing that has not been known before. There have been enlightened people, but they never brought enlightenment as a rebellion. That is what is new about it. They became enlightened, they became contented, they became fulfilled – and a great fallacy happened. I have to point it out, although I feel not to show any mistakes of the enlightened ones. I feel sad about it, but my responsibility is not for the dead. My responsibility is for those who are alive and for those who will be coming.

So I have to make it clear: Gautam Buddha, Mahavira, Adinatha, Lao Tzu, Kabir; all these people who became enlightened attained to tremendous beauty, to great joy, to utter ecstasy – what I have been calling *satyam shivam sundaram*, the truth, the godliness of the truth and the beauty of that godliness – but because they had become enlightened they started teaching people to be contented: "Remain peaceful, remain silent." This is the fallacy. They attained contentment after a long search. It was a conclusion, not a beginning. It was the very end product of their enlightenment, but they started telling people that you can be contented right now: "Be fulfilled, be silent."

That's how they became anti-rebellious – without knowing perhaps that if a poor man remains contented with his poverty it is dangerous, if a slave remains contented with his slavery, that is dangerous.

So all the enlightened people of the past attained to the great height, about which there is no doubt. But there is a fallacy, a mistake that they all committed without exception. The fallacy is that they started telling people to start with that which comes in the end. The flower comes only in the end; one has to start with the roots, with the seed. And if you start telling people to start with the roses, then the only way is for people to purchase roses of plastic. The only way to be contented without meditation is to be a hypocrite because deep down you are angry, deep down you are furious, deep down you want to freak out, and on the surface you are showing immense peace. This peace has been like a cancer to humanity.

You can see it happening in this country more clearly than anywhere else because this country was fortunate, blessed by more enlightened people than any other country. But unfortunately, because so many enlightened people committed the same fallacy, this country remained continuously enslaved for twenty centuries. And for centuries this country has remained poor, hungry, starving. No science has developed, no technology has developed. Who is responsible for all this?

Because these people were loved and respected, and they deserve to be loved and respected, when they committed fallacies, naturally nobody could figure it out that they could make mistakes. And this was their greatest mistake: to teach people things that come only in the end. If you try to bring them in the beginning you will simply become a hypocrite, a pretender; you will start having a mask. On the surface you will be one person, inside you will be just the opposite – and a house divided cannot stand for long.

Man is divided into false personality and authentic individuality. Every man on the earth who is not in deep meditation is schizophrenic; there is no need for any other symptoms. It is just the natural, almost natural, condition because for thousands of years you have been told to be hypocrites.

The alchemy of "yes" can make you one single integrated individual. It can bring you back your lost dignity; it can bring you back the capacity to stand alone in absolute blissfulness: not needing anybody, not being dependent on anything. It will take away all your spiritual diseases – greed and jealousy and violence and lust – and it will bring a tremendous showering of all that is great, incalculably great, so great that you cannot say, "I have got it," you can only say, "Existence has given it to me." It is always a gift from the beyond: your ecstasy, your blessing, your truth, your benediction – they simply shower on you.

But you will have to learn to say yes in absolute totality to nature and to existence. Your hypocrisy will not do: that you can say yes with your personality and deep down your individuality is saying no. What is deep down is more authentic than what shows on the surface. The surface is always make-up.

A very tight-haloed English vicar was preaching his sermon in a very snobbish English church when he kept being interrupted by a black American in the congregation.

"The Lord says..." began the preacher.

"Far out man!" came a cry from the back.

"The rich shall perish..."

"Hey man, right on!" the American called.

"And the mighty shall..."

"Hallelujah!" came the response from the back.

The vicar managed to get to the end of his sermon, but at the end went up to the American and said, "Excuse me. I'm afraid in this country we like to keep a bit of decorum. We try to keep a stiff upper lip. It is the Queen's own country, this is a place of God, and I frankly found your behavior rather disconcerting."

"Hey man! I'm sorry. You are right on. I just loved the quaint way you gave us all that great shit about Moses and the Ten Commandments and I thought I would throw a few thousand greenbacks in your direction for this great thing going on here."

"Cool man!" said the preacher.

It does not take much to find out what is deep inside. All decorum, all culture is so superficial; it will be a tremendous joy to see people in their authenticity, in their reality – without any decorum, without any make-up, just as they are. The world will be tremendously benefited if all this falseness disappears.

The alchemy of "yes" and the rebellion based on "yes" are capable of destroying all that is false and can discover all that is real and has been covered for centuries, layer upon layer by every generation, so that even you yourself have forgotten who you are.

If suddenly somebody wakes you up in the middle of the night and asks you, "Who are you?" it will take a little time to remember who you used to be before, in the night when you went to bed.

It happened that George Bernard Shaw was going to deliver a lecture some distance away from London. On the way in the train came the ticket-checker. Bernard Shaw looked in every pocket, opened all his suitcases, but the ticket was not there. Finally, he was perspiring and the ticket-checker said, "Don't be worried. I know who you are: the whole country knows, the whole world knows. The ticket must be somewhere, don't be worried. And even if it is lost, I am here to help you get out at the station, wherever you want to get out."

George Bernard Shaw said, "Shut up! I am already in confusion and you are making me more confused. I am trying to remember where I am going! That ticket was the only thing that told me. I am not searching for the ticket for you, you idiot! I don't care about you. Get lost! But bring me my ticket!"

The man said, "But where can I find your ticket?"

George Bernard Shaw said, "Then what am I supposed to do? Where should I get down? Because unless I know the name of the station..."

It is almost the same situation with everybody. You don't know who you are. Your name is just a label that has been put upon you. It is not your being. Where are you going? You don't have any ticket to show you where you are going to get down, and you are just hoping that somebody may push you somewhere, or maybe somewhere the terminus comes and the train stops and it does not go anywhere else... just hoping.

But why are you traveling in the first place? In fact, for all these fundamental questions you have only one answer: "I don't know." In this state of unawareness your revolutions cannot succeed. In this state of unawareness your desire for freedom is just a dream. You cannot understand what freedom is. For whom are you asking freedom?

My idea of a rebellion based on "yes" means a rebellion based on meditation, for the first time in the history of man. And because each individual has to work upon himself, there is no question of any fight, there is no question of any organization, there is no question of any conspiracy, there is no question of planting bombs and hijacking airplanes.

Some idiot at Pune airport has put on the computer, "Beware the sannyasins of Osho! They can hijack airplanes!" It is really a very insane world. One of my sannyasins who often has to go to Mumbai and come back says, "Every time I see that computer I start trembling inside. They may catch hold of me and ask, 'Why do you come again and again? Are you intending to hijack an Indian Airlines airplane? It is enough that you come once – but why do you come and go at least three times in the week?'"

He was saying, "What to do? By road, it seems you are going to hell, and on the airplane they have that computer. Every time I am there, immediately the computer says, 'Beware of sannyasins.'"

I am not interested in hijacking airplanes, neither am I interested in destroying any governments. But that will be the final result of my individual rebellion based on meditation: governments will disappear. They have to disappear; they have been nothing but a nuisance on the earth. Nations have to disappear; there is no need of any nations. The whole earth belongs to the whole of humanity. There is no need for any passports, there is no need for any visas.

This earth is ours – and what kind of freedom is there if we cannot even move? Everywhere there are barriers; every nation is a big imprisonment. Just because you cannot see the boundaries you think you are free. Just try to pass through the boundary and immediately you will be faced with a loaded gun: "Go back inside the prison! You belong to this prison. You cannot enter into another prison without permission." These are your nations!

Certainly, a rebellion of my vision will take away all this garbage of nations and discriminations between white and black, and give the whole of humanity a natural, relaxed, comfortable life. And this is possible because science has given us everything that we need to make this whole earth, even if the population of the earth is three times more than it is today. Just a little intelligence is needed – which will be released by meditation – and we can have a beautiful earth with beautiful people and a multidimensional freedom: not just a word in the dead constitution books but a living reality.

One thing finally to be remembered: the days of revolution are past. We have tried them enough, many times – and every time the same story is repeated. Now something new is urgently needed. And except this idea that I am giving to you of an individual rebellion based on meditativeness, there is no other alternative proposed anywhere in the world.

I am not a philosopher. I am absolutely pragmatic and practical. I am not only talking about meditative rebellion, I am preparing people for it. Whether they know it or not doesn't matter. Whoever comes close to me is going to become a rebellious individual, and wherever he will go he will spread this contagious health. It will make people alert to their dignity, it will make people alert to their potentiality, it will make people alert to what they can become, what they are, and why they are stuck.

My sannyasins' function is not to be missionaries, but to be so loving, compassionate; such fragrant individuals... It is not a question of converting people from one ideology to another ideology. It is a far deeper transformation – from the whole past to a totally new and unknown future. It is the greatest adventure that one can think of.

You are fortunate to be part of this great adventure.

Osho,
During your discourse the other morning, an old question arose which is disturbing my contentment. The question is: What do I do when I find that what I am looking for is what is doing the looking?

Your contentment is not much of a contentment! A contentment that can be disturbed by a small thought cannot be valued very much. This is the contentment I have been talking about that has been created by the enlightened people in the past – a superficial layer. And your thought was more significant than your contentment, so it is better it is disturbed.

The question that arose in you is more significant: "What do I do when I find that what I am looking for is what is doing the looking?" This is the ancient-most question, always asked by meditators in some way or other.

And this is the time when the master tells you, "Don't do anything." There is no need to do anything if you understand your question.

I will repeat it again: "What do I do when I find that what I am looking for is what is doing the looking?" No question of doing: you have got the point. It is not a question; it is a revelation.

Nancy Reagan had been looking over every paper fan in the push-cart, feeling them, holding them, waving them back and forth. Finally she bought the cheapest – a one-dollar fan.

The next day she returned holding the fan which was ripped down the middle.

"Look what happened," she said to the shopkeeper. "I want my money back."

The shopkeeper said, "I am not a rich man, madam. How much did I charge you for this fan?"

"A dollar," she answered.

"And what did you do with it?" asked the shopkeeper.

"I am not silly: I waved it back and forth in front of my face."

"Well," said the shopkeeper, "that is your problem. That's what you do with a five-dollar fan. With a one-dollar fan you hold the fan still and you wave your head!"

With your small contentment you should not raise such five-dollar questions!

You don't have to do anything. Just put the fan aside because you don't know the whole story, and I think nobody here knows the story's end. But I think that if you wave the fan from side to side you will destroy the fan; if you wave your head from side to side you will destroy your head. It is better not to wave anything. Put the fan back and sit still just like a buddha, doing nothing.

If you have felt the question arising in you, that "what I am looking for is really the one who is looking," this is a tremendously beautiful understanding and revelation. Now don't ask to do anything. Just sit silently, at ease with the energy that was involved in looking. You are it!

This is for all, particularly for Ronald Reagan so that he does not feel bad that I talked about Nancy Reagan. People are very disturbed if you talk about their wives and don't talk about them. Ronald Reagan is sitting in the barber's chair having a haircut, when the barber casually says to him, "Hey, Ronnie, the newspapers reported today that Osho told a great joke about you."

"Yeah? What did he say?" asks Reagan.

"It was about how you became the president of the United States after a surgeon grafted a smile onto a donkey!"

Reagan, who shows no sign of discomfort, mumbles to the barber, "Yeah, very funny. Just finish my haircut, and I will have a shave as soon as you are finished."

"Hey, Ronnie," continues the barber, "and did you hear what Osho said about you being worse than Adolf Hitler, Mussolini, and Ivan the Terrible put together?"

Ronald Reagan's face turns bright red but he does not say a word.

The barber continues, "And did you hear what Osho said about...?"

Ronald Reagan interrupts the barber, saying, "Will you just get on with the haircut. Why are you always so interested in Osho, anyway?"

"Well," replies the barber, "besides the fact that he is a very far out guy, every time I mention the name Osho, your hair stands on end and it makes it a lot easier to cut!"

27

Love and Fear

Osho,

Sitting with you, there are two parts of me operating, one opposing the other. One part loves and trusts you more than any man I've ever met. The other is just plain afraid of you: afraid of your unwavering truth and the authority that it gives you, afraid of how vulnerable I feel in front of you, afraid that you could hurt me. Yet deep inside, I know that you could never hurt me. Would you talk about the disciple's trust in, and fear of, the master?

It is a pure misunderstanding that you have two parts: one loves me and one is afraid of me. You are dividing yourself into two persons, a split personality, just because you don't understand the deep relationship between love and fear. The psychological background has to be understood.

Love is almost like a death. When you die your physical body dies and you don't experience it because most of the time you die after you have gone into unconsciousness, so you don't feel your death. Only people whose meditation has become complete can see their death because they don't go into unconsciousness.

The fear is... If you replace the word *love* with death it will not create the split in you. Love is a conscious death – not of the body but of the ego, and the ego has been dominating you for many births, for many lives. Its domination has become almost permanent. Love is the only experience that can dethrone it.

If you cannot lose your ego in love, then you can never lose it. And you are not the ego, remember: it is a false idea of yourself, accepted and acquired in ignorance. In love you need humbleness, in love a trust arises on its own. You can expose yourself to the person you love in total vulnerability. But you don't know that with love this shadow is always there: that it is a kind of death, and particularly your personality feels immensely troubled that you are in such deep love.

So as far as I can see there is no division in you. You just don't understand the relationship between love and fear. It is absolutely natural for every person who loves to feel fear because he does not know that love is nothing but a graveyard for your ego. And because you are identified with the ego you think, "It is going to be my death."

All this may not be on the conscious level; it may be going on underneath, in the darkness, in the unconscious part of your psychology. So on the conscious level perhaps you think that you are split into two opposing camps. They are not opposing camps: they are two branches of the same tree, but the tree is hidden in the unconscious and you see only the branches in the conscious. Naturally, they look like two separate things.

So the first thing is: understand exactly that love is the death of the ego, the personality, the false. There is no way to have both love and ego. Either you can have the ego or you can have love – but make it a conscious thing.

Just a few days ago, one of the most intellectual and experienced journalists of India, M.V. Kamath, wrote a review of two of my books: *The Rebellious Spirit* and *The New Man*. In his review he said a few things that perhaps he himself was not aware of – the unconscious is very deep, and nine times bigger than your conscious. He said that I am the greatest intellectual giant of the second part of the twentieth century. And at the same time, in the next sentence he said that if I were not always surrounded by controversy I would have more admirers in the world than I have today.

My secretary has written to him saying, "Can you give a single name of any intellectual giant in the whole history of man who was not surrounded by all kinds of controversies while he was alive?" He sees a little part, which comes to his conscious mind, but something unconscious erupts. Secondly, he has said in his statement that I do not have to be heard or seen: I am a master of words, just reading me is enough. And he was thinking that he was praising me, calling me a master of words, telling his readers, "There are so many statements in his writings which are quotable, and I feel a little jealous and think I would like to have written them."

My secretary wrote to him, "You have never seen Osho, you have never heard him. You seem to be an intelligent person: on what grounds are you saying that just reading him is enough? I have listened to him, I have listened to him speaking, and I can assure you that the spoken word has a life of its own. It is still warm, and the printed word is dead. If you are so much influenced by the printed word, come at least once, at our invitation, and see the difference between the spoken word and the written word. Mumbai is not far away from here, just a fifteen-minute flight."

You can also hear the spoken word on the radio or from the tape recorder, but if you see me speaking then something more is added to it. Then your two senses are working, your ears and your eyes – and ears are not that sensitive. Eyes have eighty percent of the sensitivity, and the remaining four senses have only twenty percent. To see is a totally different thing.

Seeing a master means feeling his presence, looking into his eyes, watching his grace. That is not possible from the written word. And if you are so influenced by the written word that you declare the man to be the greatest intellectual giant, it seems to be absolutely necessary that you should listen to him, that you should at least see him once.

Yesterday his letter came, a very strange letter. He does not answer any question raised by my secretary. He cannot; he knows he has committed mistakes unconsciously.

Another question was also raised by my secretary: "A man of truth does not bother about admirers. From where did you get this idea? Was Gautam Buddha interested in admirers? Was Jesus Christ interested in admirers? It would not have been difficult to get admirers; even stupid politicians manage it. It is a simple strategy: just say the things that they want to hear and you will get admirers.

"And Osho is neither a politician, nor an actor, nor a showman. He is not at all interested in getting your admiration. He is a non-compromising man. He will only say what he feels to be true. Even if the whole world condemns him, crucifies him, it won't make any difference; he will go on saying what he feels is right and true."

A crowd of admirers cannot make a lie into truth, neither does being alone against the world mean that your truth has become a lie. Truth has always been spoken by single individuals, and they were always condemned by the masses, by the crowds – for the simple reason that every truth destroys your prejudices, destroys your so-called knowledge, makes you realize that you are utterly ignorant and you don't know anything.

But he has not answered anything, although he has written a letter. On the contrary, in the letter he writes, "I will not come to listen to or to see Osho. I would not have gone to listen to and see Gautam Buddha, or Socrates, or Jesus Christ." And he himself sees the point: "Perhaps you may think that I am an egoist. Certainly I am." This is the answer, the whole answer.

But it seems he feels that to be an egoist is nothing to feel ashamed of. This is the modern education, which has given one of the most idiotic ideas to the whole educated world. The whole structure of education is based on the childish psychology of the West, which says that every person should have a strong ego, otherwise he cannot survive in the struggle of life. And the function of education is to strengthen your ego. That's why, without feeling any shame or embarrassment, M.V. Kamath says, "Perhaps you will think that I am an egoist. I am."

But I cannot conceive of a man saying that he would not have gone to listen to Gautam Buddha, or to Jesus Christ, or to Socrates. Just an ordinary journalist, with such an ego... People are so much accustomed to the ego that they don't see it. It is so close to their eyes that it keeps them blind. You are moving in a different direction from the ego.

You are moving toward love, trust; you are moving toward truth, being. The ego has to be left. It has to be completely left, and you can leave it only if you are conscious of it.

The second thing: you say, "...the other is just plain afraid of you." Everybody is afraid of love; that's why even lovers keep a little distance, and even lovers go on fighting so that the distance remains. They never come too close, where they can become one because becoming one means you have lost yourself, and that is your ego influencing you. Unless love is big enough so that you can become one with the beloved, your love will remain absolutely incomplete, and you will remain in this split between love and fear.

What have you got to lose? Why should you be afraid? Sometimes it puzzles me: you don't have anything to lose. What have you gained through your ego? What has been the benefit of it? Perhaps fights, struggles, conflict. Being very touchy, just a small thing will insult you. If somebody who used to say hello to you just passes you by one day without saying hello, that's enough to keep you awake the whole night! "I am going to show that son-of-a-bitch! He did not say hello to me."

You don't have anything to lose – just a fear of which you have not been able to be aware. But this is the time to be aware of it.

You are saying, "...afraid of how vulnerable I feel in front of you, afraid that you could hurt me." I *am* going to hurt you: there is no need to be afraid! That's my whole function here: to hurt you so much that finally you drop the ego because that is what gets hurt. Nobody can hurt, nobody can humiliate, nobody can insult your authentic being. It is the phony part that starts getting enraged, feeling wounded by small things.

But as far as I am concerned, I promise you I will hurt you. So at least you can be at ease; there is no need to hang in a limbo: "Perhaps he may hurt me." No, I am certainly going to hurt you. Unless I hurt you, I cannot change you. But I don't hurt *you*, I hurt only what is false in you.

You wanted some other kind of promise. You say, "Yet deep inside, I know that you could never hurt me." You are wrong! You cannot persuade me not to hurt you – I cannot lose my whole profession!

And finally you say, "Would you talk about the disciple's trust in, and fear of, the master?" Both are absolutely together: one. When you trust the master, the trust comes from your real being. Ego cannot trust anybody, and the fear comes from the ego. Now, if your fear is too much, then you will turn against the master and will start condemning him, saying lies about him just to protect yourself from people who will say that you are betraying your master.

It is strange that people have lived with me for ten, twelve years, worked... and when their ego was hurt in some way, they left me. Even after ten or twelve years being here with me they could not understand. How can I help if I don't operate on your ego and separate it from you?

Gautam Buddha used to say, "I am a physician." Twenty-five centuries later, I cannot say that I am only a physician; I am a surgeon! After twenty-five centuries some evolution is needed.

These people lived twelve years with me but they never wrote a single word about me, they never brought a single person to me. But the moment they left me they started writing books against me. Suddenly they became great writers. And it is simply a defense mechanism. They are trying to tell the whole world why they have left me – because I am not what they used to think. Still they are unaware that it is not my problem that they have left. It does not matter to me: thousands of people have come and gone. I don't even know their names. While they are here on my surgery table I do whatever I can do, but a few idiots escape while the surgery is only half done.

I have heard about a politician. He had gone to a great surgeon, a brain surgeon. The politician was very important and he was contesting for the presidency of the country, so the brain surgeon had called all his colleagues and told them to be very careful. But they saw so much crap in his brain that they finally thought that it was better to put him in a coma and take out the whole brain and give it a dry cleaning.

While they were cleaning his brain in another room, the man became a little conscious, and at that very moment a man came in and said, "What are you doing lying here? You have been chosen as the president of the country!"

So he jumped off the table. The surgeons saw that he was jumping off the table and they could not believe it. They said, "Wait! Your brain is being washed!"

The politician said, "For five years at least I will not need it. You can keep it and clean it completely. I have become the president of the country. What do I need the brain for?"

Shiva used to be sitting by my side every evening in *darshan*. He was a guard – not my bodyguard, just one of the guards – and his function here was that when people in *darshan* sometimes fell down, if they felt such an upsurge of energy that they could not manage to sit, his function was to take them back to their seats or take them and make them lie down by the side.

I had never seen anything that could be called intelligent in him. He never wrote a single word, he never wrote any book about his experiences here. Perhaps he was so insensitive that although he was in the midst of tremendous experiences, his insensitivity did not allow him to be aware of it.

But the day I left for America he followed me. Certainly in America there was a different arrangement. The whole commune was a different kind of functioning organization, and he was not chosen to be a guard. He came twice. I was in silence and isolation so he could not approach me and the others who were in the office said, "We don't need you as a guard because we have been confirmed by the American government as a city. So now guards are not needed: we have a police department."

Of course we did not allow any non-sannyasin to be in the police department. We sent our own people for the training. Our own people were the policemen, so there was no need for guards. Those policemen were functioning under the chief of police of Oregon.

Shiva was so hurt that his power had been taken away that he wrote a book, *Bhagwan, The God That Failed*. If he had been authentic and true he should have written, *Shiva, The Guard That Failed*. But nobody looks at himself; people always project on others.

At least you are aware of the split. Just go a little deeper in your meditation and the split will disappear. It is simply a confusion because you don't know that love is followed by fear as a shadow and unless that shadow disappears, love is never complete and flowering.

But words are sometimes very dangerous. No dictionary exists in which you will find love in any way associated with fear. But the truth is, it is always following love to the very end when the master simply takes out his sword and finishes it completely. So I cannot promise you not to hurt you, but it will be a healing wound. It will bring you to more health and to more togetherness; to your authenticity and your being.

Don't be deceived by words because words have not been coined by enlightened people.

The suave, impeccably dressed gentleman approached the menswear counter and was greeted by a beautiful, shapely, young attendant.

"Good afternoon," she murmured huskily, "and what is your desire?"

"My desire," he said, after giving her a long appreciative look, "is to take you in my arms, rush you to my apartment, open a magnum of champagne, put on some romantic music, and make hot love to you. However, what I need now is new shirts."

The word *desire* created the whole trouble. He had only come to purchase shirts. If the girl had asked, "What is your need? What is your requirement?" things would have been different. Words play such a tremendously meaningful and sometimes dangerous role in our lives. Just a single word and your ego immediately picks it up, and your whole consciousness becomes clouded and dark.

It is good that you have exposed yourself. That shows that your love is greater than your fear. Now move your energy more toward love and leave the fear without any energy. It will die by itself. It is only a shadow.

Osho,
Is it possible that instead of watching the thinking, I am thinking of watching?

It is not only possible, it is absolutely certain that instead of watching the thinking you are thinking of watching. But if you have become aware of it, the change is possible. If you can think of watching, why can't you watch thinking? Just try. It is not a difficult process; it is simple.

But most people do that. They are thinking of watching and are deceived by themselves and start feeling that great things are happening: "The watcher has come in and soon all these thoughts will disappear and the no-mind is not very far away."

When people say to me that meditation is going very well, I am a little suspicious because if the meditation is going very well, you don't have to say it to me – I can see it. It will change your eyes, it will change your posture, it will change your walk, it will change your speaking, it will make you more and more silent – a pool of peace without any ripples of thoughts.

But human mind is very cunning. It tries to the very end to deceive you. And you are very naïve; you go on being deceived.

Sadie Moskovitz took her old grandmother to the movies. It was an epic about the Roman Empire. In one scene a lot of unarmed prisoners were thrown to the lions. The old grandmother broke out into loud wails, crying out, "Ah, those poor people!"

Sadie was very embarrassed and whispered fiercely, "Don't scream like that, Grandma. Those are Christians."

Choked, Grandma said, "I see." She was quiet at once, but then began wailing louder than before.

"Grandma," demanded Sadie, "what is it now?"

"Over there," said Grandma, pointing, "that poor little lion at the back. He's not getting any Christians."

Beware of your mind more than anything else in the world. It is the greatest deceiving device, which has been created by your body, physiology, chemistry, biology. It keeps you tethered to the body and does not allow you to open your eyes to your consciousness. It keeps you engaged; it does not even give you a little holiday. The danger is that if you are given a little holiday you may become aware of your inner grandeur: the beauty of your being and the enormous truth and the glory of it. And once you have seen that splendor you are not going to be deceived anymore.

Now change: instead of thinking of watching, start watching the thinking. Even if the thinking is about watching, watch. It does not matter what the object of thinking is. It can be watching. Don't get at all disturbed. Go on watching even thinking about watching, and the watching that you will be doing will reveal secrets and mysteries of your being. And as they are revealed, mind disappears. Mind is only there while you are utterly unconscious and ignorant. When more light is brought by meditation, watching, mind disappears like darkness. It is not a strong enemy; it is just that you have never tried to go beyond it.

Watching is simply a process of going beyond the mind – far away – looking at the mind, watching what is going on. Whatever the mind is doing, simply see it: don't appreciate, don't condemn, don't judge because all these things are part of thinking.

Watching knows no judgment, no condemnation, no justification, no appreciation. Watching is simply like a mirror. Standing before the mirror you may have a beautiful face but the mirror does not smile at you. You may have an ugly face; the mirror does not feel disgusted. You may have no face at all; the mirror is unconcerned.

Watching is simply, exactly, like a mirror reflecting the mind. Whatever is going on, the mirror reflects but makes no comments. This is the secret to getting beyond the mind, farther and farther away from it. Soon you will see that your mind is just a faraway echo – you can't even figure out what it is muttering – and then it disappears.

The attachment with the mind is through your condemnation or appreciation. Even when the mind disappears, don't say to yourself, "Aha! This is it!" The mind has come back from the secret door that it knows.

Just remain silent. There is no need to say "Aha!" There is no need to say, "This is it!" Relish and enjoy the silence that has come around you.

Where mind was just a marketplace, you have entered into the silences of the heart. Enjoy, dance, but don't say a single word.

Osho,
The other morning you looked so young in my eyes. I love you.

Mukta, perhaps the other morning you became aware of my eyes and became aware of your love. But as far as I am concerned, you are the only sannyasin amongst millions who has loved me from the very first day you entered into my room some twenty years ago.

Mukta is one of those unwavering people that have become very rare in the world. She had not come for me; she had come just to accompany another sannyasin. That other sannyasin disappeared long ago. She used to come to India at least two or three times a year to see me. She was American, very rich, and was constantly thinking about when her father dies because that old fellow was holding all the money in his hands.

Then I went to America, but she never came to the commune. The old man had died. Now she was holding all the money. She was afraid if she comes to the commune and sees me it would be difficult. She used to tell me again and again, "Osho, don't be worried, he cannot live forever. Once he is gone, our commune is not going to have any trouble about money."

I said, "This is very ugly. The very idea is ugly and poisonous."

But he died and she became one of the richest women in America. She never came to see me while I was in America for five years, and the last thing she did when she found that the American government was trying to destroy the commune or in some way deport me...

The US Attorney General had said, "Our main purpose is to silence Osho absolutely." One journalist asked him, "What do you mean? Do you want to assassinate him?" He said, "No, we have more sophisticated means to silence him."

She became afraid that if the American government found out that she was my sannyasin... She sent a letter from her attorney. This is a strange world and gives tremendously hilarious moments. When I saw the letter I could not stop laughing. The letter said, "I have never been connected with Osho and I am not at all interested what happens to him or to the commune. I have never been to the commune. This is from my attorney to inform you that I have never been associated with you." She must have become afraid.

It is very difficult when you are passing through dark nights. Even your own shadows leave you. But Mukta is made of a different mettle. She had come with that sannyasin just to see India. She had no conscious intention even to meet me. She came to see me just accidentally because that woman was coming to see me. And miracles happen in the world. That woman is lost: Mukta has never left me for a single moment – here, in America, going around the world. She has left her home, she has left her husband, she has left her children, she has left all the inheritance that her old father left for her. She never went there to get the inheritance; her other sister has swallowed the whole thing.

She has never complained about anything. She was never, for a single moment, differing in her mind. She has passed from disciplehood to the state of devotee long ago.

So it may have been, Mukta, that: "The other morning you looked so young in my eyes. I love you" – but I have been loving you for twenty years. And I can remember the first day you entered into my room in Mumbai. Sitting on the sofa, I had a very clear perception that you had not come with Pratima, that sannyasin, but that Pratima had come with you, my future sannyasin. And the same day Mukta became a sannyasin.

Such unwavering trust and love is the only miracle worth calling a miracle. Jesus walking on water is not a miracle.

The Mother Superior was passing through customs and the customs officer asked her if she had anything to declare.

"Nothing at all," she said.

"What's in the bottle?" asked the suspicious inspector.

"Only holy water," declared the Mother Superior.

The inspector pulled the cork. "Aha! It is whiskey!"

"Glory to God," cried the Mother Superior, "it is a miracle!"

And this is for you all.

The morning after.

Italian girl: Now you will-a hate me!

Brazilian girl: You call that a samba?

Russian girl: My body has belonged to you, but my soul will always remain free.

American girl: Who are you? I must have been drunk.

German girl: After we rest awhile, maybe we go to the beer garden, ja?

Swedish girl: I think I go home now.

French girl: For this I get a new dress, oui?

Jewish girl: I should have held out for a new mink coat.

Japanese girl: Now you know it is not so.

English girl: There, dear, do you feel better now?

And finally, a sannyasin girl: My God, you *really* want to go to Dynamic Meditation?

28

Authentically Enjoy Your Aloneness

Osho,

More and more it happens that I'm alone, and I am beginning to love and enjoy this silent space. But a fear is coming up: I am afraid that in this way I will lose contact with others and I will become a stranger. I feel a longing that brings me toward you, but a passion and desire to fall in love with someone seems to be no longer there. Can you please tell me what is happening? Am I right or am I going astray?

The question you have asked raises many significant questions that will be useful for everybody. You are asking, "More and more it happens that I am alone, and I am beginning to love and enjoy this silent space.

But a fear is coming up: I am afraid that in this way I will lose contact with others and I will become a stranger."

To be a sannyasin is to be a stranger. To be a sannyasin is to be an outsider. You do not belong anymore to the crowd. You have chosen the path of a lion, to be alone, rather than the path of a sheep, to be always in the crowd. And now that it is happening to you, that you are beginning to love your aloneness, a fear is also arising that you may become a stranger; you may lose contact with others.

Have you ever thought what you have gained from the contact with others? What is the end result of being in the crowd except misery, anxiety? Except agony, what has been the contribution of the crowd to you? Yes, it has given you greed, it has given you violence, it has given you ambitions which are all ugly, it has given you self-hatred, it has given you a constant desiring for the future; but that is a strategy to take you away from the present. And remember, your longing for the future is never going to be fulfilled. All fulfillment is in the present.

The only people who have attained anything worthwhile are the people who had the courage to be strangers. There is certainly a fear in the beginning because the more you become a stranger, the more you are condemned; the more you become a stranger, the more you feel yourself without any support. You were always supported and you have forgotten that you can stand on your own; there is no need of any support. In fact all supports have made you crippled. If from the very beginning a child is supported, carried, he will never learn to walk on his own.

To be an outsider means you have dropped all that has been given by the past as heritage – and that heritage has nothing beautiful in it. It is full of bloodshed, wars, hatred. There is not a single thing that comes to you as a heritage that can be rejoiced in. If you are alert, and your aloneness is bound to make you very alert, you will be able to see that you have been carrying all kinds of garbage given to you by the older generation. There is not anything of any value because anything of any value has to be discovered by yourself, it cannot be given to you by anyone else.

And in the crowd, the idea is very strong that you can gain knowledge from others, that you can become wise from others' advice, that you can become religious by believing in others, that you can become spiritual if you are obedient to the commandments of God. But it is always others you have to look up to: you yourself are absolutely worthless. Anything of value is going to happen to you only through others. This idea has been propagated and everybody has been poisoned by this idea. That is the fear when you start moving on a small footpath, leaving the superhighway.

They say – or they used to say in the past, but it is no longer relevant – that all roads lead to Rome. But not all footpaths! Every footpath moves on its own, to its own destiny. Now even the roads are revolting; they have forgotten Rome completely. It is very rare that any old rotten road may be going to the Vatican.

The fear is natural, but it has to be dropped. To be carried away by the fear will be very unintelligent.

Secondly, experience shows that in the beginning, by being alone in your own silent spaces of the heart, you feel you are losing contact with others. But don't you see me? Can you find a man who is more an outsider and a stranger in the whole world? Yes, I have lost contact with all kinds of idiots. Now I only have contact with those who are thirsty and those who are understanding and those who want to evolve into spiritual beings. Now this commune of friends and fellow travelers has a totally different meaning than being in the crowd.

The crowd crushes individuality, destroys your freedom, humiliates you to such a point that you start hating yourself instead of loving yourself. The society has been dominated by a very wrong psychology. It looks logical but it is not *psychological*. And logic is something man-made; psychology is not something man-made.

The logic behind humiliating each individual to such a point that he cannot love himself is that if you love yourself, how are you going to love others? And the society and the family and the nation and the religion – everyone is interested in your loving others. Love your wife, love your children, love your parents, love your teachers – love everybody except yourself. It is a simple logic: if you love yourself you will not care much about the wife or the husband or the children or the parents or the priests.

This fear has dominated humanity for thousands of years. But this fear was absolutely wrong because it has not created what they were thinking of. It is a simple psychological fact that a man who cannot love himself cannot love anybody else; but that is not logical, that is a psychological truth.

If you cannot love yourself you don't know even the taste – what love means. So you can pretend: you love your children, you love your wife, you love your husband, you love your parents; but it is all pretension. If so many people in the world were loving, where does war come from? From where are all kinds of violence continuously coming? From where is hatred arising if everybody is so loving?

You have to love your children, you have to love your wife, you have to love your husband, you have to love your parents, you have to love your priests, elders, neighbors... There are even teachers like Jesus who say you have to love your enemies too! Just don't love yourself. This strange logic has destroyed your very roots of loving.

I say unto you: first and foremost, love yourself. And if you can love yourself, others will start getting your love very naturally, without any pretensions, very spontaneously. A man full of love soon starts overflowing. You cannot contain your love into the small space you have within you. Your love is far greater than you are. Your love can fill the whole earth. A single man's love can fill the whole universe. It is so vast that you can go on sharing with everybody.

But if your very source remains closed, then all that is left is to pretend. Everybody is pretending: that's why there is so much talk about love, so much poetry, so much literature. And if you go around you don't find love anywhere, you never encounter it.

I want the whole universe to be a loving, rejoicing universe. But I see where humanity has failed; where its teachers, messengers of God and saviors have taken a wrong route. They listened to logic and they forgot that logic is absolutely man-made; it has nothing to do with your nature. Nature has no obligation to fulfill logical conclusions. If your nature has to be heard, it will become a simple thing to understand.

Love yourself so that all your loving sources become open, all blocks are removed. And if you can love yourself – with all your frailties, with all your weaknesses, with all your errors – you can love anybody in the world. You will have tremendous compassion and understanding because you commit the same mistakes; your errors are the same, your frailties are the same.

The people who have never loved themselves have never come in contact with themselves. Yes, they are in contact with others, but it is a very strange situation. You are not in contact with yourself – how can you be in contact with others? Who is going to be in contact with others? Who are you?

At that point you simply don't know. You know that you have a contact with your friend, you have a contact with your children, you have a contact with your mother; but who are you? And the same is the situation of your mother, your friend, your children: they don't know who they are. Nobody knows who he is and everybody is in contact with everybody else. Can you think of anything more insane than this situation?

Once you become an outsider, settled, confirmed, you will be surprised that now authentic contacts start happening. Because you are now in contact with your own being you will have such a magnetic pull that those who are seeking, those who are searching, those who are longing for something to happen in their life, those who don't want to live an empty and meaningless life, will start coming in contact with you.

And this contact will have a great significance. You will be fulfilling each other without destroying each other. You will be loving but not possessive. You will help but you will not enslave. You will support, but not to exploit – just out of your love, friendliness; out of your understanding whatever happens will be right.

Of course, you will not be part of the big world of retarded people whose mental age is not more than fourteen. This is enough for being a postman or a stationmaster or a president – any trivia. I don't see any difference between a stationmaster and a president of a country. Both are small fries pretending to be something great. You will not be in contact with these psychologically retarded people, but you will come in contact with real, authentic, intelligent, loving human beings who have understanding, who have compassion. And because they can love themselves, they can also love you.

My experience is very different. The moment my blindness disappeared, the moment I found my own being, I could not believe how people started coming to me: I had not advertised myself in any newspaper! Suddenly, walking on the streets, somebody would stop me. Feeling a little embarrassed that he is stopping an absolute stranger, he would say, "Something in you makes me feel to be friendly with you."

I would say, "How many friends can I manage?"

One of the friends arranged a bungalow for me. It was big enough, but soon it was continuously full of guests coming from faraway places. I told the friend, "Something has to be done because we don't have space." I have suffered with space my whole life, and I am still suffering. A few sannyasins are continuously searching for more space because more people are coming, threatening that they are coming!

I have never found myself a stranger. On the contrary, I have found people who are on the same wavelength. I have found people who are filled with the same music. Slowly, slowly people started coming from outside India. Now perhaps this is the only gathering in the world that has its brothers, its sisters, in every country – and yet there is no church, no dogma, no belief system.

What is holding all these people together? I am not promising you any heaven or paradise, and neither am I threatening you with any hell: that if you don't believe in me, "Beware of eternal darkness and hellfire!" Neither am I making you afraid, nor making you greedy for pleasures in heaven. I am not promising you anything – in fact, I am taking away all the promises that others have given to you.

Why has this small commune of friends become an international commune?

I don't feel you will remain a stranger or an outsider for a long time if you authentically enjoy your aloneness and the beauty that showers when you are a pure silence and nothing else, and the flowers that blossom in that spring of aloneness. You will find for the first time those people to whom you belong and it will not take much effort on your part to search for them. Because it is very difficult to search, simply remain in your silence and your silence will be heard more loudly than any noise. Your love will start radiating, spreading its net, pulling people without their being even fully aware of where they are going and for what. They will realize only when they have arrived and become a part of this big caravan. What is happening to you is one of the greatest things that can happen to a person.

You say, "I feel a longing that brings me toward you." The same longing will be felt by many, and this will bring them to you just as a longing has brought you to me. Learn from this.

I have nothing to give you. I cannot give you a direct contact with God because as far as I am concerned there is no God and there is no heaven and no hell. That's how I am dismantling all the beliefs that the past has given to you. I want you to be without beliefs, without promises, without future, without past – just enjoying the moment in its fullness. And this is your moment, just as it is my moment.

And if in our rejoicing we meet, it does not create a bondage. If in our total living of the present we find ourselves in deep love, in deep friendliness, it does not create any chains, it does not make any contracts; it has nothing to do with the next moment. This moment lived totally and intensely becomes almost equal to eternity. It is enough unto itself.

You are saying, "But a passion and desire to fall in love with someone seems to be no longer there." Once you have tasted something of higher quality it is simply natural that things of lower quality will not attract you. If a longing has arisen in you to come close to me – now you cannot think of continuing your old passions and desires and love affairs, which you used to think were great. Now you are having the greatest love affair possible.

More and more only such affairs will be happening. You will live on a totally different plane of consciousness, and lower planes will be left far behind. But you are not a loser. You are a winner. You are growing.

You are worried whether you are right or you are going astray. As far as the crowd is concerned, you are not right, can never be right and you are certainly going astray. That will be the judgment of the crowd. Because you have left the crowd, their scriptures, their religions, their ideologies – you don't belong to them – naturally, according to them you are not right, can never be right, and you have certainly gone astray.

But according to me you have rightly gone astray. Nothing could have been more right than going astray from the crowd.

A doctor who worked in a psychiatric hospital got a flat tire in the parking lot, and when he took the wheel off he dropped the wheel-nuts down the drain. He was at a loss what to do when one of the inmates walked up and told him to take one nut from each of the other wheels and that would last until he got to a garage.

The doctor was very impressed and said, "That's good thinking on your part, young man. Why are you in here?"

The man replied, "I am crazy, not stupid."

It is perfectly good to be crazy here, but not to be stupid. This place is for all kinds of crazy people because they are the very cream of humanity. But this place is not for nuts, not for stupid idiots. You have certainly gone astray from the crowd, but you have found your people here.

I never for a single moment think that there is a world beyond you. You are my world. I have completely forgotten what is happening in the world: whether it exists anymore or not, whether the Third World War has happened or has yet to happen. I am not concerned with it at all. My concern is only with the people with whom I feel a synchronicity, the same heartbeat.

And once you start feeling the same heartbeat with these beautiful people who are here and around the world, you will not feel lonely. You will certainly remain alone, but you will never feel lonely. And you will remain a stranger to the world, but I have gathered all kinds of strangers.

You will not be a stranger here. Here, everybody is a stranger; everybody is an outsider. Amongst my people, nobody will condemn you, nobody will say that you are worthless. You will be loved and respected as you are, not as you should be. Shoulds's we have dropped. We live in the existential and the real. We don't insist that "First you should be according to my ideal and then I will love you."

Once when I was a child my father told me, "Unless you follow the religion of our family, which our ancestors have followed for thousands of years, you will not get my love."

I said, "If there is a condition, then you love your ancestors, you love your religion, you love your ideals, moralities – you don't love me. Unless your love is unconditional it is not love. And if it is not unconditional I am not going to accept it. Don't think that just you are capable of loving me. I am also a part of it. I can reject it. If I see even a small condition hiding behind it, I am the last person to accept it. I can live without your love, but I cannot accept a love that has a condition attached to it. It is not love at all."

The whole day he must have thought about it. In the night when I was going to sleep he came and he said, "I am sorry. I understand what you said. Perhaps in the name of love I was just imposing my ideals on you."

How can love impose ideals on anyone? Love simply accepts you as you are; there is no need to be somebody else. I call a place holy only where love is unconditional, shared without asking anything in return, not even in a subtle way.

So, don't be worried. You may be a little crazy; that is absolutely acceptable and lovable because a man who is not a little crazy is too much of a square. He does not have any juice.

Now my Veeresh is here, hiding himself. This is the crazy type of man I am talking about. He has been following me everywhere on my world tour, but always hiding, just like that. He has not even a desire to be recognized because "I have been following you all around the earth," but a pure love. He goes on working for me in Europe. In every possible way, doing whatever he can do, he puts his total energy into it. And when he comes here, and he must be wanting to come here every day, he hides.

That's the way of unconditional love. It is enough that I have looked into his eyes. It is enough that once in a while, if I can catch hold of him he is fulfilled, he is contented. I have recognized him, I remember him – that is enough.

A man who is not at all crazy, has no color, has no juice. You cannot expect anything unexpected from him. He is just an ordinary businessman type: not a poet, not a painter, not a singer, not a musician, not a dancer, not a meditator. These things are closed for your so-called sane, sober, respectable people of the society. These respectable people have not contributed anything to the world to make it more beautiful. Only the people who have been called crazy by their contemporaries have been the creative people, the contributors. The whole evolution depends on them.

Just think about the first monkey who jumped out of the tree and became a man. What do you think the other monkeys thought about him? "Look at that crazy guy! Is this the way to be a monkey, standing on two legs, on the earth? An outsider, a stranger..." They must have all laughed and enjoyed very much that this fellow has gone crazy. And it must have been talked about for centuries, from generation to generation amongst monkeys. Perhaps they still talk about it: that just one crazy monkey has created five billion crazy monkeys on the earth.

People like Gautam Buddha or Socrates or Pythagoras or Jesus are all outsiders and strangers to their contemporaries and they are all thought to be a little off the track, a little outlandish. And because the crowd, the majority, is there and they write the history books, they don't talk about the authentic contributors, they talk about the destructive people. All the histories are full of Adolf Hitlers, Benito Mussolinis, Joseph Stalins. And very rarely, in the footnotes, you will find something about Pythagoras, Heraclitus, Plotinus, Kabir... perhaps not even in the footnotes. And these are the real people who have lived, who have loved, and who have created as much humanity, as much consciousness as is possible for a single individual.

Rejoice in being a stranger; rejoice in being an outsider. That is your way to *satyam shivam sundaram*. That is the way which will bring you the truth, and the divine, and the tremendous splendor and beauty that follows on its own accord.

> Osho,
> Not counting the discourses, is twenty minutes of meditation a day enough to see me along the path and lead me to experience the satyam shivam sundaram you are pointing us toward?

Vimal, first you cannot be allowed not to count the discourses because your meditations cannot happen without these discourses. These discourses are the foundations of your meditation. I am crazy, but not that crazy that I should go on speaking four hours a day if it does not help you in meditation! Do you think I am trying to distract you from meditation?

And then you are such a miser, Vimal. I never thought you were so miserly that just twenty minutes in twenty-four hours... not even twenty- four minutes!

And you have missed my basic standpoint completely. I don't want you to think of meditation within limits. I want meditation to become your very life. In the past this has been one of the fallacies: you meditate twenty minutes, or you meditate three times a day, you meditate five times a day – different religions, but the basic idea is that a few minutes every day should be given to meditation.

And what will you do in the remaining time? Whatever you will gain in twenty minutes... What are you going to do in the remaining twenty- three hours and forty minutes? – something anti-meditative? Naturally your twenty minutes will be defeated. The enemies are too big, and you are giving too much juice and energy to the enemies and just twenty minutes for meditation. No, meditation in the past has not been able to bring a rebellion in the world because of these fallacies.

These fallacies are the reason I want you to look at meditation from a totally different standpoint. You can learn meditation for twenty minutes or forty minutes – learning is one thing – but then you have to carry whatever you have learned day in, day out. Meditation has to become just like your heartbeat.

You cannot say, "Is it enough, Osho, to breathe for twenty minutes every day?" – the next day will never come. Even while you are asleep you continue breathing. Nature has not left the essential functions of your body and life in your hands. Nature has not trusted you because if breathing were in your hands you would start thinking how much to breathe and whether it is right to breathe while you are sleeping. It looks a little odd doing two things together – sleeping *and* breathing. Breathing seems to be a kind of disturbance in sleeping. But then the sleep will be eternal!

Your heartbeat, your blood circulation are not under your control. Nature has kept everything that is essential in its own hands. You are not reliable, you can forget, and then there is no time even to say, "I am sorry, I forgot to breathe. Just give me one more chance!" Even that much opportunity is not there.

But meditation is not part of your biology, your physiology, your chemistry; it is not part of the ordinary natural flow. If you want to remain just a human being for eternity, you can remain there. Nature has come to a point of evolution where more than this is not needed by nature: you are perfectly capable of reproducing children and that's enough. You will die, your children will continue. Your children will carry on the same stupidities that you were doing. Some will be coming into the congregation, into the churches; some other idiot will be giving sermons, and the whole thing will continue – don't be worried.

Nature has come to a point where now, unless you take individual responsibility, you cannot grow. More than this nature cannot do. It has done enough. It has given you life, it has given you opportunity; now how to use it, it has left it up to you.

Meditation is your freedom, not a biological necessity. You can learn meditation in a certain period of time every day to strengthen it, to make it stronger – but carry the flavor of it the whole day.

First, while you are awake, from the moment you wake up, immediately catch hold of the thread of remaining alert and conscious because that is the most precious moment to catch the thread of consciousness. In the day you will forget many times – but the moment you remember, immediately start being alert. Never repent because that is a sheer wastage of time. Never repent, "My God, I forgot again!"

In my teachings there is no place for any repentance. Whatever has happened is gone. Now there is no need to waste time on it. Catch hold again of the thread of awareness. Slowly, slowly you will be able to be alert the whole day: an undercurrent of awareness in every act, in every movement, in everything that you are doing or not doing. Something underneath will be continuously flowing.

Even when you go to sleep, leave the thread only at the last moment when you cannot do anything because you are falling asleep. And this is one of the laws, that whatever is the last thing before you fall asleep will be the first thing when you wake up. Try it. Any small experiment will be enough to prove it.

Just repeat your own name while you are falling asleep: half awake, half asleep, go on repeating, "Vimal, Vimal, Vimal." Slowly, slowly you will forget repeating because the sleep will grow more and more and the thread will be lost. It is lost only because you are asleep, but underneath your sleep it continues. That's why in the morning when you wake up, just look around. The first thing you will remember will be "Vimal, Vimal." You will be surprised: Why? What happened? You slept eight hours, but there has been an undercurrent.

And as things become deeper and clearer, even in sleep you can remember that you are asleep. Sleep becomes almost a physiological thing and your spirit, your being becomes a flame of awareness, separate from it. It does not disturb your sleep; it simply makes your sleep very light. It is no longer the sleep of the old days, when your house was on fire and you went on sleeping. That was almost like a coma: you were so unconscious.

Your sleep will become thin, a very light layer, and your inside will remain alert. Just as it has been alert in the day, it will finally be even more alert in the night because you are so silent, so relaxed; the whole nuisance world completely silent.

Patanjali, the first man in the world to write about meditation, says that it is almost like dreamless sleep, but with one difference. In dreamless sleep you are not aware. In *samadhi*, in the ultimate state of meditation, there is just a little difference: you are aware.

Vimal, you can continue for twenty minutes every day to learn, to refresh, to give more energy and more roots – but don't be satisfied that that's enough. That's how the whole of humanity has failed, although the whole of humanity has tried in some way or other. But so few people have been successful that by and by many people stopped even trying because success seems to be so far away. But the reason is that just twenty minutes or ten minutes won't do.

I can understand that you have many things to do, so find time. But that time is not meditation, that time is only to refresh yourself – and then again you will have to work, earn, do your job and a thousand and one things. Just remain alert whether it is still there inside or it has disappeared.

This continuity then becomes a garland of twenty-four hours. Only then, Vimal, will you be able to experience *satyam shivam sundaram* – not before it.

A lion was walking through the forest taking a poll to determine who was the greatest among all the wildlife animals. When he saw the hippopotamus, he inquired, "Who is king of the forest?"

"You are," said the hippopotamus.

Next he met a giraffe. "Who is king of the forest?" he inquired.

"You are," said the giraffe.

Next he met the elephant. He gave him a good rap on the knee and said, "And who is the king of the forest?"

The elephant picked him up in his trunk and swung him against the tree. As the lion slid down, brushing himself off, he said, "You don't have to get so mad just because you don't know the right answer."

Vimal, unfortunately I know the right answer. I will not get mad at you, but certainly I will tell you where you are wrong and where you are right.

First, sitting with me in these discourses is nothing but creating more and more meditativeness in you. I don't speak to teach something; I speak to create something. These are not lectures. These are simply devices for you to become silent because if you are told to become silent without making any effort you will find great difficulty.

That's what Zen teachers have been telling their disciples: "Be silent, but don't make any effort." Now, you are putting the person into such a difficult fix: "Don't make any effort and be silent." Now, if he makes any effort he is wrong – and there is no way to be silent without making any effort. If it were possible to be silent without any effort there would have been no need of any master, there would have been no need to teach meditation. People would have become silent without any effort.

I have gone as deep into Zen efforts as possible. They have been working for almost fourteen centuries, since Bodhidharma. They are one of the greatest groups in the world, totally devoted to a single thing and that is meditation. There is no other experiment anywhere that has been done for so long a time continuously. But still there are not many Zen masters.

Yes, there are more masters in the stream of Zen than in any other stream in the world, but still they are very few compared to the people who have been working. I have been searching out what was the basic mistake. This is the basic mistake, Vimal: those Zen masters told them the right thing but not in the right way. I am making you aware of silences without any effort on your part. My speaking is being used for the first time as a strategy to create silence in you.

This is not a teaching, a doctrine, a creed. That's why I can say anything. I am the most free person who has ever existed as far as saying anything is concerned. I can contradict myself in the same evening a hundred times. Because it is not a speech, it has not to be consistent. It is a totally different thing, and it will take time for the world to recognize that a tremendously different experiment was going on.

Just a moment – when I became silent, you become silent. What remains is just a pure awaiting. You are not making any effort; neither am I making any effort. I enjoy talking; it is not an effort.

I love to see you silent. I love to see you laugh, I love to see you dance.

But in all these activities, the fundamental remains meditation.

This is for you all, absolutely unrelated with anything.

Hymie and Becky Goldberg are with their teenage son, Herschel, on holiday in California. Herschel is jogging down the beach when he happens to see someone drowning, not far from the shore. Rushing into the surf, he pulls the man out. Much to his surprise it is Ronald Reagan.

The president sits up in the sand, and when he finally manages to catch his breath, he says, "Young man, that was a heroic deed you just did. In such uncertain times as today, with the stock market crash and the Middle East crisis, the world can't do without me. Tell me son, if there is anything I can do for you, just let me know."

Herschel thinks for a minute, "You know there is one thing."

"Name it," Ronald Reagan urges.

"I would like to be buried with my surfboard in Surfers' Paradise Beach, here in California."

The request takes Ronald Reagan by surprise. "I don't understand," he says. "From the looks of you, you're in perfect health."

"Oh, I am," answers Herschel. "But when my father Hymie Goldberg finds out whose life I just saved, he's gonna kill me!"

29

When Meditation Comes to Its Completion

Osho,

While using hypnosis in the service of meditation, I have noticed that the line between therapy and meditation is dissolving. As witnessing can become easy and natural in hypnosis, it seems to provide the ground for a quantum leap into no-mind. Would you please speak on the transformation of hypnosis into meditation?

It is one of those crimes that Christianity is responsible for. There was a day when hypnosis was a recognized door toward meditation, but in the Middle Ages Christianity condemned hypnosis alongside witchcraft. That condemnation still lingers on, even in the minds of those who are not Christians but who are influenced without their knowing by Christian ideas.

Why was Christianity against hypnosis? You will be surprised to know it was against hypnosis because it leads directly to meditation. Neither the priest is needed nor the church is needed. Not even God is needed. And this was the trouble: if meditation succeeds in the world there are not going to be any religions anymore, for the simple reason that you will be in direct contact with existence and yourself. Why should you go through brokers and all kinds of agents who know nothing, except that they are knowledgeable, except that they have been disciplined for years in how to influence people and win friends?

It is not something religious that they are doing. What they are doing is the politics of numbers: gather as many numbers as possible into your fold; that becomes your strength and your power.

Hypnosis was a danger to the priesthood, and Christianity is absolutely based from the very beginning on the priesthood. Jesus does not declare himself to be enlightened, nor has any other Christian after him declared him to be enlightened. He declares something nonsensical: that he is the only begotten son of God. God is a hypothesis, and hypotheses are not Indians who go on producing children. Hypotheses are barren; they produce nothing.

Just the other day I received from Germany... There was a Protestant conference of Christians, and they invited our sannyasins, hoping to refute our sannyasins and their ideas. But the whole thing backfired.

There is nobody in the world who can refute my sannyasins because we are proposing neither beliefs nor hypotheses. We are simply living life. Our philosophy is not something beyond the clouds; it is something rooted in the earth, it is something as scientific as anything can be.

This question had arisen there, and there was great difficulty because the sannyasins said, "Osho is enlightened and Jesus Christ is not." And the priests of Protestant Christianity could not produce any evidence that Jesus was enlightened; there is no statement anywhere. All that he was proclaiming was that he is the only begotten son of God. In fact, that is a definite indication of unenlightenment.

He does not know himself and he is pretending to know God. And his prayer is just like our Vimal – twenty minutes and the religion is finished! Then the remaining time you are free to do everything irreligious, and then again for twenty minutes you refresh yourself for your irreligiousness. The statements that Jesus has made are so ordinary because he was simply repeating the old prophets.

The sannyasins have informed me that it was a strange situation when they confronted the high priests of Protestant Christianity. They looked at each other: what to do? Enlightenment has not been a Western experience, and the reason why it could not happen in the West is Christianity.

Christianity never wanted you to be directly connected with God. You have to go via the priest, the pope, the son, and then God. In between, the mediators are many, and nobody knows who is lying. Of course you can never discover because you don't have any direct line with God. The priest has a direct line with the pope, the pope has a direct line with Jesus, Jesus has a direct line with God and the numbers are not given in the telephone directories!

Hypnosis was the door, has always been the door to meditation. Once a man enters into the world of meditation, he has such clarity, such a strength, so much life arising in him that he no longer needs any father in heaven. He no longer needs any priest to pray for him. He himself has become prayer – not prayer to any God, but simply a prayerfulness, a gratitude to the whole.

It was absolutely necessary for Christianity to condemn hypnosis and to condemn it as something created by the devil. For the same reasons witchcraft was brutally destroyed. Millions of women were burned alive because they were also doing the same thing. They were trying to contact the ultimate on their own without going through the proper channel of the church.

Your question is very significant. You are asking, "While using hypnosis in the service of meditation..." Hypnosis in itself can be used dangerously unless it is used in the service of meditation. I will have to explain to you what exactly is meant by hypnosis and how it can be misused if it is not used singularly in the service of meditation.

Hypnosis literally means deliberately created sleep. It is now known that thirty-three percent, that is one third of humanity, is capable of going into the deepest layers of hypnosis. It is a strange number – thirty- three percent – strange because only thirty-three percent of people have the aesthetic sense, only thirty-three percent of people have sensitivity, only thirty-three percent of people have friendliness, only thirty-three percent of people are creators. And my only experience is that these thirty-three percent of the people are the same – because creativity and sensitivity are meditation, are love, are friendliness. All need essentially one thing: a deep trust in oneself, in existence, and a receptivity and opening of the heart.

Hypnosis can be created in two ways. Because of the first way, people became impressed by the Christian propaganda that it is dangerous. This is hetero-hypnosis: somebody else hypnotizes you, a hypnotist hypnotizes you.

There are so many wrong ideas attached, and the most fundamental is that the hypnotist has the power to hypnotize you. That is absolutely wrong. The hypnotist has the technique, not the power. Nobody can hypnotize you against yourself, unless you are willing. Unless you are ready to go into the unknown, untraveled darkness, no hypnotist can manage to hypnotize you.

In fact, hypnotists don't deny that they have the power. On the contrary, they claim that they have the power to hypnotize people. Nobody has the power to hypnotize anyone. Only you have the power to hypnotize yourself or to be hypnotized by somebody else – the power is yours. But when you are hypnotized by somebody else it can be misused.

The process is very simple, the technique, is very simple. The hypnotist hangs a crystal from a chain just over your eyes, and tells you, "Don't close your eyes until you cannot keep them open. Fight to the last! Keep your eyes open!" And the crystal shines in your eyes. Naturally, the eyes have to blink continuously to keep themselves from getting dry. They are the most delicate part of your body. You blink your eyes because your eyelids function like windshield wipers on a car. They bring liquid to your eyes and they clean your eyes of any dust, or anything that may have entered. They keep your eyes fresh and are always showering.

The hypnotist says, "Stop blinking: just stare at something shiny!" – shiny because anything shiny will soon make your eyes tired. If you are told to look at a powerful enough electric bulb hanging just above your head, naturally your eyes will get utterly tired. And you are told that you are not to close them, unless you feel they are closing by themselves.

This is one part. The other part is that the hypnotist is continuously saying that your eyes are becoming very heavy, your eyelids seem to be utterly tired... Just by your side he is repeating these words continuously: that your eyes are becoming tired, the lids want to close – and to you just the opposite direction has been given so that you are to go on fighting to the last. But how long can you fight?

It takes no longer than three minutes at the most because a double process is going on. You are focused on the light that is tiring your eyes, and the hypnotist goes on repeating like a parrot, in a very sleepy voice, that sleep is coming over you. You cannot resist; it is impossible now to keep your eyes open.

Now these suggestions... and the person is fighting, he knows that his eyes are becoming tired, and the eyelids are becoming heavy, burdened. A point comes within three minutes, not more than that, when he cannot resist the temptation to let them close. The moment the eyes are closed, the man starts repeating, "You are going into deep sleep, and you will be able only to hear my voice and nothing else. I will remain your only contact."

The person goes deeper and deeper into sleep, with continuous suggestions. There is a point when he stops hearing anything else except the sleepy voice of the hypnotist saying, "You are going deeper, deeper, deeper" – and then he tests whether you have gone deeper or not. He will prick your hand with a safety pin, but you are so asleep that you cannot know about it, you will not feel it.

In fact, in Russia they have started hetero-hypnosis even for operations. No anesthesia is needed. A person can go so deep given the right conditions: a very sleepy, dim atmosphere – neither dark nor light – a forcefully shining light focused on his eyes; very subtle music in the room, a beautiful fragrance, all these help him to go into such a deep sleep that operations can be done, have been done, and the person knows nothing.

So the hypnotist tries a few things. He takes your hand up and lets go of it, and the hand falls – because you cannot hold it, you are fast asleep; in sleep you cannot hold it up high. He lifts your eyelids up, he looks into your eyes and only the white of your eyes is seen; your pupils have moved upwards. The deeper the hypnosis, the higher your pupils will move upwards.

This happens in deep sleep every day, and this also happens when somebody dies. That's why all over the world people immediately close the eyelids of a dead person – for the simple reason that it is so frightening to see somebody with completely white eyes. In India it has been known for centuries that when a man is going to die, his eyes start slowly moving upwards, and the sign and symbol is that he cannot see the tip of his own nose.

You can see it. Remember: the day you cannot see your nose six, months at the most! – because when the pupils of the eyes are moving upwards, they cannot see the tip of the nose.

So the hypnotist opens the eyelid and sees whether it is all white, and all that used to be there, your real eye, has moved upwards. Then he is certain that you are no longer capable of hearing anybody, you are no longer capable of disobeying him; whatever he will say, you will do.

This is the danger. He can say to you, "Just take out all your money and hand it over to me," and you will immediately take out all your money and hand it over to him. He can take your ornaments, he can tell you to sign any document that may create trouble for you – that you have sold your house, or donated your house.

There is one thing more to be understood, which is very dangerous: he can give a post-hypnotic suggestion. A post-hypnotic suggestion means that he can say to you, "After ten days you will come to me, you will have to come to me, bringing all your money, all your ornaments, anything valuable that you have. Leave it on my table and simply go back."

It is possible to give a post-hypnotic suggestion that after twenty-four hours you will shoot somebody. All these orders will be followed because the person does not know, as far as his consciousness is concerned, he has no idea what has happened under deep hypnosis. Deep hypnosis reaches your unconscious.

These were the dangers that Christianity exaggerated, saying that this is against religion, against morality because a woman can be raped and she will not know, or a woman can be told, "You have fallen in love with me," and a great romance will begin from the moment she wakes up. She will feel a little hesitant because her conscious mind will not understand what has happened, but there is no communication between the conscious mind and the unconscious. The unconscious is so powerful – nine times more powerful – that when the unconscious wants to do something, the conscious may start protesting but that protest is futile.

All these things were spread, wildly exaggerated, among man. But the purpose of the church was not to save you from these dangers. The purpose was that hypnosis should become so condemned that nobody could enter from that door into the ultimate realm of *satyam shivam sundaram.*

Christianity kept people completely ignorant about another kind of hypnosis; that is self-hypnosis, not hetero-hypnosis. Only hetero-hypnosis can be misused; autohypnosis or self-hypnosis cannot be misused. There is nobody. You are alone.

You can do the same thing by yourself. You can put an alarm clock on, and then repeat three times that within fifteen minutes, when the alarm goes off, you will come back from your deep hypnotic sleep. And then the procedure is the same.

You look at the light, and you do what the hetero-hypnotist was doing. Looking at the light, you go on repeating inside, "My eyes are becoming heavy, heavy... heavier, heavier. I am falling into sleep. I cannot keep my eyes open anymore; I am trying my best, but it is impossible" – and it also takes exactly three minutes. That is the maximum; it may happen in two minutes, it may happen in one minute, but the longer you struggle, the deeper will be the hypnosis.

I have heard about a man, an old man, who was torturing his family. Every day he would figure out how many diseases he had. The doctors were tired; they said he had no diseases. He listened to the medical program on the television and learned the names of the diseases. Then he started torturing the family, "I am suffering from this, I am suffering from that. Nobody is taking care of me." This was simply a way for an old man to attract attention.

Nobody gives attention to old people, so they find their own ways. They become more irritable, more angry, more fussy. They have their own techniques to attract attention. Their whole lives they were nourished by attention, but now nobody looks at them, nobody even bothers whether they exist or are finished...

Jagjit Singh, an Indian singer, who loves me, tells a beautiful joke.

One of his friends who lives in London had come, so he asked him, "How are you?"

He replied, "All right."

Jagjit Singh said, "And how is your wife?"

He replied, "She is also all right."

"And how are your children?"

"They are also all right."

Jagjit Singh finally asked, "And what about Daddy?"

And the man said, "Daddy? He has been all right for almost four years." Four years ago he had died, so the friend is saying that he has been all right, completely all right, *forever* all right for four years!

Old people have only these methods to attract attention: that they are suffering from migraine, that they have a stomachache. The greater their medical vocabulary is, the more they will manage!

Finally, doctors started refusing, saying, "He is a mad person. He has no sickness, no disease; we have checked him so many times."

But the son said, "What can we do? We should call the doctor."

So the doctors finally suggested that there was a hypnotist and perhaps he might be helpful: "Bring this hypnotist, so he can hypnotize him and tell him that he is absolutely all right. That is the only medicine he needs. If his unconscious grips the idea of being all right, then there will be no problem."

The sons were very happy, and they brought the hypnotist to him. He looked like a doctor with his bag and paraphernalia, with his small Sigmund Freud beard, with a glass on one eye – one has to be properly dressed according to his profession. This was impressive. He asked the old man, "What are your troubles?"

The old man listed so many troubles. The hypnotist said, "Okay, just lie down and I will be holding this pendulum that shines because it has a battery behind it. You have to keep your eyes on it until you cannot keep them open."

After a long life's experience, old people become very cunning and very clever. The old man thought, "From the way he is dressed, this seems to be a con man… and what kind of treatment is going on?" He thought, "Let us see." He did not wait for three minutes, he immediately closed his eyes, and when the hypnotist took his hand, he dropped it. He knew all the tricks: an old man… he has seen everything in the world!

The hypnotist said, "He is completely at ease and asleep. Now I will give him the suggestion: 'Now you are perfectly all right. You don't have any disease and you will not harass your children with diseases that don't exist!'" And the old man remained silent.

His sons were very happy: "Why did we never think of the hypnotist? We have been wasting so much money paying the doctors, and all that they say is 'You harass us. Although you give us money, it is sheer harassment. The old man is not sick at all.' This man is the right man!"

The old man was lying completely still. All suggestions over, the hypnotist collected his fee. One of the sons went out the door to see him off to his car, but even before he returned, the old man opened one eye and asked, "Has that crackpot gone or not?"

If you immediately close your eyes, nothing will happen because you will remain conscious. And whatever the hypnotist is saying, he will look like a crank. What nonsense is he talking? "Your eyes are becoming heavy" – they will not become heavy. "You are falling deep in a sleep" – you are not falling, you are perfectly alert. And he is cheating, he is saying that you don't have any diseases!

But if you are doing a session of self-hypnosis, there is no danger. You just go through the whole process, looking at a bright thing that tires your eyes – that is its only function – and you go on repeating what the hypnotist was repeating, just inside your being. Finally, you will find you cannot keep your eyes open; they are closing. You have lost control over them. And that feeling of losing control over your eyelids immediately gives you the feeling that you are certainly falling into deep sleep.

As long as you are aware, you go on repeating, "I am going deeper, deeper..." and a moment comes when you have gone deepest into your unconscious. And after ten minutes the alarm will go off, and you will come back from your unconscious to the conscious. You will be surprised how fresh, how young you are feeling within yourself; how clean, as if you have passed through a beautiful garden full of flowers, with a cool breeze.

You can also give yourself post-hypnotic suggestions. They have to be given at the last moment when your eyes are closing and you feel that now you will be going deeper. Before going deeper you start saying, "From tomorrow my health will be better." Just choose one thing – not too many, don't be greedy – and just a fifteen-day session or a three-week session, just on yourself. Whatever you are saying, perhaps that your meditation will go deeper from tomorrow, and you will find that your meditation is going deeper and you can create a very beautiful link.

When the meditation goes deeper, then you can suggest to yourself: "Tomorrow my hypnosis will go even deeper." You can use both to bring you to the very depths of your unconsciousness. And once you have touched the depths of your unconsciousness, then you can start a second suggestion: "Although I will be in the dark unconscious, a slight awareness will remain so that I can see what is happening." And then go on repeating, "My awareness which was slight is becoming bigger and bigger and bigger..." And one day you will find the whole unconscious is lighted with your alertness – and that's what meditation is.

Hypnosis can be used, should be used, without any fear. Either together with people who trust each other and love each other, so there is no fear of exploitation, or with your very intimate friends – you know that they cannot harm you, you can open yourself, you can be vulnerable – or just yourself. By yourself it will take a little longer because you have to do two persons' work yourself. That is a little disturbance.

But now, because tape recorders are available, you can dispose of the other person completely and give the suggestion part to the tape recorder. And the tape recorder certainly cannot misuse; it cannot tell you to kill your wife – unless you have put that on the tape! Then I cannot help it. Whatever you put on the tape recorder it will repeat.

You can put the whole process on the tape recorder: all the suggestions of falling into sleep, heaviness of the lids, going deeper... And then when you are deepest – a gap of four or five minutes so you can settle in your deepness. Then from the tape recorder comes the voice saying that your meditation will become deeper from today; that you will not have to struggle with your thoughts. The moment you close your eyes, the thoughts will start dispersing themselves.

The tape recorder can be immensely helpful because there is no question of trusting anybody. You can trust your tape recorder without any fear. And you can lock the door so that nobody plays with your tape recorder: otherwise somebody may trick you!

Self-hypnosis has to be in the service of meditation; that is its greatest use. But it can serve health, it can serve long life, it can serve love, it can serve friendliness, it can serve courage. Self-hypnosis can help you with all that you want. It can dispel your fears of the unknown, it can dispel your fear of death; it can make you ready for being alone, silent, peaceful, it can make you able to continue an undercurrent of meditation for twenty-four hours. You can even suggest, "While I am asleep my small flame of awareness will continue all through the night without disturbing my sleep."

You are saying, "I have noticed that the line between therapy and meditation is dissolving." That has been my deep desire for long. Therapy should dissolve into hypnosis, and hypnosis should dissolve into meditation. Then we have created one of the greatest forces for enlightenment, which has never been used in the past.

Therapy has never been used. Therapy will cleanse you of all garbage. It will take away all your conditionings. Therapy will help you to cathart. Anything that is there and that you have been repressing inside, therapy will throw it out.

Therapy is a beautiful cleansing process, and a mind cleansed will fall into hypnosis more easily, without any struggle. Perhaps with therapy even those who are not easily available to self-hypnosis or to hypnosis – the people who don't belong to the thirty-three percent – may start belonging to the group that is available for hypnosis. Therapy can change one hundred percent of people into authentic candidates for hypnosis.

So therapy has to be used in such a way that it slowly dissolves into hypnosis, and then hypnosis has to be used so that it can become steps going toward meditation.

I propose that these three things together become my trinity. God and the Holy Ghost and Jesus Christ – forget all that nonsense! That is not a trinity. But something scientific, something that you can do yourself, something that is possible to be practiced; except for that, religion is so full of garbage that people have become more interested in the garbage and forgotten the essential. In fact, the essential has become so small in comparison with the Himalayan garbage that has accumulated over it down the centuries that it is even difficult to find where it is.

What I am proposing is a simple thing: you don't need any priest, you don't need any church, you don't need any holy scripture, all that you need is a little understanding and a little courage. Cathart totally in therapy. You don't know how much crap there is inside you. When you start catharting, then you will know: "My God, is this me or somebody else? What am I doing? What am I saying?"

Sometimes what you are saying does not even make any sense, but it was there, otherwise it could not come to you. It has been a hindrance to your meditation and it will be a hindrance to your going deep into hypnosis. It will become a barrier somewhere in-between.

So therapy has to be the first thing. The second thing is hypnosis, and the third thing will grow out of it: your meditation. The ultimate in meditation is enlightenment.

When meditation comes to its completion, then your whole being becomes full of light, full of blissfulness, full of ecstasy.

> Osho,
> The other morning in discourse, for a few moments I felt as if my face were disappearing. It was a very pleasant sensation, and at the same time a feeling of astonishment and surprise arose. Would you please say something about this?

It was not your original face that was disappearing. What was disappearing was your mask. Only the mask can disappear. The original face can be covered, but it cannot be made to disappear by any means. The mask is used to cover your face. And we have many masks. We go on changing them as the situation requires.

If you are seeing your servant, you have a different mask: you are the master. When you are facing your boss, you have a different mask: although he is humiliating you, you are still smiling. The original face cannot smile; it is only the mask. Deep down you are cursing but you have to smile, otherwise your job is in danger.

I heard about an office. The boss used to come only for one hour, but when he came, he would gather the whole office – the clerks, the typists – and tell them jokes. He had only three jokes to tell, and it was a very strange situation: those people had heard those jokes thousands of times, but still when he told them they would laugh so loudly and clap as if they had heard them for the first time and because there were only three, that meant each joke would be repeated at least twice in a week.

Even the boss sometimes thought, "What is the matter? Do these people forget all about it?"

But one day the secret was disclosed. One girl, a typist, did not laugh. Everybody looked at her: what has happened to her? She has always been laughing louder than anybody...

The boss was also very hurt that he had told a joke and she was simply sitting there, not even smiling. He said, "What is the matter with you?"

She said, "Nothing is the matter with me. I have accepted another job. Now I will laugh there, not here. Let these idiots continue to laugh. It is because of your jokes that I am changing my job! I am tired because you have told these jokes so many times that sometimes I find myself telling them to myself. It has become such a difficult thing... in the night, in my sleep, I am telling the joke and then I wake up perspiring. Just these three jokes have become my nightmare.

"I have changed my job and now for the last time I have come just to see how it feels not to laugh. I am feeling so good because for the first time it is my original face that you are seeing; otherwise all these people who are laughing and opening their mouths ear to ear... these are only masks. Inside they are cursing you, they want to kill you. They know that unless they kill you...

"They talk when you are gone, and I have been here listening to their talk. They are thinking, How to kill this fellow? – because unless you kill him, he will kill you! Those three jokes are enough to kill. They have become almost their blood, their bones, their marrow. Even while typing they forget and start typing the jokes."

If year after year you have to hear the same thing and you have to pretend...

What you felt was certainly beautiful. This is my only longing: to see you in your original faces. Let these masks disappear. Just become yourself. You will feel light; you will enjoy it. The first time you may feel astonished, but as it goes on happening again and again, astonishment will disappear and the pleasantness will become deeper. A moment comes when a person becomes absolutely original. Then his whole life is full of blissfulness.

You have been forced to wear masks because you are expected to behave in a certain way, to talk in a certain way, to dress in a certain way. You don't have any freedom. The society imposes a complete imprisonment on you, from all nooks and corners. This is your slavery and this is your misery. This is your pain and this is your hell.

Get out of all this falseness and just be simple – as simple as the birds singing, as simple as the trees enjoying the sun, as simple as small children.

Little Hymie Goldberg was taken to a seance. When he arrived, the medium asked Hymie if there was anybody he would like to contact and speak to.

"I'd like to speak to my granny," said Hymie.

"Certainly, my dear," said the medium, going into a deep trance. She began to moan and talk in a strange voice, saying; "This is your granny speaking from heaven... a wonderful place in the skies. Is there anything you would like to ask me, Hymie?"

"Yes, Granny," said Hymie, "what are you doing in heaven when you're not even dead yet?"

A childlike innocence...

Little Ronnie was growing up.

"Mom," he asked one day, "where do babies come from?"

"Why, the stork brings them," replied his mother.

"But, mom," asked Ronnie, "who fucks the stork?"

30

The Birth of Individuality

Osho,
Why is the new so scary? My wanting and need for recognition are gone along with the doing. Even though deep inside I am tremendously thankful and happy, I find part of myself feeling guilty. I see as well that laziness is not one of my qualities. I can't find the new way for me to be total in my work. It is becoming very painful. Can you please bring some light and guidance to me?

The new is always scary because of the simple fact that it is new. You don't know how to face it. All your knowledge is suddenly found to be absolutely meaningless because there is no answer in your experience and knowledge that can be an authentic response to the new – because you suddenly find yourself ignorant, helpless, not knowing what to do; hence the scariness.

Otherwise, instead of being afraid you will have a totally different experience with the new. You will explode with joy. If you are an explorer, an adventurer, then the new will fill you with tremendous ecstasy, and you will see in this new a possibility for your intelligence to function.

With the old, intelligence has no need to function: your memory functions. You know the answer already; the answer is part of your memory system. But memory is not intelligence, remember.

Intelligence is the capacity to rejoice in the new with an open-hearted welcome, with intense clarity. Just by watching the new, the response will arise from your very innermost core. That is the way of the meditator. The meditator is continuously confronted with the new. In fact, he is in search of the ultimate new, which will never become old, which will always be fresh.

That is the quality of *satyam shivam sundaram*. Truth is never old; neither is the godliness that surrounds you from all dimensions, nor the experience of beauty. The roses may come and go, the expressions of beauty may come and disappear, but the experience of beauty is always there, exactly the same.

You are asking, "Why is the new so scary?" Because you are still in the mind and you don't know what meditation is.

Mind loves the old. With the old the mind is very at ease because it knows all the answers. It does not feel helpless, it does not feel that it has to choose this way or that way. It knows exactly what is the right answer. The mind never wants you to come in contact with the new. It keeps you going round and round with the old.

Meditation is just the opposite of mind. As mind is confined with the old, meditation is an exploration of the expansion of the whole universe. The meditator wants to come each moment to the new, because only with the new does his intelligence become more sharp; only with the new does he himself become new. Only with the new is the way toward the ultimate.

The old is dead. Of course the old seems to be very comfortable. It seems comfortable because you don't have to do anything. You don't even have to be intelligent. You can remain retarded and yet pretend to the world that you are a great intellectual because you are filled with all kinds of information in your memory.

And the memory is not part of your consciousness; the memory is part of your body. The memory is just a mechanism like any computer. You feed it with information and whatever you feed it, it is perfectly comfortable with. It knows it. And knowledge gives you a certain power: you are within the territory where you are the ruler, you know everything.

The unknown, the new, suddenly exposes your ignorance, and that hurts. You don't want to know your ignorance; that's why the new is scary. But your ignorance is enormous; your knowledge is just a dewdrop. If you don't want to remain a dewdrop – closed, absolutely non-receptive and insensitive to the tremendous existence that is available to be yours any moment – gather courage and come out of your smallness. The moment the dewdrop takes a jump into the ocean is exactly the situation of a man who takes a jump from the mind into meditation.

Mind is so small. Existence and life are so vast, so infinite, that unless you come out of the mind you will live the life of a prisoner and a slave. A slave cannot know what dance is, a slave cannot know what freedom is and the joy of freedom and the blissfulness and the ecstasy of being vast, oceanic.

My work with you is to persuade you to come out of your caves which are dark – although they look very cozy to you because you are acquainted with them.

It happened in the French Revolution... France had the greatest prison, the Bastille, where only prisoners who were going to be there for their whole lives were sent. They could only enter there; they could never come out. Once a person entered there... It had only a door to enter through; it had no exit.

There are only two places like this in the world, and strangely, both are prisons. One is a Catholic monastery in Europe where whoever enters, enters forever. There are still almost ten thousand monks in that monastery. They cannot come out again, at least not while they are alive. Dead, they are free to go out – in fact others will throw them out.

And the other place, where prisoners were thrown in, was the Bastille. The Bastille had small cells for the prisoners: thousands of caves, dark caves with no light. The prisoners were handcuffed, chained, and the keys of their chains and handcuffs were thrown into a well that was in the middle of the prison because they were never going to be opened, so what was the point of collecting thousands of keys unnecessarily? There was no point. Those people would die and then their chains would be cut, not opened, so there was no need.

In the French Revolution, the revolutionaries immediately thought to open the doors of the Bastille as a priority, and allow thousands of prisoners their freedom. They were thinking that they were doing something great. They could not have expected the response of the prisoners.

The prisoners refused. They said, "We have lived here, somebody for twenty years, somebody else for thirty years..." There were a few people who had lived there fifty, sixty, seventy years.

Now a man who has lived there for seventy years must be nearabout a hundred years old. His whole life experience is confined to a small cave. He cannot come out of it; he is chained and tethered to the cave wall. He cannot even move out of the cave just to see the sky or the stars or the moon. Naturally, such a person will be afraid to go back into the world after seventy years.

Almost everybody he used to know must either be dead by now, or where is he going to find these people he used to know? Their names have faded away, their faces have faded away: a faraway seventy long years... And who knows if they will recognize him? If he cannot remember them, who is going to recognize him? – a man condemned to be in prison for life. And what will he do? From where will he get his food and his clothes, and where will he sleep? He will need a shelter too.

And now to work, to earn is almost a forgotten language. And at this age – old, sick, tattered – who is going to give him work or employment? Anyway, even ordinary prisoners who have been in prison for a few months don't easily get any employment. Who is going to trust a man who has been seventy years in jail? It is too risky.

Here everything is comfortable. It may look uncomfortable to an outsider, but for a man who has lived in the cave for seventy years, it may have been uncomfortable in the beginning for a few days, a few months, but man has a tremendous capacity of adaptability. In any situation, if you force him, he will start adapting to the situation.

And seventy years or fifty years is a long time: half a century. And now that he has started feeling perfectly cozy, comfortable: no worry about bread, no worry about tomorrow, no worry about anything. He has forgotten the names of his children, he has forgotten who used to be his wife, and what happened to all those people. No, he does not want to go out.

The revolutionaries could not believe it. "We are giving you freedom and you are as scared as if we are going to kill you."

And those prisoners said, "That's exactly what we are feeling: that you are going to kill us. We are perfectly happy here. Just excuse us. We cannot fulfill your expectations. It is too late."

But revolutionaries are stubborn people. They did not listen to the prisoners. They cut their chains, they cut their handcuffs, they forced them out with the same violence with which they had one day been forced in. Against their will they had been brought in; against their will they were brought out.

Many of them could not even open their eyes because the light was too much. Their eyes had become too weak, too delicate. Living in darkness, their eyes were no longer capable of opening in the sunlight. Many of them had forgotten how to walk. But the revolutionaries were adamant: they did not listen to their cries. They had tears, but revolutionaries are revolutionaries. They forced them, almost three thousand prisoners, out of the Bastille.

There was nobody to receive them, and they moved around the city like dead people, almost like ghosts. They could not recognize anything. Seventy years before, things had been totally different. Nor could they see anybody who was contemporary to them. And by the evening almost all of them had returned back to the prison.

They fought the revolutionaries who were preventing them from getting into the prison.

They said, "We cannot live outside. Who is going to give us food? And who is going to take care of us: medical care, shelter, clothes? Who is going to be responsible for all this – you?"

And the most amazing thing they said was, "We cannot sleep without chains and without handcuffs. We have become so accustomed to them, it feels that something is missing. We cannot sleep – we tried in the day under some trees, but unless we feel the load, the weight of the chains on the feet, on the hands, we cannot sleep. So please don't harass us. Life has harassed us enough; now at the end we don't want to change our lifestyle."

Finally the revolutionaries also recognized their problem. They had not thought about it, that man becomes adapted to a certain situation and then that is his territory. In that territory he is perfectly comfortable and cozy.

My own experience is that I have talked with beggars who had bank balances. I don't have a bank balance; I never did. It just happened by chance because I was continuously traveling, I used to come to the railway station in Jabalpur at least ten or fifteen times a month, either coming or going.

There used to be an old beggar outside the railway station. Because the first day I had given him one rupee, he would not accept less than that, and he never asked for more than that. So he had become adapted, I had become adapted: I had to give him that one rupee. In fact, if sometimes I came and I did not find the beggar, I would miss him. I would inquire, "Where is the old man?" We had become very friendly, and if sometimes I could not find him, the next time I would give him two rupees – one for the time when I missed him – because it had been very heavy on me.

One day just as I was passing the station I saw him. I was not going out of town, but I was just driving by the railway station, going to meet the doctor of the railway employees at the railway hospital.

There I suddenly saw in the corner the old man talking to a young boy, and that young boy was my student. I stopped my car and waited. When they were finished they were both shocked. The father was shocked but I could not understand why. I said, "Why do you look so shocked?"

The father said, "I cannot hide it from you. I have been hiding it from everybody, but he is my son and he is your student, and I am preparing him to become at least a doctor."

I asked the boy, "You never told me that you are the son of a beggar."

He said, "My father never allows me. He never meets me anywhere where people can see because if people come to know I am the son of a beggar it will be difficult: difficult in the college, difficult for getting further admission into new colleges. It will become impossible, and my father will be exposed: he can educate his son to become a medical doctor and still he is continuing to beg. He brings me the best of clothes." I used to see him: out of the whole class, he had the best clothes, the best shoes, everything the best.

That day I asked the old man, "How much of a bank balance do you have?"

He said, "Now I cannot hide it from you, and I trust that you will not expose the fact that he is my son. I have thirty thousand rupees in the bank."

I said, "With thirty thousand rupees you can start a shop, a small factory. Why do you go on begging in your old age?"

He said, "Begging is so comfortable. Everything else can make me bankrupt, but begging can never make me bankrupt. And my earnings are more than any shopkeeper or small factory owner. I earn nearabout fifty rupees per day." Even a doctor in India does not earn that much, nor a professor. And he said, "I have my customers, and why should I unnecessarily go into something new about which I don't know anything? Begging is my heritage: my father was a beggar, my father's father was a beggar, and they were all rich men."

For the first time I became aware of a new dimension of the human mind. It does not matter what condition you are in: slowly, slowly you settle down. And once you have settled down you don't even want to budge because then again you will have to start from *ABC*. Again you will have to start learning, again you will have to start facing problems. Right now there are no problems: you know all the answers to all the questions that can arise in a certain situation in which you have become completely enclosed.

It is cozy and it is comfortable to live in the old, but it will not bring the flowers of freedom and it will not open the whole sky for you to open your wings and fly. It will not allow you to have aspirations for the stars; it will not allow you to move in any direction or dimension. You will remain just like a dead grave where nothing moves.

The new is scary, but the new is what I teach you. You will have to drop your fears, you will have to drop your ugly coziness, you will have to drop your small comforts. These are the things with which you have to pay for the greater joys, the higher realms of being, tremendous possibilities of ecstasies. You will not be a loser, but in the beginning you have to risk something.

It is good you are aware that the new makes you scared because for centuries man, animals, everybody has been living with the old. Only man has risen once in a while to have a glimpse of the new. Think about buffaloes: can you conceive that at any time in the millions of years of evolution, buffaloes have eaten any other grass than they eat today? The same grass! Can you conceive that one day buffaloes will be different? They are so settled, so utterly settled and so contented. You cannot make a buffalo a buddha. They are perfectly at ease. Why should they bother?

The whole animal kingdom is lower than man only for one reason: man is an explorer; he has the adventurer hidden in him somewhere. His mind may be afraid, scared, but his consciousness wants to have communion with the universe, to touch the stars, to open up to all the beauties and the truth and the godliness of existence.

You will have to shift your emphasis from mind to meditation, and all fear will disappear. You will have to shift your attention from your comfortable, cozy – but old and dirty and rotten – state toward something new, fresh, young from the body to consciousness, from mind to no- mind. Then every moment you are confronting the new.

And one is thrilled with the new. Once you have learned that the new is not your enemy the fear simply disappears. On the contrary, you start searching for the new. The day you start searching for the new with joy and a dancing heart, you have become a sannyasin. That is my definition of a sannyasin.

I define my sannyasins from many dimensions; I want to give you the idea of sannyas from as many aspects as possible. The search for the new is one of the aspects of a seeker.

You are saying, "My wanting and need for recognition are gone, along with the doing. Even though deep inside I am tremendously thankful and happy, I find part of myself feeling guilty. I see as well that laziness is not one of my qualities. I can't find the new way for me to be total in my work. It is becoming very painful."

All your problems are your creations. First, you should be immensely happy that the need for recognition is gone. That is a great achievement. You are no longer dependent on others' opinions. For the first time you are just yourself and you don't need anybody to approve. This is the beginning of the birth of individuality. Otherwise people are only cogs in the wheel: whatever others say they believe, even about themselves. All that they know about themselves is what others have said. They go on collecting all kinds of opinions and that's what their self-knowledge consists of. It is a great experience that the need for recognition is gone. You should be happy with it rather than making some problem out of it.

Mind is very clever and very cunning. Even if you are feeling very ecstatic, mind will say, "Beware! You may be just having a hallucination" and it will destroy your blissfulness: "My God! It is possible it may be just a hallucination!" When you have a pain the mind never says that – not in the whole history of mankind. When you are having a migraine the mind never says that it may just be illusory.

But if you are having a beautiful space within you, as if a rose is flowering, the mind is going to jump on it immediately: "You are daydreaming, this is all hallucination, illusion. You are being hypnotized." And you immediately listen to the mind because you have listened to it for centuries. It is just a habit.

Along with the recognition, you are saying, your doing has also gone. That's an even greater achievement than the first one. If the doing is gone, the doer must have gone also. But I suspect that's where the problem is: doing is gone but the doer is there. That is creating the tension that is making you feel a part of yourself as guilty. Who is this part?

If doing is gone, nothing is wrong. In fact one of the basic fundamentals for enlightenment to happen is that your doing should go. That does not mean that you will not do things. You will do things but they will not be fulfillments of your ego or projections of your mind. They will be spontaneous. You will rejoice in doing them, or vice versa: because you rejoice you do them.

But it seems the doer is still hiding somewhere within you. So a part has disappeared, but the other part is still there creating a feeling of guilt: it is not good to be lazy, it is not good not to do anything, you should do something, you should not become a parasite. That doer goes on creating problems for you, anxiety for you. If you have been able to let the recognition go, the doing go, release the doer also. But remember, that does not mean that you will become lazy. That is a wrong interpretation by the mind.

Mind always interprets anything that is going to become a step leading beyond mind wrongly. When you feel let-go, mind will say, "This is laziness." Mind is a great condemner. It enjoys condemning others, it enjoys condemning you. Its only joy is to condemn.

You are saying, "Even though deep inside I am tremendously thankful and happy, I find part of myself feeling guilty." You have to become aware of that part and drop it. If you can just drop so much, why carry this small part of being guilty? You have not done any wrong to anyone. You are just feeling guilty because the society brings you up with the idea: "Do something, be somebody. Don't remain a nobody, don't become a good-for-nothing. Leave your footprints on the pages of history."

What kind of stupidity is this? Why should I leave my footprints on the pages of history? To torture future children? And why should I be somebody special? Those are ego trips.

Much has disappeared but something of the ego has remained, which is making you guilty and which is calling you lazy. But this is not laziness; this is relaxation, let-go. And out of this let-go, out of this relaxation will grow new flowers. That is the difference: laziness is barren, nothing grows out of it, it is a desert. So soon you will see the difference. Just don't cling to the word *laziness*. Drop it. It is a very negative and destructive word.

I have never done anything in the eyes of the world. From the very beginning my family used to say to me, "You are going to be good for nothing!" And they proved right: I am good *only* for nothing!

They were very much concerned: "How are you going to live your life? How are you going to manage?" And I always told them, "Don't be worried. If I am not worried, why should you be worried? Something or other will happen, don't be worried." But they remained concerned and they continually told me, "This is laziness, this is not good."

And I told them, "This is not laziness; it is my meditativeness. I am just simply being silent. And you will see: if it is laziness, you will find my life a desert where nothing grows. And if I am right and it is a let- go, then you will see that it may not be visible to ordinary people, but those who have eyes can see, those who have ears can hear, that my life has become a song, a dance, a celebration – so many flowers – and that I am so contented and so fulfilled."

I have not known any feeling of guilt for a single moment. Just learn the right language on the path of meditation. Your language belongs to the mind. When you change the track from mind to meditation you will have to change many words that mind uses but which are not applicable in the world of meditation. Call it let-go and suddenly you will feel a tremendous relaxation. Call it laziness and immediately some condemnation, some anxiety, something painful. Learn the new language because you have chosen to be on the path in search of the new and the unknown.

I am also against laziness. Laziness is simply dullness, it is stupidity, but let-go is the greatest quality a man can achieve. Relaxation is one of the most beautiful experiences, which can bring you so many gifts from the beyond that you are absolutely unaware of. Change the language.

If laziness is not one of your qualities, good. Let relaxation be one of your qualities. Relaxation, non-doing, don't disturb at all; your life just becomes more creative rather than being more productive. Those two words make the difference again. Mind calls productivity "activeness" and creativity is not counted. It takes time for authentic creativity to be realized.

Just the other day, one of Van Gogh's paintings was sold for forty million dollars. A few months before one of his paintings was sold for fourteen million dollars, and at that time it was said that was the most one could imagine; no painting had fetched fourteen million – now what to say about forty?

This man lived in poverty, hungry, starving because he could not sell a single painting. And he was not demanding forty million dollars; sometimes he was ready to give one painting just for one meal. Sometimes just for one cup of tea he was ready to give one of his paintings. But even for just a cup of tea people were not willing: "We don't have space, where will we put it? Just find someone else." To them it was a problem: "Where to put it? We don't have space!"

And after his death when slowly, slowly the time for his recognition came he was no longer there. It came one hundred years afterward. It is the case with almost every genius. Every genius comes, for absolutely unknown reasons, before his time. Why can't these people wait a little? It is just that they arrive when their contemporaries are not here. By the time their contemporaries are here, they are gone, so they never know.

Do you think Jesus will ever know how many Christians there are in the world now? Do you think Socrates will ever know that now his name is something that keeps Greece proud? Otherwise, without his name, Greece is nothing. It is his teachings and his disciples, Plato and Aristotle, which have kept Greece at a peak of intelligence – because I don't think anybody else in the whole of Europe has been able to transcend the sharpness of intelligence that Socrates had. Perhaps his contemporaries have not yet arrived, and twenty-five centuries have passed.

When Van Gogh's paintings were recognized people started searching them out. He must have painted thousands of paintings and just went on giving them away – to friends, as gifts, or for a cup of tea or for a meal. And people received his paintings just not to look crude, not to look uncivilized and they thought, "Once he is gone then we can put the painting in the basement." Nobody was hanging his paintings in their sitting rooms because anybody looking at the paintings would think, "This man had gone crazy! Why is he putting up this painting?" because at the time Van Gogh's ideas looked crazy. But his time came. His whole family condemned him, saying, "You have not done a single thing and you are a parasite on your younger brother" – because his younger brother went on supporting him just enough so that he could survive.

Van Gogh could never eat the whole week: four days he was eating and three days he was fasting – one day eating, one day fasting, one day eating, one day fasting – because with whatever he could save from those three days he would purchase colors, paints, canvasses, brushes for his painting. There was no other way.

Nobody has painted with such love and with such joy, with his own life and his own blood. He destroyed himself in painting. And now there is so much searching going on in the basements of Holland and France where he lived. His paintings have been found in people's basements, and now the prices of those paintings are unbelievable.

The last one was sold the day before yesterday for forty million dollars. When the painting was sold a few months ago the critics were saying, "This is the end; nobody can purchase any painting for a higher price than this." He had made a record – fourteen million dollars. Before this, the record had been only three million dollars for somebody else's painting. But this was a big jump, to fourteen million, and within three or four months another of his paintings went for forty million dollars – and I can conceive that the price of his paintings may go still higher. Just now two hundred more paintings have been found and those, too, not in good condition.

Now this man was one of the greatest creators the world has known, but he was not a doer, he was not a producer. If he had done anything else – carpentry or shoemaking or tailoring – he would have earned enough and everybody would have respected him as a man who earns his living. But he was continuously condemned as absolutely lazy – and nobody knew what he was doing.

The whole day would pass and he would forget completely about eating or even drinking water, he was so absorbed in his painting. Only when the night would descend and it became difficult to see, then he would recognize that the day was gone. He was so poor he could not even manage to purchase a few candles. Sometimes in the night he used to paint outside his house under the street lamp.

His brother must have been sensitive. He was young and certainly he understood something about paintings because he was working as a salesman in a shop where paintings and other pieces of art were sold. So he had a certain understanding. He loved his brother but what could he do? He himself was a poor man, somehow surviving, and more than that was not possible for him.

But one gift he certainly wanted to give his brother: that he should not die before seeing at least one of his paintings sold. So somehow he collected some money and asked a friend, "Go and purchase a painting from my brother. I just want to give him the consolation that his life has not been absolutely futile. At least he sold one painting."

But the man he had chosen had no sensitivity for paintings, so he simply went to Van Gogh and said, "I would like to purchase a painting."

Van Gogh said, so joyfully, "Come! I don't have a big place, but I have many paintings."

The man said, "Any will do!" That hurt Van Gogh very much.

He said, "Any will do? You don't want to see my paintings? You don't want to choose?"

He said, "It doesn't matter; don't waste my time. Any will do."

He said, "Then I am not going to sell, and it is absolutely certain you have been sent by my brother. Just get out and get lost! And tell my brother that this is not the way to console me. Now I am feeling more hurt and wounded than ever."

Then even his brother never tried again.

Creativity happens in a state of let-go. Productivity needs tension, anxiety, a doer, ego, recognition. Creativity needs no recognition, no ego, no doer – just the sheer joy of creating it.

At least Van Gogh could show his paintings. I cannot even show my paintings. But you are my paintings. I have been creating in my own way something very invisible and subtle which cannot be shown and which cannot be sold, and nobody will ever know about it. It will not be recorded anywhere how many people were transformed, how many people changed their lives from the lowest to the highest peak of illumination. But nobody can say that I have been uncreative. Day and night I am working – but I am not a doer.

One of my friends came from Russia, the Soviet Union, and he shook hands with me and he said, "You should never go to the Soviet Union."

I said, "Why?"

"Because anybody touching your hands will immediately shrink back."

I said, "But why?"

He said, "Because your hands are bourgeois, you have never done anything, and in the Soviet Union to be bourgeois is the worst condemnation. You need the proletariat's hand, the laborer's hand, rough."

I said, "My God, then first I will try – if I have to go to the Soviet Union – to make my hands as rough as I can."

This is true that I have never done anything. But I am not lazy; I have never thought for a moment that I am lazy, although I have never done anything. Even if I am feeling thirsty, I trust somebody is going to appear! And somebody always has appeared, so there is no need to distrust in the future.

In America, when my bail was set at five hundred thousand dollars – that's nearabout seventy-five lakh rupees – even the jailer who was taking me back to the jail was worried. He said, "From where? Even the figure is too big. In my whole life I have never seen or heard anybody being bailed for five hundred thousand dollars. How are you going to manage? – and you look so relaxed and so cool."

I said, "I don't bother about such things. Something will happen."

He said, "But how will it happen?"

I said, "That I don't know. 'How' is not part of my language. It will happen!"

He looked surprised; he could not believe it. But within ten minutes it happened. He came running to me and said, "You were right, your bail has been deposited!" He said, "It is unprecedented that for a person against whom no crime has yet been proved: there is no evidence against him; and yet such a large amount for bail. But you are stranger than the judge because you remain so cool and so silent."

I went into the jail and I went immediately to take my shower, because it was my shower time. The jailer was standing there and he said, "You cannot miss your shower even today? If nobody pays your bail, then for at least twenty years you will be in jail."

I said, "That is not the concern right now. Right now the concern is to take a good shower. And I have always trusted. After my shower you come to see me."

And after my shower he was standing outside the bathroom. He said, "Somebody has given the bail." He could not believe it. "How are you managing things?"

I said, "I have never managed. In my whole life I have never done anything deliberately, but things go on happening."

Once you are in a let-go, existence takes care of you. Then you are relaxed. If existence wants you to be in jail for twenty years, that's perfectly good. If it wants you to be out to prepare other people for jail, that too is good! It depends on existence, whether it is satisfied with one or many.

Now I am out, preparing many. Sooner or later, in every country, my people will be in jails – and that too, to convert the prisoners into sannyasins – because in almost every jail, I have sannyasins, and they go on asking for guidance. Now I have to send a few sannyasins to them.

It is difficult for me to guide people all over the world from here. They are in jails and they want guidance for meditation, and they have problems. The best will be for my people to start visiting – just once in a while, as a holiday!

And finally you are asking for some guidance from me. That is a very dangerous thing because I rarely give guidance, and whenever I give guidance something goes wrong! It is my experience that many times people got married and they came for my blessings. Nirvano would say, "Don't ask for his blessings because once he has blessed you, you are finished." And she was right because she had been watching: whoever gets my blessings, within a few days they are separated, something goes wrong.

Now, yesterday I had given some advice to Vimal. Vimal seems to be clever; he did not take it. But poor Rafia picked it up. Now you will see what happened to Rafia. He is writing:

The last question:

Osho

I did what you suggested.

I did not suggest this to him.

> I went to sleep saying, Vimal... Vimal... Vimal...

I was not suggesting this to him.

> ...and sure enough, I woke up saying, Vimal... Vimal... Vimal... Everything was going great until I started hugging a beautiful Indian girl, showed up for the wrong job, and started speaking with a pronounced English accent. Now I am confused. Beloved master, who am I?

...Because that girl he hugged was Vimal's girlfriend and the job he reached was Vimal's job, not his job.

But he certainly became confused repeating "Vimal... Vimal... Vimal..." the whole night. "Who am I?"

So when you ask for guidance, be very intelligent in applying it. The best is first see if somebody else applies it and what happens to him!

This beautiful silence, this is my creation. Thousands of lotuses suddenly start flowering. Thousands of hearts suddenly become a tremendous harmony, a song, a blissfulness.

Just the other day I said a few words about one of the most sincere, honest and authentic therapists. And just now as I entered I saw him again. He was crying just like a child, with utter joy.

These tears are my creation. They will not be recorded in any history book, but they will transform many who will come in contact with him. With his tears he has bridged his heart with my heart, his being with my being. He is one of the silent workers who goes on doing, without bragging about anything.

This joke is for him, not to have any more tears but to have great laughter.

A frustrated spinster was a menace to the police. She kept phoning up to say that there was a man under her bed. Before long she was sent to the mental hospital where she was treated with the latest drugs until one day she declared that she was cured.

"You mean, Miss Rustavian," asked one of the panel of shrinks, "that you can no longer see a man under you bed?"

"No, I can't," she replied, "I can see two."

The doctors consulted and diagnosed her complaint as malignant virginity, for which there was only one kind of injection that would cure her. They decided to shut her up in her bedroom with Big Don, the hospital handyman. Big Don was told of her complaint and that he would be locked up with her for an hour. He said that it would not take so long.

As the bedroom door closed an anxious group gathered outside. From inside was heard, "No, stop it, Don! Mother would never forgive you."

"Stop yelling! It has got to be done sometime! It should have been done years ago."

"Have it your way by force then, you brute!"

"It is only what your husband would have done if you had married."

The medics could not wait. They burst into the room.

"I have cured her!" cried Don.

"He's cured me!" called out Miss Rustavian. "He has chopped the legs off the bed!"

About Osho

Osho defies categorization. Mystic and scientist, a rebellious spirit whose sole interest is to alert humanity to the urgent need to discover a new way of living. To continue as before is to invite threats to our very survival on this unique and beautiful planet.

His thousands of talks cover everything from the individual quest for meaning to the most urgent social, political and environmental issues facing society today. Osho's books are not written but transcribed from audio and video recordings of his extemporaneous talks to international audiences. And he tells them, "Remember: whatever I am saying is not just for you...I am talking also for the future generations."

Osho has been described by *The Sunday Times* in London as one of the "1000 Makers of the 20th Century" and by American author Tom Robbins as "the most dangerous man since Jesus Christ." *Sunday Mid-Day* (Mumbai) has selected Osho as one of ten people – along with Gandhi, Nehru and Buddha – who have changed the destiny of India.

About his own work, Osho has said that he is helping to create the conditions for the birth of a new kind of human being. He often characterizes this new human being as "Zorba the Buddha" – capable both of enjoying the earthy pleasures of a Zorba the Greek and the silent serenity of a Gautama the Buddha.

Running like a thread through all aspects of Osho's talks and meditations is a vision that encompasses both the timeless wisdom of all ages past and the highest potential of today's (and tomorrow's) science and technology.

Osho is known for his revolutionary contribution to the science of inner transformation, with an approach to meditation that acknowledges the accelerated pace of contemporary life. His unique OSHO Active Meditations® are designed to first release the accumulated stresses of body and mind, so that it then becomes easier to experience a stillness and thought-free relaxation which can be taken into daily life.

Two autobiographical works by the author are available:

Autobiography of a Spiritually Incorrect Mystic, St. Martin's Press, New York (book and eBook)

Glimpses of a Golden Childhood, OSHO Media International, Pune, India (book and eBook)

OSHO International Meditation Resort

Each year the Meditation Resort welcomes thousands of people from more than 100 countries. The unique campus provides an opportunity for a direct personal experience of a new way of living – with more awareness, relaxation, celebration and creativity. A great variety of around-the-clock and around-the-year program options are available. Doing nothing and just relaxing is one of them!

All of the programs are based on Osho's vision of "Zorba the Buddha" – a qualitatively new kind of human being who is able *both* to participate creatively in everyday life *and* to relax into silence and meditation.

Location

Located 100 miles southeast of Mumbai in the thriving modern city of Pune, India, the OSHO International Meditation Resort is a holiday destination with a difference. The Meditation Resort is spread over 28 acres of spectacular gardens in a beautiful tree-lined residential area.

OSHO Meditations

A full daily schedule of meditations for every type of person includes both traditional and revolutionary methods, and particularly the OSHO Active Meditations®. The daily meditation program takes place in what must be the world's largest meditation hall, the OSHO Auditorium.

OSHO Multiversity

Individual sessions, courses and workshops cover everything from creative arts to holistic health, personal transformation, relationship and life transitions, transforming meditation into a lifestyle for life and work, esoteric sciences, and the Zen approach to sports and recreation. The secret of the OSHO Multiversity's success lies in the fact that all its programs are combined with meditation, supporting the understanding that as human beings we are far more than the sum of our parts.

Cuisine

A variety of different eating areas serve delicious Western, Asian and Indian vegetarian food – most of it organically grown especially for the Meditation Resort. Breads and cakes are baked in the resort's bakery.

Night life

There are many evening events to choose from – dancing being at the top of the list! Other activities include full-moon meditations beneath the stars, variety shows, music performances and "meditations for daily life."

Facilities

At the Meditation Resort you can buy all of your basic necessities and toiletries in the Galleria. In addition, the Multimedia Gallery sells a large range of OSHO media products. For those who enjoy shopping, Pune provides all the options, ranging from traditional and ethnic Indian products to all of the global brand-name stores.

Accommodation

You can choose to stay in the elegant rooms of the OSHO Guesthouse, or for longer stays on campus you can select one of the OSHO Living-In programs. Additionally there is a variety of nearby hotels and serviced apartments.

www.osho.com/meditationresort
www.osho.com/guesthouse
www.osho.com/livingin
Facebook: osho.international.meditation.resort

OSHO Books (English)

(OSHO books are available in Printed book and eBook formats, and most of them in audio format too. If a book is not available in one format, you can look up and buy it in another format.)

Early Talks

The Art of Living
Astrology
Breaking All Boundaries
Compassion and Revolution
Dimensions beyond the Known
The Eternal Quest
From Sex to Superconsciousness
The Great Challenge
Hidden Mysteries
I Am the Gate
The Independent Mind
Into the Void
Keys to a New Life
New Dimensions of Yoga
The Psychology of the Esoteric
Religion's Expiration Date
The Search for Peace
Woman and Rebellion
Work Is Love Made Visible

Meditation

And Now and Here
Body/Mind Balancing (Book & Audio)
Falling In Love with Darkness
In Search of the Miraculous
The Inner Journey
Just a Small Step
Meditation: The Art of Ecstasy
Meditation: The First and Last Freedom
The Path of Meditation
The Perfect Way
Silence: The Message of Your Being
Three Steps to Awakening

Buddha and Buddhist Masters

The Book of Wisdom
The Dhammapada: The Way of the Buddha (Vols 1-12)

The Diamond Sutra
The Discipline of Transcendence (Vols 1-4)
The Heart Sutra
The Great Secret
The Guest
The Path of Love
The Revolution

Indian Mystics

As if a Tree Starts Running (Yari))
The Beloved, Vols 1 & 2 (Baul Mystics)
Bliss:Living beyond Happiness and Misery (Shiva)
Die O Yogi Die (Gorakh)
Enlightenment: The Only Revolution (Ashtavakra)
Geeta Darshan Vol. 1 (Adhyaya 1-2)
Geeta Darshan, Vol.2 (Adhyaya 3)
Krishna: The Man and His Philosophy
The Last Morning Star (Daya)
Showering without Clouds (Sahajo)
The Song of Ecstasy (Adi Shankara)
The True Name (Vols 1&2) (Nanak)

Kabir

The Divine Melody
Ecstasy: The Forgotten Language
The Fabric of Life
The Fish in the Sea Is Not Thirsty

Western Mystics

The Art of Dying *(Hasidism)*
Come Follow to You, Vols 1-4 *(Jesus)*
Guida Spirituale (*Desiderata*)
The Hidden Harmony *(Heraclitus)*
I Say Unto You, Vols 1 & 2 *(Jesus)*
The Mustard Seed *(Jesus)*
The New Alchemy: To Turn You On (Mabel Collins)
Philosophia Perennis, Vols 1 & 2 (*Pythagoras*)
Reflections on Kahlil Gibran's *The Prophet*
Theologia Mystica *(Dionysius)*
The True Sage *(Hasidism)*
The Voice of Silence (Mabel Collins)
Zarathustra: A God That Can Dance (Nietzsche's *Thus Spake Zarathustra*)
Zarathustra: The Laughing Prophet (Nietzsche's *Thus Spake Zarathustra*)

Sufism

Just Like That

The Perfect Master, Vols 1 & 2
The Secret
Sufis: The People of the Path, Vols 1 & 2
Unio Mystica, Vols 1 & 2
Until You Die
The Wisdom of the Sands, Vols 1 & 2

Tantra

The Book of Secrets (Vigyan Bhairav Tantra)
The Tantra Experience (Saraha)
Tantra: The Supreme Understanding (Tilopa)
Tantric Transformation (Saraha)

The Upanishads

Behind a Thousand Names (Nirvana Upanishad)
Finger Pointing to the Moon (Adhyatma Upanishad)
Flight of the Alone to the Alone (Kaivalya Upanishad)
The Heartbeat of the Absolute (Ishavasya Upanishad)
I Am That (Isa Upanishad)
The Message beyond Words (Kathopanishad)
Philosophia Ultima (Mandukya Upanishad)
The Supreme Doctrine (Kenopanishad)
That Art Thou (Sarvasar Upanishad, Kaivalya Upanishad, Adhyatma Upanishad)
The Ultimate Alchemy, Vols 1 & 2 (Atma Pooja Upanishad)
Vedanta: Seven Steps to Samadhi (Akshaya Upanishad)
The Way beyond Any Way (Sarvasar Upanishad)

Tao

The Empty Boat (Chuang Tzu)
The Secret of Secrets (The Secret of Golden Flower)
Tao: The Golden Gate, Vols 1 & 2 (Ko Hsuan)
Tao: The Pathless Path, Vols 1 & 2 (Lieh Tzu)
Tao: The Three Treasures, Vols 1-4 (Lao Tzu)
When the Shoe Fits (Chuang Tzu)

Yoga (Patanjali)

Yoga: The Science of the Soul, Vols 1-10
- The Path of Yoga (Vol.1)
- The Heart of Yoga (Vol.2)
- Yoga: The Mystery beyond Mind (Vol.3)
- The Alchemy of Yoga (Vol.4)

- Yoga: A New Direction (Vol.5)
- Essence of Yoga (Vol.6)
- Yoga: The Science of Living (Vol.7)
- Secrets of Yoga (Vol.8)
- Yoga: The Path to Liberation (Vol.9)
- Yoga: The Supreme Science (Vol.10)

Zen and Zen Masters

Ah, This!
Ancient Music in the Pines
And the Flowers Showered…
And the Grass Grows By Itself…
A Bird on the Wing
Bodhidharma: The Greatest Zen Master
The Buddha: The Emptiness of the Heart
Christianity, the Deadliest Poison and Zen, the Antidote to All Poisons
Communism and Zen Fire, Zen Wind
Dang Dang Doko Dang
The First Principle
God Is Dead: Now Zen Is the Only Living Truth
The Great Zen Master Ta Hui
Hsin Hsin Ming: The Book of Nothing
I Celebrate Myself: God Is No Where, Life Is Now Here
Kyozan: A True Man of Zen
The Language of Existence
Live Zen
The Miracle
Nirvana: The Last Nightmare
No Mind: The Flowers of Eternity
No Water, No Moon
One Seed Makes the Whole Earth Green
The Original Man
Returning to the Source
The Search: Talks on the 10 Bulls of Zen
A Sudden Clash of Thunder
The Sun Rises in the Evening
Take it Easy
This. This. A Thousand Times This
This Very Body the Buddha
Turning In
The White Lotus
Yakusan: Straight to the Point of Enlightenment
The Zen Manifesto: Freedom from Oneself
Zen: The Diamond Thunderbolt
Zen: The Mystery and the Poetry of the Beyond
Zen: The Path of Paradox, Vols 1-3

Zen: The Quantum Leap from Mind to No-Mind
Zen: The Solitary Bird, Cuckoo of the Forest
Zen: The Special Transmission

Osho: On the Ancient Masters of Zen

Dogen: The Zen Master
Hyakujo: The Everest of Zen – With Basho's haikus
Isan: No Footprints in the Blue Sky
Joshu: The Lion's Roar
Ma Tzu: The Empty Mirror
Nansen: The Point of Departure
Rinzai: Master of the Irrational

Responses to Questions

Be Still and Know
Beyond Enlightenment (Talks in Bombay)
Beyond Psychology (Talks in Uruguay)
Come, Come, Yet Again Come
The Diamond Sword
From Bondage to Freedom
From Darkness to Light
From Death to Deathlessness
From Ignorance to Innocence
From Misery to Enlightenment
From Personality to Individuality
From the False to the Truth
From Unconsciousness to Consciousness
The Goose Is Out
The Great Pilgrimage: From Here to Here
The Invitation
Light on the Path (Talks in the Himalayas)
My Way: The Way of the White Clouds
Nowhere to Go but In
The Osho Upanishad (Talks in Bombay)
The Path of the Mystic (Talks in Uruguay)
The Razor's Edge
Sermons in Stones (Talks in Bombay)
Socrates Poisoned Again After 25 Centuries (Talks in Greece)
The Sword and the Lotus (Talks in the Himalayas)
Transmission of the Lamp (Talks in Uruguay)
Walk without Feet, Fly without Wings and Think without Mind
The Wild Geese and the Water
Yaa-Hoo! The Mystic Rose
Walking in Zen, Sitting in Zen
Zen: Zest, Zip, Zap and Zing

Osho's Vision for the World
The Golden Future
The Hidden Splendor
The New Dawn
The Rebel
The Rebellious Spirit

The Mantra Series
Hari Om Tat Sat
Om Mani Padme Hum
Om Shantih Shantih Shantih
Sat Chit Anand
Satyam Shivam Sundaram

Personal Glimpses
Books I Have Loved
Glimpses of a Golden Childhood
Notes of a Madman

Interviews with the World Press
The Man of Truth: A Majority of One

Meetings with Individuals
Above All Don't Wobble
Hammer on the Rock

Quotation Books
Gold Nuggets
More Gold Nuggets
Words From A Man of No Words

Letters and Writings
A Cup of Tea
Earthen Lamps
Flowers of Love
Life Is a Soap Bubble
Love Letters to Life
Seeds of Wisdom

For any information about OSHO Books, please contact:

OSHO Media International
17 Koregaon Park, Pune – 411001, MS, India
Phone: +91-20-66019999 Fax: +91-20-66019990
E-mail: distribution@osho.net
Website: http://www.osho.com

For More Information

The official website of OSHO International is www.OSHO.com

www.OSHO.com/AllAboutOSHO is a comprehensive portal to all things OSHO.

www.OSHO.com/AllAboutOSHO
www.OshoTimes.com
shop.OSHO.com
iOSHO.OSHO.com
YouTube: OSHO/OSHOinternational
Twitter: OSHO
Instagram: OSHOinternational
Facebook: OSHO.international
Facebook: OSHO.international.meditation.resort

ALSO IN THE MANTRA SERIES